THE MOST TRUSTED NAME IN TRAVEL: **FROMMER'S**

FROMMER'S EasyGuide to
AMSTERDAM, BRUSSELS AND BRUGES

2nd Edition

P9-CQS-748

By Jennifer Ceaser

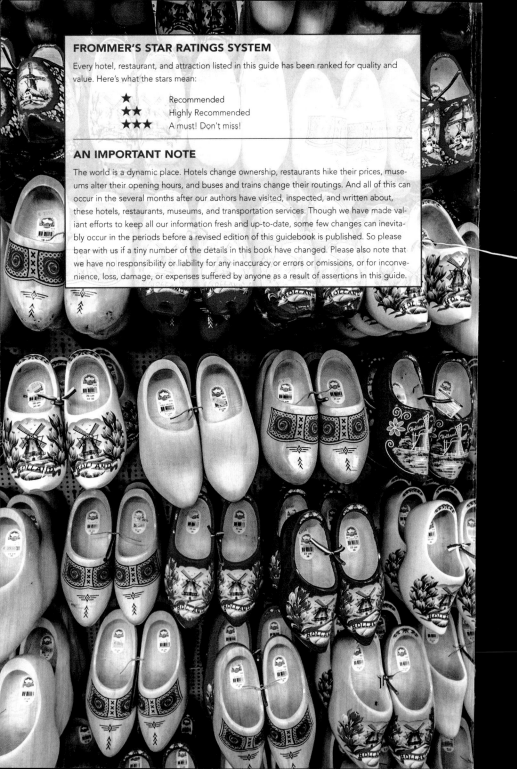

FROMMER'S STAR RATINGS SYSTEM

Every hotel, restaurant, and attraction listed in this guide has been ranked for quality and value. Here's what the stars mean:

★	Recommended
★★	Highly Recommended
★★★	A must! Don't miss!

AN IMPORTANT NOTE

The world is a dynamic place. Hotels change ownership, restaurants hike their prices, museums alter their opening hours, and buses and trains change their routings. And all of this can occur in the several months after our authors have visited, inspected, and written about, these hotels, restaurants, museums, and transportation services. Though we have made valiant efforts to keep all our information fresh and up-to-date, some few changes can inevitably occur in the periods before a revised edition of this guidebook is published. So please bear with us if a tiny number of the details in this book have changed. Please also note that we have no responsibility or liability for any inaccuracy or errors or omissions, or for inconvenience, loss, damage, or expenses suffered by anyone as a result of assertions in this guide.

CONTENTS

The municipality of Lisse holds some of Holland's loveliest tulip fields, and is an easy jaunt from Amsterdam.

A CLOSER LOOK

During separate eras, the territories that are now the Netherlands and Belgium led the Western World. For the Netherlands, the time was the 17th century, when its merchant ships ruled the oceans and brought back riches that then funded the creation of art, architecture and civil engineering projects that stunned all of Europe. For Belgium there were, arguably, several periods—the 15th century when the so-called Flemish Primitives were painting, the 17th century when Peter Paul Rubens was shaping Baroque art, and the 19th century when Magritte and his comrades were leading lights in the Surrealism movement. Today, we go to these two countries to see the art and architecture these big guns left behind. But we also make the trip—and both countries can be easily visited in one vacation—to visit two vibrant, but hugely different contemporary nations. What follows in these pages is just a quick look at what you'll see in both.

–Pauline Frommer

Every even-numbered year, Brussels' Grand-Place becomes a tapestry of blossoms, with thousands of flowers set in different patterns, for the Carpet of Flowers Festival (see p. 41).

In Amsterdam, nearly 40% of the population uses bicycles regularly (according to a European Commission report), a number far above the worldwide average.

A statue of author Anne Frank, in Westerkerk plaza, near her former home (see p. 99).

Opened as a post office in 1899, the Neo-Gothic Magna Plaza (p. 122) is an eye-catching shopping mall today.

The massive painting "The Night Watch," by Rembrandt (see p. 102) is exhibited at the Rijksmuseum and is awash in symbolism: look for the woman in yellow, who carries a dead chicken, the symbol of a defeated adversary.

The shape of the gables on Amsterdam's houses offers a clue as to when they were built. Simple triangular gables were used from the 14th through the 16th century, with more ornate stepped gables and rounded bell-shaped gables introduced in the 17th century.

Small ancestor statues from Holland's former colony of Indonesia, displayed at the Tropenmuseum (see p. 107)

Red Light District (p. 94)

Posthoorn Church Basilica

Storefront in the trendy Nine Streets district (p. 117)

The Bulldog was one of Amsterdam's first smoking coffee shops (see p. 123).

During the annual King's Day celebrations (p. 39), the canals fill with boats carrying revelers dressed in orange as a show of pride in the royal family, the House of Orange-Nassau.

A tour of the historic Heineken brewery includes ample tastings at the end (see p. 100).

The magnificent Concertgebouw (see p. 122) has been the city's premier classical music venue since 1888.

The skyline of Rotterdam, with the Erasmus Bridge, nicknamed "The Swan" for its asymmetrical but elegant winged shape (p. 155)

Delft is best known for its pottery, but the town itself is quite striking, especially around the Grote Markt. See p. 141.

The Gothic castle that is the Binnenhof (p. 146), in the Hague, today houses the country's major governmental offices. It is one of the oldest parliamentary buildings on the planet.

BRUSSELS & SIDE TRIPS

Brussels' Royal Museum of Fine Arts, established in 1803, holds extraordinary collection of art by Magritte, Rubens and the Flemish Primitives. See p. 243.

Chocolatier Pierre Marcolini works his magic. You can't say you've tasted gourmet chocolate until you try the ambrosial sweets of Belgium (see p. 201).

The Grand-Place's architecture is a stunner, containing the most important examples of medieval secular architecture in Europe. See p. 178.

Mannekin-Pis, the jaunty toddler who is the symbol of the city. Read more on

 p. 183.

A dazzling variety of Belgian waffles

Mannekin-Pis, the jaunty toddler who is the symbol of the city. Read more on p. 183.

A dazzling variety of Belgian waffles

The place du Petit Sablon features this elegant garden, created in 1890. It's found in the Upper Town of Brussels (see p. 184).

A CLOSER LOOK | Brussels & Side Trips

xi

The Belgian Comic Strip Center is set in a spectacular Art Nouveau space, formerly a department store, designed by Victor Horta. See p. 186.

The Musical Instruments Museum (p. 191)

The famed Marolles Flea Market (p. 202)

The medieval buildings of Ghent seem to glow at sunset. See p. 249.

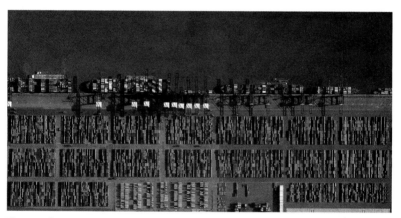

The Port of Antwerp is second-largest in Europe, and fascinating to tour (see p. 238). This geometric scene is actually thousands of shipping containers seen from above.

The market in the historic town of Mechelen, also known as Malines (p. 268)

Traditional dancers in Ypres (p. 265)

The pond of the Gravensteen (Castle of the Counts) in Ghent (p. 252)

Architect Zaha Hadid's Port House, Antwerp (p. 239)

Brabo Fountain, Antwerp

BRUGES & SIDE TRIPS

The buildings around the Markt square range in age from the 12th through the 19th century. See more on p. 219.

The Minnewater (or Lake of Love, see p. 232)

Learn about lace at the Kantcentrum (p. 232)

The view from the Belfort (Belfry tower; see p. 219) over medieval Bruges

The upper chapel of the Basilica of the Holy Blood (p. 223) was rebuilt in the Gothic style in the 16th century and renovated in the 19th century in Gothic Revival style. Its over-the-top opulence makes it one of Bruges' can't-miss sights.

Criss-crossed by canals, Bruges is known as "The Venice of the North."

THE BEST OF AMSTERDAM, BRUSSELS & BRUGES

Taken together, the nations of Belgium and the Netherlands cover a mere 72,400 sq. km (27,380 sq. miles)—around one-fifth the size of neighboring Germany, and not much larger than West Virginia. But no other comparably sized area in Europe is home to so many points of interest. Topping the list are artistic masterpieces, cultural events, and substantial reminders of a long and colorful history. Not to mention a host of other travel delights—the exquisite food and drink of Brussels, the unadulterated gorgeousness of Bruges, and the exuberant sociability of Amsterdam.

In the Netherlands, there are no dramatic canyons or towering peaks. The nation's highest point wouldn't top the roof of a New York City skyscraper, and its average altitude is just 11m (37 ft.) above sea level. Yes, it's flat, but as the famous 17th-century Dutch landscape painters showed the world, vistas in Holland are among the most beautiful anywhere, giving wide-angle views of green pastures dotted with tiny houses, church spires, the occasional windmill, and grazing cattle silhouetted against the horizon.

Amsterdam is by far its largest city and most popular destination, with some 96 percent of visitors making it the first port of call. But don't discount Holland's secondary cities: Den Haag ("The Hague"), the seat of Dutch parliament, is home to several world-class museums and the seaside resort of Scheveningen, while Rotterdam, the Dutch sea power, brims with exciting, cutting-edge architecture.

Belgium is essentially divided into two ethnic regions, with Dutch-speaking Vlaanderen (Flanders) to the north and French-speaking Wallonie (Wallonia) to the south. Brussels, the capital, sits roughly in the geographic middle, with street signs given in French and Dutch, though nearly everybody speaks English (even if it is sometimes grudgingly). The headquarters of the European Community, Brussels is a thriving international metropolis whose magnificent museums and lovely medieval and Art Deco architecture are nearly upstaged by its stellar dining scene. To the north lie the charming cities of Ghent and Antwerp, as well as the country's star attraction, the beguiling medieval walled city of Bruges.

For ease of reading, I have divided this chapter into three sections: Amsterdam and surrounding destinations; Brussels and its neighbors Ghent and Antwerp; and finally Bruges.

best AMSTERDAM EXPERIENCES

o **Chilling in a Brown Cafe:** Spend a leisurely evening in this traditional Amsterdam watering hole. After an evening of imbibing ice-cold beer in one of these, you'll understand the meaning of the Dutch term *gezelligheid*. You'll also probably find you've made lots of new friends, too. See p. 79.

o **Cruising Amsterdam's 17th-Century Canals:** Get your bearings with an hour-long canal tour of Amsterdam; you'll see all the major waterways, many famous sights, the expanding architectural landscape north of the IJ river, the workings of the port, and many beautiful canal houses. See p. 110.

o **Discovering the Jordaan:** Once a working-class district and now thoroughly gentrified, Amsterdam's most photogenic neighborhood teems with narrow, tree-lined canals and cobbled streets. It has cafes and bars aplenty to discover as well as galleries and independent stores by the dozen. See p. 60.

o **Following the Tulip Trail:** Come spring, the place to see the celebrated Dutch tulips in their full glory is Keukenhof Gardens at Lisse, about 45 minutes out of Amsterdam. Here millions of tulips and other flowers create dazzling swathes of color. Combine your visit with a trip through the bulb fields between Leiden and Haarlem. See p. 137.

o **Seeing Great Paintings:** Everything you've heard about Amsterdam's art museums is true. They are amazing; the three heavyweights are the Rijksmuseum for Dutch Old Masters, the Stedelijk for its world-beating collection of contemporary work, and the Van Gogh for . . . well, Van Gogh. See p. 60.

o **Exploring the City's Edgy North Side:** A quick free ferry ride across the IJ River gets you to the former industrial area of Amsterdam Noord, which has been transformed into one of the city's coolest districts. Check out the striking architecture of the Eye Film Museum, take a ride on a giant over-the-edge swing at A'dam Lookout, and stroll around NDSM Wharf, where old shipping warehouses now brim with trendy cafes. See p. 60.

best DUTCH FAMILY-FRIENDLY EXPERIENCES

o **Checking out the Windmills at Zaanse Schans:** In flat Holland, wind is ever present, so it's not surprising that the Dutch used windmills to assist with everything from draining water from the land to sawing wood. At one time, the Zaan district, northwest of Amsterdam, had more than 1,000

0 — 50 mi
0 — 50 km

W a d d e n   I s l a n d s
Schiermonnikoog
Ameland
Terschelling
Delfzijl
Vlieland
W a d d e n z e e
GRONINGEN
Harlingen
Leeuwarden
Groningen
Texel
FRIESLAND
Den Helder
Heerenveen
Assen
NORTH SEA
DRENTHE
NOORD-
HOLLAND
IJsselmeer
Emmeloord
Emmen
Alkmaar
Hoorn
Beverwijk
Lelystad
Zwolle
Haarlem
Zaandam
FLEVOLAND
OVERIJSSEL
Amsterdam
Almelo
Hengelo
Enschede
Leiden
NETHERLANDS
The Hague (Den Haag)
Gouda
Utrecht
Delft
UTRECHT
GELDERLAND
ZUID-
Rotterdam
HOLLAND
Arnhem
Nijmegen
Waalwijk
's-Hertogenbosch
Bergen
op Zoom
NOORD-BRABANT
Middelburg
Helmond
Vlissingen
ZEELAND
Eindhoven
Venlo
Ostend
Turnhout
Düsseldorf
Bruges
Antwerp
WEST-
VLAANDEREN
Ghent
ANTWERPEN
Mechelen
LIMBURG
Sittard
Cologne
(Köln)
Ypres
OOST-VLAANDEREN
Leuven
Hasselt
Maastricht
Kortrijk
VLAAMS-BRABANT
Brussels
GERMANY
Halle
Wavre
Lille
BRABANT-WALLON
Liège
Tournai
Ath
HAINAUT
BELGIUM
LIÈGE
Spa
Mons
Namur
Malmedy
NAMUR
Dinant
LUXEMBOURG
Chimay
Bastogne
FRANCE
LUXEMBOURG
Bouillon
Arlon
Luxembourg

National Capital
Provincial Capital

windmills. Of the 13 that survived, five have been reconstructed at Zaanse Schans, together with other historical buildings reminiscent of Holland's past. See p. 134.

o **Eating Pancakes:** The Dutch have a famously sweet tooth and pancakes are one of their national staples. There are even pancake cruises; the *Pannenkoekenboot* services Rotterdam (p. 157) and Amsterdam (p. 111).

o **Exploring Rotterdam's Gigantic Harbor:** Kids will love the chance to get out on the River Maas to discover the inner mechanics of the third-largest natural harbor in the world. The company Spido provides frequent daily multilingual tours on modern, well-equipped boats. See p. 156.

o **Seeing the Netherlands in Miniature at Madurodam:** This mini theme park has three themed zones containing detailed models of Holland's cities and landmark buildings, all scaled down to 1.25 percent. It's your chance to see all of the Netherlands in a day. See p. 150.

o **Spending a Day in Scheveningen:** The Hague's charming beach resort is a 15-minute ride on tram No. 9 from the city center and light years away in carefree vibe. The beach is safe for swimming and there are several attractions close by, including Madurodam (see above), the IMAX theater at Omniversum (p. 151), the Skyview Ferris wheel on the Scheveningen Pier, and Sea Life Scheveningen. See p. 151.

o **Visiting Amsterdam's Kid-Friendly Museums:** Amsterdam is a superb destination for family holidays; it's easy to negotiate and has plenty of green spaces, an excellent zoo at **Artis** (p. 104), and many child-friendly museums, including the **NEMO Science Museum** (p. 107), **Micropia** (p. 104), and the **Het Scheepvaartmuseum** (National Maritime Museum; see p. 105). Older kids will appreciate the powerful experience of visiting the **Anne Frank Huis** (p. 96).

best DUTCH HOTELS

o **Hotel de l'Europe, Amsterdam:** Among the plushest stays in the city, this grand hotel is rich in classic details, from the chandeliered lobby to the fine reproductions of Dutch Masters throughout. It has an enviable location right on the Amstel River, just a few minutes' walk to major sites like Rembrandtplein and Dam Square. See p. 65.

o **Hotel des Indes, The Hague:** The hotel of choice for diplomats visiting the Peace Palace (p. 149), this former palace has been a hotel since 1881. Rooms are awash with swags, flourishes, and four posters; the service is second to none. See p. 150.

o **Hotel New York, Rotterdam:** Once the HQ of the Holland-America Line, this hotel is now sandwiched between skyscrapers on the River Maas waterside; it's an historic building offering huge, airy rooms and fabulous river views. See p. 157.

o **Conservatorium, Amsterdam:** Set inside a magnificent 19th-century former music conservatory just a stone's throw from the city's three major art museums, this sleekly designed property offers some of the plushest rooms

Two of the best among the new breed of hotels awarded Green Key certificates, and run along 100-percent sustainable grounds, are the **Conscious Hotels** (p. 73) in Amsterdam and the **Court Garden Den Haag** (p. 150). The hotels get electricity from green sources, serve food that is almost entirely organic, and are stylishly designed with recycled furniture and

in town. A heavenly spa, state-of-the-art gym with pool, and flower-filled lobby lounge round out the offerings at this five-star gem. See p. 72.

o **Seven Bridges, Amsterdam:** At some hotels, the owners aren't just running a business—they're doing what they love. The Seven Bridges is that kind of place. Pierre Keulers and Günter Glaner have found both their profession and their passion in this fine hotel. All the furniture, fixtures, and fittings have been selected with loving care and guests receive the same conscientious attention. See p. 71.

o **Grand Hotel Amrâth Kurhaus, Scheveningen:** This elegant grande dame is poised over the seafront and staying here is like being wrapped in a comfort blanket. Every imaginable amenity is available, from lavish guestrooms to afternoon tea and fine dining. See p. 150.

best DUTCH RESTAURANTS

o **De Blauw, Amsterdam:** With branches in Utrecht and Amsterdam, De Blauw is the future of Indonesian cuisine in Holland. Service is skillful, the wait staff are a delight, and the *rijstaffel* dishes tasty and beautifully presented. See p. 83.

o **Ratatouille Food & Wine, Haarlem:** This Michelin-starred spot set inside a 17th-century riverfront warehouse serves up excellent French cuisine at surprisingly affordable prices. See p. 130.

o **Envy, Amsterdam:** This stylish, industrial-style bistro on the postcard-perfect Prinsengracht specializes in tapas-style dining, with multitudes of inventive, Mediterranean-inspired small plates. There's an open kitchen and guest chefs often make surprise appearances. See p. 80.

o **Kee Lun Palace, The Hague:** The Hague is home to a large Chinatown, packed with Chinese, Japanese, and Indonesian eateries; this is its best, with tasty, generous portions of Singapore noodles and chili prawns. See p. 152.

o **Restaurant de Kas, Amsterdam:** One of Amsterdam's first organic restaurants, de Kas still keeps ahead of the pack with superlative cooking and a gorgeous setting inside several restored 1920s-era greenhouses. Dining spreads out on to the terrace in summer. See p. 86.

o **Rijks, Amsterdam:** In the shadow of the Rijksmuseum, this upscale restaurant takes Dutch cuisine to another level, with staples like herring and cod given a thoroughly modern twist. See p. 82.

best AMSTERDAM BARS

o **'t Smalle:** This cozy pub in the Jordaan started as a gin distillery in 1780 and it seems little has changed within its wood-paneled walls. An original gin pump and ancient barrels that once held various spirits decorate the bar. Today the primary drink is beer, with six specialty brews on tap. Enjoy one on the splendid canal-side terrace. See p. 79.

o **De Drie Fleschjes:** Discover *jenever* (aka Dutch gin) at this traditional tasting room, which has been pouring the potent stuff since 1650. Huge wood casks hold its signature jenever blends; if you aren't won over by the malty beverage, there are plenty of specialty beers and wines to keep you in the sauce. See p. 125.

o **Vesper:** James Bond fan or no, this elegant bar excels in adventurous cocktails, with talented mixologists pushing the envelope when it comes to flavors and presentation. Expect a wild ride, from an alcoholic buttermilk punch to drinks accented with a flaming pine cone. See p. 125.

best DUTCH OUTDOOR ACTIVITIES

o **Catching Some Rays in Amsterdam Parks:** Despite the intense urbanization of central Amsterdam, the city has many green spaces in which to relax and unwind on sunny days, the Vondelpark (p. 103) and the Westerpark (p. 109) among them.

o **Hopping on a bicycle:** Cycling is the Dutch national obsession; it's healthy, it's green, and Holland is flat. Jump on a bike and explore the cobbled streets, parks, and the surrounding countryside. MacBike in Amsterdam rents out bicycles. See p. 112.

o **Pedaling Canal Bike:** One of the best ways to see the sites of Amsterdam is from the water; rent a two- or four-seat pedal boat (also called a canal bike) and leisurely wind your way through its canals. See p. 112.

best DUTCH MUSEUMS

o **Frans Hals Museum, Haarlem:** An art pilgrimage for many, this museum is located in a splendid old almshouse, which is almost as much reason to visit as the stunning display of Frans Hals's civic guards portraits in the banqueting hall. See p. 130.

o **Gementemuseum den Haag, The Hague:** The Hague's showstopper is extensive enough to keep visitors going all day. Housed in a sparse brick gallery designed by feted architect H.P. Berlage, the treasures on show range from priceless Delftware to peerless contemporary painting. See p. 147.

o **Het Grachtenhuis, Amsterdam:** Tucked away behind an elegant 17th-century facade, the Museum of the Canals brings Amsterdam's history to life through clever interactive exhibits, sound, and film. It's an ideal place to start your exploration of the Canal Ring. See p. 97.

- **Mauritshuis, The Hague:** Set in a former ducal palace, the Mauritshuis has a small but stellar collection of Dutch Old Master paintings including two major works that inspired hit novels and a film: Vermeer's "Girl with a Pearl Earring" and Fabritius's "The Goldfinch." See p. 148.
- **Rijksmuseum, Amsterdam:** With the finest collection of Dutch Old Masters in the world, the Rijksmuseum is the first stop for most visitors to Amsterdam, and deservedly so. Just be sure to get there early to escape the lines or book in advance online to secure a time slot for your visit. See p. 101.
- **Van Gogh Museum, Amsterdam:** Home to the world's largest collection of works by tortured artist Vincent van Gogh—200 paintings and counting—this is the most visited museum in the Netherlands, beating out even the neighboring Rijksmuseum. See p. 102.

best DUTCH CHURCHES

- **Sint-Bavokerk (Church of St. Bavo), Haarlem:** The moment you enter Haarlem's main square, this massive church is revealed in all its Gothic splendor. It was the subject of many a 16th-century painting and Haarlem master painter Frans Hals is buried in its cavernous interior. The young Mozart played here in 1766. See p. 132.
- **Westerkerk, Amsterdam:** The Westerkerk's tower, the Westertoren, is 85m (275 ft.) high, the tallest in Amsterdam, and provides a spectacular view of the city. Anne Frank could hear every note of the carillon's dulcet tones while in hiding from the Nazis in her house on Prinsengracht just around the corner. See p. 99.

best DUTCH SHOPPING

- **Cheese:** Holland is world famous for its great round slabs of orange and yellow cheese—in fact, the Dutch dairy industry has revenues of more than seven billion euros annually. Most delis in the main cities will sell a selection of Goudas, Edam, and holey Maasdammer vacuum-packed and ready for export. See p. 135.
- **Delftware & Makkumware:** During the 16th century, Delft factories started decorating their pottery in elaborate blue patterns in mimicry of Chinese porcelain imported into the Netherlands. Delft Blue pottery became famous the world over, along with Makkumware from the town of Makkum. Delftware and Makkumware can be bought in Amsterdam's Spiegelkwartier (p. 115) and you can see Delftware being made in the Koninklijke Porceleyne Fles in Delft. See p. 143.
- **Flower Bulbs:** It's difficult to choose from the incredible variety of bulb shapes and colors offered in the Netherlands. In Amsterdam buy them from the **Bloemenmarkt** floating market on Singel canal (p. 91) or the **Tulip Museum** on Prinsengracht (p. 99). A great array can also be bought during the spring opening of **Keukenhof** gardens in Lisse. See p. 137.

best **BELGIAN EXPERIENCES**

- **Admiring Art Nouveau, Brussels:** Considering itself the world capital of Art Nouveau, Brussels was home to architect Victor Horta (1861–1947), who was its foremost exponent. Get up with the larks to beat the endless lines outside the colorful, sinuous Horta Museum at his former home. See p. 184.

- **Taste Lambic Beer, Brussels:** Sample this distinctive style of beer at the old-fashioned, family-owned Cantillon Brewery. Founded in 1900, Belgium's last Lambic brewery still produces what's considered some of the world's finest sour beers. See p. 206.

- **Discovering Royal Brussels:** Much of Brussels was built under the stewardship of King Leopold I in the 19th century. Royal Brussels offers parks, museums, grand palaces, galleries, and gardens to explore.

- **Seeing the Grand-Place for the First Time, Brussels:** You'll never forget your first look at this timelessly perfect cobbled square, surrounded by gabled guild houses and the Gothic tracery of the Hôtel de Ville (Town Hall) and Maison du Roi (King's House). See p. 178.

- **Standing in Front of the Lamb of God, Ghent:** Some fabled artworks disappoint when you finally get to see them in the flesh. The Van Eyck brothers' superb, glowing altarpiece in Sint-Bavoskerk (St. Bavo's Cathedral) is categorically *not* one of these. It simply takes your breath away. See p. 132.

- **Touring Rubens's House, Antwerp:** The Dutch super-artist Rubens lived in some considerable style in an ornate mansion with an arcaded formal garden. See p. 245.

- **Visiting Kazerne Dossin, the Holocaust Centre, Mechelen:** This hard-hitting museum is on the site of a former holding center for Belgian Jewish deportees to the concentration camps of Germany and Poland. See p. 269.

- **Walking the Illuminated Promenade by Night, Ghent:** If you can't follow the whole route through the city center, at least see the wildly gabled ancient guild houses along Graslei, all ethereally floodlit. See p. 256.

best **BELGIAN FAMILY-FRIENDLY EXPERIENCES**

- **Cruising Antwerp Streets in the Touristram:** Take a whistle-stop tour of all Antwerp's major points of interest in a mini electric tram; you'll trundle through the Grote Markt and the cobbled lanes of the Old Town, venture through the main shopping thoroughfares, and potter along the Schelde riverfront. See p. 242.

- **Eating a Nose, Ghent:** Sample some of Ghent's iconic sweets; "noses" are conical, can be bought in an assortment of fruity flavors, and look for all the world like overweight, giant Jelly Babies. See p. 253.

- **Giggling at the Manneken-Pis, Brussels:** Heaven knows why this diminutive statue has become an icon of Brussels, but it has. Join the throng around the little fountain to photograph the city's famous peeing sculpture. See p. 183.

- **Seeing Ghent from Atop the Belfort:** The 14th-century belfry rises 90m (300 ft.) above the city of Ghent, making it the tallest tower in Belgium. Whizz to the top by elevator for unrivaled views over ancient rooftops and canals. See p. 250.
- **Spotting Comic-Strip Murals in Brussels:** Kids, keep your eyes peeled for Tintin, Asterix, and Obelix, as well as other famous Belgian cartoon characters along the streets of Brussels. See p. 192. Beyond murals, there's the Belgian Comic Strip Center, a museum that kids will adore, set in a lovely Art Nouveau gallery. See p. 186.

best **BELGIAN HOTELS**

- **Hotel Harmony, Ghent:** A family-run treasure in Patersol, Ghent's historic quarter, which is blessed with huge (even by U.S. standards) guestrooms at the front of the building, some with tiny balconies. It's all smartly kitted out in minimalist style and there's a natty little bar for early-evening drinks. See p. 258.
- **Hotel FRANQ, Antwerp:** A grand neoclassical bank building has been reimagined as a stylish boutique property complete with a Michelin-starred restaurant, buzzy bar, and an enviable location near the city's thrumming Grote Markt. See p. 247.
- **Rocco Forte Hotel Amigo, Brussels:** One of the most luscious five-star hotels in the city. Despite its size, the Amigo manages to keep that personal touch often sadly lacking in big hotels. See p. 166.

best **BELGIAN RESTAURANTS**

- **Comme Chez Soi, Brussels:** One of the city's finest gourmet dining experiences, this restaurant has been turning out expertly prepared Gallic cuisine since 1926. The setting is resplendent: an Art Nouveau dining room replete with sinuous woodwork and stained glass. See p. 171.
- **Le Wine Bar Sablon des Marolles, Brussels:** Beyond the well-curated wine list of mostly French and Italian varietals, this rustic little spot serves dishes using farm-to-table ingredients including beef sourced from France, Basque sausages, and Italian burrata. See p. 173.
- **De Graslei, Ghent:** Wonderfully situated overlooking the canal on one of Ghent's loveliest streets, this is a truly romantic spot for dining after dark. As happens everywhere in this outgoing city, you'll soon end up deep in conversation with your dining neighbors. See p. 256.
- **La Quincaillerie, Brussels:** Located in a lovely Art Nouveau building in the city's trendy Châtelain district, this brasserie serves up modern Franco-Belgian dishes using organic, sustainably grown ingredients. There's also a formidable selection of European oysters. See p. 174.
- **RAS, Antwerp:** With floor-to-ceiling windows looking out on the River Scheldt, this elegant restaurant, set inside an iconic, boat-shaped building,

offers great views—especially at sunset—and an equally excellent seafood-based menu. See p. 248.

best BELGIAN BARS

o **A La Mort Subite, Brussels:** Old-fashioned and cavernous, this traditional Belgian bar serves its home-brewed beer to hundreds of thirsty guests hourly. Just watch the wait staff work and admire their friendly professionalism. See p. 204.

o **'t Dreupelkot, Ghent:** With no shortage of fine cafes, you can just about guarantee that any one you enter in Ghent will provide happy memories. 't Dreupelkot will leave you with a particularly warm glow as it is the city's number-one spot for imbibing *jenever,* a juniper-flavored Dutch (and Flemish) spirit. Here you can find around 200 varieties to choose from. See p. 259.

o **Arthur Orlans, Brussels:** With decor reminiscent of a gentlemen's club, this clandestine bar on trendy rue Dansaert is the ideal spot to sip classic cocktails, expertly whipped up by tartan-vested bartenders. See p. 205.

best BELGIAN MUSEUMS

o **Musée Art & Histoire (Art & History Museum), Brussels:** With collections as vast as the Victoria & Albert in London, this vibrant, well-curated museum looks at civilizations from all over: Native American Indian to Indonesian, with a wonderful array of artifacts, from totem poles to wooden Balinese beds. Plan to spend several hours here or you'll miss half of it. See p. 193.

o **Design Museum Gent:** Tucked away behind the facade of a refined 18th-century townhouse, the stars of the show in Ghent's decorative arts museum are the cleverly pieced-together period Art Deco rooms and the range of *objets d'art* from Delftware tulip vases to Alessi tea services. See p. 252.

o **Mechelen Toy Museum, Mechelen:** A surprisingly extensive collection of toys means a boatload of nostalgia for most visitors. One of the largest toy museums in Europe it is as much loved by adults as by children. At last we know where all our old dolls and tin cars disappeared to! See p. 270.

o **Musée Hergé, Brussels:** This funky museum is dedicated to the works of Georges Remi, who breathed life into Tintin and his trusty terrier Snowy in 1927 under the name Hergé. See p. 198.

o **Musée Van Buuren, Brussels:** Secreted away in a posh Brussels suburb, this paean to Art Deco style hits the very apex of quality and sophistication. The house is not huge but it's been preserved with all its original furniture in situ; there's a lovely garden that is best seen in spring. See p. 194.

o **Musées Royaux des Beaux-Arts de Belgique, Brussels:** A compendium of four fabulous museums that showcase paintings by the biggest names in Belgian art—Bruegel (the Elder and the Younger), Rubens, Memling—all under one gigantic roof. The highlight, bar none, is the Magritte Museum, with over 200 works by the Surrealist master. See p. 189.

- **Museum aan de Stroom (MAS), Antwerp:** Rising above the newly trendy port district of Eilandje, this red sandstone-and-glass museum showcases the ethnographic and maritime aspects of Antwerp, most notably its dominance in trade and shipping. There's also a fascinating collection of pre-Columbian objects gifted to the museum by local collectors Paul and Dora Janssen-Arts. See p. 243.

best BELGIAN CHURCHES

- **Eglise Notre-Dame du Sablon (Church of Our Lady of the Sablon), Brussels:** The flamboyant Brabantine Gothic exterior of this church is reason enough to see it; step inside to soak in the gorgeous vaulted ceiling, murals, and baroque chapels filled with statuary. See p. 188.
- **Sint-Pauluskerk (St. Paul's Church), Antwerp:** The gleaming white Gothic edifice of St. Paul's Church hides no fewer than four Rubens masterpieces; they adorn the interior of this lovely church along with masterly paintings by other prominent Flemish artists. See p. 246.
- **Sint-Baafskathedral (St. Bavo's Cathedral), Ghent:** Awash in marble, gilded wood, and rich baroque and rococo details, this magnificent Gothic cathedral is home to one of the world's greatest art treasures, "The Adoration of the Mystic Lamb." See p. 254.

best BELGIAN SHOPPING

- **Antiques, Brussels:** You'll need luck to score a bargain at the weekend antiques market on place du Grand Sablon—the dealers are well aware of the precise worth of each item in their stock and are calmly determined to get it. But it's still fun to wander the market, browsing and haggling, and who knows? You just might stumble on a treasure. See p. 200.
- **Chocolates, Brussels:** The Swiss might disagree, but the truth is that Belgian handmade chocolates, filled with fresh-cream flavors, are the best in the universe. See p. 199.
- **Diamonds, Antwerp:** Antwerp's Diamantkwartier (Diamond Quarter) is the center of the world's market in precious stones. Much of the trading is still carried out by members of the city's Hassidic Jewish community. See p. 245.

best BRUGES EXPERIENCES

- **Time-Traveling in Bruges:** Without a doubt, Bruges is one of Europe's most handsome small cities. Its almost perfectly preserved center often feels like a film set or museum, with buildings that run the gamut of architectural styles from medieval times to the 19th century. The picturesque canals are the icing on Bruges' cake. See p. 207.
- **Climbing the Belfort in Bruges:** Perhaps no other building is more emblematic of Bruges than this ancient tower. Gird yourself for the 366 steep stairs which lead to panoramic views of the city and out to sea. See p. 219.

o **Viewing the Holy Blood, Bruges:** One of the most revered Christian relics in Europe is housed in the ancient Basilica of the Holy Blood. It is revealed to visitors twice daily in a curiously moving ceremony. It's worth attending to see the faith that believers invest in these relics as well as the over-the-top decoration of the church. See p. 223.

o **Drinking Beer at a Pub:** Steeped in brewing culture, Bruges has no shortage of historic drinking holes where beer-lovers have been imbibing potent Dubbels, Tripels, and Kwaks for hundreds of years. See p. 218.

o **Eating Moules-Frites in Markt:** Yes, it's touristy but sit at any of the terrace restaurants around Bruges' expansive main square and you'll be rewarded with great plates of mussels and piles of crispy fries as well as fantastic views. See p. 219.

o **Hearing the "Last Post," Ypres:** Stand shoulder to shoulder with proud, be-medaled veterans and heroes of recent wars to hear the daily "Last Post" ceremony in tribute to the millions who died in Flanders Fields in World War I between 1914 and 1918. It's something you'll never forget. See p. 265.

best BRUGES FAMILY-FRIENDLY EXPERIENCES

o **Making Belgian Chocolate:** Workshops in the gloriously messy art of chocolate-making take place daily at **Choco-Story** and are available by booking ahead online or occasionally on the day. See p. 231.

o **Taking a Carriage Ride:** The streets of central Bruges ring out with the clip-clopping of horses' hooves as they circle the tourist routes at a smart trot. If you're time-impaired, taking a trip by pony-and-trap is a fun way to see everything in a short (sometimes very short) time, and kids love the novelty of the experience. See p. 234.

o **Cruising on the Canals:** Bruges' ring of canals is nowhere near the size of Amsterdam's labyrinthine waterways, but the architecture and views are similarly lovely. Tours are multilingual. See p. 233.

o **Visiting Kid-Friendly Museums:** To say that Bruges is museum-rich is an understatement; luckily among all the art museums there are plenty that will appeal to children, especially the **Fries Museum** (p. 232) and **Choco-Story** (p. 231). And the **Archeological Museum** (p. 233) offers plenty of hands-on activities for kids.

best BRUGES HOTELS

o **The Pand Hotel, Bruges:** Every creature comfort is supplied at the Pand in a higgledy-piggledy series of bedrooms extending through two historic town houses. See p. 212.

o **Hotel Heritage, Bruges:** On a quiet side street just steps from the Markt, this posh Relais & Chateaux member hotel is tucked inside a stately 19th-century townhouse and features carefully preserved original details and oodles of elegant antiques throughout. A gourmet restaurant highlights seasonal local products; work off your meal in the gym, housed in the 14th-century vaulted cellar. See p. 212.

best BRUGES RESTAURANTS & BARS

o **2be:** With a glass-enclosed "beer wall" stacked with more than 1,200 Belgian beers, 2be is a popular canal-side spot in which to start a relationship with some of Bruges' local brews. See p. 218.

o **Breydel de Coninc:** Arguably the best fish restaurant in Bruges, this temple to mussels (served six different ways) is family-owned and everything is cooked from scratch so you have to forgive the occasional delays. See p. 216.

o **La Civière d'Or:** One of the best choices of the Markt restaurants for lunch-time pit stops involving bucketloads of mussels served with tomatoes, roasted fennel, and saffron. It's actually three venues rolled into one, offering brasserie, cafe, and fine dining menus. See p. 217.

best BRUGES MUSEUMS

o **Expo Picasso:** Some 300 sketches, prints, and lithographs from the famed Spanish artist are beautifully displayed in a former almshouse. Temporary exhibits by modern art greats like Warhol also on view. See p. 231.

o **Groeningemuseum:** Simply the high point of an art-lover's visit to Bruges, the museum focuses on the Flemish Primitive, dating from the 15th century when Bruges was one of the most powerful trading cities in Europe. The highlight of the collection is the horrific "Last Judgment" by Hieronymous Bosch, painted in 1482. See p. 226.

o **Gruuthusemuseum:** Housed in the ornate former residence of an aristo-cratic Belgian family, the museum is cleverly laid out to highlight the historical handiwork of a number of Bruges' guilds. Don't miss the fabulous—and original—carved woodwork doors, floors, and ceilings dot-ted about the palace. See p. 225.

o **In Flanders Fields Museum, Ypres:** Clearly an awful lot of money has been expended on this thoughtful, interactive museum housed in Ypres's remodeled Cloth Hall (the medieval original was destroyed during the dark days of World War II). It's imaginative, poignant, and heart-rending by turn. Not to be missed! See p. 268.

o **Sint-Janshospitaal.** This museum, set in a former hospital, houses Hans' Memling's finest works, including an exquisite shrine dedicated to St. Ursula. A small box, it is swathed in jewel-toned miniatures recounting the virgin's extraordinary adventures. See p. 227.

best BRUGES SHOPPING

o **Beer:** With more than 400 breweries producing over a thousand varieties, Belgium is the European home of beer. It comes in many styles, from

Trappist to white beer, and there are stores throughout Bruges selling a selection of bottles that can be wrapped for taking home in suitcases. See p. 234.

o **Chocolate:** As in Brussels, there are dozens of confectioners creating exquisite handmade chocolates in Bruges. Sample the wares before you buy to find your favorite fillings. See p. 234.

o **Lace:** There are two kinds of Belgian lace: exquisitely handmade pieces or the machine-made stuff, which is of indifferent quality to meet the never-ending demand for souvenirs. If you're looking for the real thing, there are still a few lace stores remaining in Bruges. See p. 234.

AMSTERDAM, BRUSSELS & BRUGES IN CONTEXT

B oth small and densely populated, the Netherlands and Belgium enjoy an enviable standard of living and quality of life. Their societies have become more multicultural—a development that's seen most clearly in the region's main metropolises of Amsterdam and Brussels—and these countries are among the most urbanized on earth.

For the most part, this has only added to their contemporary vibrancy, but the process has not been without stress. Amsterdam has both benefited and suffered from its rising popularity in recent years. It's emerged as a corporate hub—thanks in large part to Brexit—attracting a record 153 foreign companies in 2018 and changing the makeup of the city. But the major impact is being felt from the massive influx of tourism, with some 18 million visitors flocking annually to this city of just 820,000. Many fear Amsterdam will soon not only be known as the "Venice of the North" for its beautiful canals, but also for the way tourism has damaged its soul.

Belgium is a small country. Not so small that if you blink you'll miss it, like neighboring Luxembourg, but small enough that a couple of hours of focused driving will get you from the capital city Brussels to any corner of its realm. Yet the variety of culture, language, history, and cuisine crammed into this meager space would do credit to a land many times its size. Belgium's diversity is a product of its location at the cultural crossroads of western Europe. The boundary between Europe's Germanic north and Latin-language-speaking south cuts clear across the country's middle; the clash of culture has come home to roost in Brussels, where street signage is multilingual although the language most heard in the streets is French.

Like an Atlantis in reverse, the Netherlands has emerged over the centuries from the sea. Much of the country was once a pattern of islands, precariously separated from the North Sea by dunes. As time rolled past, these islands were patiently stitched together by Dutch ingenuity and hard work. The outcome is a canvas-flat, green-and-silver Mondrian of a country, with nearly half its land and two-thirds of its over 17 million inhabitants below sea level.

To make themselves even more welcoming and enjoyable than they already are, the cities of Amsterdam and Brussels have expanded their transport systems, redeveloped decayed inner-city and harbor zones, and revamped their cultural offerings. Amsterdam has seen its traditionally working-class neighborhoods to the east and north of the city center become rapidly gentrified, while Brussels has overhauled several of its major museums. The major Dutch satellite cities of Rotterdam, Utrecht and The Hague, are all the while nurturing, improving, and consolidating their attractions. In Belgium, Antwerp is becoming quite the destination, thanks to a revitalized harbor, new museums, and impressive architecture by the likes of Zaha Hadid.

Bruges continues to attract masses of tourists to its perfectly preserved medieval center while Ghent, once down at the heel, is gaining in popularity thanks to a major cleanup of its many historical assets.

THE NETHERLANDS

Let's clear up some matters of nomenclature. "Dutch" is the result of a 15th-century misunderstanding on the part of the English, who couldn't distinguish too clearly between the people of the northern Low Countries and the various Germanic peoples living further south and east. So to describe the former, they simply corrupted the German *Deutsch* to Dutch.

The term "Holland," is also a misnomer as, strictly speaking, it refers only to the provinces of Noord-Holland and Zuid-Holland and not to the whole country. The Dutch themselves call their country *Nederland* and themselves *Nederlanders*. But they recognize that Holland and Dutch are popular internationally, so, being a practical people, they make use of them.

The Netherlands is small enough that a burst of vigorous driving will get you from one corner of the country to the other in a morning, and you can travel by train from Amsterdam to the farthest point of the rail network in an afternoon. The nation's 42,000 sq. km (16,500 sq. miles) are among the most densely populated in the world, home to over 17 million people, or approximately 1,000 per square mile. The crowding is most noticeable in the Randstad, the heavily populated conurbation that includes the urban centers of Amsterdam, Rotterdam, The Hague, Leiden, Haarlem, Utrecht, and Delft and sprawls across the top half of the country. Elsewhere the land is much more sparsely populated.

The Netherlands is a constitutional monarchy headed by King Willem-Alexander of the House of Orange, who was inaugurated to the throne upon the abdication of his mother, Queen Beatrix on April 30, 2013. He is married to Argentinian Queen Máxima and they have three daughters.

Amsterdam Today

"The Dutch Disease" is what a conservative U.S. columnist called Holland's social liberalism. But not many of the sex workers in Amsterdam's Red Light

District are Dutch, and relatively few denizens of the smoking coffee shops are Dutch. If Amsterdam is a latter-day Sodom and Gomorrah, it's one mainly for visitors.

SEX & DRUGS

The uniquely Dutch combination of tolerance and individualism impacts areas of personal and social morality that in other countries are still red-button issues. In 2001, the world's first same-sex marriage, with a legal status identical to that of heterosexual matrimony, took place in Amsterdam. The Dutch Parliament legalized regulated euthanasia in 2000, making the Netherlands the first country in the world to do so. And then there's prostitution and drug use.

Prostitution is legal in Holland, and prostitutes work in clean premises, pay taxes, receive regular medical checks, are eligible for welfare, and have their own trade union. The majority of sex workers hail from eastern Europe, lured here by the removal of border controls within the E.U. In an effort to curb tourists gawking at them—and limit the amount of foot traffic—the city announced a ban on tours of the Red Light District starting January 1, 2020.

Authorities are not duty bound to prosecute criminal acts, leaving a loophole for social experimentation in areas that technically are illegal. It has been wryly said that the Netherlands has one of the lowest crime rates in Europe because whenever something becomes a criminal problem, the Dutch make it legal. Don't laugh—at least not in Holland—or you may find you've touched the natives where they're tender.

Popular belief notwithstanding, narcotic drugs are illegal in the Netherlands. But the Dutch treat drug use mainly as a medical problem rather than purely as a crime. The authorities distinguish between soft drugs like cannabis, and hard drugs like heroin and cocaine. Both are illegal, but the law is tougher on hard drug abuse. Ironically, improvements in Dutch cannabis cultivation techniques have increased the concentration of the active ingredient THC from 9 percent in 2000 to around 17 percent today.

The Netherlands has significantly lower rates of heroin addiction, drug use, and drug-related deaths than Britain, France, Germany, and other European countries that criticize Holland fiercely on this issue. However, the Netherlands plays a central role in the production and distribution of synthetic drugs, including MDMA, GBH, and methamphetamines, with an estimated revenue of around 19 billion euros, making it one of the world's largest producers.

Still, the Dutch "tradition" of allowing visitors to the country to pop into what's euphemistically known as a coffee shop to smoke an illegal but tolerated cannabis joint is under threat. A legal ruling in 2010 upheld the mayor of Maastricht's decision to end cross-border drugs tourism into his city by banning foreigners from its smoking coffee shops. Rosendaal and Bergen op Zoom, two other border towns plagued by drugs tourists, simply shut down all of their coffee shops in 2009. The most serious threat to Amsterdam's marijuana trade came in 2010, when the government announced its intention to force all of the country's surviving coffee shops—which numbered around 650 (down from a peak of 2,000 in 1997)—to become members-only clubs open only to residents of the Netherlands. This would have meant shutting out the tens of thousands of weed tourists who visit Amsterdam each year. With some coffee shops claiming that 99 percent of their customers are tourists—an estimate of 40 percent is probably more accurate—many coffee shops would have closed if the proposals had become law. Ultimately, the law was shelved, but the Dutch courts continued to chip away at the number of coffee shops in Amsterdam, ruling in 2017 that a coffee shop cannot operate within a 250-meter radius of a school. Today around 175 are still open and are strictly regulated: They all must be licensed and display the official green-and-white sticker in the window. Anyone caught carrying more than 5 grams (for personal use) of cannabis risks a fine, and it is officially illegal to smoke dope in the streets. It is also illegal for anyone under the age of 18 to buy drugs.

A CLASH OF CULTURES

For the visitor, the very medieval heart of Amsterdam today presents much the same face it has over the centuries—a serene canalscape interwoven with a tangle of waterways. But around the extremities of the city, much is changing. Its industrious population still hangs on to the country's age-old traditions of tolerance, and immigrants of all political, religious, and ideological persuasions are still welcomed. However, almost a million (6 percent) of the country's inhabitants are now Muslim and in recent years there have been indications that the welcome mat is wearing thin, thanks in part to threats from radical Islamists. Far-right-wing politician Geert Wilders has become a lightning rod for the racial tensions in contemporary Dutch society, inheriting the anti-Islam mantle of the gay populist politician Pym Fortuyn, assassinated in 2002 by a pro-Muslim Dutch activist; and also of filmmaker Theo van Gogh, murdered by a Dutch-Moroccan Islamist in 2004. Wilders heads the Party for Freedom (PVV), which in elections since 2010 has consistently won around 15 percent of the vote, making it one of the largest parties in the Lower House of Parliament. The PVV views Dutch society, culture, European values, and public safety as threatened by the growth of the Muslim community and of radical Islam. Wilders, who has described the Koran as a "fascist book" and who wants Muslim migration into the Netherlands halted, lives under permanent police protection due to threats to his life. Surging in popularity is the Forum for Democracy (FvD), an anti-immigration, anti-EU party led by Thierry Baudet which first participated in elections in 2017. Baudet capitalized on the March 18, 2019 suspected terrorist attack in Utrecht, a city 40km from Amsterdam, where four people were shot dead aboard a tram. His party captured 12 out of 75 seats in the provincial elections held on March 20, 2019—more than Prime Minister Mark Rutte's People's Party for Freedom and Democracy (VVD)—and is sure to shape Dutch politics in the coming years.

The Origins of Amsterdam

The earliest inhabitants of what is now the Netherlands were three tribal groups who settled the marshy deltas of the Low Countries in the dawn of recorded history. They were the Belgae of the southern regions; the Batavii, who settled in the area of the Great Rivers; and the fiercely independent Frisii, who took up residence along the northern coast. Each tribe posed a challenge to Julius Caesar when he came calling in the 1st century B.C., but the Romans managed, after prolonged and effective objections from the locals, to get both the Belgae and the Batavii to knuckle under.

After the demise of the Roman Empire, the Frisians were still going strong. They repelled the next wave of would-be conquerors in the 5th century, when hordes of Saxons and Franks over-ran the Romano-Batavians. Although many northern European peoples embraced Christianity by the late 5th century, it was not until the late 8th century that the Frisians abandoned their pagan gods, and then only when the mighty Charlemagne, king of the Franks and ruler of the Carolingian Empire, compelled them to in a massive show of force.

GOOD FOR BUSINESS

By the 13th and 14th centuries, the nobility were busy building the castles and fortified manor houses throughout the Netherlands. Meanwhile the Catholic hierarchy grew both powerful and wealthy; the bishops of Maastricht and Utrecht played key roles in politics, and they preserved their legacy by erecting splendid cathedrals, abbeys, and monasteries.

During the 14th and 15th centuries, Holland's position at the mouths of three great west European rivers made it a focal point in power struggles. The House of Burgundy became the first major feudal power in the Low Countries, consolidating its hold on the region by acquiring fiefdoms one by one through the various means of marriage, inheritance, and military force. Its day soon passed, however, and the Austrian Habsburg emperor Maximilian acquired the Low Countries from the Burgundians by much the same means.

Amsterdam began its rise to commercial prosperity in 1323, when Floris VI, the Count of Holland, established the city as one of two toll points for the import of beer from Hamburg. The city's powerful merchants established guilds of craftsmen and put ships to sea to catch North Sea herring. Soon they had expanded into trading salted Baltic herring; Norwegian salted and dried cod, and cod-liver oil; German beer and salt; linen and woolen cloth from the Low Countries and England; Russian furs and candle wax; Polish grain and flour; and Swedish timber and iron.

WARS OF RELIGION

Dutch citizens began to embrace the Protestant church at the same time that the Low Countries came under the rule of Charles V, the Catholic Habsburg emperor and king of Spain in 1506. Then known as the Spanish Netherlands, the country became a pressure point and fulcrum for the shifting political scene caused by the Reformation right across Europe. The rigorous doctrines of John Calvin and his firm belief in the separation of church and state began to take root in the country's psyche.

When Charles relinquished the Spanish throne to his son Philip II in 1555, the days darkened for the Dutch. As an ardent Catholic, Philip was determined to defeat the Reformation and set out to hunt heretics throughout his empire.

He dispatched the infamous Duke of Alba to the Low Countries to carry out the Inquisition's "death to heretics" edict. The Dutch resented Philip's intrusion into their affairs and began a resistance movement, led by William of Orange, Count of Holland. Known as William the Silent, he declared: "I cannot approve of princes attempting to control the conscience of their subjects and wanting to rob them of the liberty of faith."

Only those towns that declined to join the ensuing fight were spared destruction when the Spanish invaded in 1568. Spanish armies marched inexorably through Holland, besting the defenses of each city to which they laid siege, with few exceptions. In an ingenious if desperate move in 1574, William of Orange saved Leiden by flooding the province, allowing his ships to sail right up to the city's walls.

This victory galvanized the Dutch in fighting for their independence. In 1579, the Dutch nobles formed the Union of Utrecht, in which they agreed to fight together in a united front. Although the union was devised solely to win the battle against Spain, consolidation inevitably occurred and by the turn of the 17th century, the seven northern provinces of what had been the Spanish Netherlands was declared the Republic of the Seven Provinces.

The struggle with Spain continued until 1648, but a new, prosperous era was soon to be ushered in.

THE GOLDEN AGE

Over the first 50 to 75 years of the 17th century, that legendary Dutch entrepreneurial talent came into its own. These years have since become known as the Golden Age. It seemed every business venture the Dutch initiated during this time turned a profit and that each of their many expeditions to the unknown places of the world resulted in a new jewel in the Dutch trading empire. Colonies and trade were established to provide the luxury-hungry merchants at home with new delights, such as fresh ginger from Java, foxtails from America, fine porcelain from China, and flower bulbs from Turkey that produced big, bright, waxy flowers and grew quite readily in Holland's sandy soil—tulips.

The Netherlands was getting rich and Amsterdam soon grew into one of the world's wealthiest cities. In 1602, traders from each of the major cities in the Republic of the Seven Provinces set up the Vereenigde Oostindische Compagnie (V.O.C.), the United East India Company, which was granted a monopoly on trade in the east. It was wildly successful and established the Dutch presence in the Spice Islands (Indonesia), Goa, South Africa, and China.

This is the period that saw the planning and developing of the **Canal Ring** (p. 60) around the old heart of Amsterdam. The three great canals that form a concentric belt around the city center were years in the planning and construction, but were needed urgently as the original streets were overcrowded and disease-ridden thanks to the never-ceasing flow of immigrants into the city. Today Keizersgracht, Prinsengracht, and Herengracht stand as proud reminders of this great time of development, lined with mansions built by the nouveau riche of the Dutch Golden Age. Visit **Het Grachtenhuis** (p. 97) to learn how the canals were constructed.

Holland was becoming a refuge for persecuted groups. The Pilgrim Fathers stayed in Leiden for a dozen years before embarking for America from Delfshaven in Rotterdam in 1620, Sephardic Jews fled the oppressive Spanish and welcomed the tolerance of the Dutch, and refugees straggled in from France and Portugal. William of Orange had created a climate of tolerance in the Netherlands that attracted talented newcomers who contributed a great deal to the expanding economic, social, artistic, and intellectual climate of the country.

Golden Age Holland can be compared to Classical Greece and Renaissance Italy for the great flowering of wealth and culture that transformed society. "There is perhaps no other example of a complete and highly original civilization springing up in so short a time in so small a territory," wrote the British historian Simon Schama.

THE END OF THE GOLDEN AGE

However, the country's luck was soon to change. The Dutch call 1672 the Rampjaar (Year of Disaster). France, under Louis XIV, invaded the United Provinces by land and the English attacked by sea. This war (1672–78) and the later War of the Spanish Succession (1701–13) drained both Holland's wealth and morale. The buccaneering, can-do, go-anywhere spirit of traders, artists, and writers began to ebb, replaced by conservatism and closed horizons.

Revolutionary France invaded Holland in 1794, capturing Amsterdam and establishing the Batavian Republic in 1795, headed by the pro-French Dutch Patriots. Napoleon brought the short-lived republic to an end in 1806 by setting up his brother, Louis Napoleon, as king of the Netherlands, and installed him in a palace that had been Amsterdam's Town Hall. Louis did such a good job of representing the interests of his new subjects that, in 1810, Napoleon deposed him and brought the Netherlands formally into the empire.

When the Dutch recalled the House of Orange in 1814, it was to fill the role of king in a constitutional monarchy. The monarch was yet another William of Orange; however, because his reign was to be a fresh start, the Dutch started numbering their Williams all over again (which makes for a very confusing history). However, it was not until the Battle of Waterloo in 1815 that Napoleon was finally defeated and sent into exile.

In 1831 the Low Countries split entirely, with the southern provinces forming Belgium. The rest of the 19th century saw social reforms, an influx of Jews

---

Dutch in the English Lexicon

The 17th-century Anglo-Dutch wars were a series of skirmishes between the England and the Netherlands over maritime trade; one of the most notable conflicts was the 1667 Raid on the Medway, with the Dutch sailing boldly up the Medway River near London and trashing the English fleet. So the English added verbal abuse to their arsenal.

That's why we have "Dutch courage" (alcohol-induced courage), "Dutch treat" (pay for yourself), "going Dutch" (everybody pays their share), and "double Dutch" (gibberish). Americans were kinder to their Revolutionary War supporters, speaking of "beating the Dutch" (doing something remarkable).

from Antwerp (who formed the backbone of the diamond-cutting industry in Amsterdam), and the building of more canals, waterways, and railway lines.

MODERN TIMES

As the storm clouds gathered across Europe with the advent of World War I, the Netherlands escaped the worst ravages by maintaining strict neutrality. Holland shared in the wealth as Europe's condition improved after the war, but conditions were very bad during the 1930s, when widespread unemployment in Amsterdam brought on by the worldwide Great Depression caused the government to use the army in 1934 to control the unruly masses.

During World War II, Nazi troops invaded the country in 1940. An estimated 104,000 of Holland's 140,000 Jews were murdered, Rotterdam sustained heavy bombings, and the rest of the country suffered terribly at the hands of its invaders. The Dutch operated one of the most effective underground movements in Europe, which became an important factor in the liberation in 1945. Among those murdered in the Nazi terror was a teenage girl who came to symbolize many other victims of the Holocaust: Anne Frank (1929–45).

In the 1960s, Amsterdam was a hotbed of political and cultural radicalism. Hippies trailing clouds of marijuana smoke took over the Dam and camped out in the Vondelpark and in front of Centraal Station. Radical political activity, which began with "happenings" staged by a group known as the Provos, intensified. In 1966, the Provos were behind the protests that disrupted the wedding of Princess Beatrix to German Claus von Amsberg in the Westerkerk; they threw smoke bombs and fighting broke out between protesters and police. The Provos disbanded in 1967, but many of their principles were adopted by the Kabouters (this translates into English as "Green Gnomes," a hardline anarchist group that won several seats on the city council before fading into obscurity).

The Dutch as Giants

Maybe it's nature's way of compensating for their country being challenged size wise, but the Dutch are *tall*. The average man is 1.8m (6 ft.) and the average woman is 1.7m (5 ft., 7 in.), which in both cases is 5cm (2 in.) more than the European average. Not only that, but a government study showed that the average height of the Dutch increases by 1.5cm (½ in.) every decade.

The Provos and Kabouters had long advocated environmental programs such as prohibiting all motor vehicles from the city. They persuaded authorities to provide 20,000 white-painted bicycles free for citizens' use—this scheme was abandoned when most of the bicycles were stolen, to reappear in freshly painted colors as "private" property. But some of their other ideas very nearly came to fruition. In 1992, Amsterdam's populace voted to create a traffic-free zone in the center city, but this has yet to be realized.

The Lay of the Land

For all that the Bible says otherwise, the Dutch insist the Creation took 8 days, not 7—on the 8th day they reclaimed their country from the sea with their own hands. "God made the earth," they tell you, "and the Dutch made Holland."

The all-important dikes are designed to hold back the sea and began to evolve as far back as the A.D. 1st century, when the country's earliest inhabitants settled on unprotected coastal wetlands in the northern regions of Friesland and Groningen. These settlers first attempted to defend their land by building huge earthen mounds called *terpen,* on which they constructed their homes during recurring floods. Around the 8th and 9th centuries, they were building proper dikes; by the end of the 13th century, entire coastal regions were protected from the sea by dikes. Today they take the form of great mounds of earth and stone that extend for miles, and indeed, many of the roads you travel on around Amsterdam are built along the tops of dikes.

Around half of the country's land area has been reclaimed from the sea, lakes, and marshes. Some 2,600 sq. km (1,000 sq. miles) of the Netherlands was underwater just 100 years ago. Approximately 25 percent of Holland, an area that holds about two-thirds of its people, lies *below* sea level, protected from flooding only by sand dunes, dikes, and Dutch engineering prowess. That Amsterdam itself has not disappeared under the North Sea is largely due to this ingenuity, as most of the city is 2m (6.6 ft.) below sea level, built on piles, and shored up by a complex system of dams, canals, locks, and dykes.

In 1953, devastating North Sea storms broke through the dikes in many places along the southwest coast of the country, flooding significant areas and causing a substantial loss of life and property. To assure greater protection along its coastal areas, the Netherlands embarked upon the long-term Delta Works to seal off the river estuaries with a series of dams in the southwest of the country.

In the Netherlands, wind is ever present, so it is not surprising that the Dutch have made use of windmills to do their hard labor, from pumping water off the land to drain polders, to milling grain, and sawing timber. Nowadays you're as likely to see the whirling blades of wind turbines, generating a growing proportion of the nation's electrical power.

Amsterdam still exists, despite worries about global warming and rising sea levels. However, the government is considering bolstering the sea defenses to handle a rogue super-storm, which would be a tenfold increase over the current defense systems.

Meanwhile, the Dutch water expertise has helped Amsterdam expand: Zeeburg and IJburg are two new areas northeast of the city center where there used to be just water, much like the great Flevopolder in the eastern part of the country. This man-made island, created between 1950 and 1968, is home to half a million people, and with a surface area of 370 square miles is one of the largest artificial islands in the world.

Amsterdam in the Arts
VISUAL ART

The 17th century was the undisputed Golden Age of Dutch art. During this busy time, artists were blessed with wealthy patrons whose support allowed them free reign for their talents. Art held a cherished place in the hearts of average Dutch citizens, too. The Dutch were particularly fond of pictures that depicted their world: landscapes, seascapes, domestic scenes, portraits, and still lifes. The art of this period remains some of the greatest ever created.

One of the finest landscape painters of all time was **Jacob van Ruysdael** (1628–82), who depicted cornfields, windmills, and forest scenes, along with his famous views of Haarlem. In some of his works, the human figure is very small, and in others it does not appear at all; instead the artist typically devoted two-thirds of the canvas to the vast skies filled with the moody clouds that float over the flat Dutch terrain. His finest works are in the Rijksmuseum (p. 101).

Frans Hals (1581–1666), the undisputed leader of the Haarlem School, specialized in portraiture. The relaxed relationship between the artist and his subject in his paintings was a great departure from the formal masks of Renaissance portraits. With the lightness of his brushstrokes, Hals was able to convey an immediacy and intimacy. Visit the Frans Hals Museum (p. 130) in Haarlem to study his techniques.

One of the geniuses of western art was **Rembrandt Harmenszoon van Rijn** (1606–69). This highly prolific and influential artist had a dramatic life filled with commercial success and personal tragedy. Rembrandt was a master at showing the soul and inner life of humankind, in both his portraits and illustrations of biblical stories. His most famous work, the group portrait known as "The Night Watch" (1642), is on view in the Rijksmuseum (p. 101).

A spirituality reigns over his self-portraits as well; Rembrandt painted about 60 during his lifetime. His masterly "Self-Portrait with Saskia" shows the artist with his wife during prosperous times and is now back on show in Museum Het Rembrandthuis (p. 92) in Amsterdam—where it was painted ca. 1635—along with others of his paintings and 285 of his other etchings.

Perhaps the best known of the "Little Dutch Masters," who mainly restricted themselves to one genre of painting, such as portraiture, is **Jan Vermeer** (1632–75) of Delft. The main subjects of Vermeer's work are the activities and pleasures of simple home life. Vermeer placed figures at the center of his paintings, and typically used the background space to convey a feeling of stability and serenity. He excelled at reproducing the lighting of his interior scenes; there are fine examples of his work at the Mauritshuis in The Hague (p. 148) and in the Rijksmuseum (p. 101).

If **Vincent van Gogh** (1853–90) had not failed as a missionary in the Borinage mining region of Belgium, he might not have turned to painting and become the greatest Dutch artist of the 19th century. "The Potato Eaters" (1885) was his first masterpiece. This rough, crudely painted work shows a group of peasants gathered around the table for their evening meal after a long day of manual labor. Gone are the traditional beauty and serenity of earlier Dutch genre painting. In 1888, Vincent traveled to Arles in Provence, where he was dazzled by the Mediterranean sun. His favorite color, yellow, which to him signified love, dominated landscapes such as "Wheatfield with a Reaper" (1889). For the next 2 years, he remained in the south of France, painting at a frenetic pace in between bouts of madness. The Van Gogh Museum in Amsterdam (p. 102) has more than 200 of his paintings.

Piet Mondrian (1872–1944) was an originator of De Stijl (or neoplasticism). With Theo van Doesburg, Mondrian began a magazine in 1917 entitled *"De Stijl"* ("The Style") in which he expounded the principles of neoplasticism: a simplification of forms or, in other words, a purified abstraction; an art that would be derived "not from exterior vision but from interior life." His Impressionistic masterpiece, "The Red Tree" (1909)—which looks as though it's bursting into flames against a background of blue—marked a turning point in his career. The world's leading collection of his work is found in the Gemeentemuseum in The Hague (p. 147).

ARCHITECTURE

One of Amsterdam's most prominent architectural features is the gable. The landmark town houses and warehouses of the city's old center all have gables and it is easy to judge their age by their shape. Simple triangular, wooden gables came first, and then spout gables (see Keizersgracht 403) with a little point on top were used, mostly on warehouses, in the 14th century. These simply followed the pitch of the roof, but over time, more ornate designs crept in. Step gables were popular in the 17th century (see Brouwersgracht 2 in the Jordaan), and elegant, straight neck gables (see Herengracht 168) adorned with ornamental shoulders appeared between 1640 and 1780. Rounded bell-shaped gables (see Prinsengracht 359) were introduced in the late 17th century and remained popular until the end of the 18th century.

The hook sitting central on most of these gables is called a *hijsbalk* and is still used with a rope and pulley system for hauling cumbersome items in and out of houses with steep, narrow staircases. Most of the canalside houses lean a tad forward to prevent loads crashing into the facades.

Hendrick de Keyser (1565–1621), an architect who worked in Amsterdam at the height of the Renaissance, is known for using decorative, playful elements in a way that was practical to the structure. For instance, he combined hard yellow or white sandstone decorative features with soft red brick, creating a visually stimulating multicolored facade. The Westerkerk (p. 99) is probably his finest work. **Philips and Justus Vingboons** were architects and brothers who worked in the Renaissance style; while walking along Herengracht, Keizersgracht, and Prinsengracht, you'll see many of their buildings, including the Bijbels Museum (Biblical Museum; p. 96).

Jacob van Campen (1595–1657) built the elaborate **Town Hall** at the Dam, now the Koninklijk Royal Palace (p. 92) and was probably the single most important architect of Amsterdam architecture's classical period.

Around 1665, **Adriaan Dortsman** (1625–82), best known for his classic restrained Dutch style, began building homes with balconies and attics, leaving off the pilasters and festoons that adorned earlier facades; see his designs at the Museum van Loon (p. 98) on Keizersgracht.

A further cultural flowering took place in the late 19th century, which saw the construction of Centraal Station (p. 91) and the Rijksmuseum (p. 101) by

P.J.H. Cuypers in Neo-revivalist style as well as **A.L. van Gendt**'s neo-classical splendor of the Concertgebouw (p. 122), still the city's finest concert hall. Between 1900 and 1940, Amsterdam architects purveyed many different styles of building. **H.P. Berlage** is regarded as one of the city's first modern architects, designing the stock exchange (p. 90) and the Gemeentemuseum in The Hague (p. 147). He paved the way for the Amsterdam School of architects, whose follower **Michael de Klerk** designed Museum Het Schip (p. 109), a massive yet fluid building with stained glass, wrought iron, and corner towers.

Today the tradition of producing spectacular architecture continues in Amsterdam with the ever-changing horizons on the IJ waterway; **Science Center NEMO** (p. 107) was designed by Renzo Piano, while the gleaming-white, mantislike **EYE Film Institute** (p. 108) was the first public building to be recently constructed in Amsterdam Noord, giving a clear indication of where the Amsterdam of the future will be headed.

The Arts in Amsterdam
BOOKS
If a single individual may be said to "personify" the Holocaust, that person must be Anne Frank. Her diary, compiled as a series of letters addressed "Dear Kitty" and kept for more than 2 years until her arrest on August 4, 1944, has come to symbolize the plight of millions of Jews during the Nazi terror. Reading it is a fascinating window into Amsterdam during World War II.

"The van Gogh File: A Journey of Discovery" is Ken Wilkie's excellent exploration of Vincent van Gogh's life and art. Wilkie followed Van Gogh's trail through the Netherlands, Belgium, England, and France. Along the way, he met some of the last surviving people to have met the artist.

For more art history, Simon Schama's "The Embarrassment of Riches: An Interpretation of Dutch Culture in the Golden Age" (1987) lets you inside Amsterdam's greatest period and is simultaneously lighthearted and scholarly.

On the fiction side: Ian McEwan's "Amsterdam" (1998) and John Green's wildly successful young adult novel "The Fault in our Stars" (2012) have scenes that bring Amsterdam to life.

FILM
Amsterdam-born film director Paul Verhoeven is probably the best-known Dutch filmmaker (Basic Instinct, Robocop) and his wartime resistance drama "Soldier of Orange" (1977), is worth seeing. Amsterdam was also the backdrop in "Ocean's Twelve" (2004) and "The Hitman's Bodyguard" (2017), which featured a chase scene on the canals. And in the film adaption of "The Fault in our Stars," the bench where the couple kisses has become a pilgrimage site (it's on the Leidsegracht canal).

MUSIC
Amsterdam has been immortalized in only a few pop songs; notably the "Ballad of John and Yoko" by John Lennon, following the pair's notorious "bed-in" at the Amsterdam Hilton in 1969. And Neil Finn of New Zealand band Crowded House wrote the following lyrics after spending a wasted weekend in the

coffeehouses of Amsterdam: "Lying in the streets of Amsterdam/Nearly fell under a tram," which are hardly going to win any prizes for sentiment but probably echo the experiences of many a newbie visitor to Amsterdam.

Today, electronic dance music is one of the Netherlands' main cultural exports. Famous Dutch DJs like Tiësto, Hardwell, and Armin van Buuren perform their sets for huge audiences around the world. The Amsterdam Dance Event, held every year in October, is the biggest conference and festival of its kind, drawing around half a million visitors over 5 days.

Eating & Drinking in Amsterdam

Dutch national dishes tend to be of the ungarnished, hearty, wholesome variety—solid, stick-to-your-ribs stuff. A perfect example is *erwtensoep,* a thick pea soup cooked with ham or sausage that provides inner warmth against damp Dutch winters and is filling enough to be a meal by itself. Similarly, *hutspot,* a potato-based "hotchpotch," or stew, is no-nonsense nourishment to which *klapstuk* (lean beef) is sometimes added.

Seafood, as you might imagine in this traditionally seafaring country, is always fresh and well prepared. Fried sole, oysters, and mussels from Zeeland, and herring (fresh in early June, pickled other months) are most common. In fact, if you happen to be in Amsterdam for the beginning of the herring season, it's an absolute obligation—at least once—to interrupt your sidewalk strolls to buy a "green" herring from a pushcart such as Stubbe's Haring (p. 79). The Dutch are uncommonly fond of *paling* (an oily freshwater eel) and Zeeland oysters and mussels known as *Zeeuwse oesters* and *Zeeuwse mosselen,* from September to March.

At lunchtime you're likely to find yourself munching on *broodjes,* small buttered rolls usually filled with ham and cheese or beef; a *broodje gezond* (healthy sandwich) with cheese and vegetables is a good choice for vegetarians. Not to be missed are the delicious, filling pancakes called *pannenkoeken,* often eaten as a savory dish with bacon and cheese. *Poffertjes* are a sweet, lighter, penny-size version that are especially good topped with apples, jam, or syrup.

In the late afternoon, the Dutch like to accompany their first beer or wine with a hearty snack like *bitterballen*, deep-fried round croquettes stuffed with a meat-based goulash. Despite their name, they are not at all bitter, but were traditionally served alongside *kruidenbitter*, a strong herbal liqueur.

The popular Indonesian *rijsttafel* (rice table), a feast of 15 to 30 small portions of different dishes eaten with plain rice, has been a national favorite ever since it arrived in the 17th century. If you've never experienced this mini-feast, it should definitely be on your "must-eat" list for Holland—the basic idea behind the *rijsttafel* is to sample a wide variety of complementary flavors, textures, and temperatures: savory and sweet, spicy and mild.

For authentic Dutch dishes, look for the NEERLANDS DIS sign, which identifies restaurants specializing in the native cuisine. You'll find numerous moderately priced restaurants and brown cafes (p. 79), which are cozy social centers with simple but tasty food, sometimes served outside on sidewalk tables in good weather. Sidewalk vendors, with fresh herring and the ubiquitous *broodjes* or other light specialties, are popular as well.

Although there's no such thing as a free lunch, there is the next best thing— a *dagschotel* (plate of the day) and *dagmenu* (menu of the day). And these days, Amsterdam is increasingly a destination for fine dining, with accomplished restaurants such as **Rijks** (p. 82), **&moshik** (p. 75), and **Vinkeles** (p. 80), and many new stylish, mid-priced eateries.

BEER, GIN & WINE

What to drink when in Amsterdam? Beer, for one thing. As you make the rounds of the brown cafes, you can get regular brands such as Grolsch, Amstel, or Heineken. Recently there has been a boom in local breweries making more complex and interesting craft beers, of which Brouwerij 't IJ, Oedipus, and Walhalla are among the best.

Also popular is the potent native ginlike liqueur known as *jenever* (the name comes from the Dutch word for "juniper"), a fiery, colorless spirit distilled from grain or malt, served ice cold and drunk neat—without any mixer, or even ice. In the 16th century, it was the drink of the masses in Holland, as the drinking water was filthy and the *jenever* was believed to have medicinal properties. Dutch brands include Jonge Wees, Bols, Rembrandt Korewijn, and De Kuyper.

There are even some Dutch wines, perfectly respectable although produced in modest quantities by the 150 or so wineries around the country. Some of the finest include the sparkling wines of the Apostelhoeve, in the far south near Maastricht, and Frysling, in the upper north of the Netherlands. The wines of Wijngaard de Linie and Wijnhoeve de Kleine Schorre are also highly praised.

BELGIUM TODAY

After a long history of occupation by foreign powers, Belgium has emerged as the elected heart of Europe, the country where European nations come together to rule over their divided continent in precarious harmony. Brussels hosts the headquarters of both the European Union and NATO and is now home to the world's largest concentration of international diplomats. However, all is not well in the kingdom of Belgium.

Modern Belgium is a parliamentary democracy under a constitutional monarch, King Philippe, who ascended the throne on July 21, 2013, after his father King Albert II abdicated. Philippe is married to Queen Mathilde and they have four children. The government exists in a more-or-less permanent state of crisis due to the cultural and linguistic divide that has torn away at the heart of Belgium since the late 19th century. Ambitious regional politicians, particularly in Flanders, often push the country to the brink of dissolution; some believe that partition and subsequent accession of French-speaking Wallonia to France and Flemish- or Dutch-speaking Flanders to the Netherlands may be the only way to solve the issue.

In 2010 inconclusive election results and troubled relations between parties led to the world record longest cabinet formation, with a stunning 541 days. Although the country came out intact, a decade later there are more and more signs that Flemish and Walloon are leading increasingly disparate lives; universities in Brussels that once were open to both communities are now segregated and the denizens of Flanders towns like Bruges, Mechelen (p. 268), and Lennik firmly see themselves as Flemish, not Belgian.

Further dividing the country, in a different fashion, were the Brussels terrorist attacks on March 22, 2016, when two bombs were detonated at the Brussels Airport in Zaventem and a third in the city's Maalbeek subway station; 35 people died, including the three suicide bombers, and 320 people were injured. The bombings, for which ISIS claimed responsibility, were the deadliest act of terrorism in the country's history and they exposed the extent to which disenfranchised Muslim youths were susceptible to the message of radical Islam, primarily in the Molenbeek district of Brussels. Brussels' reputation as a global business center took a hit, and the relatively large number of Belgians who decided to join the ranks of ISIS in Syria and Iraq means that there continues to be severe national security implications for the country.

For a geographical understanding of Belgium's two ethnic regions, Flemish- or Dutch-speaking Vlaanderen (Flanders) and French-speaking Wallonie (Wallonia), draw an imaginary east-west line across the country just south of the capital city Brussels, which exists as an urban island between the two bickering factions. North of the line is Flanders, where you find the medieval cities of Bruges, Ghent, and Antwerp, and Belgium's North Sea coastline. South of the line is Wallonia.

It has been said that Belgium suffers severely from linguistic indigestion. The inhabitants of Flanders speak four variations of *Vlaams* (Flemish), two of which are considered as dialects of Dutch and two as separate, but closely connected, languages. Flanders inhabitants always claim to speak Flemish, never Dutch, although Dutch is the official language of the region. The citizens of Wallonia speak French, and a minority still speak an old Walloon dialect of French. In Brussels the two languages mingle, often to ridiculous effect (the police have both POLICE and POLITIE emblazoned on the back of their uniforms) but French has the upper hand. So strong is the feeling for each language in its own region that, along the line where they meet, it's not unusual for French to be the daily tongue on one side of a street and Flemish on the other. Throughout the country, road signs acknowledge both languages by giving multiple versions of the same place name—Brussel/Bruxelles or Brugge/Bruges, for example. There's even a small area in eastern Belgium where German is spoken. Belgium, then, has not one but three official languages: Dutch, French, and German.

In short, far from being a homogeneous, harmonious people with one strong national identity, Belgians take considerable pride in their individualistic attributes.

The vast majority of Belgians are Catholic, though there's more than a smattering of Protestants, a small Jewish community, and a rising proportion of immigrant Muslims and their locally born children. Down the centuries, Belgians—nobles and peasants alike—have proclaimed their Christian faith by way of impressive cathedrals, churches, paintings, and holy processions.

The tradition continues today, and can be seen at Bruges' centuries-old Procession of the Holy Blood (p. 39), held every year in May.

Folklore still plays a large part in Belgium's national daily life, with local myths giving rise to some of the country's most colorful pageants and festivals, such as Ypres's **Festival of the Cats,** Bruges' **Pageant of the Golden Tree,** and the stately **Ommegang** in Brussels.

Looking Back at Belgium

Julius Caesar first marched his Roman legions against the ancient Belgae tribes in 58 B.C. For nearly 5 centuries thereafter, Belgium was shielded from the barbarians by the great Roman defense line on the Rhine.

From the beginning of the 5th century, Roman rule gave way to the Franks. In 800, Charlemagne (p. 19), king of the Franks and ruler of the Carolingian Empire, instituted an era of agricultural reform, setting up local rulers known as counts who rose up to seize more power after Charlemagne's death. In 843, Charlemagne's grandsons signed the Treaty of Verdun, which split French-allied (but Dutch-speaking) Flanders in the north from the southern (French-speaking) Walloon provinces.

A Flemish mercenary known as Baldwin Iron-Arm rose to become the first Count of Flanders in 862 upon his marriage to Judith, the daughter of the King of West Francia; his house eventually ruled over a domain that included the Low Countries and lands as far south as the Scheldt (Escaut) in France. Baldwin was responsible for repelling the constant Viking incursions of the time. Meanwhile, powerful prince-bishops controlled most of Wallonia from their seat in Liège.

FLANDERS RISING

As Flanders grew larger and stronger, its cities thrived and its citizens wrested more and more self-governing powers. Bruges emerged as a leading center of European trade; its monopoly on English cloth attracted bankers and financiers from Germany and Lombardy. Ghent and Ypres (Ieper) also prospered in the wool trade. Powerful trade and manufacturing guilds emerged and erected splendid edifices as their ego-satisfying headquarters.

As medieval towns emerged as wealthy city-states, the once-mighty counts of Flanders steadily lost their power and in 1297, France's King Philip IV attempted to annex Flanders. However, he had not reckoned on the stubborn resistance of Flemish common folk. Led by Jan Breydel, a lowly weaver, and Pieter de Coninck, a butcher, they rallied to face the heavily armored French military; the decisive battle took place in 1302 in the fields surrounding Kortrijk in western Flanders. When it was over, victorious Flemish artisans scoured the bloody battlefield, triumphantly gathering hundreds of golden spurs from slain French knights. Their victory at the Battle of the Golden Spurs is celebrated by the Flemish to this day on July 11th.

THE BURGUNDIAN ERA

Philip the Good, who was Duke of Burgundy, gained control of virtually all the Low Countries in the mid-1400s, His progeny, through a series of dynastic marriages, consolidated their holdings into a single Burgundian "Netherlands," or Low Countries. Brussels, Antwerp, Mechelen, and Leuven attained new prominence as centers of trade, commerce, and the arts.

This era was one of immense wealth, much of which was poured into the fine public buildings, impressive mansions, and soaring Gothic cathedrals that survive in Brussels and Bruges to this day. Wealthy patrons made possible the brilliant works of Flemish artists such as Jan van Eyck, Hieronymous Bosch, Rogier van der Weyden, and German-born Hans Memling; Flemish opulence became a byword around Europe.

By the end of the 1400s, however, Charles the Bold, last of the dukes of Burgundy, had lost to the French king on the field of battle, and once more French royalty turned a covetous eye on the Low Countries. To French consternation, Mary of Burgundy, the duke's heir, married Maximilian of Austria and the provinces became part of the mighty Habsburg Empire.

A grandson of that union, Charles V, born in Ghent and reared in Mechelen, presided for 40 years over most of Europe, including Spain and its New World possessions. But he was beset by the Protestant Reformation, which created dissension among the once solidly Catholic populace. It all proved too much for the great monarch, and in 1556 he abdicated in favor of his son, Philip II of Spain.

THE SPANISH INVASION

Philip II ascended to power in an impressive ceremony at Coudenberg Palace (p. 188) in Brussels in 1555. An ardent Catholic who spoke neither Dutch nor French, he brought the infamous instruments of the Inquisition to bear on an increasingly Protestant—and increasingly rebellious—Low Countries population. The response from his Protestant subjects was violent: For a month in 1566, they went on a rampage of destruction; the *Beeldenstorm* (Iconoclastic Fury) saw churches pillaged, religious statues smashed, and other religious works of art burned.

An angry Philip II ordered the Duke of Alba (p. 20) to lead 10,000 Spanish troops in a wave of retaliatory strikes. The atrocities Alba and his Council of Blood committed are legendary. He was merciless—when the Catholic counts of Egmont and Hornes tried to intercede with Philip, he put them under arrest for 6 months, and then had them publicly beheaded on the Grand-Place (p. 178) in Brussels.

Instead of submission, this sort of intimidation gave rise to a brutal conflict that lasted from 1568 to 1648. Led by William of Orange (p. 20) and other nobles who raised private armies, the Protestants fought on doggedly until independence was finally achieved for the seven undefeated provinces in the north (p. 20), which became the fledgling country of the Netherlands. Those in the south remained under the thumb of Spain and gradually returned to the Catholic Church.

AN INDEPENDENT STATE

In 1795, Belgium wound up once more under the rule of France. It was not until Napoleon Bonaparte's crushing defeat at Waterloo (p. 21)—just miles from

Brussels—that Belgians began to think of independence as a real possibility. Its time had not yet come, however; under the post-Napoleonic Congress of Vienna (1814–15) Belgium was once more united with the provinces of Holland. The Dutch soon learned that governing unruly Belgium was more than they had bargained for and the 1830 rebellion in Brussels was the last straw. A provisional Belgian government was formed with an elected National Congress. On July 21, 1831, Belgium officially became a constitutional monarchy when a German prince, Leopold of Saxe-Coburg and Gotha, became king.

The new country set about developing its coal and iron natural resources, and its textile, manufacturing, and shipbuilding industries. The country was hardly unified by this process, however, for most of the natural resources were to be found in the French-speaking Walloon region, where prosperity grew much more rapidly than in Flanders. The Flemish, while happy to be freed from the rule of their Dutch neighbors, resented the greater influence of their French-speaking compatriots. And here the present-day dissension has its roots.

WAR & PEACE

It took another invasion to bring a semblance of unity. When German forces swept over the country in 1914, the Belgians mounted a defense that made them heroes of World War I—even though parts of the Flemish population openly collaborated with the enemy, hailing them as liberators from Walloon domination.

With the coming of peace, Belgium found its southern coal, iron, and manufacturing industries reeling, while the northern Flemish regions were moving steadily ahead by developing light industry, especially around Antwerp. Advanced agricultural methods yielded greater productivity and higher profits for Flemish farmers. By the end of the 1930s, the Flemish population outnumbered the Walloons by a big enough majority to install their beloved language as the official voice of education, justice, and civil administration in Flanders.

With the outbreak of World War II, Belgium was once more overrun by German forces. King Leopold III decided to surrender to the invaders, remain in Belgium, and try to soften the harsh effects of occupation. The Belgian Resistance was among the most determined and successful of the underground organizations that fought against Nazi occupation in Europe. On the other side, Flemish and Walloon quislings formed separate Waffen-SS formations that fought for the Nazis in Russia. By the war's end, the king was imprisoned in Germany and a regent was appointed as head of state. His controversial decision to surrender led to bitter debate when he returned to the throne in 1950, and in 1951 he stepped down in favor of his son, Baudouin.

UNITY & DISUNITY

During King Baudouin's 42 years on the throne, much progress was made in achieving harmony among Belgium's linguistically and culturally diverse population. In the 1970s, efforts were made to grant increasing autonomy to the Flemish and Walloons in the areas where each was predominant, and to apportion power to each group within the national government and the political parties. In 1993, the constitution was amended to create a federal state, made up of the autonomous regions of Flanders and Wallonia (and its semi-autonomous German-speaking community), together with the bilingual city of Brussels.

Baudouin died in 1993, removing one of the pillars of unity. His successor, his brother Albert II, won respect for his conscientious efforts towards unity but did not achieve the same personal connection with the people, especially in Flanders. His son Philippe, who succeeded him in 2013, has not been able to reverse this trend, and a has been the subject of a series of royal scandals.

Belgium & the Arts
VISUAL ARTS

Despite its small geographic size, Belgium has exerted a significant influence on Western art. The works of Bosch, Brueghel, Rubens, Van Dyck, Van Eyck, and Magritte represent only a fraction of the treasures you see gracing the walls of the notable art museums in Brussels, Bruges, Ghent, and Antwerp.

The golden age of Flemish painting occurred in the 1400s, a century dominated by the so-called Flemish Primitives, whose work was almost always religious in theme, usually commissioned for churches and chapels. As the medieval cities of Flanders flourished, more and more princes, wealthy merchants, and prosperous guilds became patrons of the arts.

Art's function was still to praise God and illustrate religious allegory, but **Jan van Eyck** (ca. 1390–1441), one of the earliest Flemish Masters, brought a sharp new perspective to bear on traditional subject matter. His "Adoration of the Mystic Lamb," created with his brother Hubert for Sint-Bavoskerk (St. Bavo's Cathedral, p. 132) in Ghent, incorporates a realistic landscape into its biblical theme. The Primitives sought to mirror reality, to portray both people and nature exactly as they appeared to the human eye, down to the tiniest detail, without classical distortions or embellishments. These artists would work meticulously for months—even years—on a single commission, often painting with a single-haired paintbrush to achieve a painstakingly lifelike quality. The peerless **Groeningemuseum** (p. 226) in Bruges is a top place to see their works.

The greatest Flemish artist of the 16th century, **Pieter Bruegel the Elder** (ca. 1525–69), lived and worked for many years in Antwerp. From 1520 to 1580, the city was one of the world's busiest ports and banking centers, and it eclipsed Bruges as a center for the arts. Many of the artists working here looked to the Italian Renaissance Masters for their models of perfection. Bruegel, who had studied in Italy, integrated Renaissance influences with the traditional style of his native land. He frequently painted rural and peasant life, as in his "Wedding Procession," on view at the Musée de la Ville (p. 187) in Brussels.

In 1563, Bruegel moved to Brussels, where he lived at rue Haute 132. Here his two sons, also artists, were born. **Pieter Bruegel the Younger** (ca. 1564–1637) became known for copying his father's paintings; **Jan Bruegel the Elder** (1568–1625) specialized in decorative paintings of flowers and fruits.

Peter Paul Rubens (1577–1640) was the most influential baroque painter of the early 17th century. The drama in his works, such as "The Raising of the Cross," housed in the Antwerp cathedral, comes from the dynamic, writhing figures in his canvases. His renditions of the female form gave rise to the term "Rubenesque," which describes the voluptuous women in his paintings.

Portraitist **Anthony van Dyck** (1599–1641), one of the most important talents to emerge from Rubens's studio, served as court painter to Charles I of England, although some of his best religious work remains in Belgium, including "The Bearing of the Cross" in St. Paul's Church (p. 246). More paintings by the great names mentioned above can be seen in the **Musées Royaux des Beaux-Arts de Belgique** (p. 189) in Brussels.

Belgium's influence on the art world is by no means limited to the Old Masters. **James Ensor** (1860–1949) was a late-19th-century pioneer of modern art. One of his most famous works is "The Entry of Christ into Brussels." Ensor developed a broadly expressionistic technique, liberating his use of color from the demands of realism. He took as his subject disturbing, fantastic images.

Surrealism flourished in Belgium, perhaps because of the earlier Flemish artists such as Pieter Brueghel with a penchant for the bizarre and grotesque. **Paul Delvaux** (1897–1989) became famous, but the best known of the Belgian surrealists is unquestionably **René Magritte** (1898–1967). His fantastical paintings of pipes that are not pipes, and bowler-hatted men who fall like black rain from the skies have become widely recognized images in popular culture. Many of these modern works can be seen in the **Musées Royaux des Beaux-Arts** (p. 189) in Brussels and will be seen once more in Antwerp's **Koninklijke Museum voor Schone Kunsten** (p. 243) when it reopens in 2021.

ARCHITECTURE

Examples of Gothic civic architecture abound in Belgium. The great ecclesiastical examples are **St. Michael's Cathedral** in Brussels (p. 185), in which the choir is the earliest Gothic work in Belgium, and the churches of **Our Lady** in Mechelen (p. 244) and **Sint-Bavokerk** in Ghent (p. 132). The **Onze-Lieve-Vrouwekathedraal** (Cathedral of Our Lady; see p. 244) in Antwerp is perhaps the most imposing example of late Gothic; it was begun in 1352 at the east end and the nave was completed in 1474.

Among the finest examples of commercial Gothic architecture are the Cloth Hall at Ypres (built 1200–1304), now beautifully converted in to the heart-rending **In Flanders Fields Museum,** the **Cloth Hall** in Mechelen (p. 250), the **Butchers Guildhall** in Ghent (p. 249), and the **Butchers Guildhall** in Antwerp (p. 237). Gothic style remained dominant until the early 16th century, when Renaissance decorative elements began to appear.

Around the turn of the 20th century, Belgium produced one of the greatest exponents of the new Art Nouveau style of architecture and interior design, the prime materials of which were glass and iron, worked with decorative curved lines and floral and geometric motifs. The work of **Victor Horta** (1861–1947) can be seen throughout Brussels and especially at his former home in the suburbs, now the **Musée Horta** (p. 195).

Belgium in Popular Culture

BOOKS

Belgium's most prolific man of letters—indeed, one of the most prolific authors of all time—is **Georges Simenon** (1903–89). The Liège-born author wrote some 200 novels and 150 novellas, along with other works from autobiographical books to magazine and newspaper articles, and still found time to produce dozens more novels under a variety of pseudonyms. He is best known for the Inspector Maigret detective series.

The two best-known Belgian novels would likely be *"Het Verdriet van België"* (**"The Sorrow of Belgium"**; 1983) by Hugo Claus, which deals with the Nazi occupation; and *"b-la-Morte"* (**"Dead Bruges"**; 1892) by Georges Rodenbach, which is perhaps best known for having put Bruges on the European map as a tourist destination.

More recently, English writer **Tracy Chevalier** set her 2003 historical novel, "The Lady and the Unicorn," in the tapestry workshops of Brussels. In non-fiction, David van Reybrouck's brilliantly researched **"Congo: The Epic History of a People"** (2010) describes the history of Congo, with special emphasis on the period of Belgian colonization of the African country.

COMICS

Belgium produces 30 million comic-strip books annually, and exports 75 percent of them. The **Tintin** books alone have sold more than 200 million copies since the youthful adventurer and his little terrier Snowy first appeared in 1927, created by Georges Remi, aka Hergé (the initials of his name reversed and written as they would be pronounced in French). You'll find examples of his work at the **Centre Belge de la Bande Dessiné** (p. 186) as well as **his eponymous museum** in the Brussels suburbs (p. 235).

Lucky Luke, the cowpoke who beats his shadow to the draw and whose horse, Jolly Jumper, plays a mean hand at poker, stars in more than 80 adventures; it has been adapted for television and computer games. His creator, Morris (real name Maurice de Bevere), a native of Kortrijk, died in 2001.

FILM

After decades in which Hollywood star **Jean-Claude *The Muscles from Brussels* Van Damme** was about the only thing Belgium contributed to the silver screen, the **Dardenne brothers** became among only eight directors awarded the prestigious Palme d'Or at the Cannes film festival twice.

As a location, Bruges struck gold with the 2008 international hit *In Bruges,* about two contract killers (Colin Farrell and Brendan Gleeson) who take refuge in the city. In 2011 Steven Spielberg made his first foray into animation with *The Adventures of Tintin: Secrets of the Unicorn,* based on three of the Tintin tales written and illustrated by Belgian cartoonist Hergé (p. 198).

Several Belgian comic-strip characters have received the Hollywood treatment; *The Smurfs Movie,* featuring the irritating little blue creatures from Belgian cartoonist Peyo, had films released in 2011, 2013, and 2017.

MUSIC

If it hadn't been for the Belgian designer of musical instruments **Adolphe Sax** (1814–94), there would be no saxophone—and then where would jazz be today? Probably missing the legendary Bruxellois jazz harmonica and guitar player **Jean "Toots" Thielemans,** who played theme music for movies, and is widely credited as the best harmonica player of the 20th century.

But Brussels' most famous musical son is easily the famed singer/songwriter **Jacques Brel** (1929–78), who brought unequalled passion to his performances of songs of love, comedy, and the low life. Born into an affluent family, Brel composed and sang from an early age but did not cut his first record until 1953. He then hit the big time and toured Europe almost nonstop for the next 13 years. Sentimental and caustic by turn, his songs soon captivated audiences around the world and he went on to enjoy a short movie career in the U.S. Brel's discography includes *"Quand On n'a que l'Amour"* ("If We Only Have Love") and *"Ne Me Quitte Pas"* ("If You Go Away").

Eating & Drinking in Belgium

Belgian chefs are some of the finest in the world, with Brussels considered one of the gastronomical capitals of Europe. Top Michelin-starred chefs here create a delicious cuisine based on the country's regional traditions and fresh produce, such as asparagus, chicory (endive), and even the humble Brussels sprout.

Belgium is also known for its selection of simple treats like rich, syrupy waffles topped with cream or fresh fruit, which are sold by street vendors throughout the country. Belgians also dote on their *moules-* or *steak-frites,* available at virtually every restaurant—even when not listed on the menu. *Frites* are also sold in paper cones on many street corners; they're at their best topped with lashings of mayonnaise.

Handmade **Belgian chocolates** (known generically as *pralines*) are also world-beaters in the taste stakes, so lethally addictive they ought to be sold with a government health warning. This applies in particular to those cream-filled delicacies made by artisanal chocolatier **Mary** in Brussels (p. 201), but more widely available brands like Godiva, Wittamer, Nihoul, Neuhaus, and Leonidas are just as enticing. Purchase them loose, in bags weighing from 100 grams, or boxes of 2 kilograms or more.

Everywhere in Belgium **seafood** is fresh and delicious. Almost every menu lists *tomates aux crevettes* (tomatoes stuffed with tiny, delicately sweet North Sea shrimp and light, homemade mayonnaise) and *moules* (mussels) are a specialty in Brussels, Bruges, and Antwerp. Ironically, Belgian mussels actually come from Zeeland in the Netherlands and may, in fact, be the only Dutch products Belgians will admit to being any good. *Homard* (lobster) comes in a range of dishes and in Brussels the restaurants along rue des Bouchers feature them in just about every guise you can imagine as part of vast seafood platters served on ice and encompassing crab, giant langoustines, clams, and oysters.

Don't miss the heavenly creation that is *écrevisses à la liègeoise* (crayfish in a rich butter, cream, and white-wine sauce), and eel, often served in a grass-green sauce. It's popular in both Flanders (where it's called *paling in 't groen*) and Wallonia *(anguilles au vert)*. One famous Flemish dish you'll see on almost every menu, particularly in Ghent, is the heartwarming souplike stew *waterzooï,* a seasoned, creamy mixture of chicken or fish with vegetables.

Native specialties also include *jambon d'Ardenne* (ham from the hills and valleys of the Ardennes to the south of Brussels) and savory *boudins* (succulent sausages mixed with herbs) from pigs raised on organic farms. Seasonal specialties include fresh (and expensive) asparagus from May and June, and chicory, known as *endive/witloof,* from March to October.

Most Belgian restaurants offer both a *plat du jour/dagschotel* (dish of the day) and a good-value two- or three-course menu at lunchtime as well as in the evening. No matter where you eat, service will be professional (although sometimes very perfunctory in tourist haunts) but not necessarily speedy. Belgians don't just eat—they savor each course. So if you're in a hurry, you're better off heading for a street vendor or a fast-food dive.

DRINKS

What to drink with all those tasty dishes? You're in Belgium, so drink beer. Belgium is famous for its **brewing tradition,** and this tiny country has more than 100 breweries producing around 450 different brands. The majority are local beers, specialties of a region, city, town, or village. Some famous pilsners are Stella Artois, Jupiler, Maes, Primus, and Eupener; ales to look out for include Duvel, De Koninck, and Kwak. Hoegaarden is a well-known wheat beer. Unique to the country are lambic beers (beer produced by spontaneous fermentation and brewed only in Brussels and the surrounding area), such as *faro* (a lambic sweetened with sugar), *kriek* (a fruit lambic made with cherries), and *gueuze* (a blend of lambics). Then there are the heavenly tasting beers brewed by the six Trappist breweries left in the land: Chimay, Orval, Rochefort, Achel, Westmalle, and Westvleteren.

Each local beer has a distinct bottle and shape of glass, which is why you can instantly tell what everyone is drinking in a Belgian bar. Needless to say, with so many choices, it may take quite a bit of sampling to find a firm favorite.

For a *digestif,* you might try the ginlike liqueur (p. 28) known in Flanders as *jenever* or *genever* (or, colloquially, as *witteke*), and in Wallonia as *genièvre* (colloquially as *pèkèt*); it's a potent spirit served in glasses little bigger than a thimble. Among the notable brands are Filliers Oude Graanjenever, De Poldenaar Oude Antwerpsche, Heinrich Pèkèt de la Piconette, Sint-Pol, and van Damme. *Jenever* in a stone bottle makes an ideal gift.

In recent decades, a few Belgian **vineyards** have appeared, reversing a loss that began with the onset of the Little Ice Age in the 15th century (harsh winters causing long freezes destroyed vineyards that had existed since Roman times). Most of the wineries, and five out of the seven officially recognized Belgian geographical wine regions, are in Flanders. Recently annual production reached 1 million liters (around 265,000 U.S. gallons), which is not even 5 percent of the country's total wine consumption. Among the country's best labels are those of Wijnkasteel Genoels-Elderen (www.wijnkasteel.com), and Château Bon Baron (www.chateaubonbaron.com), in the Meuse River valley between Dinant and Namur; both wineries are open for tours and tastings.

WHEN TO VISIT

Amsterdam, Brussels, and Bruges are fast-becoming all-year-around destinations with packed itineraries of festivals and public events to entice the visitor even throughout winter. Although clement weather can never be guaranteed in this little corner of northern Europe, summers are generally warm enough for T-shirts and shorts, and winters, while damp from time to time, are rarely bitterly cold. All three cities witness an influx of tourist between April and September, when the weather is on its best behavior and little can beat settling down into an *al fresco* cafe to watch the world slip unhurriedly by. Miniscule Bruges, in particular, can feel swamped with visitors during the peak months of June and July, so if you would rather have the place (relatively) to yourself, plan your visit for spring or early fall.

Amsterdam Average Temperatures & Rainfall

	JAN	FEB	MAR	APR	MAY	JUNE	JULY	AUG	SEPT	OCT	NOV	DEC
HIGH (°F)	41	46	48	54	63	66	70	70	64	59	48	43
LOW (°F)	34	32	37	39	46	52	55	55	52	46	39	37
HIGH (°C)	5	8	9	12	17	19	21	21	18	15	9	6
LOW (°C)	1	0	3	4	8	11	13	13	11	8	4	3
RAIN (IN.)	3	1.5	2.8	1.5	2	3	3	2.5	3.3	3.5	3.8	3.1

Brussels & Bruges Average Temperatures & Rainfall

	JAN	FEB	MAR	APR	MAY	JUNE	JULY	AUG	SEPT	OCT	NOV	DEC
HIGH (°F)	41	41	50	55	63	66	72	72	66	59	48	43
LOW (°F)	34	32	37	41	46	52	55	55	52	46	39	37
HIGH (°C)	5	5	10	13	17	19	22	22	19	15	9	6
LOW (°C)	1	0	3	5	8	11	13	13	11	8	4	3
RAIN (IN.)	3.6	3.1	2	2.5	1.9	2.8	4.1	3.6	3.2	3.9	3	3.1

Calendar of Events

JANUARY

New Year's in Holland. This celebration is wild and not always wonderful. Youthful spirits celebrate the New Year with firecrackers, which they throw at the feet of passersby. This keeps hospital emergency rooms busy. January 1.

International Film Festival, Rotterdam. More than 300 artistic films are screened at theaters around town. Visit www.IFFR.com or contact ℂ 010/890-9090. Late January

Brussels Antiques and Fine Arts Fair. The top Belgian antiques dealers and selected dealers from abroad get together to show off their wares in the Tour & Taxis Convention Center on avenue du port. Contact **BRAFA** (www.brafa.be; ℂ **02/513-4831**). Last 10 days of January.

FEBRUARY

Carnival ★★★, Binche, Hainaut. This is one of Europe's biggest, most colorful street carnivals, worth a day trip. On Shrove Tuesday it's led by a thousand sumptuously costumed Gilles de Binche, whose costumes are apparently modeled on Inca nobles. Contact **Office du Tourisme de Binche** (www.binche. be or www.carnavaldebinche.be; ℂ **064/ 31-1580**).

Beer Festival, Bruges. A weekend of fun sampling some of Bruges' boutique beers. The congenial festival spreads around town. Contact the Bruges Beer Festival (www. brugsbierfestival.be). Mid-February.

ABN AMRO World Tennis Tournament, Rotterdam. The world's top tennis players converge on the port city for this ATP Tour event. Contact **Ahoy Rotterdam** (www. abnamrowtt.nl; ✆ **0900 235-2469**). Second week of February.

MARCH

Windmill Days, Zaanse Schans. All five working windmills (out of eight windmills in total) are open to the public at this recreated old village and open-air museum in the Zaanstreek, just north of Amsterdam. Contact **Center Zaans Schans** (www.dezaanse schans.nl; ✆ **075/681-0000**). March through October.

Opening of Keukenhof Gardens ★★★, Lisse. The greatest flower show on earth blooms with a spectacular display of tulips, narcissi, daffodils, hyacinths, bluebells, crocuses, lilies, amaryllis, and many other flowers at this 32-hectare (79 acres) garden in the heart of the bulb country. Nearly eight million bulbs are planted every year. Contact **Keukenhof** (www.keukenhof.nl; ✆ **0252/ 465-555**). March to mid-May.

APRIL

Brussels International Fantastic Film Festival. Science fiction and fantasy films are screened at several movie theaters around the city. Contact **Peymey Diffusion** (www. bifff.net; ✆ **02/201-1713**). Mid-April.

Museumweek. A week during which most museums in the Netherlands offer free or reduced admission and have special exhibits. Contact **Museumweek** (www.nationale museumweek.nl; ✆ **045/560-5100**). Early April.

Bloemencorso van de Bollenstreek (Bulb District Flower Parade) ★★. Floats dressed to a different floral theme each year parade from Noordwijk through Sassenheim, Lisse, and Bennebroek to Haarlem. Contact **Lisse** (www.bloemencorso-bollenstreek.nl; ✆ **0252/428-237**). Mid-April.

Koningsdag (King's Day) ★★★. Countrywide celebration honoring the King's official birthday, with parades, street fairs, flea markets, and raucous street entertainment. Throughout the Netherlands, but best in Amsterdam. April 27.

MAY

Herdenkingsdag (Remembrance Day). Remembrance of the victims and fallen soldiers of World War II. Two minutes of silence throughout the Netherlands at 8pm.

Bevrijdingsdag (Liberation Day). Commemorates the end of World War II and Holland's liberation from Nazi occupation. Celebrated throughout the country, but best in Amsterdam. May 5.

National Windmill Days. Around two-thirds of the Holland's almost 1,000 working windmills spin their sails and are open to the public. Contact **De Hollandsche Molen** (www.molens.nl; ✆ **020/623-8703**). Second weekend in May.

Queen Elisabeth International Music Competition ★, Brussels. For promising young musicians, with piano, violin, and singing competitions. Generally at Bozar (Palais des Beaux-Arts; see p. 204) and a few other venues. Contact Concours Reine Elisabeth (www.cmireb.be; ✆ **02/213-4050**). Throughout May.

Kunstenfestivaldesarts, Brussels. An arts festival famed across the cultural universe for its irritatingly scrunched-up name, which means "arts festival" in both Dutch and French. It spotlights stage events, putting an emphasis on opera, theater, and dance, but finds space for cinema, music concerts, and fine-arts exhibits. Auditoriums and venues around town. Contact **Kunstenfestivaldesarts** (www.kfda.be). Three weeks in May.

Kattenstoet (Festival of the Cats) ★★, Ypres (Ieper). During the traditional Festival of the Cats, plush toy cats (they used to use live ones!) are thrown from the town hall belfry. There are parades and street entertainment too. Contact **Toerisme Ieper** (www.kattenstoet.be; ✆ **057/23-9220**). Every third year on the second Sunday in May.

Heilig-Bloedprocessie (Procession of the Holy Blood) ★★★, Bruges. The bishop of Bruges carries a relic of the Holy Blood through the streets, while costumed characters act out biblical scenes. Contact **Church of the Holy Blood** (www.holyblood. com; ✆ **050/33-6792**). Ascension Day (fifth Thurs after Easter). Usually May.

Brussels Jazz Weekend. Enjoy a long weekend of jazz of all kinds at a slew of concerts on the Grand-Place and place Ste-Catherine; at other open-air venues around town; and in jazz clubs, cafes, and hotel bars. Contact **Jazz Marathon** (www.brujazzwe.be; ✆ **02/456-0484**). End of May.

Vondelpark Openluchttheater (Open Air Theatre), Amsterdam. Runs right through the summer with weekend programs of rock and pop concerts, stand-up, drama, and dance. Contact **Stichting Vondelpark Openluchttheater** (www.openluchttheater. nl; ✆ **020/428-3360**). May through end of August.

JUNE

Holland Festival, Amsterdam. The city's big cultural buffet of music, opera, theater, film, and dance. The schedule includes all the major Amsterdam venues plus international companies and soloists. Contact **Holland Festival** (www.hollandfestival.nl; ✆ **020/788-2100**). Throughout June.

Vlaggetjesdag (Flag Day), Scheveningen. The fishing fleet opens the herring season with a race to bring the first *Hollandse Nieuwe* herring back to port (the first barrel is auctioned for charity). Contact **Stichting Vlaggetjesdag Scheveningen** (www.vlaggetjesdag.com; ✆ **070/307-2900**). Mid-June.

Brussels International Film Festival. A 9-day feast of European films, primarily of first or second features, and by independent directors, screened at the Flagey Cultural Center. Contact **Brussels Film Festival** (www.briff.be; ✆ **02/248-0872**). Mid-June.

Amsterdam Roots Festival. This festival features music and dance from around the world, along with workshops, films, and exhibits. One part is the open-air **Oosterpark Festival,** a multicultural feast of song and dance held in Amsterdam-Oost (East). Contact **Amsterdam Roots Festival** (www.amsterdamroots.nl; ✆ **020/2149652**). Mid-June.

Open Gardens Days ★★, Amsterdam. If you wonder what the fancy gardens behind the gables of some of Amsterdam's Canal Ring houses-turned-museums look like, this is your chance to find out. Six of the best are open to the public for 3 days. Contact **Museum van Loon** (www.opengardendays. nl; ✆ **020/624-5255**). Third week in June.

Couleur Café Festival, Brussels. Three days of African, Caribbean, and Latin music and dance, ably supported by heaps of soul food at the Tour & Taxis Cultural Complex, in a former warehouse zone next to the Willebroeck Canal dock. Contact **Couleur Café** (www.couleurcafe.be). Late June.

JULY

Over Het IJ Festival, Amsterdam. Performers stage avant-garde theater, music, and dance in Amsterdam-Noord beside the IJ channel, at the old NDSM-Wharf, TT Neveritaweg 15. Contact **Over Het IJ Festival** (www.overhetij.nl; ✆ **020/492-2229**). July.

Ommegang ★★★, Brussels. A dramatic annual historical pageant that dates from the 13th century and represents the city guilds, magistrates, and nobles honoring the Virgin Mary. Participants wearing period costume from the time of the "joyous entry" of Emperor Charles V into Brussels in 1549, escorted by a mounted cavalcade and waving medieval banners, go in procession from place du Grand Sablon to the Grand-Place. Contact **Ommegang-Brussels Events** (www. ommegang.be; ✆ **02/512-1961**). First Tuesday and Thursday in July.

Brosella Folk and Jazz Festival, Brussels. A small-scale specialized music fest that takes place over a weekend at the Théâtre de Verdure in Parc d'Osseghem. Contact **Les Amis de Brosella** (www.brosella.be; ✆ **02/474-0641**). Mid-July.

Cactus Festival, Bruges. A prickly summer rock festival unfolds over 3 days and attracts big names to the city. Contact **Cactus Muziekcentrum** (www.cactusfestival.be; ✆ **050/33-2014**). Mid-July.

Belgian National Day, Brussels. Marked throughout Belgium but celebrated most in Brussels, with a military procession and music at the Palais Royal (p. 188). Contact

City of Brussels Tourism (www.brussels.be; ☎ 02/279-2211). July 21.

North Sea Jazz Festival ★★, Rotterdam. One of the world's leading gatherings of top international jazz and blues musicians unfolds over 3 concert-packed days at the city's giant Ahoy venue. Last-minute tickets are scarce, so book as far ahead as possible. Contact **North Sea Jazz Festival** (www.northseajazz.com). July.

Gentse Feesten (Ghent Festivities) ★. Free street entertainment of music, dance, theater, puppet shows, and general fun and games marks the annual Ghent Festivities. Contact **Gentse Feesten** (www.gentsefeesten.stad.gent). Late July.

AUGUST

Amsterdam Gay Pride ★★. This is a big event in one of Europe's most gay-friendly cities. Watch the Boat Parade's display of 100 or so outrageously decorated boats cruising the canals, or enjoy street discos, open-air theater, a sports program, and a film festival. Contact **Amsterdam Gay Pride** (www.amsterdamgaypride.nl). Early August.

Visiting the Palais Royal, Brussels. The Royal Palace on place des Palais is open to free guided tours. King Philippe won't be there, however. Contact the **Palais Royal** (www.monarchie.be; ☎ 02/551-2020). Throughout August.

Planting of the Meyboom (May Pole), Brussels. Despite the name, this ceremony happens in August, on the eve of the Feast of St. Lawrence, at the corner of rue des Sables and rue du Marais, and celebrates Brussels' victory over Leuven in 1311 (nowadays it's more a celebration of summer). Contact **City of Brussels Tourism** (www.brussels.be; ☎ 02/279-2211). August 9.

Grachtenfestival (Canal Festival) ★★, Amsterdam. A 10-day festival of classical music plays at intimate and elegant venues along the city's canals and at the Muziekgebouw aan 't IJ. There's always a performance or two for children. The festival culminates in the exuberant **Prinsengracht Concert**, which plays on a pontoon in front of the Hotel Pulitzer. Contact **Stichting Grachtenfestival** (www.grachtenfestival.nl; ☎ 020/421-4542). Mid-August.

Tapis des Fleurs (Carpet of Flowers) ★★★, Grand-Place, Brussels. The historic square is carpeted with two-thirds of a million begonias arranged in a complex patterned tapestry. Contact **City of Brussels Tourism** (www.brussels.be ☎ 02/279-2211). Mid-August in even-numbered years.

Praalstoet van de Gouden Boom (Pageant of the Golden Tree) ★★★, Bruges. Some 2,000 costumed participants, along with giant mannequins and parade floats reenact the lavish spectacle that accompanied the wedding of the Duke of Burgundy, Charles the Bold (p. 235) and Margaret of York in 1468. Contact **Praalstoet van de Gouden Boom** (www.brugge.be/gouden-boom stoet-2). Every fifth year (Aug 2022).

Festival Oude Muziek (Festival of Early Music), Utrecht. Concerts of music from the Middle Ages to the Romantic era. Contact **Stichting Organisatie Oude Muziek** (www.oudemuziek.nl; ☎ 030/232-9000). Late August through early September.

Uitmarkt, Amsterdam. Amsterdam previews its cultural season with this open market of information and free performances in Leidseplein and Museumplein, theaters, and concert halls. The shows run the gamut of music, opera, dance, theater, and cabaret. Contact **Uitmarkt** (www.uitmarkt.nl; ☎ 020/626-2656). Last weekend in August.

SEPTEMBER

Open Monumentendag (Open Monument Day). Get to see historic buildings and monuments in the major towns around the country that usually are not open to the public, and get in free. Contact **Open Monumentendag** (www.openmonumentendag.nl; ☎ 033/209-1000). Mid-September.

Liberation Parade, Brussels. The **Manneken-Pis** statue (p. 183) is dressed in a Welsh Guard's uniform in honor of the city's liberation in 1944. Contact **City of Brussels Tourism** (www.brussels.be; ☎ 02/279-2211). September 3.

Journées du Patrimoine (Heritage Days), Brussels. Taking a different theme each year, this program allows you to visit some of the finest buildings in town that are usually closed to visitors. Contact **City of Brussels**

Tourism (www.brussels.be; ✆ **02/279-2211**). Third weekend in September.

State Opening of Parliament ★, **The Hague.** On Prinsjesdag (Princes' Day), King Willem-Alexander rides in a splendid gold coach to the Ridderzaal in The Hague to open the legislative session by delivering the Speech from the Throne. Contact **Gemeente Den Haag** (www.denhaag.nl; ✆ **070/353-3000**). Third Tuesday in September.

OCTOBER

Leidens Ontzet (Relief of Leiden). Procession commemorating the anniversary of the raising of the 1574 Spanish siege of Leiden. *Haring en witte brood* (herring and white bread) are distributed, just as the piratelike band of "Sea Beggars" did after helping drive the Spaniards away. Contact **Leidens Ontzet Secretariaat** (www.3october.nl/international; ✆ **071/532-4724**). October 3 (Oct 4 when the 3rd is a Sun).

Film Fest Gent. Belgium's top international film festival, and an event that has grown in stature to become one of Europe's main movie showcases. As many as 150 full-length movies and 100 shorts are screened over 12 days. Contact **Film Fest Gent** (www.filmfestival.be; ✆ **09/242-8060**). Mid-October.

Amsterdam Dance Event (ADE). Five-day electronic music conference and festival with over 2,000 DJs spinning in more than 100 venues. Contact **ADE** (www.amsterdam-dance-event.nl). Mid-October.

NOVEMBER

Crossing Border, The Hague. Literature, poetry, and music are combined in this 4-day festival. Contact **Crossing Border** (✆ **070/346-2355**; www.crossingborder.nl). Mid-November.

Snow & Ice Sculpture Festival ★, **Bruges.** Cool works of ice sculpture can be viewed on Stationsplein in front of the train station. There's an ice bar too. Contact **Snow & Ice**

Sculpture Festival (www.ijs.be). Mid-November to early January.

Sinterklaas Arrives. Holland's Santa Claus (St. Nicholas) launches the Christmas season when he sails into Amsterdam, accompanied by black-painted assistants, called Zwarte Piet (Black Peter), who hand out candy to kids. During the next 2 weeks, he makes his way to towns across the country. Contact local tourist offices. Third Saturday in November. He arrives the next day in Amsterdam.

DECEMBER

Christmas Markets: Antwerp, Brussels, Bruges and Ghent. Stands selling seasonal trinkets, craft items, and food and drink are set up on Grote-Markt in Antwerp (www.visitantwerpen.be), on place Ste-Catherine in Brussels (ww.brussels.be), at the Markt and on Simon Stevinplein in Bruges (www.visitbruges.be) in Bruges, and on Sint-Baafsplein in Ghent (visit.gent.be).

Amsterdam Light Festival. The center of Amsterdam is illuminated with contemporary light installations. The festival kicks off with a boat parade around the canals. Contact **Amsterdam Light Festival** (www.amsterdamlightfestival.com; ✆ **020/420-2060**). Early December through mid-January.

Nativity Scene and Christmas Tree, Grand-Place, Brussels. The crib on display at this Christmas nativity scene has real animals. Contact **City of Brussels Tourism** (www.brussels.be; ✆ **02/279-2211**). Throughout December.

Winter Fun, Brussels. An ice-skating rink and a big wheel are set up on the Marché aux Poissons; there's a carousel on neighboring place Ste-Catherine. Contact **City of Brussels Tourism** (www.brussels.be; ✆ **02/279-2211**). Throughout December.

Sinterklaas. St. Nicholas's Eve is the traditional day in Holland for exchanging Christmas gifts. December 5.

SUGGESTED ITINERARIES

Getting around Belgium and the Netherlands is remarkably easy thanks to its excellent network of trains. What *will* be difficult is sandwiching everything you want to see into your itinerary, so take as much time with you as you can—you won't run out of things to do in this corner of the world.

You'll also want to plan carefully. That means booking tickets online ahead of time for such hugely popular attractions as the Van Gogh Museum and Anne Frank Huis in Amsterdam, plus the Ridderzaal in The Hague. And in some cases it may make sense to choose a couple of "home bases," just so you can see more. What follows is our suggestions on how to make the most of your time on a vacation to Holland and/or Belgium.

BELGIUM & THE NETHERLANDS IN 1 WEEK

Few countries can boast of cities more justly celebrated than Amsterdam, Brussels, and Bruges. They all are blessed with wonderful museums, galleries, shops, restaurants, and day-trip opportunities, and this whistle-stop tour will allow you to see their main attractions—just about. For this is a week where you'll barely be able to catch your breath.

The best way to travel between cities is by using the excellent network of trains and buses. **Skip the car!** Driving in Amsterdam is exceedingly difficult due to its maze of one-way streets, plus the parking is quite expensive. And the roads in and around Brussels are among the most congested in Europe.

Day 1: Arrive in Amsterdam ★★★

Arrive on an early flight and get going—time is of the essence this week! First up is a 1-hour **canal cruise** (p. 110). This is the very best way to view much of this canal-threaded city in a reasonable time. Then head to the **Rijksmuseum** (p. 101), whose collection of masterpieces from the Dutch Golden Age (Vermeer, Frans Hals, and most notably, Rembrandt's "The Night Watch) is unparalleled. A stroll around the grassy **Museumplein** (p. 101) will clear your head. Follow up with drinks on the terrace of **Café Cobra** (p. 82). Dine in the evening at a traditional Dutch brown cafe like **'t Smalle** (p. 79) or an Indonesian restaurant like **De Blauw** (p. 83).

Day 2: Amsterdam & The Hague ★★

Plan ahead to visit the **Anne Frank Huis** (p. 96) in the morning; you'll need to have booked your timed ticket 2 months in advance to the day on the website. Hop the train to The Hague, a 50-minute train ride from Amsterdam Centraal. Store your luggage in a locker at the train station (Den Haag Centraal) and walk 10 minutes to the Dutch Parliament Buildings, the **Binnenhof** and **Ridderzaal** (p. 146), and admire the magnificent 13th-century architecture. If you've booked ahead, take the brief guided tour of the Ridderzaal (Hall of the Knights), which houses the royal throne. Wind things up with a visit to the superb collection of Dutch Old Masters in the nearby **Mauritshuis** (p. 148). Catch an early-evening train for the 2- to 2 1/2-hour ride to Brussels (note that there are no direct trains and you'll have to change in Breda or Rotterdam). In Brussels, have dinner at a classic Belgian brasserie like **Taverne du Passage** (p. 172), in the centrally located Galeries Royales St-Hubert.

Day 3: Brussels ★★★

Since you don't want to be packing and unpacking every day, you will lodge in Brussels and visit Belgium's other historic cities as easy day trips. But you'll explore the "capital of Europe" first, starting at the **Grand-Place** (p. 178), taking time to absorb the magnificent old square's architectural details and animated spirit. A date with Rubens, Bruegel Magritte, and other notable Belgian artists awaits you in the elegant **Musées Royaux des Beaux-Arts de Belgique** (p. 189). Next you might want to stroll amid trees, fountains, and lawns in the **Parc de Bruxelles** (p. 162), and view the **Palais Royal** (p. 188) and the Belgian Parliament building, the **Palais de la Nation,** on opposite sides of the park. In the evening, have a beer at **A La Mort Subite** (p. 204) and dine on seafood at any of the restaurants around the **Marché aux Poissons (Fish Market),** a short walk from the Grand-Place around place Ste-Catherine (p. 170).

Day 4: Bruges ★★★

By train, Bruges is an hour from Brussels. Once you arrive, hop the bus or walk about 20 minutes to the connected medieval central squares of **Burg** (p. 223) and **Markt** (p. 219). On the Markt, climb the 366 steps to the top of the **Belfort** (p. 219) for splendid city views. Relax after your long climb at any of the casual Belgian cafes flanking the Markt; **La Civière d'Or** (p. 217) is a good option. On the Burg, visit the **Basiliek van het Heilig-Bloed** (p. 223) for a glimpse of a relic that's said to be drops of Christ's blood, and the splendid 14th-century town hall, **Brug-gemuseum-Stadhuis** (p. 224). Then head to the **Groeningemuseum** (p. 226) to view masterpieces by Flemish artists including Bosch and van

Eyck, and pop in to the nearby **Sint-Janshospitaal** (p. 227) to small but stunning assemblage of paintings by Hans Meml wouldn't be a visit to Bruges without beer; grab a seat on the terr pub **2be** (p. 218) and soak in the lovely canal views with a cold o time permits, wander through the tranquil gardens of the **Begijnhof** convent (p. 232) on your way back to the station. Back in Brussels, have dinner at the brasserie **Lola** (p. 173) near the place du Grand Sablon.

Day 5: Ghent ★★

Just a half-hour train ride from Brussels, Ghent is a buzzing university town with a thoroughly Flemish vibe. Get your bearings by taking the elevator up above the city's rooftops to the viewing platform of the 14th-century **Belfort** (p. 266). Next stop has to be **Sint-Bavokerk** (p. 132) to see Jan van Eyck's magnificent altarpiece "The Adoration of the Mystic Lamb" (1432). From the cathedral, stroll to the medieval inner harbor along **Korenlei** and **Graslei** (p. 257 and 256), which are both lined with spectacular medieval guild houses. From here, head to the restored medieval district of **Patershol** (p. 253), which is chock-a-block with bars and restaurants. Stay until night falls to see the city dramatically illuminated with artistic light displays; you can follow the entire 2-hour circular **Light Plan** walk (p. 257) or concentrate on the waterfront areas of Korenlei and Graslei. Return to Brussels after dinner.

Day 6: Antwerp ★★

Forty minutes by train from Brussels, Antwerp is Belgium's second-largest city. Bring your luggage if you'll be leaving from Amsterdam tomorrow as you'll be heading back by train tonight; there are luggage lockers in the Antwerp Centraal Station. Catch a tram to city center's **Grote Markt** (p. 242) to view the dramatic Brabo Fountain and glorious, lacy guild houses, and then stop for a coffee or a *bolleke* (round glass) of Antwerp's De Koninck beer at the grand old tavern **Cafe den Engel** (Grote Markt 3; www.cafedenengel.be; ✆ **03/233-1252**), also on the square. Antwerp means Rubens; to learn more about the artist, visit his former home, the **Rubenshuis** (p. 245), view his four masterly paintings at the Gothic **Sint-Pauluskerk** (p. 246), and see more of his works as well as his tomb at **Sint-Jacobskerk** (p. 245), which is open but is currently undergoing restoration. Back at Antwerp Central Station, stroll briefly around the city's celebrated (although not exactly handsome) **Diamond Quarter** (p. 245) before catching your train; it's just over an hour ride to Amsterdam Centraal on the high-speed Thalys or 2 hours on the far less expensive Intercity train. It's your last night in Amsterdam, so make it special by splurging on a fancy meal at one of the city's Michelin-starred spots like **Rijks** (p. 82) or **&moshik** (p. 75).

Day 7: Amsterdam ★★

Try to arrange your flight so that you can fit in one last bit of culture before winging your way home (there are a number of evening transatlantic flights out of Amsterdam). Spend your last morning at the **Van Gogh Museum** (p. 102). As with the Anne Frank House you'll need to get advance tickets, but it's a stellar way to cap off a week of culture.

A 2-WEEK HOLLAND & BELGIUM ITINERARY

If you have 2 weeks in your itinerary to dedicate to Amsterdam and Brussels and all stops in between, you'll breathe more easily. You can stroll where you might otherwise have needed to hop on a city tram or bus, and you'll be able to head off the beaten track every once in a while. This itinerary is designed for travel by train. If you're driving, you'll need to modify some elements to allow for the additional time it will take to get around.

Day 1: Arrive in Amsterdam ★★★

With 2 weeks, you can take your time exploring the delights of Amsterdam. The first thing to do is step onboard a **cruise boat** (p. 110) for an hour-long cruise around the city's iconic canals. Afterward, take a leisurely stroll around the 17th-century Golden Age **Canal Ring** (p. 60)—comprising the Herengracht, Keizersgracht, and Prinsengracht canals. Pop in to the many boutiques and art galleries that line the **Nine Streets** (p. 117), a cluster of narrow, charming streets that cross the three canals. For dinner, head to the smart canal-side restaurant **Envy** (p. 80), then wrap up your evening in the nightlife hubs of **Leidseplein** and **Rembrandtplein.**

Day 2: More of Amsterdam's Best ★★★

Today you'll devote yourself to two of the world's greatest art museums: the **Rijksmuseum** (p. 101) and the **Van Gogh Museum** (p. 102), both set on the city's vast green **Museumplein** (p. 101). Start with the Rijksmuseum and allow at least 3 hours to explore its vast collection, but head first to the Gallery of Honour to see masterpieces from the Golden Age, including Rembrandt's grand painting "The Night Watch." Break for a casual lunch of Dutch fare at **Café Cobra** (p. 82), then cross Museumplein to the Van Gogh Museum, housing more than 800 of the Dutch artist's paintings and drawings. (*Note:* You'll need to book a timed ticket in advance on the museum's website.) After a long museum day, you'll want a hearty dinner; try **De Blauw** (p. 83) for an Indonesian feast.

Day 3: Amsterdam Again ★★★

In the morning, visit the **Anne Frank Huis** (p. 96) but be sure to book timed tickets online in advance; very few tickets are released on the day of. In her diary, Frank mentions the chimes of **Westerkerk** (p. 99); the church is just around the corner and also houses the unmarked grave

Rembrandt. Follow with a wander through the old artisans' district of **Jordaan** (p. 60), now prettily gentrified. Stop at **'t Smalle** (p. 79), a traditional Dutch brown café, for lunch. If it's not raining, take the free ferry from behind Centraal Station across the IJ River to the burgeoning new city north of the waterway. Among the attractions are the striking architecture of the **EYE Film Institute** (p. 108) and the observation deck of the **A'dam Lookout** (p. 108), which offers spectacular panoramic views of the city. Otherwise, duck inside **Museum Het Rembrandthuis** (p. 92) to see where the Dutch Old Master lived and view the remarkable collection of Rembrandt etchings. By dusk, you'll want to make your way over to the city's famous **Red Light District** (p. 94)—the later it gets, the more drunk, rowdy tourists fill its streets. Enjoy an excellent seafood supper at **Visrestaurant Lucius** (p. 78) in the city center followed by a nightcap at **Freddy's** cocktail bar in the posh **Hotel de l'Europe** (p. 65).

Day 4: Amsterdam & Haarlem ★★★

Hop the train from Amsterdam Centraal for the 15-minute ride west to Haarlem. Head straight for the **Grote Markt** (p. 130) to admire the splendor of its gabled, medieval buildings, then visit the grand interior of **Sint Bavoskerk** (p. 132), where a 10-year-old Mozart played an organ recital in 1766. Spend a couple of hours in the **Frans Hals Museum** (p. 130), located in a dreamy former almshouse, noted for its exceptional collection of Hals's civic portraits. Have lunch along the scenic Spaarne River at **Ratatouille Food & Wine** (p. 130). From there, move on to the oldest museum in the Netherlands, the **Teylers** (p. 132), established in 1778, for its eccentric displays of minerals and scientific instruments. Stop for a craft beer at **Jopen** (Gedempte Voldersgracht 2; www.jopen bier.nl; ℂ **023/533-4114**), a gorgeous brewery housed in a former church. Back in Amsterdam, if it happens to be a summer weekend, catch an evening performance at **Vondelpark**'s **Open-Air Theater** (p. 126); otherwise check out the musical offerings at the hip church-turned-nightclub **Paradiso** (p. 126).

Day 5: The Hague ★★

Pack your bags and take the 50-minute train ride to The Hague, where you will be based for the next 3 days before heading to Belgium. After checking in to your hotel—the centrally located **Hotel Indigo** (p. 150) is a great choice—your first stop should be the fine medieval buildings of the **Binnenhof** and **Ridderzaal** (p. 146) at the home of the Dutch Parliament (book guided tours in advance; see p. 146). Then head to see the superb collection of Dutch Old Masters in the **Mauritshuis** (p. 148). It's a short stroll to the historic Grote Markt packed with cafes and restaurants; try the terrace of **['t] Goude Hooft** (p. 150) for excellent Duch fare. Finish with a drink or live music at one of the many bars and clubs in the area.

Day 6: The Hague & Scheveningen ★★

Start your day with a visit to the **Panorama Mesdag** (p. 148) for its "painting in the round" of 19th-century **Scheveningen** (p. 151). Then hop a tram and take the short ride to the seacoast to see the real thing. Breathe in the brisk sea air and head for the **Museum Beelden aan Zee** (p. 151) to see its cluster of modern sculpture strewn alongside the boardwalk. Enjoy lunch in one of the many restaurants along the boardwalk or out on the **Scheveningen Pier** (p. 151). Head back to city in the afternoon; it's a 15-minute tram ride from Scheveningen to the **Gemeentemuseum** (p. 147), renowned for its huge Mondrian collection and other works by De Stijl artists. Plan to spend a couple of hours here before heading to dinner. The Hague is blessed with a wonderful Chinatown packed with Chinese, Japanese, and Indonesian shops and restaurants; try the outstanding Singapore noodles at **Kee Lun Palace** (p. 152).

Day 7: The Hague, Delft & Rotterdam ★★

Hop Tram 1 and in about 25 minutes you'll be in tiny, postcard-perfect **Delft** (p. 141). Stroll the cobblestone streets of Vermeer's hometown, threaded with pretty canals and dotted with lovely churches. Make your way to the historic Grote Markt, an enormous square flanked by cafes and dominated by the ancient **Nieuwe Kerk** (p. 143) and the Renaissance-style **Stadhuis** (Town Hall) at opposite ends. If your visit is on a Thursday, you can see the thrumming weekly market take place here. See the famous Delftware being made by hand at **De Koninklijke Porceleyne Fles** (p. 142); the porcelain factory offers tours of its workshop and you can shop for pieces at its on-site store. Head back to the station for the 15-minute journey to the modern metropolis of Rotterdam; get off at Rotterdam Blaak (not Rotterdam Centraal) as the station is more conveniently located. Emerging from the station, you're immediately confronted with the edgy architecture the city is known for, namely the towering futuristic indoor food hall **Markthal** (p. 156), where you can have a bite at one of its many multi-ethnic eateries. A few minutes' walk leads you to the cube-shaped houses known as **Kubuswoningen** (p. 155), built in the 1970s; one is perfectly preserved as a museum and it's worth a visit. From there, walk along the River Maas, spanned by the magnificent **Erasmusbrug cable bridge.** At its foot, leave for a 75-minute **boat trip** (p. 155), which takes you along the city's waterfront, dotted with cutting-edge buildings, and around the world's third largest natural harbor. Unfortunately, the city's great art museum, the **Museum Boijmans van Beuningen,** is closed for renovations until 2026; some of its works are on display at **Kunsthal Rotterdam** (p. 155), a sleek contemporary art space designed by Rem Koolhaas. Nearby, the trendy drinking and dining strip of **Witte de Withstraat** (p. 157) offers plenty of fun dinner options. Catch the train back to The Hague from Rotterdam Centraal or Rotterdam Blaak.

Day 8: Brussels ★★★

Today, you'll bring your bags on board the train for a trip to Be
capital, about a 2-hour journey with a change of trains in Breda ⸗
terdam. You'll be based here for 5 nights while making day trips ↳
surrounding cities. Drop your luggage at the hotel and head to the n ↙g-
nificent **Grand-Place** (p. 178), an ideal starting point for your sightseeing,
and fit in a "pilgrimage" to the miniscule **Manneken-Pis** statue (p. 183)
nearby. Following this, stop off at the **Musées Royaux des Beaux-Arts
de Belgique** (p. 189) to view works by Rubens, Brueghel, Magritte, and
other notable Belgian artists. Then stroll amid Masonic symbols in the
Parc de Bruxelles (p. 162), stopping to view the **Palais Royal** (p. 188)
and the Palais de la Nation—on opposite sides of the park. In the evening,
enjoy a Belgian beer on the Grand-Place and then dive into the maze of
pedestrian streets around rue des Bouchers for a seafood supper.

Day 9: Brussels ★★★

Go window-shopping in the 19th-century **Galeries Royales St-Hubert**
(p. 203) and be sure to stop for a sweet treat at one of the many chocolate
shops here, including Neuhaus and **Pierre Marcolini** (p. 201). Then
make your way to the **place du Grand Sablon** (p. 183) to browse its
antiques stores; if you're visiting on a weekend, stop at the famous
antiques market in front of **Notre-Dame du Sablon.** Cross over rue de la
Régence to tranquil **place du Petit Sablon** (p. 184) and stop a while by
the fountain. In the afternoon, take a tram trip to the **Cantillon Brewery**
(p. 206), just southwest of the city center, for traditional lambic beer.
Head back by tram to the Ixelles district, which is chock-full of hip eateries like the tapas-style **Ötap** (p. 175). For a nightcap, it's a short stroll to
Alice Cocktail Bar on avenue Louise.

Day 10: Brussels & Ghent ★★

Follow the Ghent itinerary from our 1-week tour (see p. 45).

Day 11: Bruges ★★★

Follow the Bruges itinerary from our 1-week tour (see p. 44) except you
will be staying 2 nights in Bruges, so bring your bags and check into your
hotel before the start of sightseeing.

Day 12: More of Bruges' Best ★★★

Explore the historical collection in the **Gruuthusemuseum,** housed in
a 15th-century palace (p. 225), then head to the nearby **Xpo Picasso**
(p. 231) to see over 300 graphic works by the Spanish master. After a
morning spent in museums, hop on a 30-minute **canal cruise** (p. 232) to
see the city's layout and character from the water. Have a light lunch at
the airy bistro **Nomad Kitchen + Bar** (p. 218), then make your way to
the grand **St. Saviour's Cathedral** (p. 229) and visit its remarkable
seven-room treasury, which is only open in the afternoon. Take some
time to wander around Bruges' cobbled streets shopping for lace and

chocolate; for the latter, head to Katelijnestraat, where around a half-dozen chocolatiers are mere steps from one another. Have an early dinner at the excellent seafood spot **Breydel-De Coninc** (p. 216).

Day 13: Antwerp ★★

Follow the Antwerp itinerary from our 1-week tour (see p. 45). It's a 1½ hour train ride to Antwerp from Bruges, so leave early in the morning to make the most of your time.

Day 14: Amsterdam ★★

Head back to Amsterdam to catch your flight home. If you have time to kill in Amsterdam before your flight home but don't want to stray too far from Centraal Station, catch the free Buiksloterweg ferry (p. 62) from behind the station; it's just a 5-minute ride across the IJ waterway to the architecturally striking **Eye Film Museum** (p. 108).

AMSTERDAM, BRUSSELS & BRUGES FOR FAMILIES

Along with world-class museums filled with works by Old Masters, all these cities offer a wealth of kid-oriented museums and family-friendly activities. You certainly don't need to worry about a language barrier since most natives of these multilingual cities speak English. There are also plenty of choices on the menus beyond mussels—don't forget that fries and chocolate are almost the national dish of Belgium, while immense piles of child-friendly sweet pancakes sate the Dutch national sweet tooth.

Day 1: Brussels ★★★

Since you don't want to be packing and unpacking every day, especially with kids, you will lodge in Brussels for the next 3 days and visit Bruges as an easy day trip. Start in the center of town with a visit to the bold little **Manneken-Pis** statue (p. 183); grown-ups usually wonder what all the fuss is about, but kids love him. Then hop the tram for a 45-minute ride out to the space-age **Atomium** (p. 197), an enormous silver structure built for the 1958 World's Fair; kids will enjoy scampering through its tubes and spheres and seeing the views from on high. Combine it with a visit to **Mini-Europe** (p. 198) located at the foot of the Atomium; the theme park is filled with 350 miniature models of member states of the European Union, including a tiny Venice complete with gondolas.

Day 2: More of Brussels ★★

Kids will want to will want to take a look under the hood of **Autoworld** (p. 192) and most will enjoy discovering the cavernous underground excavations at **Coudenberg** (p. 188) underneath the Palais Royale. The comic strips and characters at the **Centre Belge de la Bande-Dessinée** (p. 186), home to Tintin and the Smurfs, are appealing to all ages. And children will jump at the chance to take a guided tour around the **Musée du Cacao et du Chocolat** (p. 197).

Day 3: Bruges ★★★

The train to Bruges takes about an hour from Brussels. Starting the visit with a canal cruise on an open-topped **boat** (p. 233) is a great choice. It's also completely safe to get around Bruges by rented **bike** (p. 210) and even more exciting to see the sights by **pony and carriage** (p. 234). Several city museums should peak children's interest: **Choco-Story: The Chocolate Museum** (p. 231), which features a chocolate-making demonstration where you can taste the sweets afterwards, and the **Friet Museum** (p. 232), devoted to the humble French fry. Both are small enough that kids won't get bored. The **Archaeological Museum** (p. 233) is also designed with kids in mind, with interactive displays, skeletons, and medieval costumes to dress up in. Then take them for sweet crepes or waffles at the family-friendly bistro **'t Minnewater** (p. 218).

Day 4: Rotterdam ★★

Today, pack your bags and board the train to Rotterdam; you can store your luggage in the lockers at Rotterdam Centraal station and start exploring. Make your way up to the top of **Euromast** (p. 154), near the River Maas; kids will love riding in the revolving glass elevator to the viewing platform, which offers incredible panoramic views of Rotterdam and the harbor below. Follow with a cruise on the bright-yellow **Pannenkoekenboot (Pancake Boat),** moored at the foot of the Euromast; the 2½-hour ride around the vast harbor is made even more exciting with all-they-can-eat pancakes. Head back to the station for the 45-minute train ride to Amsterdam, where you'll spend the next 2 nights.

Day 5: Amsterdam ★★★

Start by seeing the sights of the city on a 1-hour **canal boat tour** (p. 110). A visit to the **Anne Frank Huis** (p. 96) is thought-provoking for older children; for younger kids, a visit to the compact **Artis Zoo** (p. 104), complete with an aquarium, planetarium, and petting zoo, is hugely enjoyable. From there, it's less than a 10-minute walk to the city's maritime museum **Het Scheepvaartmuseum** (p. 105); a highlight is climbing aboard and exploring the replica of the Dutch East India Company ship Amsterdam moored just out front. Then head over to the nearby **NEMO Science Museum** (p. 107), which has all sorts of kid-friendly exhibits covering science and technology with an emphasis on hands-on, interactive activities. If the kids are too tired for another museum, NEMO's sloping, stepped roof is also a big attraction—especially during the summer, when it turns into a giant water fountain with 30 shallow pools that little ones will love to splash around in. Bonus: the roof is completely free.

Note: Getting around Amsterdam by **tram** (p. 61) is safe fun for the whole family, but steer away from cycling around the city center, as the resident cyclists are often downright dangerous. You'll also want to avoid taking kids to the Red Light District, not only because of the lurid sex shops and scantily-clad sex workers in the windows, but also because it's usually chock-a-block with drunk and/or stoned tourists.

Day 6: Zaanse Schans ★★

Spend a half-day visiting Zaanse Schans, a living history open-air museum replicating 17th- and 18th-century village life in northern Holland, complete with working windmills. It's located just a half-hour outside of Amsterdam; consult p. 134 for information on how to get to there. When you're back Amsterdam, if the kids are still buzzing with energy, hop a tram to **Vondelpark** (p. 103), which offers plenty of green space to run around plus several playgrounds scattered around the park.

Day 7: Back to Brussels ★★

Before leaving Amsterdam for Brussels, take a ferry ride across the IJ waterway to the **A'dam Lookout** (p. 108). (You can store your luggage at Amsterdam Centraal station and ferries depart every 5 minutes from right behind the station.) The views from the sky deck will amaze kids, as will the cool light and sound effects in the elevator ride up; thrill-seekers over 4 feet tall can get strapped in for a ride on Europe's highest swing. The train trip to Brussels will take about 2 hours.

AN ART LOVER'S TOUR

A tour of the world-class art offerings of Amsterdam, Brussels, Bruges, and several other cities in between could take weeks. Here's how to shoehorn a lifetime's dose of culture into just a week.

Day 1: Amsterdam ★★★

Two world-beaters in 1 day is pushing it a bit, but start early at the **Rijksmuseum** (p. 101), and cherry pick your way through the acres and acres of magnificent Dutch art, silverwork, and the glorious glass- and Delftware, before ending up at Rembrandt's "The Night Watch" in the second-floor Gallery of Honor. Grab lunch and then head to the **Van Gogh Museum** (p. 102). His eponymous museum is just across the Museumplein (p. 101), and offers up the world's biggest collection of his works.

Day 2: Amsterdam & Haarlem ★★★

It's back to Museumplein this morning for a trawl around the **Stedelijk Museum** (p. 102), for stellar modern work from a roster of great international names including Chagall, Warhol, Pollock, Mondriaan, and Lichtenstein. Also on Museumplein, the **Modern Contemporary Museum,** known colloquially as Moco (p. 100), makes for a nice complementary visit, with works by Pop Art masters Andy Warhol and Roy Lichtenstein as well as graffiti artists Keith Haring and Banksy. In the afternoon train it to Haarlem to admire the peerless Frans Hals civic guard portraits and other Old Master showstoppers in the **Frans Hals Museum** (p. 130).

Day 3: The Hague ★★★

Take the 50-minute train ride from Amsterdam to The Hague, which houses the world's leading collection of works by Piet Mondriaan in the H.P. Berlage-built **Gemeentemuseum Den Haag** (p. 147). You'll also find a sterling collection of Old Masters by the likes of Vermeer and Holbein in the **Mauritshuis** (p. 148), home to the famous "Girl With a Pearl Earring."

Day 4: Brussels ★★★

Depart from Amsterdam for the 2-hour train ride to Brussels, where you will be based for the next 3 days. Head for the masterpiece galleries at the **Musées Royaux des Beaux-Arts de Belgique** (p. 189) and plan on staying there all day, but save the **Musée Magritte** (see below) for tomorrow. Focus on the **Musée d'Art Ancien** (Museum of Old Masters), which covers the 15th to the 17th centuries and includes works by Breughel, Rubens, and Van Dyck. **Musée d'Art Moderne,** with works from the 19th century onward, includes masterpieces by Francis Bacon and Dali; spot famous artists such as Bonnard and Sisley among lesser-known Belgian artists in the **Musée de la Fin de Siècle.**

Day 5: Brussels & Ghent ★★★

Head back to the **Musées Royaux des Beaux-Arts de Belgique** (see above) and devote the better part of the morning to the **Musée Magritte** (p. 189), which holds more than 230 of the Belgian artist's eccentric, surreal works and covers all periods of his oeuvre. Then hop the train to Ghent, a half-hour train ride from Brussels, to see Jan van Eyck's newly restored 13-section altarpiece "The Adoration of the Mystic Lamb" (1432) in **Sint-Bavokerk** (p. 132). Follow with a visit to **Museum voor Schone Kunsten Gent (Ghent Fine Arts Museum)** (p. 253), which houses works by Bosch, van Dyck, and Rubens, as well as paintings from the great 19th-century Belgian artist James Ensor. Nearby is the **Stedelijk Museum voor Actuele Kunst Gent** (p. 256), better known by its acronym SMAK; see works by Karel Appel of CoBrA fame as well as those of Andy Warhol and Christo.

Day 6: Bruges ★★★

The train to Bruges takes about an hour from Brussels. Start your Bruges art tour at the **Groeningemuseum** (p. 226) to view the world-beating collection of works by the Flemish Primitives. After that, stop off at **Xpo Picasso** (p. 231) to see sketches and prints by its namesake, Picasso. Pop in to **Sint-Janshospitaal** (p. 227) to catch the golden Shrine of St. Ursula by Hans Memling, then wind up your day at the **Dalí Xpo-Gallery** (p. 222) in the Belfort.

Day 7: Back to Amsterdam ★★

The train from Brussels to Schiphol Airport takes about 2 hours. Content yourself with a quick visit to the Rijksmuseum's airport outpost (p. 58), which houses a few treasures from the state collection.

A MINI MILITARY MEMORIAL TOUR OF BELGIUM

Belgium has been the scene of some of the world's fiercest battles three times in the last 200 hundred years. First, Napoleon carved up the region south of Brussels, then the advent of World War I saw more than 500,000 Allied and German soldiers killed in the trenches of Flanders. Sadly, the country saw action again just 20 years later, with heavy fighting between Allied troops and the German army in the Ardennes.

Note: For this itinerary, you should base yourself in Brussels and rent a car to see these sites.

Day 1: Waterloo ★

South of Brussels, the French emperor Napoleon Bonaparte met final defeat at the **Battle of Waterloo** (p. 21) in 1815. A tour of this largely preserved battlefield and a visit to the Duke of Wellington's military HQ, now the **Musée Wellington** (www.museewellington.be) both afford a fascinating insight into the great and decisive battle.

Day 2: Drive to Ypres (Ieper) ★★★

A 2-hour drive north from Brussels brings you to the medieval cloth town of **Ypres** (p. 265), a crucible of fighting on the World War I Western Front that claimed the lives of 500,000 Allied and German soldiers in just 100 days in 1917. The now peaceful Flanders fields are sprinkled with a few remaining sections of trenches and plenty of military cemeteries, including Tyne Cot, which is the largest Commonwealth War Graves cemetery in the world. Don't miss Ypres's superb **In Flanders Fields Museum** (p. 268) or the emotional Last Post ceremony held at the **Menin Gate** (p. 267) daily at 8pm.

Day 3: Bastogne & World War II ★★

Drive southeast from Brussels past Tournai and Mons to the River Meuse at Namur. Continuing eastward into the rolling Ardennes hills, you'll pass many scenes of hard-fought action from the Battle of the Bulge in the winter of 1944 to 1945, at places such as Marche-en-Famenne, Rochefort, and La Roche-en-Ardenne. None was harder than the epic struggle U.S. troops fought to hold the strategic crossroads town of **Bastogne** in those closing days of World War II. The greatest memorial to American soldiers can be found at the star-shaped **Mardasson Memorial;** a short walk brings you to the thoughtfully presented Bastogne War Museum.

AMSTERDAM

O pen-hearted, welcoming, and prosperous, Amsterdam is a good-time city that merrily welcomes all comers. It embraces its tourists, its cyclists, its boatfolk, and its multi-cultural community. It is friendly, unflappable, and approachable; a city confident in its own skin but with one eye fixed on the future, buzzing with creativity and bonhomie.

But it is also a city of surreal juxtapositions; an elegant cityscape of 165 waterways, 1,280 bridges, and thousands of venerable 17th-century mansions exist side by side with the sleazy alleyways of the Red Light District. A city with some of the most impressive art museums in the world that tolerates sex clubs and dope smoking; that has one of Europe's best concert halls but also a gritty nighttime scene springing up around Westerpark and NDSM-Wharf; and a city that offers Michelin-starred restaurants alongside grungy brown cafes.

It's a long-outdated cliché to regard Amsterdam as some sort of latter-day Sodom and Gomorrah, for the winds of change are blowing through the streets. Tolerance may be embedded deeply in the Dutch psyche, but even the most open-minded of people can run out of patience. Amsterdam's notorious coffee shops have dropped in number, from around 350 citywide in the 1990s to about half that today, while in the Rosse Buurt (also known as De Wallen), the famous Red Light District, druggie haunts have been closed down as have some 40 percent of the prostitutes' infamous windows in the last decade. Starting in January 2020, group tours of the Red Light District will be banned in an effort to combat tourists gawking at sex workers. In turn, smart restaurants, bars, and upmarket independent stores are starting to move in to Rosse Buurt's pretty side streets, which ironically hides some of the most unspoiled architecture in Amsterdam. In any case, Amsterdammers themselves have never drifted around town in a drug-induced haze.

Between visits to Amsterdam's artistic and historical treasures, be sure to give yourself time out to absorb the freewheeling spirit of one of Europe's most vibrant cities.

ESSENTIALS

Arriving

BY PLANE   Amsterdam Airport Schiphol (www.schiphol.nl;
© **0900/0141** for general and flight information, 31-20/794-0800

Amsterdam

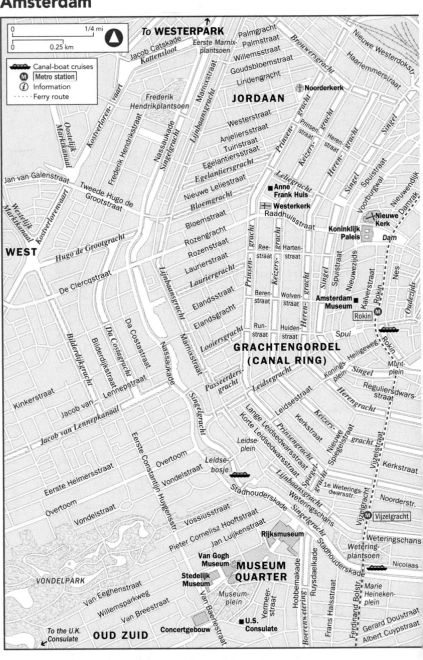

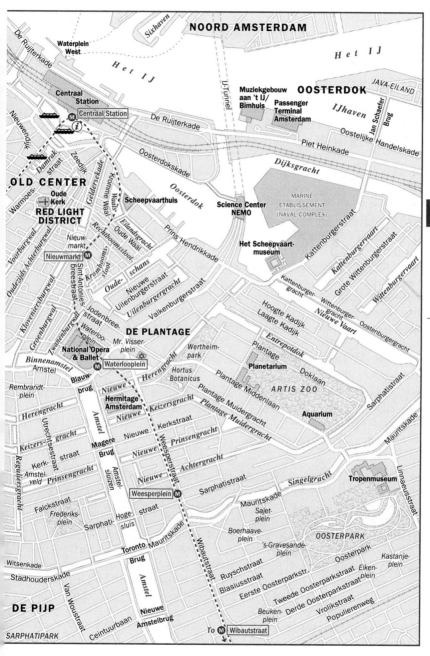

from outside Holland; airport code AMS), 14km (9 miles) southwest of Amsterdam is pronounced *Skhip*-ol and is universally regarded as one of the best airports in the world for its ease of use, its massive duty-free shopping center, and its outpost of the Rijksmuseum (p. 101). Located southwest of the city center, it is the main airport in the Netherlands, handling the country's international arrivals and departures.

There are three terminals close together and imaginatively numbered 1, 2, and 3. Moving walkways connect passengers with the Arrivals Hall and Passport Control, Baggage Reclaim, and Customs. Conveniences like free luggage carts, baby rooms, and showers are all on tap. Beyond Customs is Schiphol Plaza, a one-stop destination that combines tourist office, transport ticket office, rail station access, YOTELAIR Amsterdam Schiphol and Mercure Hotel Schiphol Terminal for transit passengers, a shopping mall, bars and restaurants, baggage lockers, tourist info desks, car-rental, and hotel-reservation desks all in the one location. Bus and shuttle stops plus a taxi stand are just outside the terminal.

For tourist information go to I amsterdam's **Visitor Information Center** in Schiphol Plaza (www.iamsterdam.com; ✆ **020/702-6000;** daily 7am–10pm).

BY CAR A network of major international highways crisscrosses the Netherlands. European expressways E19, E35, and E231 converge on Amsterdam from France and Belgium to the south and from Germany to the north and east. These roads also have Dutch designations; as you approach the city they are, respectively: A4, A2, and A1. Amsterdam's ring road is A10. Distances between destinations are relatively short. Traffic is invariably heavy and delays are frequent but road conditions are otherwise pretty good, service stations are plentiful, and highways are plainly signposted.

BY CRUISE SHIP Cruise-ship passengers arrive in Amsterdam at the **Passenger Terminal Amsterdam,** Piet Heinkade 27 (www.ptamsterdam.nl; ✆ **020/509-1000**), on the IJ waterway within easy walking distance of Centraal Station, where all modes of transport can be picked up to travel anywhere in the city.

BY FERRY DFDS Seaways (www.dfdsseaways.co.uk; ✆ **0871/522-9955** in Britain, 44/330-333-0245 outside the UK) has daily car-ferry services between Newcastle in northeast England and Ijmuiden, west of Amsterdam on the North Sea coast. The overnight travel time is 15½ hours. From IJmuiden, you can go by bus to Amsterdam Centraal Station.

P&O Ferries (www.poferries.com; ✆ **44/1304-44-8888** in Britain, 020/200-8333 in Holland) has daily car-ferry service between Hull in northeast England and Rotterdam Europoort. The overnight travel time is 10 to 11 hours. Ferry-company buses shuttle passengers between the Europoort terminal and Rotterdam Centraal Station, from where there are frequent trains to Amsterdam Centraal Station.

Stena Line (www.stenaline.co.uk; ✆ **08447/707-070** in Britain) has a twice-daily car-ferry service between Harwich in southeast England and Hoek van Holland (Hook of Holland) near Rotterdam. The travel time is 6 hours, 45

AMSTERDAM | Essentials

minutes for the daytime crossing, and 7½ hours overnight. Frequent trains depart from Hoek van Holland to Amsterdam Centraal Station.

BY TRAIN   Rail services to Amsterdam from other cities in the Netherlands and elsewhere in Europe are frequent and fast. International trains arrive at Centraal Station from Brussels, Paris, Berlin, Cologne, and other German cities, and from the main cities in Austria, Switzerland, Italy, and Eastern Europe. **Nederlandse Spoorwegen** (**Netherlands Railways;** www.ns.nl) trains arrive in Amsterdam from towns and cities all over the Netherlands. Schedule and fare information on travel by train is available by calling ✆ **0900/9292** (0.90€ per minute) for national service, and **030-230-0023** for high-speed international services; or by visiting www.ns.nl.

The burgundy-colored **Thalys high-speed train,** with a top speed of 300kmph (186 mph), connects Paris, Brussels, Amsterdam, and (via Brussels) Cologne. Travel time from Paris to Amsterdam is 3 hours, 20 minutes, and from Brussels 1 hour, 50 minutes. For Thalys information and reservations, call **32/7066-7788** (0.30€ per minute) or visit www.thalys.com. Tickets are also available from railway stations and travel agents.

On **Eurostar** high-speed trains (top speed 300kmph/186 mph), the travel time between London St. Pancras Station and Amsterdam is just under 4 hours. All trains stop in Rotterdam and Brussels' Bruxelles-Midi Station (no change of train required). For Eurostar reservations, call ✆ **08432/186-186** in Britain; ✆ 44/1233-617-575 from outside the UK; www.eurostar.com.

BY BUS   **International coaches** arrive at the bus terminal at Sloterdijk rail station (Metro: Sloterdijk) in the south of the city. **Flixbus** and **National Express** operate bus service between London Victoria Bus Station and Sloterdijk rail station. Travel time is around 12 hours. For reservations, contact Flixbus (www.flixbus.com; ✆ **49/30-300-137-300)** or National Express (www.nationalexpress.com; ✆ **08717/818-181**).

From Sloterdijk, you can go by train or Metro to Centraal Station, or by Tram 19 to the Museumplein area and to connecting points for trams to the center city. For the Leidseplein, take tram 19.

Visitor Information

Amsterdam's main **Visitor Information Center** is run by I amsterdam and is located at Stationsplein 10, right outside Centraal Station (www.iamsterdam.com; ✆ **020/702-6000**); it's open daily 9am to 6pm and in addition to a helpful, if busy staff, there are touch screens where you can access general information about the city. There's also a branch in Schiphol Plaza at the airport, with the same phone number but longer opening times: daily from 7am until 10pm.

City Layout

Amsterdam is not a huge city and its central district, where most of the tourist attractions are concentrated, can be walked easily. The canals and streets fan out in a series of concentric circles from the historic city center. However, despite its size, this city is very diverse in mood and style, changing in feel almost from one street to another.

The Neighborhoods in Brief

The Old Center The oldest, most central district of Amsterdam encompasses Dam Square, Oude Kerk (p. 94), and the Nieuwmarkt and is probably best known for containing the infamous Red Light District (p. 94), which lies between the two canals Oudezijds Voorburgwaal and Oudezijds Achterburgwaal. Despite its seedy reputation, it's safe and well policed. A recent gentrification policy has seen more restaurants and design stores moving in.

Canal Ring The concentric band of three canals that surround the Old Center was built in the 17th century as the cramped, disease-ridden old city drastically needed to expand. Herengracht, Keizersgracht, and Prinsengracht today form an aristocratic enclave of grand townhouses overlooking the three canals. Some of the city's smartest hotels, and many major attractions, lie within this belt, including the Westerkerk (p. 99), the Anne Frank Huis (p. 96), the Canal House Museum, and the Willet-Holthuysen Museum (p. 99) along with more niche attractions like the pipe museum (p. 95).

Jordaan This picturesque former working-class area, with low-rise gabled houses, narrow canals, and hump-backed bridges, is now the favored residential area of Amsterdam's intelligentsia. There are lots of bars and traditional brown cafes to discover as well as innovative art galleries and design studios. Jordaan also has scores of canal-house hotels tucked into its pretty lanes, a world away from the Red Light District, yet only a 15-minute walk.

Museum Quarter Home to Amsterdam's triumvirate of heavyweight art museums—the Rijksmuseum (p. 101), Stedelijk Museum (p. 102), and the Van Gogh Museum (p. 102)—this quarter also holds the Concertgebouw concert hall (p. 122), embassies, and upmarket stores as well as one of the city's most glorious public spaces, the Museumplein (p. 101). The Heineken Brewery is close by (p. 100).

Oud Zuid Adjoining the Museum Quarter and the Vondelpark (p. 103), Amsterdam's poshest residential area is also its most exclusive shopping district, with chi chi hotels, and top international brands and jewelry stores along PC Hooftstraat (p. 121).

De Pijp Multi-ethnic and beguiling, De Pijp is packed with well-priced restaurants of every nationality, and features the city's best street market along Albertcuypstraat. Although the area is smartening up with the arrival of stylish hotels and trendy restaurants, it is still a quarter of immigrants, students, and Amsterdam's least-known red light district along Ruysdaelkade (p. 95).

De Plantage Incorporating the Artis Royal Zoo (p. 104), the Hortus Botanicus (p. 106), and Amsterdam's Jewish Quarter (p. 112), Plantage is an area of wide boulevards surrounded by residential streets. Its pricey 19th-century townhouses are popular with young, upwardly mobile professionals. The Jewish Historical Museum (p. 106) and Portuguese Synagogue (p. 106) mark the district's western limits, the housing developments around Oosterdok its northern edges.

Amsterdam Noord The opening of EYE Film Institute started the migration across the IJ waterway to this new bastion of cool, an alternative area of street art mixed with shiny new high-rise apartments. Here, dilapidated old docks and industrial buildings have been repurposed into cultural centers such as the Tolhuistuin, housed in an abandoned Shell factory. There's a trendy cafe scene around NDSM Wharf.

Westerpark Westerpark is a funky corner of the city, home to formerly working-class housing that has largely been turned into apartments. Its focal point is the trendy entertainment complex that has seen the old Westergasfabriek (p. 109) turned into one of the city's biggest leisure destinations.

Oosterdok Amsterdam's new residential areas consists of manmade islands redeveloped from the ruins of former dockyards. The housing stock is low-level and

4

AMSTERDAM | The Neighborhoods in Brief

contemporary, with plenty of on-trend cafes, bars, and design boutiques along the IJ-front promenades. Residents are mainly a young bunch working in creative industries. The Scheepvartmuseum (p. 105) and NEMO Science Museum (p. 107) are close by.

Outlying Areas Amstelveen lies south of Amsterdam, a middle-class suburban area that has little to distinguish itself other than for being the home of the exceptional Cobra Modern Art Museum (p. 110).

Getting Around

BY PUBLIC TRANSPORT   Most of Amsterdam is easily navigable on foot or by bicycle, but it's a rite of passage to take a ride on the clanging trams that wind through the city streets. The underground Metro can also come in handy if you're visiting farther-flung destinations; buses you'll likely use less frequently. The city's public transportation system, **GVB Amsterdam,** is entirely cash-free. A single-use ticket (3.20€) is valid for 1 hour and can be purchased from automated ticket vending machines which take cash and credit cards. Onboard trams and buses, non-chip-and-pin credit and debit cards, which most Americans use, will not work.

Note: You will see locals using a plastic electronic card called an **OV-chipkaart** to pay for public transportation; this is probably not the best option for a short-term stay as the card alone costs 7.50€.

If you plan to use public transportation often, your best bet is to buy a **1-day or a multiday card:** 24 hours (8€), 48 hours (13.50€), 72 hours (19€), 96 hours (24.50€), 120 hours (29.50€), 144 hours (33.50€), and 168 hours (36.50€). There are reduced fares for children aged 4 to 11 and ages 3 and under travel free. Public transport in the city is also free when you purchase an I amsterdam City Card (see p. 90). With any of these cards, you must check in and out—just hold your card up against the electronic reader at both the start and the end of the ride.

The central information and ticket sales point for GVB Amsterdam is **GVB Tickets & Info,** Stationsplein (www.gvb.nl; ✆ **0900/8011** for timetable and fare information and other customer services), in front of Centraal Station and next to the Amsterdam Tourist Information Office. It's open Monday to Friday from 7am to 9pm, Saturday from 8am to 9pm, and Sunday from 9am to 9pm. In addition, tickets are available from GVB and Netherlands Railways ticket booths in Metro and train stations and from ticket vending machines at Metro and train stations and at certain stops along the Tram 2 line.

The network of trams, buses, and the Metro is in service starting at 6am until 12:30am; there are also night buses between 3am and 7am, which cost 5.50€.

BY TRAM   Half the fun of Amsterdam is walking along the canals. The other half is riding the blue-and-gray trams that roll through most major streets. There are 14 tram routes, 9 of which (lines 2, 4, 11, 12, 13, 14, 17, 24, and 26) begin and end at Centraal Station, so you know you can always get back to that central point if you get lost and have to start over. The city's other tramlines are 1, 3, 5, 7, and 19. Lines 2, 3, 5, and 12, are useful for visiting the sights south of the city around Museumplein, while 1, 4, 7, 11, 12, 19, and

If you're keen on your green credentials, use a bike taxi or rickshaw to get around the city. They're clean, relatively comfortable, and can zip along the cobbled streets giving Amsterdam's cyclists a run for their money. The rickshaws are easy to spot all over the city, but especially around Centraal Station, Leidseplein, Museumplein, and Waterlooplein, or you can order your eco-taxi in advance. Contact Amsterdam Fietstaxi (www.amsterdam-fietstaxi.nl; © 065/348-1860). Charges start at 10€ for rides in the city center; half-hour tours are 25€.

24 serve the city center. Tram 2 travels from Centraal past many of the city's major sites including Dam Square, the Prinsengracht and Keizersgracht canals, Leidseplein, and the Rijksmuseum.

Trams have one access door that opens automatically, normally toward the rear; arrowed indicators point the way to the door. To board a tram that has no arrowed indicators, push the button beside the door on the outside of any car. To get off, you may need to push a button with an "open-door" graphic. Tram doors close automatically, and they do so quite quickly, so don't hang around. Always remember to hold your card against the reader as you get on and off the tram. *Note:* If you don't "check out" as you get off, your card will carry on being charged and will run out of credit.

BY BUS   An extensive bus network complements the trams and Metro, with many bus routes beginning and ending at Centraal Station, but it's generally much faster to go by tram or Metro.

BY METRO   Although it can't compare to the labyrinthine systems of Paris, London, and New York, Amsterdam does have its own Metro, with five lines—50, 51, 52, 53, and 54—that run partly over ground and transport commuters in and out from the suburbs. From Centraal Station, you can use Metro trains to reach both Nieuwmarkt and Waterlooplein in the old city center. The newest line, 52, opened in July 2018 and travels between Amsterdam-Noord (North), and Amsterdam Zuid (South) in just 15 minutes.

BY FERRY   Free **GVB ferries** (www.gvb.nl) for passengers and two-wheel transportation connect the center city with Amsterdam-Noord (North), across the IJ waterway (p. 58). The short crossings are free, which makes them ideal micro-cruises as they afford fine views of the harbor. Most ferries depart from Waterplein West behind Centraal Station. The two most popular routes are to Buiksloterweg (for attractions like the Eye Film Institute and A'dam Tower), with the journey taking 5 minutes and ferries running every 4 to 12 minutes around the clock, and to NDSM-Werf, a 14-minute trip, with ferries running from 6:45am to midnight on weekdays and from 7:15am on weekends. A third route goes to IJplein, a more easterly point on the north shore, with ferries every 7 to 15 minutes from 6:30am to midnight.

BY TAXI   It used to be that you couldn't hail a cab from the street in Amsterdam; occasionally they will now stop if you do. Best is to find one of the taxi stands sprinkled around the city, generally near the luxury hotels, at major squares such as the Dam, Spui, Rembrandtplein, Westermarkt, and Leidseplein, and of course at Centraal Station. Taxis have rooftop signs, blue license plates, and are metered. Hotel reception staff can order a cab for you, too.

Fares are regulated citywide and all cabs are metered; the meter starts at 3.19€ and there is a charge of 2.35€ per kilometer. If you don't see a cab stand you can call the generally reliable **Taxi Centrale Amsterdam** (**TCA;** www. tcataxi.nl; ✆ **020/777-7777**). The fare includes a tip, but you may round up or give something for an extra service, like help with your luggage or for a helpful chat. In fact, most Amsterdam cab drivers like to talk and are pretty knowledgeable about their city, so take full advantage of them.

Uber (UberX and UberBLACK) is also available in the city and to and from Schiphol airport. Generally, the airport rates are slightly less expensive with an UberX than by taxi (around 35€–40€ vs. 45€–50€).

BY CAR There's no point whatsoever in renting a car if you are intending to stay in Amsterdam and not venture out of the city, as the public transport system works efficiently and most attractions are within walking distance of each other. In addition, the streets are narrow, many are one-way, some are pedestrianized, and all are crowded with bonkers cyclists; in short, driving in the city is a nightmare. However, if you are travelling outside Amsterdam, it's usually cheapest to book a rental car online before you leave home. Try **Auto-Slash.com,** which applies current coupons against the cost of your rental, whether it be from Avis, Hertz or any of the other major companies. Then, it tracks your rental, so if the daily cost drops before you pick it up, they rebook you at the lower price.

If you must have a car, know that there are limited **parking facilities** in the city itself but plenty of Park + Ride options in the suburbs, with rates of 8€ per 24 hours. Useful P+R parking lots include Olympisch Stadion and RAI in the southern part of the city, and Noord and Zeeburg in the north; all are near public transport facilities. If you insist on parking in town, there are designated car parks centrally, the most useful for tourists being at Waterlooplein (Valkenburgerstraat 238) or Beursplein 15 and charging 3€ to 8€ per hour.

Don't risk leaving your car on the street as the limited public parking in the city is managed with a gauntlet-grip by Cition, which will **tow your car away** at the drop of a hat for the slightest parking violation and then whack you with a 373€ fine; cash payments not accepted. If you do have the misfortune to get towed, the collection depot is at Daniël Goedkoopstraat 9 and it's open 24/7.

[FastFACTS] AMSTERDAM

ATMs There are ATMs all over Amsterdam, and many are open 24/7, although you'll want to be a bit cautious about withdrawing cash in quiet areas after dark.

Business Hours Stores usually open from 10am to 6pm Tuesday, Wednesday, Friday, and Saturday. Many are closed on Monday morning, opening at noon or

1pm, and most shops outside the center close all day Sunday (although many are open in the main shopping district around Kalverstraat). Some stay open until 8 or

9pm on Thursday. Most museums close 1 day a week (often Mon), but open some holidays, except for Koningsdag (King's Day on Apr 27; see p. 39), Christmas, and New Year's Day. (Even then, the Rijksmuseum is open every day of the year, regardless of public holidays.)

Consulates The **U.S. Consulate:** Museumplein 19 (https://nl.usembassy.gov); ℂ **020/575-5309;** tram 2, 3, 5 or 12). **The British Consulate:** Koningslaan 44 (www. gov.uk; ℂ **070/427-0427;** tram 2). The Australian, Canadian, Irish, New Zealand, UK, and U.S. embassies are all in The Hague (p. 144).

Emergencies For any **emergency** (fire, police, ambulance), the number is ℂ **112** from any landline or cellphone. For 24-hour urgent but **nonemergency** medical or dental services,

call ℂ **088/0030-600;** the operator will connect you to an appropriate doctor or dentist. To **report a theft,** call ℂ **0900/8844.** Residents of E.U. countries must have a European Health Insurance Card (EHIC) to receive full health-care benefits in the Netherlands.

Internet Access Most hotels in Amsterdam offer Wi-Fi access as a matter of course. **KPN hotspots** are scattered throughout the city; cost starts at 5€ per hour. **(www.kpn.com/internet/ wifi-hotspots.htm).**

Pharmacies In the Netherlands, a pharmacy is called an *apotheek* and sells both prescription and nonprescription medicines. Regular open hours are Monday to Saturday from around 9am to 6pm. A centrally located pharmacy is **Dam Apotheek,** Damstraat 2

(www.dam-apotheek.nl; ℂ **020/624-4331;** tram 4, 14, or 24) close to the National Monument on the Dam. Pharmacies post details of nearby **all-night and Sunday pharmacies** on their doors.

Post Office The city of Amsterdam doesn't have post offices as such anymore; instead various branches of newsagents, supermarkets, and grocery stores have postal points run by **PostNL** (www.post.nl). The stationers Gebroeders Winter (Rozengracht 62), the branch of Albert Heijn supermarket at Jodenbreestraat 21, and Primera (Waterlooplein 169) all have postal points where you can mail a parcel or postcard home. Stamps can also be purchased from your hotel reception and any newsstands that sell postcards.

WHERE TO STAY

Whether you are after glitzy luxury with every conceivable amenity, a cozy townhouse hotel, family-friendly facilities, or bare-bones bed and board that frees up hard-earned cash for other purposes, Amsterdam will have just the right accommodation for you.

The city's popularity soars during spring and summer, but most hotels offer rate reductions between November and March simply to fill their rooms—with the notable exception of the Christmas and New Year periods, of course. Amsterdam is an all-year-around destination and has many charms in the off season, such as less-crowded museums, slashed prices during sales in the stores, and a full calendar of winter cultural events (p. 38).

Apartment Rentals in Amsterdam

Renting an apartment for your visit can be a really smart move in Amsterdam, where the accommodations stock includes dreamy canal-side townhouses, spacious studios, houseboats out in the IJ, and barges moored up along the Canal Ring. Generally, renting an apartment, private room, or houseboat will cost less than staying a hotel, but demand for properties soars during the busy summer months; that means you will likely have to book a multi-day or even weeklong stay in order to get this type of accommodation. Also keep in mind that most residential buildings in the city do not have elevators and stairs can be steep.

Airbnb (www.airbnb.com), **HomeAway** (www.homeaway.com), and **VRBO** (www.vrbo.com) have thousands of Amsterdam properties on their sites; most are apartments in canal houses but you can also find the occasional full townhouse or houseboat. Prices typically range from 120€ to 210€ per night for a studio or cozy one-bedroom apartment. If you don't mind sharing an apartment, Airbnb is your best bet for booking a private room, often with a shared bathroom; prices run the gamut depending on the property and location, but most average around 80€ per night.

If you have your heart set on staying on a houseboat, the sites **www.house boatrental.amsterdam** and **www.houseboathotel.nl** both rent either studio apartments on boats or entire boats. Rates are similar to those for the houseboats found on Airbnb, HomeAway, and VBRO, but there are far more properties listed one these two sites. Studios average around 150€–200€ per night while entire houseboats, which usually sleep 4 to 6 people, start at around 250€ and go up to 700€ per night for a luxurious five-bedroom boat.

A final option for very friendly travelers: **Couchsurfing** (www.couch surfing.org) and **GlobalFreeloaders** (www.globalfreeloaders.com) connect travelers with folks willing to share their room/sofa/apartment for free or a very minimal charge.

APARTHOTELS

There are also several aparthotel and serviced apartment options in the city, which offer a bit more space than the average hotel room (an especially good option for families), come equipped with kitchens and usually include daily maid service. **Dutch Masters** (http://en.dutch-masters.com; ✆ 06/1020-5504) are 9 upscale contemporary apartments tucked inside a 17th-century building on the Keizersgracht canal. Sleeping 2 to 4 people (though bedrooms are small), the one- to three-bedroom flats feature subtle decor inspired by Dutch artists like Karel Appel and Mondrian and offer fully equipped kitchens, washer/dryers, and free Wi-Fi; some have access to a private garden. The minimum booking is generally 1 week and prices range from 1,200€ to 2,400€ weekly. A more flexible choice, allowing for single-night stays, is **Eric Vökel Amsterdam Suites** (www.erikvokel.com; ✆ 020/808-0487), located on Oosterdok island, just a stone's throw from Amsterdam Centraal station. Decked out with sleek, Scandinavian-inspired furnishings, the spacious one- to three-bedroom apartments sleep 4 to 6 people and feature huge windows (many with views of the IJ River) and a 24-hour manned reception desk. Rates average 190€–450€ per night.

The Old Center
EXPENSIVE
Hotel de l'Europe ★★   The grande dame of Amsterdam's luxury hotels occupies a prime location overlooking the Binnenamstel. Its rooms are

Amsterdam Hotels

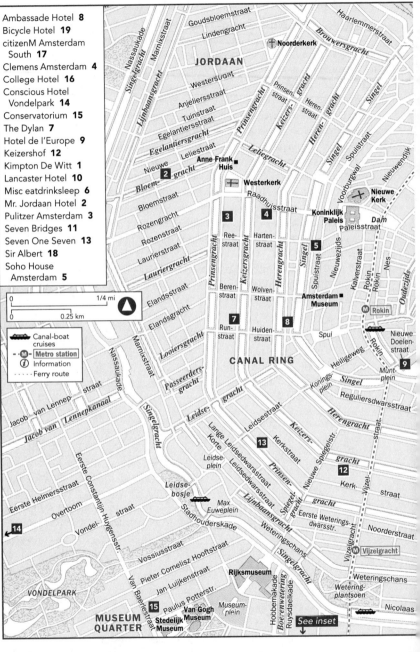

Canal-boat
cruises
Metro station
Information
Ferry route

4

AMSTERDAM | Where to Stay

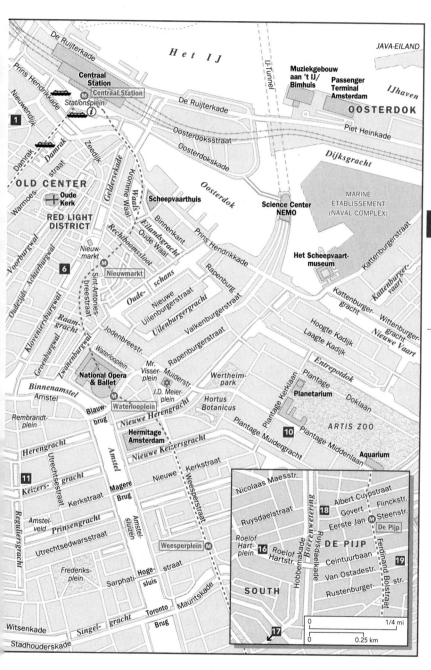

sumptuous, spacious, and flooded with light, all with barn-sized marble bathrooms. An all-suite Dutch Masters Wing has 23 extravagant apartments, each boasting a copy of a famous oil painting from the Rijksmuseum. Along with its superb foodie pilgrimage restaurant **Bord'Eau** ★★★, a spa with an indoor pool, and a summer terrace with river views, l'Europe also boasts the swanky **Freddy's** cocktail bar and what might well be Amsterdam's last *fumoir*, where the smoking of (only) cigars is still very much permitted.

Nieuwe Doelenstraat 2-14. www.deleurope.com. ✆ 020/531-1777. 111 units. 490€–720€ double. Parking 65€/day. **Amenities:** 2 restaurants, 2 bars, sauna, spa, indoor pool, free Wi-Fi.

Kimpton De Witt ★★★

Just a few minutes' walk from Centraal Station, this hotel is exceedingly convenient. But it's the friendly, prompt service that make it a real standout. In 2017, Kimpton overhauled the former Crowne Plaza, a 1980s building that incorporated three 17th-century houses. The result is a marvelous blend of stylish contemporary Dutch design with period accents like wood beamed ceilings. The open-plan lobby is particularly welcoming, with Delft-inspired tile floors, floor-to-ceiling windows, and lots of comfortable seating nooks where you can enjoy the complimentary all-day tea bar and free wine and snacks at the 5pm social hour. Rooms are spacious and blissfully quiet, with comfortable beds, large walk-in rainforest showers, and plush touches such as Frette robes and local Marie-Stella-Maris bath products. The ground-floor **Wyers** restaurant offers a serviceable menu of American comfort food, but the new **Super Lyan** bar is the true star, a candy-colored 1950s-style haunt masterminded by award-winning British mixologist Mr. Lyan.

Nieuwezijds Voorburgwal 5. www.kimptondewitthotel.com. ✆ 020/620-0500. 274 units. 290€–400€ double. Parking 50€/day. **Amenities:** Restaurant, bar, room service, fitness center, free bike rental, free Wi-Fi.

Soho House Amsterdam ★★

The monumental 1930s Bungehuis, which most recently served as university faculty offices, is now home to the Amsterdam outpost of this hip hybrid hotel/members' club. The impressive renovation, completed in 2018, retained much of the original building's Art Deco flavor, with wood-lined corridors, glazed wall tiles, and stained glass and brass accents—all complemented by new and vintage mid-century-style furnishings. The design scheme carries over into the rooms, which come in all shapes and sizes due to the building's landmark status; they feature parquet floors, soaring ceilings, and clever touches like gable-shaped headboards and retro mini-bars. Many of the canal-fronting rooms sport tall bay windows with lovely views of turreted canal houses across the Singel, but the single-pane glass can make for a noisy stay (it's the reason we've docked this hotel one star). Most appealing are the club amenities—all open to hotel guests—that surpass those of the city's most luxurious hotels. Best is the rooftop terrace, complete with heated outdoor pool and comfy loungers where you can soak up the sunset over neighboring Dam Square; a close runner-up is the private cinema, outfitted with 36 plush velvet seats and screening free first-run movies nightly. Mingle with members—mainly young, fashionable creative

Staying in an elegant 17th-century canal house in the UNESCO World Heritage-listed district may offer all the charm and atmosphere you could possibly dream of, but the fact remains that it's nigh on impossible to shoehorn an elevator into the cramped confines of most of these multi-story, narrow buildings. So many simply don't have them. If that's a problem, ask for a room on a low floor or choose another hotel where elevators are installed and working.

types—at the exclusive fifth-floor **House** kitchen and bar; the latter serves particularly good cocktails.

Spuistraat 210. www.sohohouseamsterdam.com. ✆ **020/888-0300.** 79 units. 250€–500€ double. Parking 55€/day. **Amenities:** 2 restaurants, 3 bars, lounge, gym, outdoor pool, cinema, spa, free Wi-Fi.

MODERATE

Misc eatdrinksleep ★★ This quirky six-room guest house is just a short walk to bustling Nieuwmarkt square. Each room in the four-story 17th-century canal house is uniquely decorated and spans a range of styles, from brightly colored contemporary furnishings in the Design Room to a Baroque-inspired room replete with a canopied bed, gilded mirrors, and a chandelier. The quieter accommodations are, naturally, at the back and overlook a pretty courtyard garden but there are trade-offs: the canal-fronting rooms are larger, brighter, and have air-conditioning. Bear in mind that negotiating the steep, narrow staircase can be difficult (though the friendly staff will transport your luggage). The cozy, tchotchke-filled lobby lounge transforms into a lively cocktail bar come evening.

Kloveniersburgwal 20. www.misceatdrinksleep.com. ✆ **020/330-6241**. 6 units. 199€–350€ double. Rates include full breakfast. **Amenities:** Breakfast room, bar, free Wi-Fi.

Canal Ring
EXPENSIVE

Ambassade Hotel ★★ A far cry from the minimalist styling adopted by so many city hotels, the designers of the Ambassade evidently believed that more is best; the ten 17th- and 18th-century gabled townhouses sandwiched together to form this elegant frippery are gaily festooned with swags of curtain, chandeliers, and antiques—plus a collection of priceless CoBrA artwork (p. 110). The guest rooms have statement color palettes, fancy gilt mirrors, and walls filled with Dutch paintings. The three joyfully appointed suites all have views over the canal, as does the first-floor apartment. A sumptuous library bar stocks 5,000 books, many of them first editions. A few doors down at Herengracht 321, you'll find the hotel's blissful **Koan Float** massage center; guests receive a discount on treatments. Although not all rooms are accessible by elevator, plenty are; breakfast is not included in the room rate.

Herengracht 341. www.ambassade-hotel.nl. ✆ **020/555-0222.** 57 units. 260€–450€ double. Public parking nearby. **Amenities:** Restaurant, bar, spa, free Wi-Fi.

The Dylan ★★★ Offering truly individual guest rooms with stripped oak floors, exposed beams, blindingly white bathrooms, and four-poster beds that you could lose a family in, Amsterdam's glossiest boutique hotel is located in a former 17th-century theater on lively Keizersgracht and well deserves its accolades. Facilities include top-notch concierge service, a secluded courtyard garden for afternoon tea and evening drinks, and light-filled top-floor suites. As if that's not enough, the fabulous Michelin-starred Restaurant **Vinkeles** (p. 80) has its home in the Dylan. For a hotel so upmarket, the ambience is surprisingly chill, but with room rates starting at around 400€ it is a very exclusive treat.

Keizersgracht 384. www.dylanamsterdam.com. ℂ **020/530-2010.** 40 units. 400€–1,400€ double. Rates include continental breakfast. Parking 95€/day. **Amenities:** 2 restaurants, bar, gym, room service, free Wi-Fi.

Pulitzer Amsterdam ★★★ Long considered the boutique hotel of choice in Amsterdam, the Pulitzer underwent a thorough renovation and refurbishment in 2017; the result is a more cohesive and contemporary design sensibility that still retains its charming historic character. Rooms (a jumble of shapes and sizes) are dressed in sophisticated muted colors with bright, jewel-toned accents; of particular note are the four themed Collector's Suites that are larger than some New York City apartments. As the hotel is a combination of 25 interlinked canal houses, negotiating your way around the maze-like property can be frustrating at times. But once you've found the path to the famous **Pulitzer's Bar,** where you can sip classic cocktails in a plush, clubby setting, all will be well. What hasn't changed is the hotel's prime location, on the Prinsengracht canal between the quaint Jordaan and the tourist hotspots of the Old Center, and among the retail delights of the buzzy Nine Streets (p. 117).

Prinsengracht 323. www.pulitzeramsterdam.com. ℂ **020/523-5235.** 225 units. 350€–1,300€ double. Parking 62.50€/day. **Amenities:** Restaurant, cafe, bar, private boat, gym, room service, free Wi-Fi.

Seven One Seven ★★ This magical, suite-only and award-wining temple of style is furnished in lavish 19th-century style, complete with antique furnishings and with every possible amenity on tap. With views either over the canal or a leafy patio to the rear, there's no bad choice of room here. An elegant drawing room, a sun-spot terrace, views over the canal, a flower-filled breakfast room, and smooth service all contribute to making this a truly unforgettable experience in Amsterdam, far removed from impersonal chain hotels. A small irritant is the extra charge for breakfast over and above an already expensive stay. *Note:* Be aware that there is no elevator and the stairs are steep.

Prinsengracht 717. www.717hotel.nl. ℂ **020/427-0717.** 9 units. 320€–530€ double. Public parking nearby. **Amenities:** Breakfast room, free Wi-Fi.

MODERATE

Clemens Amsterdam ★★ A little hotel that packs a big punch, this two-star hotel isn't long on amenities but the rooms are all pristine and welcoming with en-suite baths and rain showers. Bear in mind when booking that the Clemens sits on one of the city's main thoroughfares so rooms can get quite noisy, although those at the front of the building do have the added pull of cute wrought-iron balconies to perch on. Typically for a small hotel in central Amsterdam, it occupies four floors in a narrow townhouse and there's simply no place to put an elevator, but the hotel is fantastically located near the Anne Frank Huis and the Westerkerk.

Raadhuisstraat 39. www.clemenshotel.nl. © **020/624-6089.** 14 units. 150€–249€ double. Rates include breakfast. **Amenities:** Free Wi-Fi.

Seven Bridges ★★★   Quite simply one of the most gorgeous hotels in the city, with individually decorated room boasting genuine antique furnishings in a variety of opulent Biedermeier, Art Deco, or rococo styles with original 17th-century wooden floors. The attic rooms have sloped ceilings and exposed wood beams and provide the perfect romantic hideaway for couples, while room number 5 has a lovely private terrace. There are no public spaces beyond the entrance lobby, which cuts overhead and may explain the exceptionally reasonable prices for a hotel of such comfort and opulence. As with so many Canal Ring hotels, there's no elevator.

Reguliersgracht 31. www.sevenbridgeshotel.nl. © **020/623-1329.** 5 units. 140€–205€ double. **Amenities:** Free Wi-Fi.

INEXPENSIVE

Keizershof ★★   Offering exceptional value in the expensive city center, the Keizershof occupies a four-story, narrow canal house that dates back to 1672, so of course there's no elevator. Guestrooms are beamed and plain with simple, modern furnishings, and only two have private bathrooms; they either overlook the bustle of the canal or a tranquil pocket-size, flower-filled courtyard to the rear, where breakfast is served in summer. Downstairs a TV lounge shares its space with a grand piano, but what makes this place memorable is the warm welcome from its owners, the hospitable De Vries family, who will go that extra mile to make your stay comfortable.

Singel 301. www.hotelkeizershof.nl. © **020/622-2855.** 5 units. 130€–150€ double. Rates include breakfast. **Amenities:** TV lounge, free Wi-Fi.

> ### An Alternative to Amsterdam for Lodgings
>
> Despite there being thousands of rooms in more than 550 hotels up for grabs in Amsterdam, it can be nigh on impossible to find a room between May and September, when the weather is at its best and the festivals are in full swing. If you get stuck for accommodation, you could consider staying in Haarlem (p. 128), a charming Golden Age city only a 15-minute train ride from Amsterdam city center.

Jordaan

MODERATE

Mr. Jordaan Hotel ★   Set on the quiet, tree-lined Bloemgracht canal in the heart of the Jordaan district, this modest boutique hotel is just a 5-minute walk to major sites like the Anne Frank Huis (p. 96) and the Tulip Museum (p. 99). Exposed brick walls, vintage furniture, and pendant lighting in the common areas give it a hip vibe and its small, simply decorated rooms have clever design touches, like wood headboards mimicking the surrounding gabled canal houses. The double beds are comfortable though a bit tight for two; the marble bathrooms are extremely petite, but do sport rainforest showers. Best is the attic room, which feels large thanks to its pitched roof and windows on three sides.

Bloemgracht 102. www.mrjordaan.nl. ℂ **020/522-2345.** 34 units. 155€–250€ double. **Amenities:** Coffee bar, free Wi-Fi.

Museum Quarter
EXPENSIVE

Conservatorium ★★★ Occupying the former neo-Gothic Sweelinck Conservatory of Music, the Conservatorium is owned by bespoke hotel chain The Set and sets a new benchmark for luxury. Standard rooms have crisply contemporary appeal, with wood floors and marble bathrooms equipped with rainfall showers, its 46 suites (including three signature suites) take things up a notch with vaulted ceilings, oversized bathtubs, and balconies. There are several eating options under the stewardship of super-chef Schilo van Coevorden including the signature restaurant **Taiko** ★★★, which serves exquisite Asian cuisine. The hotel is mere steps away from the Museumplein attractions, although when you spy the gorgeous **Akasha Holistic Wellbeing Centre,** it'll be a toss-up between spending the day floating around in its giant pool or elbowing your way through the crowds to stand in front of Rembrandt's fabled "The Night Watch" in the Rijksmuseum.

Van Baerlestraat 27. www.conservatoriumhotel.com. ℂ **020/570-0000.** 129 units. 550€–800 double, suites 670€–3,200€. Parking 65€/day. **Amenities:** 2 restaurants, bar, pool, spa, gym, free Wi-Fi.

MODERATE

College Hotel ★★ A sleek and urbane boutique hotel found in a former school (hence the name), the College is a couple of minutes from Amsterdam's Big Three museums, the Rijksmuseum, Stedelijk, and Van Gogh. It's also dangerously close to the shockingly expensive designer stores on PC Hooftstraat so you'll get to spy on plenty of self-consciously glam 30-something European professionals among the vaguely Art Nouveau surroundings of the hotel's luscious, shady courtyard and bar. The spacious guest rooms are the last word in contemporary cool, in soothing beiges and tans, with stacks of pillows and smart fixtures and fittings.

Roelof Hartstraat 1. www.thecollegehotel.com. ℂ **020/571-1511.** 40 units. 169€–245€ double. Parking 45€/day. **Amenities:** Restaurant, bar, room service, free Wi-Fi.

De Pijp
MODERATE

Sir Albert ★★ The first of the hip Sir Hotels chain, which has since expanded to cities including Berlin and Barcelona, this boutique property is nicely situated on the border of De Pijp and the Museum Quarter, within easy walking distance of the city's Big Three museums and the bustling Albert Cuyp Market. It's housed in a redbrick former diamond-cutting factory, somewhat unsettlingly around the corner from one of Amsterdam's smaller Red Light districts. The book-lined lobby lounge, outfitted with generous leather seats, cowhide poufs, and a gas fireplace, is a cozy spot for casual drinks and snacks, while the adjacent restaurant **Izakaya** is a neighborhood favorite serving Japanese-inspired small plates. Many of the rooms feature high ceilings and equally tall windows letting in plenty of light; opt for a suite if you want a bit more privacy than the standard open-plan bathrooms afford.

Albert Cuypstraat 2-6. www.sirhotels.com. ℂ **020/710-7258.** 90 units. 160€–275€ double. Parking 45€/day. **Amenities:** Restaurant, bar, gym, free Wi-Fi.

BUDGET

Bicycle Hotel Amsterdam ★ Homey and basic, the Bicycle Hotel is fiercely proud of its sustainable ethos; it is powered by solar heat, has a "green" roof, and uses recycled furniture wherever possible. The miniscule bedrooms are no great shakes in terms of luxury but are spotlessly clean; be warned, however, that the very cheapest rooms at 50€ don't have private bathroom. A few have kitchenettes and there are also a couple of triples for families. Amazingly for these prices, a decent Dutch breakfast of bread, ham, and cheese is included in the room rate. Foolhardy guests who choose to explore Amsterdam by bike can rent cycles for 7.50€ per day. There's no elevator and payment is preferred in cash.

Van Ostadestraat 123. www.bicyclehotel.com. ℂ **020/679-3452.** 16 units. 50€–135€ double. Rates include breakfast. **Amenities:** Free Wi-Fi.

Oud West

INEXPENSIVE

Conscious Hotel Vondelpark ★★ This hotel shouts its green cred, with living plant walls, an eco-roof, and rooms kitted out with sustainably made furnishings (including a "stone" bathroom counter crafted from pressed paper). It's run by a young, handsome, and very cool staff that goes the whole hog to help visitors. They let their collective hair down on weekends when every night is party night, with music and dancing in the bar. Bedrooms are compact and wittily adorned with pithy slogans on energy conservation, and the breakfast bar is an organic delight. It's just a few minutes' walk to leafy Vondelpark, and Tram Line 1 stops right outside the hotel, getting you to the city center in less than 5 minutes. There are three other outposts in the city, including one near Museumplein that is ideally placed for visiting the Rijksmuseum and Van Gogh Museum though the room rates are significantly higher.

Overtoom 519. www.conscioushotels.com. ℂ **020/820-3333.** 81 units. 96€–175€ double. Parking 22.50€/day. **Amenities:** Bar, discounted gym next door, free Wi-Fi.

Zuid

INEXPENSIVE

citizenM Amsterdam South ★★   One of a gaggle of no-frills accommodation options that seem to be flooding European cities, CitizenM has washed up close to the World Trade Center and RAI and caters largely to short-stay business travelers, although there's the fast Tram 5 service right into the city center for sightseers. Check in is automated, barista-standard coffee is on tap 24/7, and a canteen serves up sushi and salads at lunch. The zingy, ultramodern room designs include podlike showers, touch-screen remotes, huge, comfortable beds, and free movies; breakfast is extra at 17€ if ordered in advance, 3€ more on the day. There's a second location in De Plantage and another within spitting distance of Schiphol airport.

Prinses Irenestraat 30. www.citizenm.com. © **020/811-7090.** 215 units. 89€–150€ double. **Amenities:** 24/7 snack room, bar, free bike rental, free Wi-Fi.

De Plantage

MODERATE

Lancaster Hotel ★   Located on the eastern, gentrified side of the city, a world away from the leery Red Light District, this hotel is perfectly placed for family visits to Artis Zoo, the Tropenmuseum, and the Botanical Gardens. Even better, it's just a 10-minute ride on trams 9 or 14 to all the central amenities and action. Prices are reasonable with spacious bedrooms furnished in neutral, inoffensive tones and gigantic black-and-white images over the beds. If you're traveling with kids, there are several triple rooms available.

Plantage Middenlaan 48. www.thelancasterhotelamsterdam.com. © **020/535-6888.** 91 units. 138€–188€ double. Public parking nearby. **Amenities:** Restaurant, bar, free Wi-Fi.

WHERE TO EAT

Amsterdam's cuisine is a perfect mirror image of the city itself: multi-ethnic, and exciting. As a trading city with tentacles that spread all over the world, Amsterdam has welcomed immigrants from the Far East, South America, Africa, and Eastern Europe ever since the Golden Age days of the 17th century, a phenomenon reflected in the diverse cooking styles seen in its many restaurants. In Amsterdam, it seems, you can eat in any language and certainly at any price, taking your pick from Michelin-starred gastronomic feasts, multi-plated Indonesian *rijstaffel* banquets, or comforting snacks of Dutch *bitterballen*.

As with most northern European countries and certainly in comparison with Spain and Italy when families are still munching away at midnight, Amsterdam eats early. Even the smartest restaurants open around 6pm, which makes dining out a family-friendly experience.

Beyond the restaurants recommended below, we're also big fans of three hotel-based eateries: **Taiko ★★★** (see p. 72) which serves seriously stellar Asian fare in the Museum Quarter, the swank **Bord'Eau ★★★** (see p. 68) which features fabulous views of the city center and equally stunning, very creative tasting menu meals, and the Japanese small plates restaurant **Izakaya ★★** (p. 73), in De Pijp.

Old Center
EXPENSIVE
&moshik ★★ INTERNATIONAL Set on the small island of Oosterdok just east of Centraal Station, &moshik is one of just four two-Michelin-starred restaurants in the city. It's masterminded by chef Moshik Roth, whose ethereal, ever-changing tasting menus take you on a whirlwind gastronomical journey with flavors from such far-flung places as Morocco, Japan, and Turkey as well as the Netherlands. The exquisitely crafted seven-course menu might feature a raw scallop topped with pheasant jelly and Dutch caviar; roasted sweetbreads with anchovies and a squeeze of Amalfi lemon; and tender milk-fed lamb dotted with apricots. There's also a full vegetarian tasting menu and a handful of dishes available a la carte. Enormous floor-to-ceiling windows in the intimate, 55-seat dining room afford lovely harbor views.

Oosterdokskade 5. www.moshikrestaurant.com. ✆ **06/260-2094.** Mains 50€–120€. Fixed-price menu 165€–220€. Wed–Sat 7–9:30pm, Sun 7–8:30pm, lunch Fri and Sun noon–2pm.

The White Room ★★★ EUROPEAN An opulent white and gold dining room—the oldest in the city, dating back to 1885—sets the stage for chef Jacob Jan Boerma's inventive dishes. Each jewel-like plate is a skillful balance of acidity, sweetness, and spice, as with a starter of raw tuna and foie gras dotted with peppery shiso leaves or roasted pigeon with baby carrots in a rich hazelnut sauce. Depending on the day, dinner tasting menus range from four to nine courses and are surprisingly well-priced given the sumptuous setting on Dam Square, just across from the Royal Palace.

Dam 9. www.restaurantthewhiteroom.com. ✆ **020/554-9454.** Fixed-price lunch menus 32.50€–37.50€, dinner 69€–119€. Mains 49€. Thurs–Sat noon–1:30pm; Tues–Sat 6:30–10pm.

MODERATE
Kapitein Zeppos ★★ INTERNATIONAL A casual cafe tucked away down a little alley off Spui, Zeppos offers sandwiches, salads, and burgers by day and fried fish platters, fondue, and huge shared plates of antipasto by night. Dishes are satisfying, but it's the lively atmosphere that brings in the crowds. It's popular, in particular, with students from the University of Amsterdam across the street and has a slightly cheesy decor that's compounded when the equally cheesy 1980s disco music starts up late on weekend nights. There's live music every evening except Sunday and kitschy sing-alongs around a grand piano the first Sunday brunch of the month in winter.

Gebed Zonder End 5, Spui. www.zeppos.nl. ✆ **020/624-2057.** Mains 17€–26€. Mon–Thurs 11–1am, Fri–Sat, 11–3am, Sun noon–1am. Tram 1, 2, or 5 to Spui.

Amsterdam Restaurants

&moshik **27**
Café Cobra **17**
Café de Sluyswacht **23**
Café Restaurant
   Mamouche **18**
Coffee & Coconuts **18**
d&a hummus bistro **2**
Envy **8**
EYE Bar-Restaurant **29**
Foodhallen **9**
Golden Temple **19**
Kapitein Zeppos **11**
Koffiehuis de Hoek **7**
La Rive **20**
Lion Noir **13**
Mata Hari **26**
Momo **14**
Nam Kee Chinatown **25**
Pancake Bakery **3**
Pllek **28**
Restaurant Blauw **15**
Restaurant de Kas **21**
Restaurant-Café
   In de Waag **24**
Restaurant Plancius **22**
Rijks **16**
Stubbe's Haring **4**
Supperclub
   Amsterdam **12**
Toscanini **1**
Vinkeles **10**
Visrestaurant Lucius **6**
The White Room **5**

| 0 | | 1/4 mi |
| 0 | 0.25 km | |

Canal-boat cruises
Ⓜ Metro station
ⓘ Information
- - - - Ferry route

JORDAAN

Goudsbloemstr.
Lindengracht
Frederik Hendrik-plantsoen
† Noorderkerk
Haarlemmerstraat
Brouwersgracht
Westerstraat
Anjeliersstraat
Tuinstraat
Egelantiersstraat
Egelantiersgracht
Leliestraat
Nieuwe
Bloemgracht
Anne Frank Huis
Leliegracht
⊕ Westerkerk
Raadhuisstraat
Bloemstraat
Rozengracht
Rozenstraat
Laurierstraat
Lauriergracht
Elandsstraat
Elandsgracht
Looiersgracht
Passeerders-gracht
Leidse-gracht
Lijnbaansgracht
Marnixstraat
Nassaukade
Singelgracht
Lijnbaansgracht
Singelgracht

Prinsengracht
Keizersgracht
Herengracht
Singel

Ree-str.
Harten-straat
Beren-straat
Wolven-straat
Run-straat
Huiden-straat
Prinsengracht
Keizersgracht
Herengracht
Singel
Spuistraat
Nieuwezijds
Kalverstraat
Rokin
Rokin
Nes
Oudezijds
Voorburgwal
Nieuwendijk
Spuistraat

Koninklijk Paleis
Nieuwe Kerk
Dam
Paleisstraat
Amsterdam Museum
Rokin Ⓜ
Nieuwe Doelenstraat
Spui
Muntplein

CANAL RING
Heiligeweg
Koningsplein
Singel
Reguliersdwarsstraat
Herengracht

Leidse-plein
Lange Leidsedwarsstraat
Korte Leidsedwarsstraat
Leidsestraat
Kerkstraat
Prinsengracht
Keizers-gracht
Nieuwe Spiegelstr.
gracht
Kerk-straat
Vijzelgracht
Leidsebosje
Overtoom
Eerste Constantijn Huygensstr.
Max Euweplein
Stadhouderskade
Lijnbaansgracht
Singelgracht
Eerste Weteringdwarsstr.
Noorderstraat
Ⓜ Vijzelgracht
Weteringschans
Weteringplantsoen
Nicolaas
kade

VONDELPARK
Vondel-straat
Vossiusstraat
Pieter Cornelisz Hooftstraat
Jan Luijkenstraat
Van Baerlestr.
Paulus Potterstr.
Rijksmuseum
Museumplein
Van Gogh Museum
Stedelijk Museum

MUSEUM QUARTER

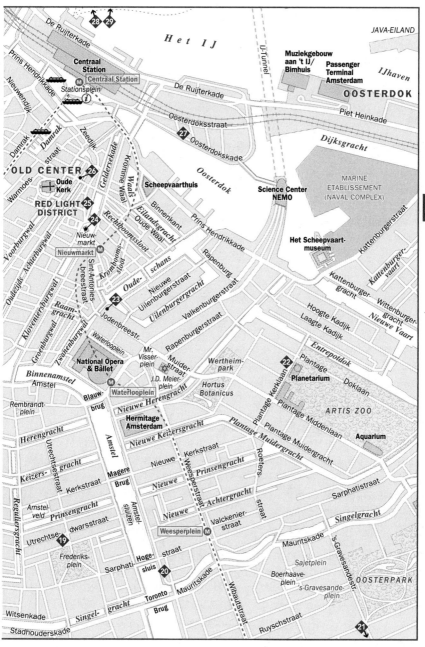

Mata Hari ★★ EUROPEAN   In the sea of mediocre, touristy dining spots that fill the Red Light District, this restaurant stands out for its vintage living-room-like atmosphere and first-rate Mediterranean menu, which includes oven-roasted feta wrapped in phyllo, ricotta and saffron-stuffed ravioli, and a hearty braised lamb shank. For a quick snack, share a generous mezze plate on the retro sofas in the front windowed nooks, or sit down for a full lunch or dinner at one of the candlelit wood tables. Evenings can get quite busy, so best to head to the upper level, where things are a bit quieter away from the bar.

Oudezijds Achterburgwal 22. www.matahari-amsterdam.nl. ℂ **020/4205-0919.** Mains 12€–22€. Daily 11–1am (Fri–Sat till 3am).

Restaurant-Café In de Waag ★★ DUTCH   Bang in the middle of vibrant Nieuwmarkt, the historic Waag buzzes day and night; its outdoor cafe is filled to bursting all afternoon and serves a decent, if unremarkable daytime menu of soups, sandwiches, and salads. Late-night snacks of *bitterballen* and platters of Dutch cheeses and meats soak up any surfeits of alcohol. The restaurant inside the Waag is made for romance, with a candlelit dining room and long trestle tables ideally suited to one of Amsterdam's oldest buildings. The evening menu is short but solidly tasty, offering mostly steak and fish; a dinner deal of three courses runs 39.75€.

Nieuwmarkt 4. www.indewaag.nl. ℂ **020/422-7772.** Mains 24€–32€. Mon–Wed 11am–10:30pm; Thurs–Sun 9am–10:30pm. Metro to Nieuwmarkt.

Visrestaurant Lucius ★★ SEAFOOD   A top choice for fresh fish in Amsterdam, Lucius is decked out like a traditional fishmongers with tiled walls and marble tabletops, wooden seating, and ceiling fans. It has been going great guns for more than 40 years. The spectacular seafood platter includes piles of fresher-than-fresh mussels, oysters, clams, and shrimp, plus a half lobster, and there's a reasonably priced set menu for 39.50€, consisting of three courses that could include langoustines, grilled octopus, or earthy pike perch. Cooking styles are unfussy, allowing the true taste of the fish to shine on the plate. Reservations are recommended on the weekend.

Spuistraat 247. www.lucius.nl. ℂ **020/624-1831.** Mains 22.50€–32.50€, fixed-price menu 39.50€, seafood platters to share 65€–155€. Daily 5pm–midnight. Tram 1, 2, or 5 to Spui.

INEXPENSIVE

Café de Sluyswacht ★★ DUTCH   Tilting at a precarious angle over the Oudeschans canal, this former 17th-century lock-keeper's cottage is one of the oldest and most famous pubs in Amsterdam. Inside all is crooked, with wooden bars and uneven stone floors. Sample the *wit bier* (white beer) and a plate of strong Dutch cheese and enjoy the tiny, crowded terraces with views over the canal or towards the Museum Het Rembrandthuis.

Jodenbreestraat 1. www.sluyswacht.nl. ℂ **020/625-7611.** Mains 7.50€–18€. Mon–Thurs 12:30pm–1am, Fri–Sat 12:30pm–3am, Sun 12:30–7pm.

Nam Kee Chinatown ★★★ CHINESE   The most famous restaurant in Amsterdam's Chinatown is also one of its best; this family-run venue looks

AMSTERDAM'S brown cafes

Traditional Dutch taverns or "brown cafes" are great places to mix with local Amsterdammers, as they are the very embodiment of *gezellighied*, that particularly Dutch mixture of charm, conviviality, and comfort all wrapped into one splendid welcoming package. Some brown cafes date right back to Rembrandt's day; all are warm and cheery, with dark interiors and simple wooden furniture and bars. Some have kitchens where short-order chefs rustle up all manner of moderately priced breakfasts, all-day dishes, *broodjes* (sandwiches), and simple suppers. Opening hours are anywhere between 8 and 10am and 1 and 3am the following day.

Hoppe ★★ is an ancient brown cafe that dates back to 1670. It has a convivial, English-pub atmosphere, and is standing-room-only in the early evening, when the place fills up with a merry after-work bunch. Things can become rowdy after a couple of samplings of Dutch *jenever*, a ginlike liqueur with recipes dating back to the 18th century. Main dishes are 7.50€ or less. It's open daily 8am to 1am (Fri–Sun till 2am). You'll find it at Spui 18–20 (www.cafe-hoppe.nl; **© 020/420-4420**).

't Smalle ★★★ is on the edge of the cute Jordaan area. It's a traditional locals' cafe decked out in wood and glass and offering a small menu of snacks (dishes 3.60€–11.50€). The primary business here is the beer, so grab a glass and join the local drinkers at the bar, or on warm evenings sit outside on the decking over the canal. 't Smalle is on Egelantiersgracht 12, and open daily 10am to 1am, Fri–Sat till 2am. (www.t-smalle.nl; **© 020/623-9617**).

like nothing from the outside and frankly not that much in the neon-lit sparse interior but it's always packed out with local Chinese families. The plates piled high with noodles, Peking duck, and beef spare ribs dripping in honey simply fly out of the kitchen. There are now two more equally successful outposts of Nam Kee at Geldersekade 117 and Marie Heinekenplein 4. If you don't fancy eating out, there's also a delivery service.

Zeedijk 111–113. www.namkee.nl. **© 020/624-3470**. Mains 7.50€–25€. Daily 11:30am–10:30pm.

Stubbe's Haring ★★ FISH   Raw herring is a Dutch specialty, and there are dozens of *haringhuis* stands in town, but this one is regarded as the best. Located on a bridge near Centraal Station overlooking the Singel canal, the stall is something of a local institution and long lines form here come lunchtime. It's a great spot to sample raw herring served in a bread roll with pickles and sweet onions; tip your head back and try and eat the fish whole for a quintessential Amsterdam experience.

Singel bridge. Sandwiches 5.50€. Midday–evening. No credit cards.

Canal Ring
EXPENSIVE
Supperclub Amsterdam ★ FUSION   This stark white, wildly popular spot is a restaurant, nightclub, and performance space all rolled into one.

Diners lounge on couches or sit at tables to listen to whatever the DJ is playing and watch acrobatic performances, and there is no menu—you will be served a five-course feast of whatever is available seasonally. Inform your waiter of any dietary restrictions and sit back to see what arrives. Post-supper is party time with live music and wild dancing. Reservations required.

Singel 460. www.supperclub.com. © **020/344-6400.** Fixed-priced menu 69€. Sun–Wed 7:30pm–2am, Thurs–Sat 7:30pm–5am. Tram 1, 2, or 5 to Spui.

Vinkeles ★★ FRENCH   Housed in the converted bakery of a 17th-century almshouse that is now the Dylan hotel (see p. 70), Vinkeles has been overseen by top chef Dennis Kuipers since 2006. He whips up unusual dishes such as Zeeland lobster with white asparagus, wild garlic, and sea lavender. Should you decide to splash out and eat the chef's signature menu, the bill will set you back 290€ for two; for that you get to feast on eight extravagantly tasty courses teamed with exquisite wine pairings (85€ per person) as recommended by sommelier Natasja Noorlander.

Dylan hotel, Keizersgracht 384. www.vinkeles.com. © **020/530-2010.** Mains 45€–110€, fixed-price menus 115€–145€. Tues–Sat 7–10pm. Tram 1, 2, or 5 to Spui.

MODERATE

Envy ★★ MODERN MEDITERRANEAN   The emphasis at this matte-black citadel of Zen is grazing on small plates of food, tapas-style. Small but perfectly executed crab, pork belly, mussels, and lamb dishes emerge from the open kitchen; most of the ingredients are organic. The showpiece is the boundary-pushing 8-course chef's table menu created by its young star Floris van Straalen who earned his stripes at Vinkeles (above).

Prinsengracht 381. © **020/344-6407.** www.envy.nl. Mains 10€–16€, tasting menus 49€–69€, chef's table menu 69€. Daily 6pm–1am, Fri–Sun noon–3pm. Tram 13, 14, or 17 to Westerkerk.

Golden Temple ★★ VEGETARIAN   Housed in a narrow, candle-lit dining hall with an open kitchen, low-slung tables, and rugs as decoration, the menu here goes one step beyond the normal veggie options with its unlikely roster of Indian, Middle Eastern, and Mexican plates, along with pizza. Mixed *thalis* and *mezze* are delicious; there is also a choice of chunky salads with quinoa, tempeh, and soba noodles. Downsides? The ethnic music can get a bit irksome, there's no alcohol, and it's closed at lunchtime (a shame as this would make a great sightseeing pit stop).

Utrechtsestraat 126. www.restaurantgoldentemple.com. © **020/626-8560.** Mains 14€–21€. Daily 5:30–9:30pm. Tram 4 to Frederiksplein.

Lion Noir ★★ FRENCH   Among the slew of Asian eateries and gay bars peppering Reguliersdwarsstraat, the city's most famous gay street, Lion Noir stands out not only for its French menu, but also for its eccentric interior. A hodgepodge of taxidermy, animal skeletons, and other curios dot the dual-level space, which attracts scenesters who come for the quirky ambiance as much as the food. As for the grub, it's quite good, with classic French choices like Fine de Claire oysters on the half shell, duck liver terrine, steak tartare, and at lunch, a nice selection of salads. Dinner service stops at 10pm but the first-floor bar and lounge offers drinks and snacks till the wee hours. The back terrace (open only when it's warm) is an oasis of calm surrounded by flower-filled private gardens.

Reguliersdwarsstraat 28. www.lionnoir.nl. ℂ **020/627-6603.** Main courses lunch 10€–21€, dinner 25€–30€, fixed-price dinner 39.50€–55€. Tues–Thurs and Sunday noon–1am, Fri–Sat noon–3am, Mon 6pm–1am.

INEXPENSIVE

Koffiehuis de Hoek ★ DUTCH   An old-style Amsterdam cafe on the corner of the Nine Streets shopping enclave and overlooking the canal, this place positively bursts at the seams with local workers at lunchtime. Grab a table for an all-day breakfast or a Dutch snack of croquettes or *bitterballen* washed down with an excellent espresso. We can't recommend the acidic house wine, however—try a local beer instead. All tables are shared; takeaway sandwiches piled high with salami and salad are also available.

Prinsengracht 341. ℂ **020/625-3872.** Snacks from 5€. Mon–Fri 8am–4pm, Sat–Sun 9am–4:30pm. Tram 13, 14, or 17 to Westerkerk.

Pancake Bakery ★ PANCAKES   There are many, many pancakes houses in Amsterdam but this is one of the best. Set in a 17th-century canal warehouse houses its pancakes come with a choice of 70 toppings and stuffings, from Indonesian chicken to honey, nuts, and whipped cream. The selection of breakfast options includes organic muesli, scrambled eggs, and giant omelets. A terrific place to take kids, plus it's on Prinsengracht and suitably placed for a treat after a visit to the sobering Anne Frank Huis.

Prinsengracht 191. www.pancake.nl. ℂ **020/625-1333.** Pancakes 6.25€–16.25€. Daily 9am–9:30pm. Tram 13, 14, or 17 to Westerkerk.

Jordaan

MODERATE

Toscanini ★★ ITALIAN   The chefs at Jordaan's superlative Italian restaurant make almost everything on the premises, from the organic bread to the pasta, which comes in myriad shapes and colors. The vaulted restaurant leads on to an open kitchen that operates like clockwork, with homemade charcuterie, tagliatelle with rabbit ragu, stewed oxtail, and chargrilled steaks constantly pouring forth.

Lindengracht 75. www.restauranttoscanini.nl. ℂ **020/623-2813.** Mains 18€–25€, tasting menu 57.50€. Mon–Sat noon–2:30pm and 6–10:30pm. Tram 3 to Haarlemmerplein.

INEXPENSIVE

d&a hummus bistro ★★ MEDITERRANEAN   This homey little spot is celebrated for its extensive hummus menu; the creamy original is topped with whole chickpeas and fresh herbs and comes with warm, freshly baked pita, but you can order a more filling version with roasted root veggies or meat, including a tender, slow-cooked beef stew. Other standouts are the shakshuka, a spicy tomato-and-egg dish, and *siniya*, a hearty Palestinian meal of chopped lamb and beef ladled atop a crispy pita. There is a second outpost on the east side of the city at Oostenburgergracht 185, not far from the Artis Zoo (p. 104) and the Tropenmuseum (p. 107).

Westerstraat 136. www.dna-hummusbistro.com. (℃) **020/341-6487.** Mains 9€–18€. Daily 11am–11pm.

Museum Quarter
EXPENSIVE

Momo ★★ ASIAN-FUSION   A stone's throw from Vondelpark, this sleek, high-end Asian-Fusion hotspot is known for its extensive menu of small plates, designed for sharing. Seafood is king here, with an array of sushi, sashimi, and ceviche, as well as steamed fish and grilled lobster. Perennial favorites include crispy duck with pancakes and hoisin sauce, and tuna tartare, whimsically presented inside a small cave of ice. By day, the light-filled, minimalist space is relatively subdued, with business types lunching on one of the four-course bento boxes. Come evening, Momo morphs into a buzzy dining destination, with the music turned up—and occasionally live DJs spinning—and its long, curving bar peopled by a fashionable crowd.

Hobbemastraat 1. www.momo-amsterdam.com. (℃) **020/671-7474.** Mains 23€–46€, fixed-price lunch bento box 23€–25€, fixed-price dinner tasting menus 69€–99€. Daily 10am–1am (Sat–Sun till 2am).

Rijks ★★★ DUTCH   The restaurant of the Rijksmuseum has earned accolades galore, thanks to young chef Joris Bijdendijk's brilliant modern interpretation of Dutch cuisine. Nearly everything on the menu is sourced from the Netherlands, from cheeses to Zeeland oysters to local beef; the vegetable dishes, with many products cultivated in the restaurant's own garden, are particularly outstanding. Dishes change seasonally and might include roasted young leeks with truffles and chanterelles; a goat terrine with cranberries and bitter lettuce; or dry-aged farm duck served with the bird's heart and tongue. Most come as small plates, which make for a fun, experimental meal, or spring for the six-course tasting menu. Even the wine list features Dutch varietals, rarely seen outside the country. In summer, make a reservation on the spacious terrace, where you can dine while taking in views of the Rijksmuseum next door.

Museumstraat 2. www.rijksrestaurant.nl. (℃) **020/674-7555.** Mains 17€–32€, fixed-price menu (price changes with the seasons) 79€. Mon–Sat 11:30am–10pm, Sun 11:30am–3pm.

MODERATE

Café Cobra ★★ DUTCH   Little beats sitting outside at Café Cobra on a sunny afternoon, watching the great and good of Amsterdam come out for Sunday brunch. The food is not fancy but the spicy croquettes and *bitterballen* (meatballs) accompanied with fat fries, mayo, and a glass of Prosecco certainly hit the spot. By day, the light-filled cafe interior is always heaving with tourists as amazingly it is the only affordable restaurant adjacent to the Rijksmuseum, Stedelijk, and Van Gogh museums, but the young wait staff cope admirably with the multilingual crowds and service is always smooth. In winter there's an ice rink outside.

Hobbemastraat 18. www.cobracafe.nl. ℂ **020/470-0111.** Mains 7€–17.50€. Daily 9:30am–7pm. Tram 2, 3, 5, 12, 16, or 24 to Museumplien.

Oud Zuid
MODERATE

Restaurant Blauw ★★★ INDONESIAN   Part of the new breed of Asian restaurants in the Netherlands, Restaurant Blauw may serve traditional Indonesian dishes but its minimalist decor and service from the beautiful, charming wait staff are thoroughly 21st century. There's even a decent wine list—a rarity in Indonesian eateries! It's filled to the rafters on two noisy floors every night of the week and even then people line up for the chance of a table. The *rijsttafel* consists of an amazing 17 plates, including pickles, fried and sticky rice, pork balls, plantain, satay, and chili-laden beef, pork, chicken, and fish dishes. Other tasty mains include chicken cooked with lemongrass and tamarind, or slow-braised beef in coconut sauce. Heaven! Remember to book ahead.

Amstelveenseweg 158–160. www.restaurantblauw.nl. ℂ **020/675-5000.** Mains 22.50€–27.50€, *rijstaffel* 30€–35€. Mon–Thurs 6–10pm, Fri 6–10:30pm, Sat 5–10:30pm, Sun 5–10pm. Tram 1 to Overtoomsesluis.

INEXPENSIVE

Foodhallen ★★ INTERNATIONAL   A converted tram depot is now home to this lively indoor food hall, with around 20 international street food stalls dishing up a bit of everything, from summer rolls at Viet View to Spanish *jamon* at Jabugo Bar Iberico to falafel plates at Maza. Also look for offshoots of popular local eateries, including The Butcher, with its wonderfully juicy flame-grilled burgers, and De Ballenbar for trendy takes on Dutch specialties, like gourmet *bitterballen*. Though lunchtime is less busy, it's also far less fun, and you'll miss out on the frequent free live music and DJs in the evenings. Aim to get there early to score a seat at the communal tables or a stool at one of the four bars, including one devoted to the favorite Dutch drink, gin and tonic, then tag-team to get your food. Be sure to save room for the delectable jewel-like French tarts at Petit Gateau.

Bellamyplein 51. www.foodhallen.nl. ℂ **020/218-1776.** Mains 7€–10€. Daily 11am–11pm (Fri–Sat till 1am).

De Pijp
MODERATE

Café Restaurant Mamouche ★★ MOROCCAN   The styling of this intimate little restaurant is a romantic blend of French brasserie (mirrors, smartly laid tables) and North African (tagines and candlesticks) flourishes, and that is reflected in the trans-Mediterranean menu—a happy blending of North African dishes and French influences. Hence confit of duck, grilled fish with *charmoula* (a spicy Maghreb marinade), and couscous *mechoui* appear on the brief menu. The specialty of the house: a delicious lamb tagine with prunes, almonds, beans, and coriander. Unusually for a restaurant, the bar staff can whip up a punchy cocktail, too.

Quellijnstraat 104. www.restaurantmamouche.nl. ⓒ **020/670-0736.** Mains 16€–24€. Tues–Sun 5–11pm. Tram 16 or 24 to Ferdinand Bolstraat.

Coffee & Coconuts ★★ KOREAN   Yes, they do serve excellent coffee (from local micro-roaster Friedhats) and yes, there are many coconut-themed offerings on the menu, but this all-day dining spot offers so much more. A 1920s cinema has been beautifully transformed into an airy, open-plan restaurant that sprawls across three levels, with whitewashed walls and floors and lots of comfy linen cushioned seats to lounge on. The menu is packed with healthy options, from spelt granola to quinoa and cauliflower bowls to snapper steamed in a banana leaf, but the star is the red beet veggie burger, topped with roasted eggplant and sheep's cheese and served on a fresh whole-wheat bun. Weekend brunch is exceedingly popular—try the coconut pancakes with whipped coconut cream.

Ceintuurbaan 282-284. www.coffeeandcoconuts.com. ⓒ **020/354-1104.** Mains 9€–19€. Daily 8–11pm.

De Plantage
MODERATE
Restaurant Plancius ★★ EUROPEAN   The perfect spot for sitting outside on a sunny day—its right opposite the Artis Royal Zoo and next door to the Dutch Resistance Museum—the cavernous interior of Plancius fills up quickly with local families and glamorous women loudly treating each other to lunch. Lunchtime menus include heaping salads, hearty sandwiches, burgers, and a pasta of the day, and there's an indulgent afternoon tea featuring a mix of savory sandwiches and sweets along with a glass of Prosecco. Dinner offerings range from grilled tuna to mushroom risotto to baked guinea fowl, while the meal-sized salads are ideal for vegetarians.

Plantage Kerklaan 61. www.restaurant plancius.nl. ⓒ **020/223-6946.** Mains 14€–19€. Daily 10am–10pm. Tram 9 or 14 to Artis.

Amsterdam's Street Food

Popular snacks include **bitterballen** (fried meatballs) available in most bars and bistros and served with cold beer, or **patat** (fries) bought from street vendors and eaten dunked in mayonnaise, straight from the paper cone.

Haring (herring) is the most popular fish in Amsterdam, traditionally eaten whole and pickled from street vendors such as the famous Stubbe's Haring (p. 79) on the Singel Bridge.

For sweet Dutch street food options, see p. 87.

Noord Amsterdam
MODERATE
EYE Bar-Restaurant ★★ INTERNATIONAL   The spectacular, smooth planes of the EYE form one of the coolest buildings in Amsterdam (p. 108), with views through great glass windows over the ever-changing architectural

Thanks to the influx of immigrants from across the world into the Netherlands, anything goes in the country's cuisine, particularly in the capital Amsterdam and the port city of Rotterdam (p. 152). Chinese, Surinamese, Turkish, Indian, Indonesian, Italian, and Mediterranean cooking has been accepted into the Dutch gourmet lexicon since immigration first began in the 17th century. Indonesian *rijstaffel* (meaning "rice table") is virtually a staple national dish, originating with Dutch plantation overseers in what was then called the East Indies.

The basic concept of *rijstaffel* is to sample many different tastes on one plate, relying on a backdrop of plain rice to help blend textures and flavors. Restaurants in Amsterdam offer a shared feast of up to 30 small plates; these can include *loempia* (classic Chinese-style egg rolls); *satay* or *sateh* (small kabobs of pork, grilled and served with a spicy peanut sauce), *perkedel* (meatballs), *gado-gado* (vegetables in peanut sauce), *daging smoor* (beef in soy sauce), *babi ketjap* (pork in soy sauce), *kroepoek* (crunchy, puffy shrimp toast), *serundeng* (fried coconut), *roedjak manis* (fruit in sweet sauce), and *pisang goreng* (fried banana).

One of the best Indonesian restaurants in the city is **Restaurant Blauw** in Oud Zuid (p. 83); other tasty alternatives include **Kantjil en de Tiger** on Spiustraat (www.kantjil.nl) and **Long Pura** on Rozengracht (www.restaurant-longpura.

horizons of the IJ waterway. The suntrap terrace of the bar-restaurant gets two stars for its location (take the free ferry from Buiksloterweg at Centraal Station; see p. 62), but one star for its gourmet offerings: insubstantial and predictably Dutch dishes are served during the day, offering aged Gouda cheeses, salads, soups, and sandwiches. The evening offerings are a little more imaginative, incorporating fish, steak, and vegetarian risottos, but flickering nighttime views across the harbor more than compensate.

IJpromenade 1. www.eyebarrestaurant.nl. (℗ **020/589-1402.** Main courses lunch 5.50€–14€, dinner 18€–22€. Tues–Thurs and Sun 10am–1am, Fri–Sat 10am–2am. Free ferry from Buiksloterweg at Centraal Station.

Pllek ★★ INTERNATIONAL   Pllek is one of the original of the many urban "beach bars" popping up all around the waterfronts of Amsterdam. It's set in the rapidly gentrifying former shipyard of NDSM wharf. A free 15-minute ferry ride from Centraal Station transports you to this trendy hangout constructed entirely from old shipping containers; the corrugated-metal exterior hides a surprisingly attractive restaurant, whose industrial vibe is warmed by bright artwork, cozy leather sofas, an indoor fireplace, and huge windows offering views of the IJ River. Its expansive man-made beach is the real draw, when warm weather draws crowds to the picnic tables and beanbag loungers. Though many come here just to drink, the food is quite good, with sandwiches, salads, and main dishes emphasizing fresh, organic produce—nearly 75 percent of the menu is vegetarian, and a quarter of it vegan.

T.T. Neveritaweg 59. www.pllek.nl. (℗ **020/290-0020.** Main courses lunch 8.50€–13€, 4.50€–8.50€, dinner 18€–22€25. Daily 9:30am–1am (Fri–Sat till 3am). Free ferry from Buiksloterweg at Centraal Station.

Oost

VERY EXPENSIVE

La Rive ★★★ FRENCH/MEDITERRANEAN Michelin-starred master chef Rogér Rassin has been at the very top of his game since 2008 and consistently puts out superlative cooking using the very finest of seasonal ingredients. Located in Amsterdam's elegant InterContinental Hotel, La Rive's dining rooms have the unruffled ambience of an English gentlemen's club but the service from the accomplished waiting staff is happily unstuffy; however, it is advisable to look smart when you visit. The food itself is a thing of unparalleled beauty, each plate a delicate masterpiece of peerless modern cooking. Every night two menus are presented with seven courses in each; dishes vary seasonally and may include Wagyu beef with asparagus and morels sea bass, or veal sweetbreads with risotto. Mains from the tasting menus are also available a la carte. Reservations required.

InterContinental Hotel Amstel, Professor Tulpplein 1. www.restaurantlarive.nl. ℂ **020/520-3264.** Mains 60€–85€, fixed-price menu 110€–130€. Daily 6:30–10pm. Metro to Weesperplein.

South of Amsterdam

EXPENSIVE

Restaurant de Kas ★★★ INTERNATIONAL Award-winning de Kas was one of the first organic restaurants in Amsterdam when it opened in 2001, and is run on totally green principles and supplied with fruit, vegetables, and herbs grown in the nursery next door. The spacious, light-filled dining rooms inhabit former greenhouses and in summer, the huge patio is filled with fragrances from the herbs. Three- to six-course prix-fixe menus are served each day, and are dependent on what's available in the market or garden; expect skillfully presented dishes such as locally raised beef with Hollandaise or roasted Jerusalem artichoke with dashi beurre blanc. Imaginative vegetarian alternatives are always available. Each course is carefully paired with quality wines. Reservations are required.

Kamerlingh Onneslaan 3, Park Frankendael. www.restaurantdekas.nl. ℂ **020/462-4562.** Fixed-price lunch 35€–45€, fixed-price dinner 57€–65€. Mon–Fri noon–2pm, Mon–Sat 6:30–10pm. Tram 9 to Hogeweg.

EXPLORING AMSTERDAM

Where to start in this city of 165 canals, 1,250 bridges, countless cobbled streets, the UNESCO World Heritage-listed Canal Ring (p. 60), and more than 70 museums? The answer to that question is easy. Your first adventure in Amsterdam should be a canal cruise (p. 110), both to get your bearings and appreciate the city's beauty from the perspective of the water. The magnificence of the elegant canal houses, and the mystique of the labyrinthine waterways will spark your curiosity to explore the myriad wonders on offer in this city. Whatever your interest or itinerary, culture vulture or low-brow, Amsterdam rarely disappoints.

The Dutch Sweet Tooth

The Dutch have a particularly sweet tooth and happily devour pannenkoek (pancakes) and thick, sweet poffertjes served with heart-busting butter and sprinkled with sugar at any given opportunity. Other calorie-laden treats include stroopwafels (wafers oozing with caramel) and deep-fried oliebollen (donuts) filled with raisins and dusted with sugar, which can be bought on street stalls all over the city center during the winter holidays. Amsterdammers also have a thing for chocolate sprinkles, which you'll find shaken over breakfast rolls as well as all sorts of broodjes (sandwiches), sweet and savory; a favorite combination is chocolate sprinkles with peanut butter. Or you could try adding a dollop of thick, syrupy appelstroop made from sugar and apple, to your lunchtime cheese broodje (sandwich).

And on a practical note, tramlines 2, 3, 5, and 12 are useful for visiting the sights south of the city around Museumplein, while 1, 2, 4, 7, 11, 12, 19, and 24 serve the city center sights.

Old Center

Amsterdam Museum ★★ MUSEUM   Telling the story of Amsterdam's progression from simple fishing village to world power in the 17th-century Golden Age, the city's superb historic museum kicks off with the interactive exhibition "Amsterdam DNA." It takes a whistle-stop tour through the main stages of the city's history, illustrated by Old Dutch Master paintings, maps, tools, armor, and religious sculpture. After that, however, things tail off as visitors are led through gallery after gallery of poorly organized artifacts. One highlight, however, is the 1677 scale model of the Koninklijk Paleis (p. 92). The city's historical museum is partly housed in a former convent and partly in a 17th-century orphanage. The Schuttersgalerij (Civic Guards Gallery; see p. 95) stands outside the museum entrance.

Kalverstraat 92. www.amsterdammuseum.nl. ✆ 020/523-1822. Admission 15€ adults, 12.50€ students, free ages 17 and under. Daily 10am–5pm. Closed Apr 27, Dec 25.

Begijnhof ★★ HISTORIC BUILDING   Entered through an ornate gate off Spui, this cluster of photogenic gabled houses around a leafy garden courtyard is the perfect place to feel the ambience of old Amsterdam. Built as a hofje (almshouse; see p. 97) intended to offer beguines (devout women) the option to live independently of husband and children, but without becoming a nun, the 47 houses of the Begijnhof today provide sheltered residence for elderly people. Amsterdam was a destination for religious pilgrims and an important Catholic center before the Calvinist rebellion and Alteration in 1578. It remained in operation for centuries after the changeover of the city from Catholicism to Protestantism and the last beguine died in 1971 at the age of 84. In the southwest corner of the cloister, at no. 34, stands Het Houten Huys, one of Amsterdam's pair of surviving timber houses, built around 1425. The Engelse Kerk (English Church) dates to 1607 and is used today by British

Amsterdam Attractions

4

AMSTERDAM | Exploring Amsterdam

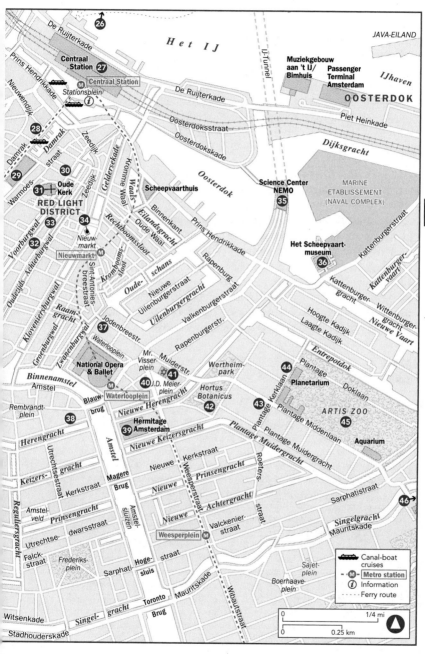

De Ruijterkade

Het IJ

JAVA-EILAND

26

Centraal
Station 27

Prins Hendrikkade

Nieuwendijk

Centraal Station

Stationsplein

De Ruijterkade

U-Tunnel

Muziekgebouw
aan 't IJ/
Bimhuis

Passenger
Terminal
Amsterdam

IJhaven

OOSTERDOK

Piet Heinkade

Oosterdoksstraat

Oosterdokskade

28

Damrak

straat

Damrak

Zeedijk

Kromme Waal

Waals

Geldersekade

Oosterdok

Dijksgracht

MARINE
ETABLISSEMENT
(NAVAL COMPLEX)

4

AMSTERDAM | Exploring Amsterdam

29

Warmoes-

30

31

Oude
Kerk

RED LIGHT
DISTRICT

33

34

32

Voorburgwal

Nieuw-
markt

Nieuwmarkt

Oudezijds Achterburgwal

Scheepvaarthuis

Binnenkant

Eilandsgracht

Oude Waal

Prins Hendrikkade

Science Center
NEMO

35

Het Scheepvaart-
museum

36

Kattenburgerstraat

Kattenburger-
vaart

Sint-Antonies-
breestraat

Rechtboomssloot

Kromboomssloot

Oude-

schans

Nieuwe

Uilenburgerstraat

Uilenburgergracht

Rapenburg

Valkenburgerstraat

Kattenburger-
gracht

Hoogte Kadijk

Laagte Kadijk

Wittenburger-
gracht

Nieuwe Vaart

Kloveniersburgwal

Raam-
gracht

Groenburgwal

37

Jodenbreestr.

Waterlooplein

Zwanenburgwal

Rapenburgerstr.

Entrepotdok

National Opera
& Ballet

Binnenamstel

Amstel

Mr.
Visser-
plein

41

40 J.D. Meier-
plein

Blauw-
brug

Waterlooplein

Muiderstr.

Wertheim-
park

Hortus
Botanicus

42

43

44

Plantage

Plantage Kerklaan

Planetarium

Doklaan

ARTIS ZOO

45

Plantage Middenlaan

Nieuwe Herengracht

Plantage Muidergracht

Plantage Muidergracht

Aquarium

Rembrandt-
plein

38

Herengracht

Hermitage
Amsterdam

39

Nieuwe Keizersgracht

Nieuwe Kerkstraat

Keizers-
gracht

Utrechtsestraat

Kerkstraat

Magere
Brug

Nieuwe

Prinsengracht

Roeters-

straat

Sarphatistraat

Amstel

Amstel-
sluizen

Nieuwe

Achtergracht

Weesperstraat

Singelgracht

Mauritskade

46

Amstel-
veld

Prinsengracht

dwarsstraat

Utrechtse-

Valckenier-
straat

Weesperplein

Reguliersgracht

Falck-
straat

Frederiks-
plein

Sarphati-

Hoge-

sluis

straat

Sajet-
plein

Boerhaave-
plein

Witsenkade

Stadhouderskade

Singel-

gracht

Toronto

Brug

Mauritskade

Wibautstraat

Canal-boat
cruises

M Metro station

i Information

Ferry route

0 ——— 1/4 mi

0 ——— 0.25 km

89

ex-pats. Opposite the church, at no. 30, is the Begijnhofkapel, a secret Catholic chapel dating from 1671 that's also still in use today.

Spui and Gedempte Begijnensloot. Free admission. Daily 9am–5pm.

Beurspassage ★★★ PUBLIC ART   Tucked between the busy shopping corridors of Damrak and Nieuwendijk, this eye-popping, 165-foot-long passageway is an Instagrammer's dream: a wonder of colored mosaic tiles, gilded chandeliers, stained glass, and patterned mirrors. A trio of Dutch artists reimagined the bland 19th-century arcade in 2016, turning the massive, barrel-vaulted ceiling into a underwater world inspired by the city's canals, complete with fish, anchors, and of course, a bicycle. Other amusing details include clog-shaped wall sconces and a fountain inside in the mouth of a large fish.

Beurspassage, between Damrak and Nieuwendijk. Free admission. Open 24/7.

Beurs van Berlage ★★ HISTORIC BUILDING   Amsterdam's redbrick former stock exchange was built in 1903 by Hendrik Berlage and is now an occasional concert venue and temporary exhibition space. This monumental building was one of the precursors of the Amsterdam School and is exceptional for its use of patterned brickwork and clean lines, which broke away from the fancy Dutch Revivalist styles of the time (as seen at the Stedelijk Museum and Centraal Station). A frieze decorates the facade showing man's (questionable) evolution from Adam to 20th-century stockbroker. It's rarely open, so you'll have to content yourself with looking from the outside.

Beursplein 1. www.beursvanberlage.nl. ℂ **020/530-4141.**

I amsterdam City Card: Buy or Not?

Will the **I amsterdam** sightseeing pass save you money in the end? That depends. Yes, it does provides entry into most of Amsterdam's museums and free travel on public transport. It also entitles cardholders to a canal cruise (p. 110), discounts in certain stores and restaurants, a free city map, and admission to attractions outside Amsterdam including Zaanse Schans (p. 134) and the museums in Haarlem (p. 130).

But the card isn't cheap. To have it pay off would require visits to at least two major museums per day (about 20€ each), multiple tram rides (3.20€ per ride), and a canal cruise (around 14€). Note that one of the museums *won't* be the Anne Frank House, as it's not covered by the card. We should note that beyond the cost, the card is a time-saver as bearers don't need to wait in ticket lines (especially advantageous at the busy Rijksmuseum) or rummage around for separate public transport tickets. But if money is your main concern, you'll have to keep VERY busy each day to actually save any money. Which might be counterproductive: you are supposed to be on vacation, right?

Prices in 2019: I amsterdam City Card for 24 hours 60€, 48 hours 80€, 72 hours 93€, 96 hours 105€, 120 hours 115€. You can buy the passes at I amsterdam at Stationsplein 10, right outside Centraal Station (www.iamsterdam.com; ℂ **020/702-6000**), open daily 9am to 6pm, or at the branch in Schiphol Plaza at the airport (same phone number), open daily 7am to 10pm.

Bloemenmarkt (Flower Market) ★ HISTORIC MARKET Amsterdam's last remaining floating market is a permanent fixture housed on a row of moored barges along the Singel canal. Once famous for its many flower shops, the market has since ceded to tourism, with the last florist closing up shop in 2019. You can still purchase seeds, bulbs, gardening tools, and the odd houseplant, but its stalls now mainly trade in cheesy souvenirs: clog-shaped keychains, wooden tulips, magnets, and the like.

Singel between Koningsplein and Muntplein. Free admission. Mon–Sat 9am–5:30pm, Sun 11am–5:30pm.

Centraal Station ★★ HISTORIC BUILDING Amsterdam's humongous main railway station is an architectural masterpiece. Designed by Dutch architect P.J.H. Cuypers, who also built the Rijksmuseum, it was built between 1884 and 1889 on three artificial islands in the IJ waterway. Amsterdammers thoroughly disliked the building when it debuted, but it's now beloved for its extravagantly ornate, two-tone Dutch Revivalist facade covered in allegorical tributes to Amsterdam's maritime past. The left-hand tower is adorned with a gilded weathervane; the right one with a clock. Apart from being the jumping-off point for thousands of adventures in Amsterdam, the terminus also acts as a transport hub, with trams and taxis leaving from Stationsplein in front and buses from outside the new retail-packed IJ-hall on the back side; ferries also depart from the piers behind the building. The main I amsterdam Visitor Center is in Stationsplein, and it is the starting point for canal cruises. It's worth catching your breath here and taking time to absorb the buzz that swirls around the station in a blur of people, backpacks, bikes, trams, buses, vendors, pickpockets, and junkies. The air of crazy chaos is augmented by the station being in a fairly constant state of renovation.

Stationsplein, off Prins Hendrikkade. Free admission. Open 24/7.

De Waag ★★ HISTORIC BUILDING You'll find Amsterdam's only surviving medieval fortified gate on the fringe of Chinatown. The many-towered, squat Waag was constructed in 1498 of red-and-white brick and is now the oldest secular building still standing in Amsterdam. The building had many functions over the centuries; it was the site of public executions before morphing into a public weigh house for merchandise brought into the city and later becoming a guild house. One of the wealthy, powerful guilds that lodged here was the Surgeon's Guild; a fact that is immortalized in Rembrandt's graphic painting "The Anatomy Lesson" (1632), which depicts a dissection being conducted in the upper-floor Theatrum Anatomicum. Today the Waag is purely dedicated to pleasure; it's the perfect spot for people watching from the buzzy outdoor bar of the historic **Restaurant-Café In de Waag** (p. 78).

Nieuwmarkt 4. Free admission. Mon–Wed 11am–10:30pm; Thurs–Sun 9am–10:30pm (when restaurant is open).

Erotic Museum ★ MUSEUM Even less erotic than the (unsexy) Sex Museum (p. 95), this ludicrous homage to erotica is spread over five dusty floors, with one entirely dedicated to some rather alarming aspects of S&M.

Otherwise there are tons of lewd antique figurines on display, some sketches by John Lennon, and a flea-bitten re-creation of a red-light window.

Oudezijds Achterburgwal 54. www.erotisch-museum.nl. © **020/627-8954.** Admission 7€. Sun–Thurs 11am–1am, Fri–Sat 11am–2am.

Hash Marihuana & Hemp Museum ★★ MUSEUM   Along one of the Red Light District's main drags, this museum will entertain anyone curious about the history of soft drugs and modern-day medicinal applications of hemps. There's the predictable display of pipes—some beautifully carved—and bongs, some lovely old paintings depicting 16th-century farmers smoking dope, and lots of items made out of hemp, including a surfboard. If you're after a smoke, however, drugs are not sold here nor is their use promoted.

Oudezijds Achterburgwal 148. www.hashmuseum.com. © **020/624-8926.** Admission 9€ adults (8.50€ online), free for children 12 and under (must be accompanied by adult). Daily 10am–11pm. Closed Apr 27.

> ## A Party Fit for a King
>
> Put simply, Amsterdam loves a party, and the celebration that brings Amsterdammers out on to the streets like no other is **Koningsdag (King's Day)** celebrated on April 27 in honor of their monarch, King Willem-Alexander. The whole city grinds to a halt for the day, parties spring up on every corner, and the canals are chock full of barges blaring music. The crowds wear orange and float orange balloons, the bars overflow, everybody gets happily drunk, and dances and sings their hearts out. A jolly good time late, late into the night.

Koninklijk Paleis ★★ HISTORIC BUILDING   The behemoth building plonked in the middle of Amsterdam's focal Dam Square is the official residence of the reigning Dutch House of Orange (p. 21), although these days the Royal Family prefers to reside in The Hague. This palace was originally designed by Jacob van Campen in 1655 as the City Hall and has a solid, neoclassical facade. It was repurposed into a royal palace by Louis Bonaparte, brother of the better-known Napoleon, when he was crowned king of Holland in 1806, and its public rooms are now open to view. The interior is crammed with early-19th-century furniture, chandeliers, sculptures, and vast oil paintings reflecting Amsterdam's wealth during the Golden Age in the 17th century. Highlights include the highly ornate Council Chamber, and the high-ceilinged Burgerzaal (Council Chamber), where maps inlaid on the marble floors place Amsterdam at the center of the world. The palace is closed to visitors during periods of royal residence and state receptions.

Dam, off Damrak. www.paleisamsterdam.nl. © **020/522-6161.** Admission 10€ adults, 9€ seniors and students, free children 17 and under. Daily 10am–5pm (check website before visiting, as there are frequent changes and closures).

Museum Het Rembrandthuis ★★★ MUSEUM   Just east of the city center on the edge of the former Jewish quarter sits the former home of Rembrandt van Rijn, Dutch Old Master artist extraordinaire. He bought this elegant townhouse in 1639 when his career as Amsterdam's premier portrait painter at its peak. Alas, he overstretched himself with a massive mortgage that plagued his life for years. The house brought him little personal happiness as his adored first wife Saskia died here in 1642; he was declared bankrupt in 1656. Rembrandt's belongings were all sold off and he moved to a smaller house on Rozengracht, where he died in 1669. This house was re-opened as a museum in 1911, and, thanks to a notary's inventory of his possessions, has the same type of period furnishings the master would have had. The layout of the house is typical of the 17th century, with servants' quarters in the basement, and three floors atop that. Rembrandt's hallway served as his gallery, with his dealing room off this, and the family's living quarters are hung with his masterful oil paintings. Upstairs you'll find his cabinet of curiosities and the airy studio where he painted "The Night Watch." Bequests of his prints and paintings continue to grow and are displayed in a contemporary wing adjacent to the historical house.

Jodenbreestraat 4. www.rembrandthuis.nl. ✆ **020/520-0400.** Admission 14€ adults, 10€ students, 5€ children 6–17. Daily 10am–6pm. Closed Apr 27, Dec 25.

Museum Ons' Lieve Heer op Solder (Our Lord in the Attic) ★★

MUSEUM   One of Amsterdam's best-kept historical secrets is tucked away on Oudezijds Voorburgwal. Following the Alteration (p. 141) and the sacking of all Catholic churches in 1578, practicing Roman Catholicism was banned, so the Catholics had to find ways to worship in secret. Between 1661 and 1663, the wealthy Catholic merchant Jan Hartman bought this stately town house and two others behind it, converting all three attics into a clandestine but lushly decorated Catholic chapel. Worshipers entered from a side street and climbed the narrow stairs to the hidden third-floor chapel, which could accommodate a congregation of 150. The secret chapel is beautifully preserved with Baroque flourishes, an organ, marble columns, and oil paintings behind the altar. It's the highlight of the visit, but there are other curious spaces worth a peek, such as the miniscule bedchamber carved out in a mezzanine alongside the staircase. A modern visitor's center in the adjoining house features an unremarkable collection of religious artifacts that you can quickly breeze through on your way to the main attraction.

> ### The Narrow View
>
> The **narrowest house** in Amsterdam is at **Singel 7.** It's just 1m (3.3 ft.) wide—barely wider than the front door. However, it's a cheat. Only the front facade is really so narrow; behind this it broadens out to more usual proportions. The genuine narrowest house is **Oude Hoogstraat 22,** near Nieuwmarkt. With a typical Amsterdam bell gable, it's 2m (6½ ft.) wide and 6m (20 ft.) deep. A close rival is nearby at **Kloveniersburgwal 26,** the cornice-gabled **Kleine Trippenhuis,** 2.4m (8 ft.) wide.

Oudezijds Voorburgwal 38. www.opsolder.nl. ✆ **020/624-6604.** Admission 12.50€ adults, 6€ students and children 5–17. Mon–Sat 10am–6pm, Sun and holidays 1–5pm. Closed Apr 27.

Nieuwe Kerk (New Church) ★★ CHURCH   This beautiful church is

the most important in the Netherlands. It was built in the last years of the 14th century, and in 1814, King William I first took the oath of office and was inaugurated here (Dutch royalty are not crowned). It still retains its relevance into the modern era, with His Majesty King of the Netherlands Willem-Alexander marrying Argentinian Princess Máxima here in 2002. Although many of its original priceless treasures were removed or painted over in 1578 when it passed into Protestant hands, much of its original grandeur has since been recaptured. The church has a stately arched nave, an elaborately carved altar, a great pipe organ that dates from 1645, several noteworthy stained-glass windows, and sepulchral monuments for many of Holland's most revered poets and naval heroes. It's also the venue for a lively program of events and exhibitions; see the website for more information.

Dam, off Damrak. www.nieuwekerk.nl. © **020/626-8168.** Admission varies by event; free when there's no exhibit. Daily 10am–5pm. Closed Apr 19 and 27, May 4, Dec 25, Jan 1.

Oude Kerk (Old Church) ★★ CHURCH/MUSEUM   This late-Gothic, triple-nave church has its origins in 1250 but was only completed with the extension of the bell tower in 1566. Behind its grand brick facade, the barnlike interior was stripped of all its adornment in the Alteration of 1578. Rembrandt's beloved first wife lies in vault 28K, which bears the simple inscription "Saskia Juni 1642." The magnificent 1728 organ is regularly used for recitals. The church, which officially was designated as a museum in 2016, hosts two annual site-specific contemporary art installations, in summer and winter. The tower, which once was open to guided tours, is currently undergoing restoration with no reopening date set.

Oudekerksplein 23. www.oudekerk.nl. © **020/625-8284.** Admission 12€ adults, 7€ students, free ages 12 and under. Mon–Sat 10am–6pm, Sun 1–5:30pm. Closed Apr 27, Dec 25.

Rosse Buurt (Red Light District) ★★ HISTORIC AREA   A few steps away from the Oude Kerk and De Waag and you're immersed in the sleazy underbelly of Amsterdam's infamous Red Light District. Here barely clad prostitutes advertise themselves behind illuminated glass windows along the medieval canals and alleyways; if the curtains are closed, then you know that a deal has been struck, but if they are open, sometimes you can even glimpse the stark beds upon which the deal is done. Currently most of the women seem to be from Eastern Europe and some (although by no means all) are exceptionally beautiful. Needless to say, throngs of testosterone-driven men circle these tiny alleyways egging each other on either to visit a prostitute or one of the live, hardcore sex shows that leave nothing to the imagination.

Despite all this, the Red Light District is seedy rather than dangerous; although you should keep an eye out for pickpockets, the area is generally safe. However, a word of warning: Don't photograph the sex workers; it might be tempting to take pictures of half-naked women posing in windows but it will not be appreciated by the thuggish bouncers who parade the area, and you may well find your camera in the canal. Dusk is the best time to visit, before the drunken/stoned hordes of Euro-trash youth arrive to ogle the girls.

Along Oudezijds Achterburgwal and surrounding alleyways. Free admission. Daily 24/7.

Schuttersgalerij (Civic Guards Gallery) ★ MUSEUM   Outside the entrance to the Amsterdam Museum, this narrow, glass-roofed walkway links Kalverstraat to the Begijnhof and has been transformed into a public art gallery currently displaying 15 bigger-is-better, 17th-century portraits of the city's heroic musketeers, the Civic Guards. Elegantly uniformed and coiffed, these militia companies once played an important role in the city's defense but degenerated into little more than decadent banqueting societies. Their portraits are accompanied by a vast wooden sculpture of Goliath and a miniscule David, plus photos of Amsterdam's contemporary elite; running the length of the walkway is a fab Barbara Broekman carpet representing the 179 nationalities of Amsterdam.

Kalverstraat 92. www.amsterdammuseum.nl. ✆ **020/523-1822.** Free admission. Daily 10am–5pm. Closed Apr 27, Dec 25.

Sexmuseum Amsterdam ★ MUSEUM   Located on scruffy Damstraat, Amsterdam's so-called "Venustempel" opened in 1985 and is the oldest sex museum in the world. Thanks to its position on the edge of the Red Light District, it attracts more than half a million giggling visitors per year. There's not much about the history of sex here, just lots of erotic ephemera such as a Delft blue tile showing a man playing cards with an erection, Chinese and Japanese figurines in compromising positions, and wax work figures in various states of undress and decay.

Damrak 18. www.sexmuseumamsterdam.com. ✆ **020/622-8376.** Admission 5€ ages 16 and over (15 and under not admitted). Daily 9:30am–11:30pm. Closed Dec 25.

Canal Ring

Amsterdam Pipe Museum ★★ MUSEUM   For what sounds like a museum of niche appeal, the pipe museum turns out to be actually quite good fun. The eccentric curator-owner is an entrancing character and also runs the old-fashioned Smokiana shop in the basement, which sells pipes and books about pipes. Upstairs is the world's largest collection of Dutch clay pipes, intricately carved and bejeweled Meerschaum pipes, and bronze cast pipes

---

Cleaning Up the Red Light District

Amsterdam's Red Light District is notorious the world over for its anything-goes vibe, but recently the warren of streets, also known as *Rosse Buurt, De Wallen,* or *De Walletjes,* has been undergoing a gentrification. Several of the city's infamous coffee shops and around half the brothel windows have been closed; at press time, the city fathers were halfway through a decade-long plan to sanitize the area and more closures will follow.

Although the most famous Red Light District is around the Oude Kerk, there are two others. **Singelgebied** is bounded by the Singel canal and Nieuwezijds Voorburgwal; a few of the prostitutes here are transsexuals and there are gay sex shops and movie theaters. The city's smallest, least-known Red Light district is south of the city center in De Pijp, on **Ruysdaelkade** along the east side of Boerenwetering canal.

from Cameroon in Africa. You'll also get to drink in the rarified atmosphere of the traditional 17th-century house renovated in 19th-century fashion.

Prinsengracht 488. http://pipemuseum.nl. ☏ **020/421-1779.** Admission 10€ adults, 5€ ages 6–18, free children under 5. Mon–Sat noon–6pm. Closed Jan 1, Apr 27, Dec 25.

Anne Frank Huis ★★★ MUSEUM You shouldn't miss experiencing this typical Amsterdam canal house, where eight people from three separate Jewish families lived together in near silence for more than 2 years during World War II. The hiding place in Het Achterhuis—literally "the back house," but more commonly translated as "The Annex"—that Otto Frank found for his family, the van Pels family, and Fritz Pfeffer, kept them safe until tragically close to the end of the war, when it was raided by Nazi forces and its occupants deported to concentration camps. It was in this house that Anne, whose ambition was to be a writer, kept her famous diary as a way to deal with both the boredom and her youthful array of thoughts, which had as much to do with personal relationships as with the war and the Nazi terror raging outside.

During the war, the building was an office and warehouse, and its rooms are still as bare as they were when Anne's father returned, the only survivor of the eight onderduikers (divers, or hiders). Nothing has been changed, except that Plexiglas panels now protect the wall on which Anne pinned up photos of her favorite actress, Deanna Durbin, and of the little English princesses Elizabeth and Margaret. As you tour the building, it's possible to imagine Anne's experience growing up in this place, awakening as a young woman, and writing down her secret thoughts. Sound bites from her diary and a heartrending final word from her father augment the somber atmosphere. Despite the crowds filling the rooms, this haunting museum has the power to silence everyone.

Important: Due to the museum's popularity, tickets are only available online and for a specific time slot. To be sure you get one (only about 20 percent are given out on the day of the visit, and they go fast), be sure to go to the site exactly 2 months before you plan to visit, as that's when the tickets for your date will be released, and when they're gone, they're gone. *Also important:* The interior stairs are quite steep, which means that those in wheelchairs, and those with mobility impairments, may only be able to see the modern section of the museum.

Prinsengracht 263–267. www.annefrank.org. ☏ **020/556-7105.** Admission 10.50€ adults, 5.50€ children 10–17, free children 9 and under. Nov–Mar Sun–Fri 9am–7pm, Sat 9am–10pm; Apr–May 29 and Sept–Oct daily 9am–10pm; May 30–Aug daily 8:30am–10pm. Closed Yom Kippur.

Bijbels Museum (Biblical Museum) and Cromhouthuis ★ MUSEUM Two of a group of four majestic 1660s houses (nos. 364–370 Herengracht) form Cromhouthuis, and on the upper two floors, house the Biblical Museum. The houses, featuring delicate neck gables, were designed for wealthy timber merchant Jacob Cromhout. The Biblical Museum is nothing to write home about, with a ramshackle layout and an odd assortment of exhibitions—a model of the temple in Jerusalem, some religious tapestries,

Amsterdam's Hofjes

Amsterdam has many secret courtyards surrounded by almshouses—they could be considered an early form of care in the community where the poor or disadvantaged of the parish could be housed and supported. The best known is the **Begijnhof** (p. 87), where a community of pious women lived for several centuries. The **Hermitage Amsterdam** (p. 105) is also housed in a former *hofje*, where homes were provided for elderly women of slender means. **Zon's Hofje** at Prin-sengracht 159–171 is an example of a tranquil *hofje* with courtyard garden; the outer door is open Monday through Friday between 10am and 5pm, and you can walk quietly through the passageway to the serene courtyard. A walk around the pretty streets of the Jordaan will reveal several *hofjes*, including the **Raepenhofje** at Palmgracht 28-38, and the **Suykerhofje** at Lindengracht 149-163.

Egyptian mummies. Focus your energy on the house itself, which showcases marvelous ceiling frescoes by Jacob de Wit and an ever-changing, eclectic assortment of artifacts in the Cabinet of Curiosities room. On sunny days, enjoy coffee and cake from the museum cafe out in the lovely landscaped garden.

Herengracht 366–368. www.bijbelsmuseum.nl and www.cromhouthuis.nl. ℰ **020/624-2436.** Admission to both 12.50€ adults, 10€ students, free ages 17 and under. Daily 10am–5pm. Closed Jan 1, Apr 27.

FOAM ★ MUSEUM Dedicated to contemporary photography, this cool gallery is tucked behind a traditional canal-house facade. Its displays the work of established photographers like Erwin Blumenfeld, multi-media exhibits from the likes of controversial Chinese artist Ai Weiwei, plus newly discovered Dutch talent. There's a smart bookshop and a little cafe here, too.

Keizersgracht 609. www.foam.org. ℰ **020/551-6500.** Admission 12.50€ adults, 9.50€ students, free children 12 and under. Sat–Wed 10am–6pm, Thurs–Fri 10am–9pm. Closed Apr 27.

Het Grachtenhuis (Canal Museum) ★★★ MUSEUM This brilliant museum shares the secrets of Amsterdam's expansion through a cleverly curated series of interactive displays. First off, a sound-and-light show centers on a model of the city in medieval times; it was grim, overcrowded, and unhygienic. By the 17th century, expansion became imperative. The planning and construction of the ring of three canals around the medieval city is dealt with in a lively series of interactive displays, films, models, and holograms. The final exhibit romps home with an all-singing, all-dancing celebration of multicultural Amsterdam today. You couldn't wish for a more instructive or entertaining introduction to Amsterdam and its social and cultural development. To get here, take the tram to Herengracht on the Grachtengordel (Canal Ring).

Herengracht 386. www.hetgrachtenhuis.nl. ℰ **020/421-1656.** Admission 15€ adults, 7.50€ ages 4–12. Tues–Sun 10am–5pm. Closed Apr 27 and Dec 25.

Amsterdam's Historic Buildings

The **Munttoren** on Muntplein sits at a busy traffic intersection on the Rokin and Singel canals. In 1487, the Mint Tower's base was part of the Reguliers Gate in the city wall. In 1620, Hendrick de Keyser (p. 99) topped it with an ornate, lead-covered tower, from which a carillon of Hemony brothers bells sings out gaily every 15 minutes and plays a 1-hour concert on Saturdays at 2pm. The tower got its present name in 1672, when it housed the city mint. It's near the following tram stops: 4, 9, 14, 16, 24, or 25.

The tilting **Montelbaanstoren** is known as the "Leaning Tower of Amsterdam," a fortification at the juncture of the Oudeschans and Waalseilandsgracht canals that dates from 1512. It's one of only a few surviving elements of the city's once-powerful defensive works. In 1606, Hendrick de Keyser added an octagonal tower and spire. The building now houses local Water Authority offices. Near Metro: Nieuwmarkt.

Huis Marseille Museum voor Fotografie ★★ MUSEUM   One of two Amsterdam photography museums (see also FOAM, above), the Marseille is privately owned and housed in two spectacularly neck-gabled aristocratic town houses along Keizersgracht (the Emperor's Canal). Fourteen exhibition rooms alternate photos from the museum's permanent collection with worthy exhibitions of contemporary images that change every 3 months. As with so many Amsterdam galleries and museums in the Canal Ring, the building is part of the attraction; the house at Keizersgracht 401(the museum merged with neighboring Keizersgracht 399 in 2013) dates from the 17th century and takes its name from the plaque on the front of the house that depicts a map of Marseille harbor in France. The interior maintains many original features, including fireplaces, wooden floors, and plaster moldings as well as a ceiling fresco by Jacob de Wit. Out the back there's a summer cafe in the delightful leafy courtyard garden.

Keizersgracht 401. www.huismarseille.nl. ℂ **020/531-8989.** Admission 9€ adults, 4.50€ seniors and students, free children 17 and under. Tues–Sun 11am–6pm. Closed Jan 1, Apr 27, Dec 25.

Museum Van Loon ★★ MUSEUM   The Museum Van Loon is housed in an elegant mansion first owned by Ferdinand Bol, who was a student of Rembrandt. Between 1884 and 1945 it was the property of the Van Loons, who were founders of the Dutch East India Company and one of the richest families in Amsterdam. This beautiful house with a double frontage and vast dimensions befits the family's social standing, with rooms that showcase how the Dutch aristocracy lived among scores of family portraits, Louis XV furniture, and fine porcelain. The marble staircase with its ornate brass balustrade is a highlight of the interior, while out back in the restored coach house, which is modeled on a Greek temple, a splendid horse-drawn carriage takes center stage. There are occasional music recitals in the beautifully landscaped garden.

Keizersgracht 672. www.museumvanloon.nl. ℂ **020/624-5255.** Admission 10€ adults, 8€ students, 5.50€ children 6–18. Daily 10am–5pm. Closed Jan 1, Apr 27, Dec 25.

Westerkerk ★★ CHURCH   Just around the corner from the Anne Frank Huis, the Protestant Westerkerk is yet another ecclesiastical masterpiece by the Dutch celebrity architect of the 17th century, Hendrick de Keyser (who also designed the Noorderkerk and the Zuiderkerk), as part of the new development of the Grachtengordel (Canal Ring). The foundation stone was laid in 1620 (de Keyser died a year later), and the tower was finally completed in 1638; it is more than 85m tall (270 ft.) and is topped with the gilded Crown of Maximilian. Every 15 minutes the carillon bells ring out across the city but the church itself is austere inside; in keeping with the Calvinist beliefs of the time there is no altar, but the gold and silver pipes and Baroque sculpture adorning the organ make up for the lack of ornamentation. It is the burial place of Rembrandt—although no one knows where his grave is on the unmarked stone floor—as well as his wife Saskia and son Titus. At press time the church's interior was being restored and closed to visitors; check the website to make sure it's open before heading over.

Prinsengracht 281. www.westerkerk.nl. ℂ **020/624-7766.**

Willet-Holthuysen Museum ★★★ MUSEUM   This is a wonderful museum with a pristine interior dating from the 19th century in a perfectly restored canal house that shouts money. It's redolent of the sybaritic lifestyle of Amsterdam's prosperous merchant classes and every curtain, every piece of furniture displayed, and every scrap of wallpaper, down to the deep-blue fabric in the gentleman's parlor, is in keeping with the period. Displays include an introduction to the aristocratic family who lived here, and a collection of painstakingly detailed silver figurines. There's an exquisite formal knot garden at the rear of the house.

Herengracht 605. www.willetholthuysen.nl. ℂ **020/523-1822.** Admission 12.50€ adults, 10€ students, free ages 17 and under. Daily 10am–5pm. Closed Apr 27, Dec 25.

Jordaan

Tulip Museum ★ MUSEUM   The Tulip Museum is just across Prinsengracht from the Anne Frank Huis, and is the perfect antidote if you need cheering up after a visit. It offers an upbeat, contemporary, and informative slant on the story of Amsterdam's obsession with tulips, which were imported from the Himalayas and nearly brought the country down when trade in the bulbs collapsed in 1637. It's all showcased in a short, well-designed basement exhibition with superb poster-sized photos of swathes of tulips and cleverly designed woodcuts showing the journey of tulips from the Far East into the Netherlands. On ground level is a top-quality souvenir store selling bulbs, pretty plant holders, and other classy tulip-related ephemera.

Prinsengracht 116. www.amsterdamtulipmuseum.com. ℂ **020/421-0095.** Admission 5€ adults, 3€ students. Daily 10am–6pm. Closed Apr 27, Dec 25.

Woonbootmuseum (Houseboat Museum) ★ MUSEUM   The Houseboat Museum is found on board the *Hendrika Maria*, a freighter that was built in 1914, and was busily transporting sand up until the 1960s. A self-guided tour won't take more than 15 minutes, as there's not that much to see, but it offers the opportunity to glimpse life aboard one of Amsterdam's 2,500 houseboats. Moored on the Prinsengracht near Elandsgracht.

Prinsengracht 296K. www.houseboatmuseum.nl. ℂ **020/427-0750.** Admission 4.50€ adults, 3.50€ children 5–15. Jan–June and Sept–Dec Tues–Sun 10am–5pm, July–Aug daily 10am–5pm. Closed Jan 1 and 2 weeks in Jan, Apr 27, 1st Sat in Aug (Canal Parade), Dec 25.

De Pijp

Heineken Experience ★★ BREWERY One of Amsterdam's most popular attractions, the Heineken Experience is always crowded with fans of the famous beer brand. It's housed inside the redbrick former brewery, which functioned from 1867 until 1988 before production was moved to modern facilities in The Hague and Den Bosch. The intro to Heineken the company, delivered by human hologram from behind a well-stocked bar, sets the pace for a rollicking journey through the growth of the brand from microbrewery to multi-million-euro, international company with liberal use of interactive exhibits and funny simulated rides. The tour also incorporates the original copper brewing vats, malt silos, and vintage brewing equipment, plus a stable full of Shire horses used to pull the promotional drays. The ultimate goal for most is to glug back Heineken (two beers are included with admission) so expect a bit of a scuffle when trying to get served at the bar.

Stadhouderskade 78. www.heinekenexperience.com. ℂ **020/721-5300.** Admission 21€ adults (18€ if booked online), 14.50€ children 12–17, free children 11 and under. Mon–Thurs 10am–7:30pm, Fri–Sun 10:30am–9pm, July–Aug daily 10:30am–9pm.

Museum Quarter

Modern Contemporary Museum (Moco) ★★ MUSEUM Joining the trio of Amsterdam's notable art institutions on Museumplein is this small museum devoted mainly to street art. Inside a lovely turn-of-the-century mansion in the shadow of the Rijksmuseum, local gallerists Lionel and Kim Logchies have assembled an impressive number of works by rock-star graffiti artist Banksy, including one of his most iconic stencils, "Girl with Balloon." The permanent collection also includes pieces by pioneering street artist Keith Haring, as well as works by Pop Art masters Andy Warhol and Roy Lichtenstein.

Art Galleries in the Jordaan

Bohemian Jordaan is an area of narrow cobbled streets–and even narrower canals–crammed with around 40 specialist art galleries. Check out Diana Stigter's gallery **Stigter van Doesburg** (Elandsstraat 90; www.stigtervan doesburg.com; ℂ **020/624-2361**); she has her finger on the pulse of what's hot and what's not. For more than 2 decades,

Galerie Ron Mandos (Prinsengracht 282; www.ronmandos.nl; ℂ **020/320-7036**) has presented internationally renowned contemporary artists alongside emerging Dutch talent. And the Edouard Planting Gallery (Eerste Bloemdwarsstraat 2 L; www.eduardplanting. com; ℂ 020/320-6705) exhibits the best of contemporary photography.

Temporary exhibitions have featured contemporary virtuosos such as Yayoi Kusama and Iranian street art duo Icy and Sot.

Honthorststraat 20. www.mocomuseum.com. © **020/370-1997.** Sun–Thurs 9am–7pm (July–Aug till 8pm), Fri–Sat 9am–8pm (July–Aug till 9pm). Admission 15€ adults, 12.50€ students, 9.50€ ages 10–15, free children 9 and under.

Museumplein ★★★ PARK   After the crush of the Rijksmuseum, take a breather in the vast green space that is Museumplein, home to all three of Amsterdam's great art museums—Rijksmuseum, the Van Gogh, and the Stedelijk—as well as edgy newcomer Moco. The elaborate facade of **Het Concertgebouw** (p. 122) faces the Rijksmuseum across the piazza, which has become a buzzing public space with lawns, buskers playing South American pan pipes, the brilliant open-air terrace of **Café Cobra** (p. 82), museum stores, and a kids' playground. In winter the area in front of the Rijksmuseum is transformed into an ice rink.

Museumplein. Free admission. Daily 24/7.

Rijksmuseum ★★★ MUSEUM   The Rijksmuseum is the world's biggest repository of Dutch Golden Age treasures, stacked over four sprawling floors in the redbrick P.J.H. Cuypers monolith opened in 1855. A decade-long refurbishment completed in 2013 did a spectacular job in sprucing up the elegant Cuypers decorations in the central Voorhal (Great Hall) but the layout of the museum remains confusing. It's almost sacrilegious to criticize this venerable institution, but the biggest mistake made in laying out the displays is crowding all the famous **Dutch Old Masters** ★★★ together in the Gallery of Honour on the second floor. Over 2 million people visit this museum annually and they all want to see Rembrandt's "The Night Watch" from 1642 (or, to give it its official title, "The Militia Company of Captain Frans Banning Cocq and Lieutenant Willem van Ruytenburch"; see box p. 102) and the wonderful works by Jan Steen, Jan Vermeer, and Frans Hals, so be prepared for impenetrable throngs. "The Milkmaid" and "The Merry Drinker" are truly mesmerizing close up, so you'll have to bear with the crowds.

Elsewhere in the museum are glorious collections of tulip vases, fine silver, glassware, and Delftware, forming the greatest collection of Dutch Golden Age treasures in the world. There are endless galleries stuffed with Asian and Indonesian artifacts brought back by marauding Dutch trading vessels. In a nod to more modern times, there are works by CoBrA artist Karel Appel and De Stijl designer Gerrit Rietveld. Don't forget the sculpture exhibitions in the gardens.

A note for families: Two rare furnished 17th-century dollhouses should be a highlight for children, by bringing the Dutch Golden Age to life for them in a way no amount of "real" stuff could. The dollhouses' owners commissioned craftsmen to copy objects and ornaments, and the contents are exactly as they were in those days, only in miniature. Tiny seashells occupy a display cabinet. The tapestry room walls are covered with silk, the ceiling and the fireplace mantel are painstakingly painted, and Italian marble paves the hall floor. Silver spoons rest on the dining table and the family initials are embroidered on the napkins. Look carefully, and you'll even see pins stuck in pincushions.

ALL ABOUT "the night watch"

One painting defines Holland's Golden Age: Rembrandt's **The Militia Company of Captain Frans Banning Cocq and Lieutenant Willem van Ruytenburch** (1642), better known as "The Night Watch." The scene it so dramatically depicts is surely alien to most of the people who flock to see it: Gaily uniformed, but not exactly warrior-looking, militiamen checking their weapons and accouterments before moving out on patrol. Captain Cocq (once described as the stupidest man in the city, and whose house at Singel 140-142 still stands), Lieutenant van Ruytenburch, the troopers, and observers (including Rembrandt himself) gaze out at us along the corridor of time, and we're left wondering what's going on underneath the paint, inside their minds.

One sentiment might be irritation with this upstart artist, who painted some of their faces in profile or partly hidden, yet charged the full-face fee per man—the militiamen hated the artistic freedom Rembrandt had exercised on their group portrait. In 1975, the masterpiece was restored after having been attacked and slashed.

Contrary to popular belief, Rembrandt's "The Night Watch" (1642) actually shows a daytime scene. Centuries of grime dulled its luster until restoration revealed sunlight glinting on the militia company's arms.

Lines are always long so either reserve a ticket online before your visit or turn up on the dot of opening time. And—like everywhere else in Amsterdam—watch out for the bikers who stream through the museum's underpass with little regard for milling tourists.

Museumstraat 1. www.rijksmuseum.nl. ℂ **020/674-7000.** Admission 20€ adults, free ages 18 and under. Daily 9am–5pm.

Stedelijk Museum ★★★ MUSEUM   This is the second of the triumvirate of great art museums in Amsterdam, and is devoted to modern and contemporary art and design. The stark original 1895 building by A.W. Weissman got a new wing in 2012—a curious structure that locals refer to as "the bathtub"—which houses the foyer, cafe, and gift shop, as well as temporary exhibitions on the lower level. The Stedelijk's interior is bright and white, all the better to show off its stellar collections of works by the most famous names of the 19th to 21st centuries. Things get off to an excellent start with the sparkly mural by CoBrA artist Karel Appel in the first gallery, and the roster of great names exhibited here includes Mondrian, Chagall, van Gogh, Spencer, Matta, Newman, Pollock; pop artists Warhol and Liechtenstein; and contemporary provocateur Jeff Koons. The museum's design collection is less successful as the layout is cramped, but there are many standout pieces here, including De Stijl designer Gerrit Rietveld's famous painted chair.

Museumplein 10. www.stedelijk.nl. ℂ **020/573-2911.** Daily 10am–6pm (Fri till 10pm). Admission 18.50€ adults, 10€ students, free ages 17 and under.

Van Gogh Museum ★★★ MUSEUM   More than 200 paintings by Vincent van Gogh (1853-90), along with nearly every sketch, print, etching, and piece of correspondence the artist ever produced, have been housed here since the museum opened in 1973. Van Gogh's sister-in-law and a namesake nephew presented the collection to Holland with the provision that the canvases not leave Vincent's native land.

Displays start with various works from different points in Vincent's career hung alongside contemporary work by Pissarro, Gauguin, and Monet to provide useful historical context. You can also trace this great artist's artistic development and psychological decline by viewing the paintings displayed in chronological order according to the seven distinct periods and places of residence that defined his short career. (He painted for only 10 years producing over 800 works and was on the threshold of success when he committed suicide at age 37.) Only one of van Gogh's paintings sold during his lifetime (his brother Theo sold it), but he did give others out to pay for food, drink, and lodgings—worth millions today, some perhaps went for little more than a song.

In 1888, van Gogh traveled to Arles in Provence. He was dazzled by the Mediterranean sun, and his favorite color, yellow (it signified love to him), dominated such landscapes as *Wheatfield with a Reaper* (1889). Until his death 2 years later, van Gogh remained in the south of France painting at a frenetic pace, between bouts of madness. In *The Night Café* (1888), a billiards hall's red walls and green ceiling combine with a sickly yellow lamplight to charge the scene with an oppressive, almost nightmarish air. (With red and green, Vincent wrote, he tried to represent "those terrible things, men's passions.") We see the halos around the lights swirl as if we, like some of the patrons slumped over their tables, have had too much to drink. The very famous Still Life *Vase with Fourteen Sunflowers,* best known simply as Sunflowers, is another highlight of the collection. By the time you reach the vaguely threatening painting of black crows rising from a waving cornfield, you can almost feel the mounting inner pain the artist was finally unable to bear.

The Van Gogh Museum has surged in popularity in recent years, becoming the most-visited museum in the Netherlands. That means that despite the switch to online-only timed tickets, there are always snaking queues of visitors out front, no matter the time of year.

Museumplein 6. www.vangoghmuseum.nl. ℂ **020/570-5200.** Admission 19€ adults, free ages 17 and under (all tickets must be purchased online). Mar–late June and Sept–Oct, daily 9am–6pm (Fri till 9pm); late June–Aug and Dec 23–31 daily 9am–7pm (Fri and Sat till 9pm); Nov–Feb 9am–5pm (Fri till 9pm).

Vondelpark ★★ PARK   A 5-minute stroll from the Van Gogh down Van Baerlestraat (head down to PC Hooftstraat to gawp at the expensive stores; see p. 118) brings you to Amsterdam's biggest, greenest public park, providing 44 hectares (109 acres) of peace and quiet. This is a cherished open space crammed with trees, lawns, lakes, and bridges criss-crossed with walking, biking, and jogging tracks, although as usual cyclists take precedence, so watch your step. Summer sees the lakeside cafes filling up and open-air festivals and concerts (p. 126).

Multiple entrances, including Van Eeghenlaan at the corner of Jacob Obrechtstraat. Free admission. Daily 24/7.

When the Germans arrived in Amsterdam on May 16, 1940 after a day of intense bombing that all but destroyed Rotterdam (p. 152), they were cautiously welcomed into the Netherlands. But slowly the Nazis clamped down on the city and its open-minded people; more brutal laws were enforced taking away individual freedom, and underground resistance to the Nazis mounted. The 10 percent of the population that was Jewish were persecuted, forced to wear yellow Stars of David, and stripped of their jobs. In 1942, the roundup of Jewish families began; thousands of people were taken to the Hollandsche Schouwburg (p. 105) before being deported to labor camps, Bergen-Belsen in Germany, or Auschwitz in Poland. Of the 140,000 Sephardic and Ashkenazi Jews who lived in Amsterdam before WWII, less than 30,000 survived until Liberation on May 5, 1945. The most famous Dutch victim of the Holocaust was Anne Frank, whose tragic story is told at the Anne Frank Huis (p. 96) on Prinsengracht. To learn more about opposition to the German occupation of Amsterdam, visit the Resistance Museum (p. 107).

4

AMSTERDAM | Exploring Amsterdam

Plantage/Oost

Artis Royal Zoo ★★ ZOO   Amsterdam's wonderfully family-friendly zoo was established in 1838 and covers more than 14 hectares (35 acres) of tree-lined pathways and landscaped gardens. It has more than 900 species of animals, successfully combining 19th-century layouts and buildings with a 21st-century commitment to conservation and breeding. Here lions, elephants, lemurs, giraffes, and gazelles range fairly freely, and the ticket price grants admission to Artis's Aquarium, the Insect House, Geological Museum, and Planetarium where 3-D films on the birth of the planet are shown. If you're traveling with kids, head to the children's farm (with assorted small animals to pet) and take note of the daily keeper talks, vulture and lion feeding sessions, and sea lion training demonstrations to fit in to your day as well. On Saturdays between June and the end of August the zoo stays open into the late evening.

Also worth visiting (though admission is 6.50€ extra) is the adjacent **Micropia,** a surprisingly entertaining interactive museum delving into the invisible world of microbes.

Plantage Kerklaan 38–40. www.artis.nl. © **0900/278-4796.** Admission 24€ adults, 20.50€ children 3–9. Nov–Feb daily 9am–5pm, Mar–Oct daily 9am–6pm.

Dockworker Statue ★★ MONUMENT   Just to the left side of the Portuguese Synagogue complex is Jonas Daniël Meijerplein, where many Dutch Jews were herded together while awaiting deportation to concentration camps in Germany and Poland. The bronze figure is always surrounded by wreaths of flowers; it was created by Mari Andriessen and was erected in 1952 in commemoration of the February 1941 strike by workers protesting against the Jewish deportations, which was violently suppressed by Amsterdam's Nazi occupiers and ended in a bloodbath.

Jonas Daniël Meijerplein. Free admission. Daily 24/7.

Hermitage Amsterdam ★★ MUSEUM   The Amsterdam branch of St. Petersburg's Hermitage is a delight to visit; it's housed in the Amstellhof, a former almshouse for elderly women built in 1680 behind a serene neoclassical facade. Centered on a giant courtyard and all but surrounded by canals and the Amstel River, the building has been transformed into a state-of-the art gallery displaying the rich pickings from the Russian state collection. Exhibitions run for about 6 months, so check online before you visit, but with the Hermitage's holding more than 3 million works of art, chances are the current exhibition will be spectacular. The permanent Golden Age portrait gallery features 30 large-scale 17th-century paintings; there is also an outsider art museum with a rotating series of works by self-taught artists.

Amstel 31. www.hermitageamsterdam.nl. ✆ **020/530-8755.** Admission varies depending on exhibitions, 18€ adults, free children age 11 and under. Daily 10am–5pm. Closed Apr 27, Dec 25.

Het Scheepvaartmuseum (National Maritime Museum) ★★ MUSEUM   Housed in a mammoth, Venetian-style 17th-century arsenal, Amsterdam's Maritime Museum is a gem of a museum whose displays showcase the importance of Amsterdam's maritime history. There are many paintings and models of ships, seascapes, navigational instruments, cannons, and other weaponry scattered through the displays, which have all been spruced up with the clever use of interactive light, sound, multimedia, and audio-visual aids. The best exhibits detail the growth of the Dutch East India Company and sensitively address the slave trade and today's whaling issues. Youngsters will enjoy boarding the gaily painted, full-size replica of the merchant ship Amsterdam, moored on the quay outside. Everything on board is as it was in 1749 when the original boat foundered on its maiden voyage to the East Indies (present-day Indonesia). Actors playing the part of sailors fire cannons, sing sea shanties, mop the deck, hoist cargo on board, and attend a solemn burial at sea. Kids can join sail makers and rope makers at work and see the cook prepare meals in the galley.

Kattenburgerplein 1. www.hetscheepvaartmuseum.nl. ✆ **020/523-2222.** Admission 16.50€ adults, 8€ students and children 4–17. Daily 9am–5pm. Closed Jan 1, Apr 27, Dec 25.

Hollandsche Schouwburg ★★ MUSEUM/MEMORIAL   The imposing white Hollandsche Schouwburg was originally a theater, but in World War II hundreds of Dutch Jewish families were forcibly detained here before deportation to the concentration camps of Poland. The former theater is now the official memorial to the Nazi Holocaust in Amsterdam, with a deeply moving documentary highlighting the persecution of the Jews through a series harrowing interviews with victims. The small museum on the upper floor is mainly notable for its pictures of the ingenious hiding places used to conceal Jewish people from the Nazis. However, it is the monument out in the rear courtyard that grabs attention—a simple cast column scattered with flowers.

Plantage Middenlaan 24. https://jck.nl/en. ✆ **020/531-0310.** Free admission, contribution suggested. Daily 11am–5pm. Closed Apr 27, Rosh Hashanah, and Yom Kippur (check online as dates change).

Hortus Botanicus (Botanical Garden) ★★ PARK   Established in 1638, these gardens are home to around 4,000 species of rare plants and trees, brought here from former Dutch colonies around the world. In summer the landscape explodes with the colors and scents of more than 250,000 flowers. The three-climate greenhouse gets progressively warmer as you walk through it—most of the plants in there come from Australia and South Africa. There's also an herb garden, a desert greenhouse, a tree-spotting route through the gardens, and a butterfly house that kids love.

Plantage Middenlaan 2A. www.dehortus.nl. ℂ **020/625-9021.** Admission 9.75€ adults; 5.50€ seniors, students, and children 5–14. Daily 10am–5pm (Sun till 7pm in July–Aug). Closed Jan 1, Dec 25.

Joods Historische Museum (Jewish Historical Museum) ★ MUSEUM   Built by Ashkenazi Jewish refugees from Germany and Poland in the 17th and 18th centuries, it was sheer luck that the four synagogues that make up this complex survived the Nazi occupation in World War II. They have now been turned into a disappointingly dull museum covering the history of the Jewish community in Amsterdam from the 17th century to present day, and displaying some of the artifacts looted by the Nazis during the war. (Interestingly, the temporary exhibits tend to be far better than the permanent one, dealing with such topics as the Kabbalah and the legacy of singer Amy Winehouse). The adjoining **Kindermuseum (Children's Museum)** ★★ is much better, cleverly set up as the home of a traditional Orthodox Jewish family, with such interactive activities as matzo baking, Yiddish lessons, and celebrations of the Sabbath.

Nieuwe Amstelstraat 1. https://jck.nl/en. ℂ **020/531-0310.** Admission with single ticket for 5 locations in the Jewish Quarter 17€ adults, 8.50€ students and children 13–17, 4.25€ children 6–12. Daily 11am–5pm. Closed Apr 27, Rosh Hashanah, and Yom Kippur (check online as dates change).

Portuguese Synagogue ★★★ SYNOGOGUE   In continuous use since it was built in 1675 by Sephardic Jews who moved to Amsterdam from Spain and Portugal, this monumental, square-shaped building—one of the largest synagogues in Europe—looks pretty much as it did 3 centuries ago. It still has no electricity, so during evening services it is illuminated by large, low-hanging brass chandeliers that together hold 1,000 candles. The women's gallery on the upper floor is supported by 12 stone columns representing the Twelve Tribes of Israel In the courtyard complex that surrounds the synagogue, effectively cutting it off from the rest of the city, are the mikvah ritual baths; the mourning room complete with a coffin stand; and the synagogue's treasure chambers containing precious menorahs, torahs, and ornate clerical robes.

Mr. Visserplein 3. https://jck.nl/en. ℂ **020/531-0310.** Admission with single ticket for 5 locations in the Jewish Quarter 17€ adults, 8.50€ students and children 13–17, 4.25€ children 6–12. March–Apr and Sept–Oct Sun–Thurs 10am–5pm, Fri 10am–4pm; May–Aug daily 10am–5pm; Nov and Feb Sun–Thurs 10am–5pm, Fri 10am–2pm; Dec–Jan Sun–Thurs 10am–4pm, Fri 10am–2pm. Closed Apr 27, Passover, Rosh Hashanah, Yom Kippur, Sukkot (check online as dates change).

NEMO Science Museum ★★★ MUSEUM As much children's play space as museum, NEMO is the number one place to hit with kids if it's a rainy day. Housed in a magnificent, pale green, ship-shaped building designed by Renzo Piano, this interactive science center introduces kids to science and technology, but never feels like school. Through games, experiments, and demonstrations, they learn how chain reactions work, search for ETs, blow a soap bubble large enough to stand inside, and other fun stuff. NEMO's broad, stepped, and sloping roof is an attraction in itself: a place to hang out, have a light meal (there's a restaurant), and take in the views. At the top, you are 30m (100 ft.) above the IJ waterway and have sweeping views over the Old Harbor and Eastern Dock.

Oosterdok 2. www.nemosciencemuseum.nl. © **020/531-3233.** Admission 17.50€, free for children 4 and under. Tues–Sun 10am–5:30pm. Closed Apr 27 and several Mondays throughout the year.

Tropenmuseum ★★★ MUSEUM One of the city's most intriguing museums belongs to the Royal Institute for the Tropics, a foundation devoted to studying the cultures of tropical areas around the world. Its focus reflects Holland's centuries as a landlord in areas such as Indonesia, Surinam (on South America's northern coast), and the Caribbean islands of St. Maarten, Saba, St. Eustatius, Aruba, Bonaire, and Curaçao. The Tropical Institute building complex alone is worth the tram ride to Amsterdam East; its heavily ornamented 19th-century facade is an amalgam of Dutch architectural styles: Turrets, stepped gables, arched windows, delicate spires, and a monumental galleried interior court.

The museum's approach to its subject has matured considerably from its original 19th-century colonial pride and condescension—indeed, it's become an antidote to those kinds of views. Its representation of contemporary issues such as the causes of poverty in the developing world and the depletion of the world's tropical rainforests is both considered and balanced. The new ground-floor "Things That Matter" exhibition, on view through 2023, highlights cultural identity throughout the world through religious artifacts, music, fashion, and more. The top floor houses a series of rotating exhibits, which have included shows on iconic Japanese culture, from ancient samurai to Hello Kitty to *kawaii* street fashion. The first and second floors are devoted to the permanent collection and will be undergoing renovations in the near future; check the website for the latest updates.

Linnaeusstraat 2. www.tropenmuseum.nl. © **31/880-042-800.** Admission 16€ adults; 10€ students, 8€ children 4–17. Tues–Sun 10am–5pm. Closed Jan 1, Apr 27, Dec 25.

Verzetsmuseum (Dutch Resistance Museum) ★★★ MUSEUM Take a trip back in time to Holland's dark World War II days, during the Nazi occupation (1940-45). With authentic photographs, documents, weapons, communications equipment, spy gadgets, and other materials actually used by the Dutch Resistance, exhibits show the ingenuity—along with courage—the freedom-fighters brought to bear on German occupation forces. A pedal-powered printing press is a good example of items that evoke the period and bring it to life. The fate of Amsterdam's Jewish community, herded into a ghetto, then rounded up for deportation to concentration camps, has a prominent place, as do the actions of workers who in 1941 went on strike to protest the first deportation of 400 Jewish Amsterdammers. Yet the museum doesn't shrink from less palatable aspects of Holland's wartime record, like the actions of collaborators, including those who joined Dutch Nazi SS units. The **Resistance Museum Junior** (for children 8 and up) is found in a newer wing of the museum and focuses on the experience of Dutch children under Nazi occupation. The entrance is opposite the Artis Royal Zoo.

Plantage Kerklaan 61. www.verzetsmuseum.org. © **020/620-2535.** Admission 11€ adults, 6€ children 7–16. Mon–Fri 10am–5pm, Sat–Sun 11am–5pm. Closed Jan 1, Apr 27, Dec 25.

Wertheim Park ★ PARK   The little scrap of grass overlooking Nieuwe Herengracht canal holds one of Amsterdam's most poignant commemorations of the Holocaust: a 1993 memorial by sculptor Jan Wolkers, dedicated to the millions killed at Auschwitz. Six large cracked glass shards lie flat on the ground reflecting a shattered sky and covering a buried urn that contains ashes of the dead from the concentration camp. The glass legend reads NOOIT MEER AUSCHWITZ ("Never Again, Auschwitz"), with the words reflecting back from the glass.

Plantage Middenlaan. Free admission. Daily 24/7.

Amsterdam Noord

A'dam Lookout ★★ ATTRACTION   Just across the harbor from Centraal Station, a staid former office tower has been transformed into an entertainment destination, with several dining options, a nightclub, a hotel, and on its rooftop, 21 stories up, a sky deck offering spectacular 360-degree views of the city. Thrill-seekers strap into a harness for a ride on Europe's highest swing, which shoots out over the edge of the building at a height of 100 meters (328 feet). If the weather isn't agreeable, the indoor observation deck one floor below offers equally great vistas.

Overhoeksplein 5. www.adamlookout.com. © **020/242-0100.** Admission 13.50€ adults, 7.50€ children 4–12. Swing 5€ extra. Daily 10am–10pm.

EYE Film Institute ★★★ MUSEUM/MOVIE THEATER   Built in 2012 by Austrian firm Delugan Meissl Associated Architects, the EYE is the first major public building to be constructed north of the river. The all-white aerodynamic structure appears to float above the waterfront promenade, and the shallow steps leading up to the museum are usually filled with people posing for a selfie with the eye-catching building. Inside, the gleaming complex houses four movie theaters, exhibitions, a store, and a restaurant with a sought-after terrace with views back to Centraal Station. Although there's an admission fee for the movies and temporary exhibitions, the 360-degree

Panorama film display in the basement is free. EYE is a totally cash-free zone so make sure you go armed with plastic.

IJpromenade 1. www.eyefilm.nl. ⓒ **020/589-1400.** Admission movies: 11€ adults, 9.50€ students, 7.50€ children 11 and under; exhibitions: 11€ adults, 9.50€ students, free ages 18 and under. Exhibition: daily 10am–7pm. Box office: Thurs 10am–10pm, Fri–Sat 10am–11pm. Take free ferry across IJ waterway from Waterplein West dock behind Centraal Station to Buiksloterweg.

NDSM-Werf (NDSM-Wharf) ★★ CULTURAL CENTER   The Nederlandsche Dok en Scheepsbouw Maatschappij (Netherlands Dock and Shipyard Corporation) had been long derelict before it was taken over by an artists' community known as Stichting Kinetisch Noord, who have spruced up the dilapidated buildings and strewn the streets with recycled sculpture and heavy-duty graffiti, including an enormous, colorful mural of Anne Frank. Among this urban jungle, studios and galleries have sprung up as well as a theater, forming a cutting-edge cultural center that is growing in reputation as the Westergasfabriek becomes more mainstream. Here, also is one of the city's quirkiest accommodations: the Faralda Crane Hotel, with three luxury suites inside a converted 50m-high crane (we don't think its worth at a stay at 700€ per night, but it's interesting to see from afar). The elegant old triple-masted schooner *Pollux* (now home to an Indonesian restaurant) is moored up alongside the Botel; nearby the *Pannenkoekenboot* (Pancake boat; see p. 111) offers tours of the IJ along with unlimited pancakes.

NDSM-Werf. www.ndsm.nl. Free admission 24/7. Take free ferry across IJ waterway to NDSM-Werf from behind Centraal Station.

Westerpark

Museum Het Schip ★★ MUSEUM   The city's most famous example of Amsterdam School architecture is a bus ride west to Zaanstraat. The movement's designs were influenced by the socialist ideals of architect Hendrik Berlage and are epitomized by heavy use of brickwork, elaborate masonry, spiky towers, painted glass, and wrought-iron work. Michel de Klerk (1884–1923) was the leading exponent of the school and designed his seminal building Het Schip to resemble an ocean liner; the brick complex incorporated social housing, a school, and a post office. The latter is the only one of De Klerk's interiors currently open to the public but must be visited with a guided tour; the 3pm tour is in English. The permanent collection includes furniture and objects designed by artists of the Amsterdam School.

Spaarndammerplantsoen 140. www.hetschip.nl. ⓒ **020/686-8595.** Admission 15€ adults, 7.50€ students, 5€ children 5–12. Tues–Sun 11am–5pm. Closed Jan 1, Apr 27, Dec 25.

Westerpark ★★ PARK   Until the early 2000s the Westerpark was a scrubby patch of green in the otherwise grimy industrial wasteland around the gas works that lay on its western flank, which became redundant and fell into disrepair after the advent of North Sea gas in the 1960s. Since then new life has been breathed into the area with the Westerpark remodeled to include open lawns and shady trees, tennis courts, skate parks, and play areas for kids. The gasworks have been repurposed into the Westergasfabriek, one of Amsterdam's coolest entertainment venues, with plenty of chances for beer or coffee as well as exhibition spaces, design studios, and Het Ketelhuis movie theater. Summer sees plenty of free open-air concerts here and there's often a fair for kids.

Westerpark, off Haarlemmerweg. www.westergasfabriek.nl. © **020/586-0710.** Free admission 24/7.

Amstelveen

CoBrA Modern Art Museum ★★ MUSEUM
Art lovers will find this breathtakingly contemporary museum worth the trek to its off-the-beaten-path location. The most enjoyable way to get here is the 20-minute Tram 5 ride from Amsterdam city center, giving you a chance to see leafy, suburban Amstelveen as you rattle through the streets. The museum is a light-filled brick-and-glass affair with plenty of white space for framing the artwork; it was designed by Dutch architect Wim Quist and opened in 1995. The collection overflows with the post–World War II abstract expressionist art and ceramics of the short-lived CoBrA Group, named for the initials of the founding artists' home cities: Copenhagen, Brussels, and Amsterdam. Karel Appel (1921–2006) and Constant (1920–2005) were the Dutch proponents, both controversial painters, sculptors, and ceramicists whose work, like their fellow CoBrA artists, have a childlike quality, employing strong colors and abstract shapes, seen in Constant's oil painting "Figure of the Night" and Appel's delightfully simple ceramics.

Sandbergplein 1, Amstelveen. www.cobra-museum.nl. © **020/547-5050.** Admission 12.50€ adults; 8€ students, and children 6–18. Tues–Sun 10am–5pm.

Organized Tours

BUS TOURS We think that Amsterdam's unique alternative to the bus tour—canal boat cruises—are by far the best way to get an overview of the city. But for those who don't like boats, and those nervous about doing a lot of walking, Amsterdam also has hop-on, hop-off circular bus tours from **City Sightseeing.** These buses stop at all the major sights and run every 15 to 20 minutes from 9:15am to 6pm in summer and 9:30am to 5:15pm in winter (www.citysightseeingamsterdam.nl; © **020/420-4000**). Prices start at 21€ (10.50€ for children 4–13) for 24 hours of access to the service.

   Tours & Tickets (www.tours-tickets.com; © **020/420-4000**) and **Stromma** (www.stromma.com; © **020/217-0501**) run bus tours around the city and also across the Netherlands. A favorite trip from March to May is out to the Keukenhof bulb fields at Lisse (p. 137). Rates vary with the particular tour on offer, but begin at 34€.

CANAL CRUISES There's no better way to discover Amsterdam than from its waterways. Canal cruises leave from 14 different points throughout the city, but most depart from the pier to the left of Centraal Station. A 1-hour cruise is included with the I amsterdam City Card (p. 90); there are four participating operators, among them **Lovers Canal Cruises** (www.lovers.nl; ℰ 020/530-1090) and **Stromma** (see above). Frankly, we've never been able to find much difference between one cruise operator and the next (all are just fine). Depending on the tour line, boats during the summer season (mid-March–early Nov) leave daily every 15 minutes from 9am to 10pm; in winter (early Nov–mid-March), departures are every 30 minutes from 9:30am to 9:30pm. From Centraal, most cruises loop northwards into the IJ, which is bordered by the gleaming contemporary architecture of EYE Film Institute (p. 108), Muziekgebouw aan 't IJ (p. 123), and NEMO Science Museum (p. 107) before entering the Canal Ring and passing along the eastern canals, giving sight of the Magere Brug (Skinny Bridge) connecting Keizersgracht and Prinsengracht and illuminated at night with hundreds of lights. Then it's up Herengracht past mighty mansions to the "Nine Bridges" viewpoint, which actually permits sight of 15 bridges on the corner of Reguliersgracht. There's a rather lackluster commentary in English on board the boat, but it is still an entertaining way to learn about Amsterdam in a short time.

Other canal tour-boat lines are: **Amsterdam Canal Cruises** (www.amsterdamcanalcruises.nl; ℰ 020/676-0302); **Reederij P Kooij** (www.rederijkooij.nl; ℰ 020/623-3810; **Rederij Plas** (www.rederijplas.nl; ℰ 020/624-5406), and **Blue Boat Company** (www.blueboat.nl; ℰ 020/679-1370). Prices vary from company to company, but a basic hour-long tour is around 12€ for adults, 8€ for children 4 to 12, and free for children 3 and under. Evening tours are available through most of these companies; 3-hour candlelit dinner cruises are among the most popular.

Still other canal cruising options include the hop-on, hop-off **City Sightseeing** (www.citysightseeingamsterdam.nl; ℰ 020/420-4000) which stops at (or near) all the major attractions and allow you to build your own sightseeing itinerary. Looking for a lunchtime treat for the kids? Try the **Pannenkoekenboot** (**Pancake Boat;** www.pannenkoekenboot.nl; ℰ 020/638-8817) for unlimited servings of pancakes with sweet or savory fillings with your boat trip.

CYCLING TOURS One of the great joys of Amsterdam is being part of its bike culture. But its streets can sometimes feel like a minefield: Cyclists zip around town at high speeds—bikes are the main form of transportation for locals—there are lots of pedestrians, and crossing tram rails can be dangerous. That's not to say you shouldn't hop on two wheels, but a guide can help with navigating busy streets and understanding the rules of the road. There are several tour companies offering tours of the city by bike. **Yellow Bike** (www.yellowbike.nl; ℰ 020/620-6940) and **We Bike Amsterdam** (www.webikeamsterdam.com; ℰ 06/1007-1179) both offer multiple options, from 2- to 3-hour canal jaunts to all-day rides out into the country past windmills and through nature reserves. Prices start at around 25€.

HORSE & CARRIAGE TOURS These romantic, family-friendly vehicles run by **Karos Citytours** (www.karos.nl; ℰ 020/691-3478) depart from just outside the Royal Palace on the Dam for traipses through the Old Center, along the canals, and into the Jordaan. Tours operate April to October daily

11am to 6pm and on a limited schedule in winter. Rides are 45€ for 25 minutes, 70€ for 40 minutes, and 95€ for 1 hour.

WALKING TOURS   It's easy enough to make up your own walking tour of Amsterdam and include all the important sights, but if you want guidance, there are also multiple free walking tours of the city that cover essential sites and areas including the Canal Belt, the Jewish Quarter, and the Anne Frank House. One of the most popular is the three-hour, tips-based walking tour from **Sandemans New Europe** (www.neweuropetours.eu; **49/305-105-0030**) which meets in Dam Square; tours run from 10am to 3pm. Another is from **FreeDam Tours** (www.freedamtours.com; ℰ **06/4079-0279**), which departs from Oude Kerk in the Red Light District.

WATER BIKE TOURS   It's fun to toodle around on the sturdy paddleboats called canal bikes. You can rent them from **Stromma** (www.stromma.com; ℰ **020/217-0501**). They seat two or four and come with a guidebook with map and route suggestions. The Canal Bike moorings are at Leidseplein; Westerkerk, near the Anne Frankhuis; and Stadhouderskade, beside the Rijksmuseum. Rental is 9€ per person hourly plus a deposit of 20€.

Outdoor Activities

BOATING & SAILING   Sailboats, kayaks, and canoes can be rented on the Sloterplas Lake from **Watersportcentrum De Duikelaar,** Noordzijde 41 (www.deduikelaar.nl; ℰ **06/8146-6991**). From mid-March to mid-October, you can go to the Loosdrecht lakes, southeast of Amsterdam, to rent sailing equipment from **Ottenhome,** Zuwe 20, 1241 NC Kortenhoef (www.otten home.nl; ℰ **035/582-3331**). Canoes can be rented in **Amsterdamse Bos,** south of the city, for use in the park lakes.

CYCLING   Amsterdam is flat, flat, flat, but you take your life in your hands trying to ride a bike in the center of the city—local cyclists take no prisoners. Luckily there are plenty of options for enjoying a less frenetic bike ride. You can cycle along the canals; follow the path of the River Amstel south to Amstelpark and out to the photogenic village of Ouderkerk aan de Amstel;

Amsterdam's Beaches

Amsterdam has no natural beaches of its own, so it decided to create some. **Sloterpark** ★★, in the western part of the city, is home to a large lake (Sloterpas) with a man-made beach; it's a popular family-friendly spot that's ideal for picnicking and swimming and is open year-round. From the center, it's a half-hour ride on Tram 13 and admission is free. Perched on a lake just to the south of the city center, **Strandzuid** ★★ at Europaplein 22 (www.strand-zuid.nl; ℰ **020/639-2589**) is an urban beach complex attracting a sophisticated clientele. Its small beach is surrounded by a restaurant, chill-out lounge, and cocktail bar all connected by a series of wooden boardwalks. It's open from May to October. Another option is **Pllek** (see p. 85), a hip bar with a sandy beach set on the banks of the River IJ in NDSM Wharf.

head into the forest park of Amsterdamse Bos. Or venture further afield to the UNESCO-listed Amsterdam Stelling; this former defense line is 10km (8 miles) out of the city and gives 135km (85 miles) of scenic cycling past nature reserves and waterways. **MacBike** (www.macbike.nl; ✆ 020/620-0985) is the best-known bicycle rental company. You'll need passport ID and a 50€ deposit per bike (cash or credit card). Rates (excluding insurance) are 7.50€ for 3 hours and 9.75€ for 1 day for a pedal-brake bike, 11€ and 14.75€ respectively for a bike with a handbrake. MacBike is open daily 9am to 6pm. A range of bikes is available, including tandems, six-speed touring bikes, and smaller ones for kids. There are five MacBike rental outlets (same web details)—on Waterlooplein, Stationsplein outside Centraal Station, Oosterdokskade 63A Weteringschans 2 at Leidseplein, and Overtoom 45 at Vondelpark.

GOLF   Among public courses in or near Amsterdam are: 9-hole **Golfbaan Sloten,** Sloterweg 1045 (www.golfbaansloten.nl; ✆ **020/614-2402**); 18-hole **Waterlandse Golf Club,** Buiksloterdijk 141 (www.waterlandsegolfclub. nl; ✆ **020/636-1010**); and **Golfbaan Spaarnwoude,** Het Hoge Land 2, 1981 Velsen-Zuid (www.golfbaanspaarnwoude.nl; ✆ **023/538-5599**).

HORSEBACK RIDING   If you want to experience the magical forest park of Amsterdam Bos by horseback, **Manege Nieuw Amstelland,** Jan Tooropplantsoen 17 (www.manegenieuwamstelland.nl; ✆ **020/643-2468**) offers lessons.

ICE-SKATING   If temperatures drop low enough for long enough in winter, the canals of Amsterdam become sparkling highways through the city and the Dutch get their skates on. Classical music plays over the ice and kiosks are set up to dispense warming liqueurs. There are very few places that rent out skates, however. One that does is **Jaap Eden IJsbanen,** Radioweg 64 (www.jaapeden.nl; ✆ **020/694-9652**), from October to February.

JOGGING   The two main jogging areas are **Vondelpark** in the center city and **Amsterdamse Bos** on the southern edge of the city. You can run along the Amstel River. If you choose to run along the canals, watch out for uneven cobbles, loose paving stones, and dog poop.

ROLLER BLADING   You can hire blades from **De Skate Dokter**, Jan van Galenstraat 161 (www.skatedokter.nl; ✆ 020/260-0055) then join the hundreds of skaters on Amsterdam's regular—and free—**Friday Night Skate** (www.fridaynightskate.com). It begins at 8:30pm, weather permitting. Meet at 8pm in summer and 8:15pm in winter outside the VondelCS cultural center in the Vondelpark, and take a circular route of around 20km (12½ miles) through the city. It's a sensible idea to wear a helmet and knee protection.

SWIMMING   Amsterdam's state-of-the-art swimming facility is **Het Marnix,** Marnixplein 1 (www.hetmarnix.nl; ✆ **020/524-6000**), which has two heated pools along with a fitness center and spa, and a cafe-restaurant. The **Zuiderbad,** Hobbemastraat 26 (✆ **020/252-1390**), is a handsome, refurbished place close to the Rijksmuseum and built in 1911; it even has times set aside for those who like to swim in their birthday suit. **De Mirandabad,** De

Mirandalaan 9 (© **020/252-4444**), features an indoor pool with wave machines, slides, and other amusements, and an outdoor pool that's open May to September.

TENNIS   Find indoor courts at **Frans Otten Stadion,** IJsbaanpad 43 (www. fransottenstadion.nl; © **020/662-8767**), close to the Olympic Stadium. **Sportcentrum Amstelpark,** Koenenkade 8, Amsterdamse Bos (www.amstelpark. nl; © **020/301-0700**) has 18 outdoor clay courts and 11 indoor hard courts.

Especially for Kids

From toddlers to teenagers, Amsterdam offers plenty of family-friendly activities. There are modern, interactive museums carefully designed to appeal to youngsters; canal trips; trams to ride; and bikes to rent. With playgrounds in all the parks, kids' shows in several theaters, and pancakes on almost every menu, there's always something to do when youngsters get fractious or it pours with rain (which it often does). However, as anyone with toddlers will tell you, pushing baby strollers across all those cobbles isn't much fun.

Best options for a happy family day out include **canal cruises;** if you don't think they'll last an hour without getting bored, you might like to blackmail them into behaving by promising a lunchtime treat aboard the *Pannenkoekenboot* (**Pancake Boat;** see above) for unlimited pancakes with sweet or savory fillings. There are parent-child tandem bikes and kids bikes from **MacBike** (see above). Even **riding the trams** can be quite a novelty.

And as for **museums,** there are plenty to choose from. The Tropenmuseum (p. 107) is full of color and noise while teaching about culture and race in an unpreachy manner, and the hands-on **NEMO Science Museum** (p. 107) cleverly unravels the mysteries of science. All kids will fall in love with the sea lions and penguins at **Artis Royal Zoo** (p. 104), while older kids will dig the weird world of microorganisms at **Micropia** (p. 104). The tales of piratical derring-do aboard the good ship *Amsterdam* at **Het Scheepvaartmuseum** (**National Maritime Museum;** p. 105) will enthrall most kids, too.

The heartache of **Anne Frank Huis** (p. 96) will challenge and interest children 9 and older but can confuse younger kids, and it is not strollerfriendly. **Madame Tussauds** (Dam 20; www.madametussauds.nl; © **020/522-1010**) is perennially popular with older kids for its waxwork models of Johnny Depp, pop stars Ariana Grande and Lady Gaga, and tennis ace Rafael Nadal; costs 24.50€ adults, 20€ children 5 to 15, and free for children 4 and under. It's open daily 10am to 9:30pm. Although the **Amsterdam Dungeon** (Rokin 78; www.thedungeons.com/amsterdam; © **020/530-8500**) may well terrify youngsters, teens will adore it for the gory interpretations of the Spanish Inquisition and burning witches at the stake. Admission is 24€ adults, 20€ children 5 to 15, and free for children 4 and under. It's open daily 11am to 6pm (Fri and Sat till 7pm). The views from the **A'dam Lookout** (p. 108) will amaze older kids, as will the cool light and sound effects in the elevator ride up, and little daredevils over 4 feet tall can get strapped in for a ride on Europe's highest swing.

SHOPPING

Although Amsterdam is no Paris or Milan, it's no slouch either. **Leidsestraat** and **Koningsplein** are among the most popular shopping spots, with mid-range boutiques and design stores. Upping the ante are young designers changing the face of the retail scene around the **Nine Streets** (p. 117), in the trendy De Pijp, and in the **Museum Quarter,** where independents are giving the international designers such as Louis Vuitton and Gucci a run for their money on shopping streets **Pieter Cornelisz Hoofts-traat** and **van Baerlestraat.** The **Spiegelkwartier** at the south end of the Canal Ring is famous for antique and art stores, and is the place to head for genuine blue-and-white Delftware. Typically Dutch products such as cheese and flower bulbs are bargains, as diamonds can be if bought carefully from a reputable dealer such as Gassan (p. 121).

> ## Amsterdam Shop Opening Hours
>
> Shops normally open from 10am to 6pm Tuesday, Wednesday, Friday, and Saturday. Some stay open until 8 or 9pm on Thursday. Many close on Monday morning, opening at noon or 1pm, and most stores around the city center also open Sunday around midday; outside the center many are closed all day Sunday.

Shopping areas you can skip? We'd suggest you ignore the tatty souvenir stores selling plastic tulips and mass-produced clogs around Dam Square; and **Rokin** and pedestrianized **Kalverstraat** which only offer mainstream shopping brands that can be found anywhere in the world.

Art & Antiques

Antiekcentrum Amsterdam ★★ The largest indoor antiques market in the Netherlands is situated in Jordaan. Formerly known as De Looier, it's a cornucopia of Delftware, porcelain, silverware, wonderfully restored furniture, and bizarre statuary straggling through several old warehouses. There are 55 dealers with permanent stalls here, specializing in everything from Bakelite phones to priceless pocket watches. Wednesday, Saturday, and Sunday sees dealers from all over the country bring their wares to a table market just outside the antiques center; get there early and you just might find that elusive Old Master oil painting. Open Monday and Wednesday to Friday 11am to 6pm, and Saturday and Sunday 11am to 5pm. Elandsgracht 109. www.antiekcentrum amsterdam.nl. © **020/624-9038.**

Art Plein Spui ★ Sundays in the Old Center see a gathering of local artists who show their works under canvas just off the busy street of Spui. Standards and subject matter vary considerably as 25 artists from a pool of 60 exhibit each week. As well as predictable canal-side views badly executed in watercolor, you might find lovely ceramic vases by Jos van Alphen or wacky etchings from Janny Endstra, handmade ethnic jewelry, or silk-screen printing. You have to take potluck. It runs from 11am to 6pm. Spui. www. artamsterdam-spui.com. © **06/2499-2403.**

Galerie Lieve Hemel ★★ Located in the exclusive Spiegelkwartier in the Canal Ring, Lieve Hemel is a refined gallery selling the very best of contemporary Dutch art from a carefully selected gaggle of fine artists who may prove to be the Damien Hirsts of the future. Styles range from slightly surreal to 21st-century takes on the 17th-century still-life genre. Also on sale here is a charming selection of contemporary silverware, including vases, bowls, and tea services. Nieuwe Spiegelstraat 3. www.lievehemel.nl. ℂ **020/623-0060.**

> ### Smart Shops
>
> Amsterdam's "smart shops" sell natural stimulants such as *guarana* and supposed aphrodisiacs such as *ginkgo biloba*, as well as magic mushrooms, growing kits for weed, and seeds. Check out the **Magic Mushroom Gallery** (Spuistraat 249), or **Azarius** on Kerkstraat behind the Leidseplein.

Mathieu Hart ★★ Still family owned and considered one of the leading experts in fine art since 1878, Erik Hart's antiques emporium in the Old Center is stuffed to the gunnels with rare prints of Dutch cities, elaborate French Empire chandeliers and candlesticks, top-quality 18th-century Delftware, Chinese porcelain, and an array of loudly ticking clocks. A courier service is available for shipping overseas. Rokin 122. www.hartantiques.com. ℂ **020/623-1658.**

Premsela & Hamburger ★★ Opened in 1823, this historic store in the Old Center deals in antiquities at the luxury end of the market. Although some modern jewelry is sold here, the shop specializes in antique silver and gold collectables, from beautifully crafted 17th-century galleons under full sail to exquisite pre-loved diamond rings. It's a reputable choice if you're considering buying gemstones, gold, or jewelry in Amsterdam. Rokin 98. www.premsela.com. ℂ **020/624-9688.**

Van Gogh Museum Shop ★★★ One of the better Amsterdam museum shops, selling hundreds of items smothered with van Gogh's familiar artworks. There's a choice of books detailing the story of the tortured artist's life and postcards and posters by the hundred as well as puzzle books for kids and pretty silk scarves patterned with sunflowers. Paulus Museumplein 6. www.vangoghmuseum.nl. ℂ **020/570-5200.**

Books

American Book Center ★★ From best-selling novels to travel guides, remaindered titles, and the latest celeb magazines, this vast bookstore is handsomely stocked. Book readings are frequent, there are discount vouchers for students, and if you are an aspiring author, there's even a self-publishing advisory service. This main branch is in the Old Center, but there is another branch in The Hague (p. 144). Spui 12. ℂ **020/625-5537.**

Evenaar ★★★ In the Canal Ring, Amsterdam's first stop for travel literature is a light-filled space filled with travel maps, mainstream guides, and gorgeous coffee-table tomes containing stunning color photography. There's also a section on armchair travel and anthropology as well as antique travel books. Korsjespoortsteeg 2. ✆ **020/624-6289.**

Delftware

Galleria d'Arte Rinascimento ★★★ Buying authentic Dutch Delftware can be difficult in Amsterdam, but you'll never have an issue here as all the blue-and-white pottery on sale is authenticated. Dealing in pottery old and new, the gallery has a fine collection of antiquarian Delft tiles depicting Dutch views. The cream of the crop is the pricey, exquisite, and subtly multi-colored Makkumware from Koninklijke Tichelaar Makkum. Prinsengracht 170 (at Bloemstraat). www.delft-art-gallery.com. ✆ **020/622-7509.**

Heinen Royal Delftware ★★ There are three Amsterdam and three Delft branches of this family-owned chain that makes and sells its own-brand porcelain as well as being official dealers in fine De Porcelyne Fles and leaded crystal. It's the go-to place for many-spouted tulip vases, the legacy of 17th-century tulip madness, as well as cute Delftware charm bracelets and cufflinks. One store is based in the historic Muntoren. Prinsengracht 440 (at Leidsestraat). www.delftsblauwwinkel.nl. ✆ **020/627-8299.**

negen straatjes—AMSTERDAM'S NINE STREETS

Tucked away between the historic Old Center and the bohemian Jordaan, the Nine Streets are a classy one-stop shopping destination crisscrossing the western side of the 17th-century Canal Ring between Reestraat and Runstraat. The streets provide a welcome relief from the tatty souvenir stores of Dam Square, as they offer chic stores selling designer labels, artisan jewelry, offbeat vintage fashions, and luxury toiletries, all interspersed with plenty of stylish bars and restaurants.

L'étoile de Saint Honoré (Oude Spiegelstraat 1; www.etoile-luxuryvintage. com; ✆ **020/330-2419**) is the best place for vintage handbags, **Hester van Eeghen** (Hartenstraat 37; hesterva-neeghen.com; ✆ **020/626-9212**) has bold color blocked contemporary purses and wallets. **Anecdote** (Wolvenstraat 15; www.anecdote.nl; ✆ **020/330-4300**) is the pick for simple, stylish fashion. **United Nude** (see below) sells cool shoes and boots for women, **Parisienne** (Berenstraat 4; www.nlstreets.nl/EN/shop/parisienne; ✆ **020/428-0834**) offers lovely vintage jewelry, and **MINT Mini Mall** (Runstraat 27; www.mintminimall.nl; ✆ **020/627-2466**) sells cushions, pottery, and furniture in all shades of pastel. **Skins Cosmetic** (Runstraat 11; www.skins.nl; ✆ **020/240-0199**) is the place for organic toiletries, and **La Savonnerie** (Prinsengracht 294; www.savonnerie.nl; ✆ **020/428-1139**) for handmade soaps.

Last but not least, **De Kaaskamer van Amsterdam** ★★★ (Runstraat 7 at Keizersgracht. www.kaaskamer.nl. ✆ **020/623-3483**) is the city's most famous cheese emporium, with more than 300 cheeses to pick from. They will value pack for travelers, and have "variety packs" of six selections of organic cheese for those who want to experiment.

For more info about the Nine Streets in English, visit **www.theninestreets.com.**

Department Stores

de Bijenkorf ★★   Amsterdam's answer to Harrods and Bloomingdales is a four-story shopping addict's dream in the Old Center, selling everything from Gucci belts to Chanel headphones. The city's most prestigious and expensive department store is a delight, with high-brand designs such as Missoni and Alexander Wang for women as well as Petit Bateau and Hilfiger for kids, and Armani or Nike sports gear for men-about-town. A duty free shopping service allows overseas visitors to claim their tax back on leaving the country. Dam 1. www.debijenkorf.nl. ✆ **088/245-4488.**

Peek & Cloppenburg ★★   This elegant shop is in pole position just off Amsterdam's main square, the Dam. It does fashion for both sexes brilliantly at a range of price levels, from designer brands such as D&G and Armani to the less pricey Fred Perry and Geox. With stores now in 15 European countries, P&C is introducing more European clothing lines to its repertoire. Dam 20. www.peek-cloppenburg.nl. ✆ **020/623-2837.**

Design

Moooi ★★   Dutch designer Marcel Wanders co-founded this eclectic furniture company whose sprawling Jordaan flagship displays bold, playful, and outrageously pricey pieces by top international designers. Even if the fantastical mesh chandeliers, furry white space-age armchairs, end tables cleverly crafted to resemble lace, and giant resin rocking horses don't quite fit with your personal aesthetic, it's great fun to poke around. Westerstraat 187. www.moooi.com. ✆ **020/528-7760.**

Pol's Potten Amsterdam B.V. ★★   Housed in a former warehouse right at the coal face of Amsterdam regeneration in the eastern docks, this funky design store concentrates on selling simple, stark designs for the home. From colorful glassware to plastic kitchen utensils and desk accessories, the shop's style is reminiscent of an upmarket Swedish Ikea. A visit might unearth funky Italian furniture, dog-shaped watering cans, and pretty sets of tinted glasses. KNSM-Laan 39. www.polspotten.nl. ✆ **020/419-3541.**

Fashion

Azzurro Due ★★   A stone's throw from the chi-chi shopping boulevard PC Hooftstraat, Azzurro Due presents established high-end designers such as Saint Laurent, Chloe, and Isabel Marant alongside lesser known Dutch labels like Loes Vrij in its airy, dual-level showroom. Two more locations nearby outfit budding fashionistas (Azzuro Kids) and streetwear-savvy men (Four Amsterdam). Van Baerlestraat 3. www.azzurrodue.com. ✆ **020/671-9708.**

De Maagd & De Leeuw ★★   A pretty boutique in the lovely shopping enclave of the Nine Streets, selling jeans and stylish tops for off-duty wear, smart day dresses, and elegant gowns for the evening, all sourced from the latest Paris fashions on a monthly basis. There's also a selection of stylish shoes and boots, belts in many colors, and leather bags at reasonable prices. Hartenstraat 32. ℂ **020/428-0047.**

Episode ★★★   This was one of Amsterdam's original thrift stores and has been a huge eco-friendly success story, adhering to principles of sustainability that see almost nothing thrown away. Everything sold here is secondhand— tatty old jeans are up-cycled into shorts, gauzy evening frocks given a new lease on life, and fresh items of clothing are cleverly created out of old. Three more stores are found at Berenstraat 1 in the Nine Streets, in the city center at Spuistraat 96, and at Nieuwe Speigelstraat 37H. Waterlooplein 1. www.episode. eu. ℂ **020/320-3000.**

Kiki's Stocksale ★★   This designer outlet in the Nine Streets is always crammed with fashionistas searching for that elusive bargain. Discounted brands include Gucci, Lanvin, Jil Sander, and Miu Miu. New styles on the upper level are less of a bargain, but downstairs, fashion from bygone seasons comes at a whopping 70-percent reduction. No need to do math; color-coded dots indicate the prices, which start at 98€. Hartenstraat 32. www.kikiniesten.nl. ℂ **020/638-3073.**

X Bank ★★   Occupying the second floor of a 1908 bank building that also houses the W Hotel, this sprawling concept store stocks cutting-edge Dutch fashion and accessories for both men and woman. Look for established ready-to-wear brands such as Scotch & Soda and Denham alongside ethereal haute couture pieces by the likes of David Laport (whose fans include Solange and Sia). It's also a place to discover emerging Dutch designers like Atelier Reservé, whose one-of-a-kind kimono-like jackets are crafted from recycled denim. Spuistraat 172. www.xbank.amsterdam. ℂ **020/811-3320.**

Webers Holland ★★   A hoot of a shop hidden behind the facade of one of Amsterdam's narrowest houses. Yes, the 17th-century Klein Trippenhuis (Little Trippenhuis) in the Old Center is the unlikely venue for the wacky, outlandish fetish designs of Désirée Webers, who has been creating rubber and leather outfits since 1995. Apart from huge, stacked platforms by Pleaser and cat suits with cut outs, not all her clothes are so out there; a recent collection of hand-knit dresses was even quite demure. Kloveniersburgwal 26. www. webersholland.nl. ℂ **020/638-1777.**

Flea Markets

Noodermarkt op Zaterdag (Northern Market on Saturday) ★★
The Noorderkerk (North Church) was built in 1623, the final masterpiece of Hendrik de Keyser (p. 25). The square surrounding the church is the site of a sprawling flea market on Saturday (and a slightly smaller one on Monday), where stalls are a mixed bag of decent paintings, a few antiques, handmade jewelry, rugs, and old books at rock-bottom prices. Everything starts to close up around 2pm so get there at 9am to snap up some great vintage finds. The Boerenmarkt (see below) is adjacent. Noordermarkt. www.noordermarkt-amsterdam.nl.

Waterlooplein Flea Market ★   The big daddy of Amsterdam street markets has around 300 stands flogging anything and everything from rubbishy oil paintings to jugglers' balls by way of knock-off DVDs, beat-up army jackets, and dainty ethnic jewelry. You can still find genuine treasures under all the second-hand junk but you have to look hard; be prepared to bargain, but accept that Dutch speakers will probably get a better deal. Whether you turn up that vintage Burberry trench or not, Waterlooplein makes for a great hour or two rummaging around in what is effectively other people's castoffs. It's open Monday through Saturday 9:30am to 6pm. Waterlooplein. www.waterlooplein.amsterdam.

Flowers

A.P. Bloemen ★★   Creating artful arrangements of bright blooms inspired by the Golden Age, this award-winning floral studio is located in the historic Spiegelkwartier among a bevy of antique shops and galleries. Kerkstraat 151a. www.apbloem.nl. ℂ **020/223-1616.**

Gerda's Bloemen ★★★   This enticing flower shop in the center of Amsterdam has a regular gig creating all the flower arrangements for the Grachtenfestival (see p. 41). Every day there's a fresh selection of riotously colored blooms for sale in the stylish store, and a delivery service spans the city. Runstraat 16. www.gerdasbloemen.nl. ℂ **020/624-2912.**

Food Markets

Albert Cuypmarkt ★★★   Amsterdam's biggest street market stretches for 1km (½ mile) and takes place Monday through to Saturday from 9am to 5pm. Although it is fast becoming a tourist attraction in its own right, the market still functions as the daily food market for De Pijp residents. Reflecting the multi-ethnic nature of the district, everything is on sale here from raw herring to sweet baklava pastries and rice noodles. It's also the place to stock up on cheery patterned sarongs, flip-flops, daft headgear, and kitchen mops. Albert Cuypstraat btwn. Ferdinand Bolstraat and Van Woustraat. www.albertcuypmarkt.amsterdam.

Boerenmarkt (Farmers Market) ★   Amsterdam's premier organic market is known locally as **the Bio** and runs alongside Saturday's flea market on Noordermarkt. As it has a captive audience of middle-class shoppers from genteel Jordaan, the market's quality produce has proved a great hit and, despite the high prices, it is fast expanding. This is the spot for you if you're after an al fresco picnic lunch; search out delicious organic breads, homemade salads, luscious fresh fruit and vegetables, salamis, and cheeses, then scarf down the lot on a tranquil Jordaan canal bank. Open Saturday 9am to 4pm. Noordermarkt. www.boerenmarktamsterdam.nl.

Gifts

Condomerie ★   The world's first condom shop is cleverly sited on the edge of the Red Light District for those little emergencies in life. Even though it's notorious the world over, the store is surprisingly small, but it packs in all manner of protection in numerous flavors, patterns, and shapes from common brands to flashing or sparkly oddities as well as a variety of other sex aids. Warmoesstraat 141. www.condomerie.com. ✆ **020/627-4174.**

Robins Hood ★★★ This sweet little concept store tucked in the Jordaan sells a finely curated mix of quirky, mostly Dutch-designed items, including edgy candlestick holders from van tjalle & jasper and adorable handcrafted ceramic Amsterdam houses and stroopwafel coaster sets by Kesemy Design. Wood cutting boards in the shape of gabled canal houses and bicycle-printed objects—from tote bags to vases to scarves—are scattered among vintage teak shelving. Tweede Tuindwarsstraat 7. www.robinshood.nl. ✆ **020/363-7486.**

Smokiana ★★ Like a relic of a bygone age, this odd little store underneath the bizarrely compelling and informative Amsterdam Pipe Museum (p. 95) offers tobacco in a multitude of flavors, snuff, and smoking memorabilia as well as an enormous selection of wooden and clay pipes from across the world. An anachronism in an era where smokers are virtually alienated from society, the store carries on regardless of popular opinion. Prinsengracht 488. www.pipeshop.nl. ✆ **020/421-1779.**

Tony's Chocolonely Super Store ★★ Easily recognizable by their pop-art style wrappers, these beloved local chocolate bars can be found on store shelves all around the Netherlands, but a visit to the newly opened shop in the historic Beurs van Berlage is a real treat. Pull the lever on the towering vending machine to dispense the bar of your choice, from caramel sea salt to pretzel toffee to pecan coconut, or create your own flavor and wrapper design using the in-store iPad. Limited-edition varieties of the Fair Trade chocolate bars are also available, along with gift boxes and Tony's-branded Tees and tote bags. There is a second location at Pazzanistraat 1 in Westergasfabriek. Oudebrugsteeg 15. www.tonyschocolonely.com. ✆ **020/205-1200.**

Jewelry

Gassan Diamonds ★★★ An international company of some repute, Gassan's jewelry stores have spread into airports across the world, but their HQ is still based in the remarkable Amsterdam School building designed by J.N. Meyer in 1897, overlooking the Oudeschans canal. It is here that the founder of Gassan first learned to cut diamonds; free, guided tours of the factory are available daily and incorporate a visit to the onsite boutique, where whopping great precious stones are sold at whopping great prices. There are multiple stores in Amsterdam: one on PC Hooftstraat, another at Rokin 1–5 in the Old Center, plus three more out at Schiphol airport. Considering the company's size and standing, it is one of the better options to head for if you are thinking of investing in gemstones. Nieuwe Uilenburgerstraat 173–175. www. gassan.com. ✆ **020/622-5333.**

Kids

Het Muizenhuis (The Mouse Mansion) ★★ "The Mouse Mansion" is a hit children's book series created by Dutch author Karina Schaapman that tells the adventures of two mice best friends, Sam and Julia, who live together in an elaborately crafted dollhouse. Their tales come to life in this charming shop in the Jordaan, which displays intricate, handcrafted Mouse Mansion sets—delightful even if you're not familiar with the stories. It also sells all manner of Mouse Mansion items, from Sam and Julia dolls to postcards to the books (translated into 27 languages). You can also peek into the on-site studio to see the creators hard at work. Eerste Tuindwarsstraat 1HS. www.themouse mansion.com.

Tinkerbell ★★★ *The* place in Amsterdam to purchase traditional wooden toys, puzzles, and gentle learning tools for kids 9 and under. Located in the exclusive Spiegelkwartier among the antiques shops, there's a refreshing lack of plastic in favor of quality and sustainability. Best sellers include cuddly teddy bears, model farm animals, books, and animal glove puppets. Spiegelgracht 10. www.tinkerbelltoys.nl. ✆ **020/625-8830.**

Malls

Magna Plaza ★★ Housed in the city's former main post office, which dates back to 1899, this elegant mall features an attractive, colonnaded, and arcaded interior. Arranged around three levels under a soaring vaulted roof, the 16 mid-range stores include the gleaming crystal animals of Swarovski and the hip Dutch fashion chain Sissy Boy as well as Lacoste and America Today. A new food court opened in 2019 on the second level with around 15 international food stalls plus several bars. Nieuwezijds Voorburgwal 182. www.magnaplaza.nl.

Shoes

United Nude ★★ On the outer reaches of the city center, this wackily designed boutique is owned by avant-garde designer Rem Koolhaas, who has pushed boundaries in shoe design in the same way that his uncle of the same name storms forward with his architecture. A collaboration with Iranian-English architect Zaha Hadid produced a series of gravity-defying boots, but more practical and wearable styles include wedge sandals and neon-colored mules. Molsteeg 10. www.unitednude.com. ✆ **020/626-0010.**

ENTERTAINMENT & NIGHTLIFE

The Performing Arts

Amsterdam's top orchestra—indeed, one of the world's top orchestras—is the renowned **Royal Concertgebouw Orchestra** (www.concertgebouworkest.nl), whose home is the **Concertgebouw ★★★**, Concertgebouwplein 10 (www.concertgebouw.nl; ✆ **0900/671-8345;**), which first opened its doors in 1888 and still is touted as one of the most acoustically perfect concert halls in

Soft Drugs Tolerance

Amsterdam's reputation as a party town is due in part to its tolerance toward soft drugs. But in fact the practice is technically illegal. Whereas it's fine to carry 5 grams (⅙ oz.) for personal use, it's not fine to buy dope anywhere other than in a **coffee shop.** These are licensed and controlled venues where you can purchase marijuana or hashish, and can sit and smoke all day if you want to. Around 175 coffee shops still exist in Amsterdam, most concentrated around the Red Light District; **The Bulldog** at Oudezijds Voorburgwal 90 is the best known. Many coffee shops have been closed down since 2010 as civic leaders have tried to clean up the city's act. There was even talk back in 2012 of introducing an ID system for coffee shop users that would have banned overseas tourists from utilizing them, but this was vetoed as financially unviable for the city. However, it is still illegal to smoke dope in the streets, to buy drugs in the streets, and to buy drugs at all if you are under 18. And don't be tempted to take any drugs out of the country with you.

Europe. The Netherlands Philharmonic Orchestra and the Netherlands Chamber Orchestra are also based here, and both have the same contact details (www.orkest.nl; ℂ **020/521-7500**). World-class orchestras and soloists appear in the hallowed Grote Zaal (Great Hall), chamber and solo recitals are given in the smaller Kleine Zaal (Little Hall). Tickets cost 25€ to 100€. The main concert season is September to mid-June. A mixed-bag of free concerts are held at the Concertgebouw every Wednesday at 12:30pm except in July and August.

At the other end of the musical spectrum, lovers of avant-garde and experimental music should head to the **Muziekgebouw aan 't IJ,** Piet Heinkade 1 (www.muziekgebouw.nl; ℂ **020/788-2000**), which opened in 2005 on the ever-expanding IJ waterfront east of Centraal Station. It's the hub of modern and old jazz, electronic, and non-Western music in Amsterdam, as well as small-scale musical theater, opera, and dance. The waterside terrace of the cafe-restaurant is one of the most idyllic in town. Tickets are 12.50€ to 39€. Right next door is the Bimhuis, Piet Heinkade 3 (www.bimhuis.com; ℂ **020/788-2188**), Amsterdam's much-loved improvisational jazz and blues club, where ticket prices range from 15€ to 33€.

The **Dutch National Opera** (www.operaballet.nl) is one of the leading companies in Europe. They perform at the **Dutch National Opera & Ballet,** Waterlooplein 22 (www.operaballet.nl; ℂ **020/625-5455**). The box office is at Amstel 3, and the theater is also home to the **Dutch National Ballet** (www.operaballet.nl), which offers both classical ballet repertoire and contemporary works. The **Netherlands Dance Theater** (www.ndt.nl), known for its contemporary repertoire, also stages productions here, although its home is in The Hague. Most performances begin at 8:15pm and tickets cost between 17€ and 186€, depending on the program.

For last-minute admission to a wide variety of theater and dance performances as well as concerts, visit the website for **Last Minute Ticketshop** (www.lastminuteticketshop.nl), which sells half-price tickets for same-day performances after 10am every morning. There's a nominal booking charge of 2.50€ for each ticket. Although the website is only in Dutch, the Visitor Information Center at Stationsplein 10 can assist with translation. However, you will have to purchase tickets directly through the site.

Theater

Internationaal Theater Amsterdam ★★ The Internationaal Theater Amsterdam (ITA) stages mainstream Dutch productions inside a grand neo-Renaissance building, formerly known as the Stadsschouwburg, on Leidseplein. There are two theaters here: one is the historic 900-seat Great Hall; the other is a modern 500-seat New Hall. Though productions are almost always in Dutch, English subtitles are often provided a Thursday performances. Opera and ballet performances are occasionally staged here, as are the occasional classic and modern plays in English. Ticket prices vary according to production, but average between 10€ and 50€. Leidseplein 26. www.ita.nl. ℗ **020/624-2311.**

Royal Theatre Carré ★★★ A lovely old theater that was once Amsterdam's circus arena; these days a circus performs here only over Christmas. The theater hosts a few English-language productions of opera, contemporary dance, and ballet, as well as best-selling big-name shows such as "The Book of Mormon." International acts (Glen Hansard, Bryan Ferry) also perform here from time to time. Amstel 115–125. www.carre.nl. ℗ **0900/252-5255.** Tickets 20€–140€.

Comedy Theater

Boom Chicago ★ Amsterdam's foremost comedy theater, set in a century-old former cinema in the Jordaan, brings delightful English-language improvisational comedy to the city. The partly scripted, partly improvised humor takes potshots at life in Amsterdam, politics, tourists, and any other available target. There's a ginormous bar and the audience sits at candlelit tables during the show. Tickets are 12.50€ to 35€. The box office is open daily from 4pm until show time, with doors opening at 8pm. Rosengracht 117. www.boomchicago.nl. ℗ **020/217-0400.**

Bars & Pubs

Brouwerij 't IJ ★★ The biggest draw of this brewery and pub, set on the eastern fringes of the city, is the chance to drink next to Amsterdam proper's only surviving windmill. But the beer is pretty fine, too; the microbrewery's craft beers range from bright blondes to uber-hoppy IPAs to sweet-and-smoky double bocks. Most are organic and unfiltered and pair well with the hearty meat and cheese plates on offer. Line up for your beer and if it's pleasant, enjoy it out on the sprawling patio, in the shadow of the Netherlands' tallest windmill. Funenkade 7. www.brouwerijhetij.nl. ℗ **020/261-9800.**

Bubbles & Wines ★★ An oh-so-sophisticated champagne and wine bar in the Old Center makes a little oasis of hushed red decor and subdued lighting among the chaos of the city's tourist heartland. Along with the extensive and reasonably well-priced selection of new and old world wines, there are champagnes sold by the glass. Some of the most delicious tapas bites in the city are served as accompaniment to the wines, but with prices starting at 23€ for a tiny dollop of caviar, you'd be better off sticking to the delicious jamon Iberico or Wagyu beef salami. Nes 37. www.bubblesandwines.com. ✆ **020/422-3318.**

Café Pollux ★★ A real treasure just a short walk from Centraal Station, primarily due to the charismatic and slightly bonkers owner Frits and his enigmatically smiling wife. It has a garish scarlet interior reminiscent of an old-fashioned American diner on acid, and a simple menu of Dutch favorites like *bitterballen* and croquettes is served all day. Come evening, there is often live music—but if not, you can fall back on the well-stocked jukebox and dance around the stripper's pole. It's often open very late, dependent on the mood of Frits. Prins Hendrikkade 121. www.cafepollux.com. ✆ **020/624-9521.**

De Drie Fleschjes ★★★ There's sawdust on the floor and wooden barrels line the walls in this traditional *proeflokaal* (tasting room), which is a real find and a welcome escape from the Red Light District hinterland. De Drie Fleschjes is run by informed and relaxed bartenders who are only too pleased to pass on their secrets for sampling *jenever* (a ginlike liqueur) in wholesome, old-fashioned surroundings. Although one or two tourists may find their way in here, most of your fellow drinkers will be Dutch. Gravenstraat 18. www. dedriefleschjes.nl. ✆ **020/624-8443.**

Glouglou ★★★ Set on the edge of the hip De Pijp neighborhood, this corner wine bar pioneered the natural wine movement in the Netherlands when it opened in 2015. It gets its name from the French term for glug glug, and indeed, that's exactly what you'll do here, thanks to an incredibly well-curated selection of unfiltered wines, mostly hailing from France, with around 40 available by the glass. Be sure to accompany your *vin naturel* with a generous charcuterie and cheese plate. Inside is all warm wood and cozy tables, but on sunny days, the terrace can't be beat. Tweede van der Helststraat 3. www. glouglou.nl. ✆ **020/233-8642.**

Vesper ★★★ One of a new breed of super-smooth cocktail bars with some wacky concoctions, Vesper is widely regarded as employing the coolest mixologists in Amsterdam. In Jordaan, it's one step beyond the usual fare of mojitos and gin slings as the bartenders go off piste to create new wonders in a cocktail glass. The little wooden bar is also the original home of the alcoholic high tea, which puts a pleasant new slant on scones with clotted cream. Vinkenstraat 57. www.vesperbar.nl. ✆ **020/846-4458.**

Dance Clubs & Live Music

De School ★ Home to the city's only round-the-clock nightclub, De School is an entertainment complex set in a repurposed school building in Amsterdam West. It draws a young, trendy crowd, with alternative music concerts and DJs spinning house music until dawn. If hardcore clubbing isn't your thing, there's a buzzy scene happening most evenings in the venue's restaurant, bar, and out on the spacious terrace in the courtyard garden. Jan van Breemenstraat 1. www.deschoolamsterdam.nl. © **020/737-3197.** Club admission 9€–16€.

Paradiso ★★   An Amsterdam institution, Paradiso is based in a former church that has converted well into a majestic, multi-purpose club with lofty ceilings and high balconies encircling the dance floor. Big-name DJs and musical theme nights draw dance fans at the weekend, and in recent times Arcade Fire, Robbie Williams, and Adele have all played here. Weteringschans 6–8. www.paradiso.nl. © **020/626-4521.** Admission 15€–25€.

Vondelpark Openluchttheater (Open Air Theater) ★★★   Summer is festival and party time in Amsterdam, and June through August see alfresco fun kick off in the Vondelpark with a series of concerts at the moon-shaped, open-air stage. There are Sunday afternoon jazz sessions plus a program of pop, rock, Latin, classical music, and stand up as well as special shows for kids. Best of all everything is free, although a small donation of around a euro is requested. Bring a picnic or eat at Vondelpark before the concert starts. Vondelpark. www.openluchttheater.nl. © **020/428-3360.** Free admission.

WesterUnie ★★   Secreted away in the Westergasfabriek cultural complex west of Centraal Station, WesterUnie is a venue of three parts. By day it's an industrial-chic, cavernous bar and cafe with a suntrap terrace, but at night it morphs into either a concert hall or a heavy-duty music club that gets packed with fans of hip-hop, garage, and pretty much anything danceable. Numerous DJ parties are held here over summer, when the action goes on until the wee, wee hours; it's the go-to club of choice for the post, post-party crowd. Westergasfabriek, Klönneplein 4–6. www.westerunie.nl. © **020/684-8496.** Admission free–75€.

Gay & Lesbian

Amsterdam is an extremely LGBTI-friendly city, with bars sporting rainbow flags in just about every neighborhood. There are several quintessentially gay areas, most notably the nightlife districts in and around **Reguliersdwarsstraat** and in **Zeedijk** and **Warmoesstraat** at the edge of the Red Light District. For

---

Amsterdam Gay Pride

The summer's biggest street party is the riotous Amsterdam Gay Pride, which normally takes place the last week of July. A celebration of the open-hearted, welcoming, and tolerant culture of the Netherlands, Pride kicks off with a canal parade of lavishly decorated barges around the Canal Ring and the week that follows is a non-stop round of street parties, concerts, and drag queen Olympics. The Amsterdam Gay Pride program is available on the website (www.amsterdamgaypride.org).

a good overview, including information on gay nightlife, gay-friendly hotels, and local gay organizations, visit **Pink Point** (Westermarkt; www.pinkpoint. nl; © **020/428-1070**), the city's official LGBTI information kiosk. Located on the Keizersgracht canal near Westerkerk, it's open Monday to Saturday from 10am to 6pm and Sunday from noon to 6pm.

Saarein ★★   A happy-go-lucky, essentially lesbian environment that is open to all comers, straight, bi, or gay, Saarein is typical of the Jordaan's brown cafes (p. 79) in that the bar staff and clientele are cheery, welcoming, and happy to talk. With a decent selection of draught and bottled beers, live music, DJs, and one of the few pool tables in the Jordaan, the bar becomes the center of much of the action during Amsterdam Gay Pride. Elandsstraat 119. www.saarein2.nl. © **020/623-4901.**

SoHo Amsterdam ★   The city's quintessential gay venue is a typical pub during the week, but hits party time at the weekend. Nothing really gets going until after 11pm, and there are DJ nights and themed parties right in the heart of Amsterdam's gay area in the Old Center. Reguliersdwarsstraat 36. www.soho-amsterdam.com.

SIDE TRIPS FROM AMSTERDAM

The Netherlands may start with Amsterdam, but it certainly doesn't end there. This crowded little country has much more up its sleeve, from the stately pleasures of genteel Hague, which is after all the country's political capital, to the laid-back charm of Haarlem. You can step back in time to visit a Holland almost forgotten at the open-air museums of Zuiderzee and Zaanse Schans, or look to the future among the gritty, urban architecture of Rotterdam. There are chart-topping art museums to discover in virtually every city, beaches to stroll in Scheveningen, and blazes of color to admire in the bulb fields of Lisse.

5

Most of the side trips suggested below can be achieved as a day out from Amsterdam; however, if you really want to get a feel for the ultra-modern vibe of Rotterdam or the provincial gentility of The Hague, then a stay of at least 1 night is recommended, so a couple of eating and sleeping options have been included in both cities. You might choose to spend an entire day among the flower displays at Keukenhof (only open between March and May) but others may prefer to see iconic Holland in a day, combining Keukenhof with a visit to the exceptional Frans Hals Museum in Haarlem. Likewise, a jaunt to the pottery factory at Delft or the botanical gardens at Leiden can easily be appended to a stay in either The Hague or Rotterdam.

HAARLEM

18km (11 miles) W of Amsterdam

Haarlem is the little sister of Amsterdam; it's thoroughly provincial, prosperous, and gets along just fine without the big-city hassles of Amsterdam, which is only a 15-minute train commute away. The micro-city (pop. 150,000) was founded around the 10th century, so technically it is older than Amsterdam, but has a similar 17th-century ambience. You can easily get around this quaint, quiet center of music and art—it's home to one of Holland's premier art museums—on foot.

Being so close to Amsterdam, there's no need to make an overnight stopover in Haarlem, but there is a scattering of classy

restaurants to choose from around the tangle of pedestrianized streets in the old city center. Options include **Dijkers** (Warmoesstraat 5–7; www.restaurant dijkers.nl; ✆ **023/551-1564**) serving a casual menu of salads and *flammkuchen* (Alsatian pizza) in the chic shopping streets south of the Grote Markt; **Grand Café Xo** (Grote Markt 8; www.xo-haarlem.nl; ✆ **023/551-1350**), a great burger spot near the tourist office; or **Ratatouille Food & Wine** (Spaarne 96; www.ratatouillefoodandwine.nl; ✆ **023/542-7270**) for Michelin-starred French cuisine with a marvelous riverfront locale.

Essentials

GETTING THERE   **Trains** for Haarlem depart at least every half hour from Amsterdam Centraal Station; the ride takes 15 minutes. A round-trip ticket is 9€. For more details, visit **www.ns.nl**.

By **car** from Amsterdam, take N200/A200 west; parking is around 3€ an hour.

VISITOR INFORMATION   **VVV Haarlem,** Grote Markt, 2; (www.haarlem marketing.nl; ✆ **023/531-7325**), is housed in the Stadhuis, one of the city's oldest buildings. The office is open April through September Monday to Friday from 9:30am to 5:30pm, Saturday 9:30am to 5pm, and Sunday noon to 4pm; October through March Monday 1 to 5:30pm, Tuesday to Friday 9:30am to 5:30pm, and Saturday 10am to 5pm.

Exploring Haarlem

Granted municipal status by Count Willem II of Holland in 1245, this is where Frans Hals, Jacob van Ruisdael, and Pieter Saenredam were living and painting their famous portraits, landscapes, and church interiors at the same time that Rembrandt was working in Amsterdam.

The old center of Haarlem is a 10-minute walk from the graceful Art Nouveau rail station dating from 1908, most of it via pedestrian-only shopping streets. First-time visitors generally head straight for the **Grote Markt ★★★**, the beautiful central market square adjacent to **Sint-Bavokerk** (p. 132). The monumental buildings around the tree-lined square date from the 15th to the 19th centuries and are a microcosm of the development of Dutch architecture. The glorious 15th-century **Stadhuis (Town Hall),** Grote Markt 2 (✆ **023/511-5115**), has an ornate bell tower, gables, and elaborate balconies. It was once a hunting lodge of the Counts of Holland and is now—rather prosaically—the home of the tourist information office. And while it can't compete with the glorious canals of Amsterdam, Haarlem has lovely waterways snaking through the historic city. **Smidtje Canal Cruises,** Spaarne 11a (www.smidtje canalcruises.nl; ✆ 02/353-57-723) offers daily 50-minute tours departing every hour from 11am to 4pm (till 4:30pm Friday to Sunday) from in front of the Teyler Museum. The cost is 14€ for adults, 7€ for children 4 to 12.

Frans Hals Museum ★★★ MUSEUM   The finest attraction in Haarlem, this may be a high point of your trip to Holland. The museum is housed in the elegant former Oudemannenhuis, a home for retired gentlemen dating from 1608 during the Dutch Golden Age. Consequently, the wonderful paintings by

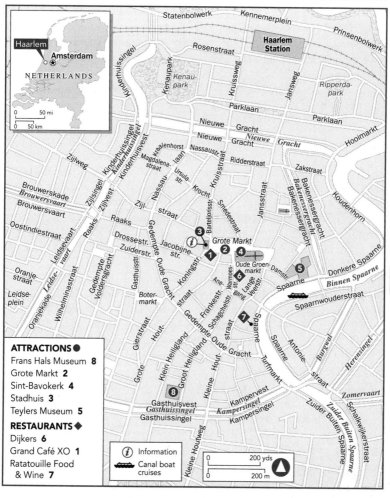

ATTRACTIONS ●
Frans Hals Museum **8**
Grote Markt **2**
Sint-Bavokerk **4**
Stadhuis **3**
Teylers Museum **5**

RESTAURANTS ◆
Dijkers **6**
Grand Café XO **1**
Ratatouille Food
& Wine **7**

ⓘ Information
🚢 Canal boat cruises

Frans Hals (1580–1686), and other masters of the Haarlem School, hang in a setting reminiscent of the 17th-century houses they were intended to adorn. The dynamic permanent exhibition, "The Hals Phenomenon," provides an informative introduction to this great artist, who earned a living by painting portraits of members of the local guilds.

Five of his civic-guard pictures are on display in the museum, lining the walls of the former refectory, which is set up as for a Golden Age banquet, with a long wooden table piled high for a feast. This is where Hals's consummate "A Banquet of the Officers of the Civic Guard of St. George" (1616) is hung. Other showcase pieces include landscapes by Jacob van Ruisdael,

Gerrit Berckheyde's famous "Grote Markt" (1696), and the disturbing "The Monk and the Beguine" (1591) by Cornelisz van Haarlem, which depicts a monk tweaking a nun's bare breast (it has been interpreted variously as a satire on lecherous behavior in cloisters, or as being symbolic of purity and virginity). Among other highlights are a superb wooden replica of a merchant's town house from around 1750 and fine collections of antiques, silver, porcelain, and clocks.

Groot Heiligland 62. www.franshalsmuseum.nl. ✆ **023/511-5775.** Admission 16€ adults, 8€ students 19–24, free for ages 18 and under. Tues–Sat 11am–5pm, Sun noon–5pm. Closed Jan 1, Apr 27, and Dec 25.

Sint-Bavokerk (St. Bavo's Church) ★★ CHURCH   The tall spire of St. Bavo's Church, also known as the Grote Kerk (Great Church), looms over the central pedestrianized streets like a beacon; once in the Grote Markt, it's revealed in all its massive splendor. The colossal late-Gothic church was begun in 1445 under the direction of Antwerp's city architect, Evert Spoorwater. It was complete by 1520 and has a pleasing unity of structure and proportion. The interior is light and airy, with whitewashed walls and sandstone pillars. Its elegant wooden tower is covered with lead sheets and adorned with gilt spheres.

The Grote Kerk was so popular as a subject with 16th- and 17th-century Dutch painters that it immediately feels familiar; Gerrit Berckheyde and Pieter Saenredam repeatedly featured it in their work. And indeed Haarlem's greatest artist, Frans Hals, was buried under a simple stone slab near the choir stalls in 1666. The famous Christian Müller organ, built in 1738, is considered one of the best in Europe; when the precocious prodigy Mozart played this magnificent instrument in 1766 at just 10 years old, he is said to have shouted for joy. Handel, Mendelssohn, Schubert, and Liszt also visited Haarlem to play the organ. Free organ concerts are held at 8:15pm every Tuesday and occasional Thursdays at 4pm between mid-May and mid-October, and there's a program of services, festivals, and concerts running throughout the summer; check the website for details.

Grote Markt 22. www.bavo.nl. ✆ **023/553-2040.** Admission 2.50€ adults, 1.25€ ages 12–16, free 11 and under. Mon–Sat 10am–5pm, July and Aug also open Sun 12–5pm.

Teylers Museum ★ MUSEUM   Strange but oddly compelling for its very eccentricity, this museum was the very first to open in the Netherlands, in 1784. It's named after the 18th-century merchant Pieter Teyler van der Hulst, who willed his entire fortune to the advancement of art and science. You'll find a diverse collection in the galleried display rooms: drawings by Michelangelo, Raphael, and Rembrandt (which are shown in rotation); fossils, minerals, and skeletons; instruments of physics; and an odd assortment of wacky inventions plus some ancient globes showing Holland at the apex of the world.

Spaarne 16. www.teylersmuseum.eu. ✆ **023/531-9010.** Admission 14€ adults, 2€ ages 6–17, free 5 and under. Tues–Fri 10am–5pm, Sat–Sun 11am–5pm. Closed Jan 1 and Dec 25.

VOLENDAM & MARKEN ★

Marken: 16km (10 miles) NE of Amsterdam; Volendam: 18km (12 miles) NE of Amsterdam

Volendam and Marken are in the area north of Amsterdam labeled the "Waterland" and have long been combined on bus-tour itineraries from Amsterdam as
a kind of pre-packaged "clogs, cheese, and windmills" day trip. Many people
even attach that damning label "tourist trap" to these two lakeside communities. We won't lie: they ARE touristy in the summer months, but you're a
tourist, for heaven's sake. It's still possible to have a delightful day in the
bracing air there, and you might even see a few residents in traditional dress.

Essentials

GETTING THERE **R-Net** (www.rnet.nl) and **EBS** (www.ebs-ov.nl) buses
depart every 15 to 30 minutes from the upper bus terminal behind Amsterdam
Centraal Station. No. 316 goes to Volendam; to get to Marken, you will have
to go back toward Amsterdam and change in Broek to the no. 315 to Marken.
You can also take the no. 315 bus to Marken from Amsterdam's Station
Noord. The ride to Volendam takes 35 minutes and to Marken 45 minutes. The
round-trip bus fare is 10€ for the all-day "Waterland Ticket."

By **car,** go north on N247. When driving to Marken, which was once
an island, you cross a 3km (2-mile) causeway from the quiet backwater
Monnickendam. Leave your car in a parking lot outside the main village
before walking through the narrow streets to the harbor. Operating year-
round, the **passenger-and-bike ferry** *Marken Express* (www.markenexpress.
nl; ✆ **0299/363-331**) sails every 45 minutes daily 10:30am to 7:15pm between
Volendam and Marken. The ride takes 30 minutes, and fares are 13.50€ round-
trip and 8.75€ one-way for adults, 6.75€ round-trip and 4.38€ one-way for
children 4 to 11, and free 3 and under; bicycles are carried for an additional
1.75€ one-way.

VISITOR INFORMATION **VVV Volendam,** Zeestraat 37 (www.vvv-
volendam.nl; ✆ **0299/363-747**), is just off Julianaweg in the heart of town.
The office is open mid-April to October Monday to Saturday 10am to 5pm,
and Sunday 11am to 3pm; and November to mid-April Monday to Saturday
11am to 4pm.

WHAT TO SEE & DO

A small, Catholic town on the mainland, **Volendam** lost most of its fishing
industry to the enclosure of the Zuiderzee. It now makes its living from tourism, which means plenty of souvenir and gift stores. Lots of people come to
pig out on the town's near-legendary *gerookte paling* (smoked eel) and to visit
such attractions as the fish auction, diamond cutter, and clog maker. Still,
Volendam's boat-filled harbor, tiny streets, and traditional houses have an
undeniable charm. If you must have a snapshot of yourself in the traditional
Dutch costume—local women wear white caps with wings—this is the place
to do it.

Smaller and less touristy than Volendam, **Marken** was a historically Protestant insular island until a narrow causeway connected it to the mainland in 1957. It is rural, with clusters of quaint farmhouses dotted along the waterfront. Half of Marken village is called Havenbuurt and consists of green-and-white houses on stilts grouped around a tiny harbor. Even if you don't plan on integrating traditional Dutch clogs into your wardrobe, the **Wooden Shoe Factory,** Kets 52 (https://thisisnl.com; © **0299/601-250**) puts on an interesting free clog-making demonstration; it also sells a huge variety of the shoe in every color. Four old smokehouses in the other half of the village, Kerkbuurt, serve as the **Museum Marken,** Kerkbuurt 44–47 (www.markermuseum.nl; © **0299/601-904**), which displays traditional furnishings and costumes. The museum is open mid-March to September Monday to Saturday 10am to 5pm and Sunday 12 to 4pm, and October 11am to 4pm and Sunday 12 to 4pm. Admission is 3€ for adults, 1.50€ for children 5 to 12, and free 4 and under.

Marken does not go overboard for its tourists. It merely feeds and waters them and allows them to wander its pretty streets gawking at the locals as they go about their daily routines of hanging out laundry, washing windows, and shopping for groceries. Some residents occasionally wear traditional dress—for women, caps with ribbons and black aprons over striped petticoats—as much to preserve the custom as for you.

ZAANSE SCHANS

16km (10 miles) NW of Amsterdam

Incorporated into the town of Zaandam on the east bank of the River Zaan, Zaanse Schans is an historic area dedicated to replicating 17th- and 18th-century village life in northern Holland. This living, working slice of history is made up of houses, windmills, and workshops that were moved to the 8-hectare (20-acre) site when industrialization leveled their original locations.

The Zaanstreek (Zaan District) was historically a shipbuilding area and its backstory is told in the contemporary, glass-and-brick **Zaans Museum & Verkade Pavilion** ★, Schansend 7 (www.zaansmuseum.nl; © **075/681-0000**), at the entrance to the site. The museum is open April to September daily 9am to 5pm and October to March daily 10am to 5pm (closed Jan 1 and Dec 25). Admission is 12€ adult, 6€ children aged 4 to 17. Pick up a brochure here to identify all the buildings outside and enjoy a self-guided tour of the area.

At one time, the Zaanstreek had more than 600 windmills; of those only 15 have survived. You'll discover ten here, including a sawmill, and mills specializing in producing paint, vegetable oil, and Zaanse mustard, all prettily located on the Zaan riverside.

Tucked among the gabled wooden houses are several excellent museums exhibiting traditional crafts, including the **Bakkerijmuseum (Bakery Museum)** ★★, Zeilenmakerspad 4, where cookies and candy are made to old recipes, and the **Nederlandse Uurwerk (Dutch Clock) Museum** ★★,

HOLLAND'S TRADITIONAL cheese markets

The cheese markets that were once a weekly occasion in many Holland towns are now largely defunct with the exception of the colorful summertime happenings in Edam and Alkmaar.

Just 18km (11 miles) northeast of Amsterdam and a fraction north of Volendam, **Edam** (pronounced Ay-dam) was a whaling port during the 17th-century Golden Age and today is a pretty town centered around its canals. It's quiet enough most of the year but Edam's major claim to fame is its world-renowned Edammer cheese. If you're there in summer, time your visit to coincide with the historic *kaasmarkt* (cheese market; www. kaasmarktedam.nl), which only takes place on Wednesdays in July and August, from 10:30am to 12:30pm on Kaasmarkt. Yes, it's a tourist attraction, but nevertheless it's a wonderfully colorful event, taking place with much ringing of church bells, stirring music from local bands, hand clapping, and dramatic "bargaining" by the straw-boater-and-clog-clad cheese carriers. Most of the action takes place outside the gaily frescoed **Kaaswaag (cheese weigh house)**, which dates from 1592 and features cheese-making displays over summer. By the way, don't expect to see the luscious rounds of cheese in its familiar red skin—that's purely for export. In the Netherlands, the Edammer's skin is always canary yellow.

Edam can be reached on **R-Net** (www. rnet.nl) and **EBS** (www.ebs-ov.nl) buses departing every 15 to 30 minutes from the upper bus terminal behind Amsterdam Centraal Station. Nos. 314 and 316 go to Edam. By **car**, go north on N247 via Volendam (p. 133). **Tourist info** is at **VVV Edam** in the Stadhuis (Town Hall), Damplein 1 (www.vvv-edam.nl; ℰ **0299/315-125**), in the center of town. Should you wish to tour a local Edammer cheese factory, this is where you get the details.

Alkmaar is 30km (19 miles) north of Amsterdam and its famous cheese market takes place every Friday morning between April and September, when a torrent of tourists pour in to this handsome, canal-lined town founded in the 10th century. At precisely 10am, the white-uniformed cheese carriers enact an ancient scene in the Waagplein. There's much rushing around with brightly painted wooden cheese hoppers, which are weighed under supervision and brought to the market square to be laid out in rows in front of the ancient **Waaggebouw (weigh house).** Haggling over price and quality is conducted with much hand clapping and good-natured shouting and it's great fun to watch. Get there by 9:30am for the kickoff at 10am, otherwise you won't see a thing thanks to the crowds. If you want to learn more about how Dutch cheese has been made throughout the centuries, there's the small but entertaining **Hollands Kaasmuseum (Dutch Cheese Museum),** in the Waaggebouw, Waagplein 2 (www.kaasmuseum.nl; ℰ **072/511-4284**). April to September it's open Monday to Saturday from 10am to 4pm (Fri 9am–4pm and Sun 1–3:30pm; closed Apr 27), October to March closed Sunday. Admission is 5€ for adults, 2€ for children 4 to 12, and free for 3 and under.

Get to Alkmaar on trains departing every 15 minutes or so from Amsterdam Centraal Station; the ride takes around 40 minutes. A round-trip ticket is 15€. By **car** from Amsterdam, take A8, N246, N203, and A9 north. Tourist information is at the **VVV Alkmaar** at Waagplein 2 (www.vvvalkmaar.nl; ℰ **072/511-4284**).

Kalverringdijk 3, which displays timepieces from the period 1500 to 1900, and also has a functioning workshop. Also worth a peek are the **Klompenmakerij (Clog Maker's Workshop),** a workshop where wooden *klompen* (clogs) are made and sold; and **De Catharina Hoeve Kaasmakerij,** which does likewise with cheese. And for an idea of how a well-heeled Zaan resident lived, visit **Museum Het Noorderhuis,** Kalverringdijk 17, a merchant's house from 1670 containing furnishings, utensils, and traditional costumes.

Most of these mini museums are open April to October daily 11am to 5pm, and November to March Saturday and Sunday 11am to 5pm. Admission varies from free to 10€.

Daily 25-minute **river cruises** on the Zaan River take place aboard **Windmill Cruises** (https://windmillcruises.nl; © **075/3030-020**) and depart every half hour weekdays from noon to 3pm and weekends from 11am to 4pm. Trips are 9.50€ for adults, 5€ for ages 4 to 12.

Trains depart around every 15 minutes from Amsterdam Centraal Station via Zaandam to Zaandijk Zaanse Schans station, from where it's a 1km (⅔-mile) walk, across the Zaan River, to Zaanse Schans. The train ride takes 20 minutes, and a round-trip ticket is 6.60€. Or take **Connexxion bus** no. 391 (www.bus391.nl) from bus platform E at Amsterdam Centraal Station for the 40-minute ride. Fares are 6.50€ one way or 11.50€ for an unlimited day ticket for all buses in the region. By **car** from Amsterdam, take A8 north and then switch to A7/E22 north to exit 2, from where you follow the signs to Zaanse Schans. Parking is 10€ per day.

Zuiderzee Museum at Enkhuizen ★★ MUSEUM   The economy of several coastal towns was devastated when the Afsluitdijk was constructed in 1932, transforming the Zuiderzee into the freshwater IJsselmeer. To commemorate a lifestyle long gone, the Zuiderzee Museum showcases the 19th-century fishing-based industry on which the ports around the former seacoast depended. Split into two sections, the museum features the **Binnenmuseum** ★★, housed in a 17th-century Dutch Renaissance building that once served as warehouses of the Dutch East India Company. Here you'll find a display of the fishing boats that provided an income for the Zuiderzee folk. The open-air **Buitenmuseum** ★★★ stands on the IJsselmeer shore; more than 130 historic buildings—farmhouses, public buildings, stores, a church—were shipped here intact from defunct lakeside communities across northern Holland and furnished in period style. Two bottle-shaped limekilns, a working windmill, a functioning smokehouse, and other structures, pay tribute to the area's industrial heritage, alongside a chandler, an apothecary, a cheese warehouse, and a steam laundry. Just south of the Buitenmuseum is a recreation of Marken's old harbor, with smokehouses for preserving herring and eels standing on the dike, and fishing boats tied up at the dock. Cafes and restaurants are found on site.

Wierdijk 12–22. www.zuiderzeemuseum.nl. © **0228/351-111.** Admission 17€ adults, 11€ ages 4–12, free ages 3 and under, 45€ family. Binnenmuseum: daily 10am–5pm. Buitenmuseum: Apr–Oct daily 10am–5pm. Trains from Amsterdam Centraal Station to Enkhuizen run every 30 min., taking an hour, for 23.40€ round trip. Apr–Oct a free ferry departs every 15 min. from dock next to Enkhuizen station to Buitenmuseum, otherwise it's a 10-min. walk from station. Car parking is 5€/day.

KEUKENHOF & THE BULB FIELDS

35km (22 miles) W of Amsterdam

The heaviest concentration of the tulip bulb fields that contribute millions of euros to the Dutch economy lie in the **Bloemenbollenstreek (Bulb District)** ★, a strip of land 16km (10 miles) long and 6km (4 miles) wide between Haarlem and Leiden. In the spring, it's a frenzied Dutch rite of passage to traipse through this colorful district and view the massed, varicolored regiments of tulips on parade. Every year from around the end of January to late May, the fields are covered at various times with tulips, crocuses, daffodils, narcissi, hyacinths, and lilies.

Viewing the flowers is easy. Just follow all or parts of the circular, sign-posted **Bollenstreek Route** (40km/25 miles) by car or bike—although you could find your way there by the trail of roadside stalls flogging bunches of cut flowers and bulbs. To get to the bulb fields from Amsterdam, drive to Haarlem, then go south on N206 through De Zilk and Noordwijkerhout, or on N208 through Hillegom, Lisse, and Sassenheim. There are also scores of **bus tours** leaving for Keukenhof from all the main cities, including Amsterdam, Rotterdam, and The Hague; **Tours & Tickets** (www.tours-tickets.com; ✆ 020/420-4000) and **Stromma** (www.stromma.com; ✆ 020/217-0501) provide several different Keukenhof tours. Special seasonal buses transport eager-beaver visitors on the direct service no. 858 from Schiphol Airport, and tourists staying over in Leiden can catch bus service no. 854 from Leiden Central train station.

Keukenhof ★★★ GARDEN   Open for barely 2 months between March and May when the flowers are at their peak, Keukenhof is the most-visited attraction in the Netherlands. Every year more than 800,000 flower fans from all across the world flock to more than seven million bulbs explode into life in intricate patterns in gardens that are a scented, visual paradise (such is the rush to get here that buses run directly from the airport). The meandering, 32-hectare (79-acre) estate in the heart of the bulb-producing region is all-too-briefly a riot of tulips and narcissi, daffodils and hyacinths, bluebells, crocuses, lilies, and amaryllis. Swathes of color are seen in greenhouses, beside brooks and shady ponds, along paths, in neat little plots, and helter-skelter on lawns. There's also a boat tour of the neighboring bulb fields; lines are inevitably long. Keukenhof claims to be the greatest flower show on earth, and certainly it is Holland's annual spring gift to the world. The spectacular annual **flower parade** (p. 39) takes

---

Flower Power

During Holland's 17th-century "tulip mania" (p. 139) when trading in bulbs was a lucrative business and prices soared to ridiculous heights, a single tulip bulb could be worth as much as a prestigious Amsterdam canal house, with the garden and coach house thrown in.

place in mid-April. There are four decent cafes on-site where you can grab a quick bite and contemplate your bulb purchases.

Stationsweg 166A, Lisse. www.keukenhof.nl. © **0252/465-555**. Admission 18€ adults, 8€ ages 4–11, free 3 and under. Parking 6€. 3rd week of Mar to 3rd week of May daily 8am–7:30pm.

LEIDEN

36km (22 miles) SW of Amsterdam; 20km (12 miles) NE of The Hague

Stately yet bustling, the old heart of Leiden is classic Dutch, filled with handsome, gabled brick houses along canals spanned by graceful bridges. The Pilgrim Fathers lived here for 11 years before sailing to North America from Delfshaven in Rotterdam. Leiden's proudest moment came in 1574, when it became the only Dutch town to withstand a Spanish siege, although William of Orange *was* forced to flood the land around the city to win that battle. The town is also the birthplace of Rembrandt, the Dutch tulip trade, and the oldest university in the Netherlands (founded in 1575). The 12th-century citadel of De Burcht stands on a mound in the town center between two branches of the Rhine, the Oude and Nieuwe, providing a great view of the surrounding rooftops. And with a choice of 14 museums, covering antiquities, natural history, anatomy, clay pipes, windmills, and coins, Leiden seems perfectly justified in calling itself Holland's *Museumstad* (Museum City).

Essentials

GETTING THERE   Up to eight **trains** per hour run from Amsterdam Centraal Station to Leiden Centraal Station. The ride takes around 35 minutes, and the round-trip fare is 20€. The center of Leiden is a walk of around 1.5km (1 mile) south from the station. For more details, visit **www.ns.nl**. By **car**, take A4/E19.

VISITOR INFORMATION   **Leiden Visitor Centre,** Stationsweg 26 (www.visitleiden.nl; © **071/516-6000**), is just outside the train station. The office is open Monday to Friday 7am to 7pm, Saturday 10am to 4pm, and Sunday 11am to 3pm.

Exploring Leiden

American Pilgrim Museum ★ MUSEUM   This tiny museum is set in a beautifully preserved ca. 1370 house that is Leiden's oldest building. Two authentically recreated rooms reveal what life was like for the Pilgrims who were exiled from England and settled in Leiden in 1609 before eventually founding the Plymouth Colony in 1620. Along with furnishings and artifacts dating from Pilgrim times, there's a fascinating collection of 16th- and 17th-century books, maps, and engravings.

Beschuitsteeg 9. www.leidenamericanpilgrimmuseum.org. © **071/512-2413**. Admission 5€ adults, free children 6 and under. Wed–Sat 1–5pm. Closed Jan 1, Good Friday, Apr 27, Oct 3, Dec 24–26, and Dec 31.

Rembrandt in Leiden

In 1606, the great artist Rembrandt van Rijn was born in Leiden. He later moved to Amsterdam, where he won fame and fortune—and later suffered bankruptcy and obscurity. In his hometown, a **Rembrandt Walk** takes in the site of the house (since demolished) where he was born, the Latin School he attended as a boy, and the first studio where he worked. A booklet outlining the walk route is available from Leiden Visitor Centre for 2.95€.

Hortus Botanicus Leiden (Botanical Garden Leiden) ★★ GARDEN   Leiden's botanical gardens were established by the University of Leiden in 1590 to cultivate tropical trees and plants such as banana plants, ferns, and flesh-eating plants brought back from overseas trading forays. Carolus Clusius, who was the first professor of botany at Leiden University, was also the man responsible for first introducing tulip bulbs into the Netherlands, and in so doing he may have brought about the abrupt end of the Golden Age. Such was their popularity that they quickly became a status symbol among the Dutch aristocracy and the crazy trading in tulip bulbs led to the downfall of the economy in 1637. Today may of the original specimens are still thriving in the Clusiustuin, a garden dedicated to the botanist.

Rapenburg 73 (at Nonnensteeg). www.hortus.leidenuniv.nl. ℂ **071/527-5144.** Admission 8€ adults, 3.50€ ages 4–12. Apr–Oct daily 10am–6pm, Nov–Mar Tues–Sun 10am–4pm. Closed Jan 1, Oct 3, and last week of Dec.

Museum De Lakenhal Leiden ★★ MUSEUM   Located in Leiden's fine cloth hall, dating from 1640, the city's civic museum focuses on a collection of paintings by Dutch artists of the 16th and 17th centuries including Rembrandt and Jan Steen. The masterpiece of the exhibits is the masterly "Last Judgment" triptych by Lucas van Leyden, which was rescued from Leiden's main church, the Pieterskerk, during the Alteration of 1578. In among the guild silverware and decorative arts found in the museum's modern wing, purpose-built in the 1920s, is a bronze cooking pot believed to have belonged to William of Orange himself. The museum was closed for renovations at press time; go to the website to see what its current pricing and hours are.

Oude Singel 32. www.lakenhal.nl. ℂ **071/516-5360.**

Rijksmuseum van Oudheden (National Museum of Antiquities) ★★★ MUSEUM   Quite simply one of the best museums in the Netherlands, so if you're short of time in Leiden, make this your priority for the collection of Egyptian, Near Eastern, Greek, and Roman treasures. Opened in 1818, the showpiece of the museum is the Egyptian Temple of Taffeh, dedicated to Isis, the Egyptian Goddess of Fertility; it was assembled here in 1978. Other highlights include treasures from Dutch Bronze Age graves, statuary from Roman villas, and ancient Greek amphorae. With so much to see,

5

SIDE TRIPS FROM AMSTERDAM | Leiden

139

it's sensible to follow one of the suggested themed routes through the collections.

Rapenburg 28. www.rmo.nl. ℰ **071/516-3163.** Admission 12.50€ adults, 4€ ages 5–17, free 4 and under, 29€ family. Tues–Sun 10am–5pm (during school holidays also Mon 10am–5pm). Closed Jan 1, Apr 27, Oct 3, and Dec 25.

Rijksmuseum Volkenkunde (National Ethnological Museum) ★

MUSEUM   Housed in a grand town house dating from 1837, this enchanting ethnographical museum is founded on a superb collection of thousands of *objets d'art* squirreled together between 1823 and 1830 by German-born Philipp Franz von Siebold, who was the physician at the Dutch trading post on Deshima Island in Nagasaki Bay in Japan. From this beginning, the displays have grown to include intriguing artifacts from across the world, such as Inuit snowshoes, Balinese *gamelans,* and a roomful of Chinese Buddhas. An ever-changing series of temporary exhibits might include anything from rare black-and-white images to interactive displays about world music.

Steenstraat 1. www.volkenkunde.nl. ℰ **071/516-8800.** Admission 15€ adults, 6€ ages 4–18. Tues–Sun 10am–5pm (during school holidays also Mon 10am–5pm). Closed Jan 1, Apr 27, May 5, Oct 3, and Dec 25.

5 GOUDA

40km (25 miles) S of Amsterdam; 25km (16 miles) NE of Rotterdam

Essentials

GETTING THERE   There's frequent train service from Amsterdam to Gouda, with up to six trains an hour (some are direct, while others require a change in Utrecht) and six an hour from Rotterdam. The direct ride from Amsterdam takes 45 minutes, and a round-trip ticket is 25€. From Rotterdam it's around 20 minutes, and fares are 11€ round trip. For more details, visit **www.ns.nl**.

By **car,** the town is just off the A12 expressway from Amsterdam to The Hague or Rotterdam.

VISITOR INFORMATION   VVV Gouda, Markt 35 (https://welcometo gouda.com; ℰ **0182/589-110**), is open mid-March through October daily 10am to 5pm; November through mid-March Wednesday through Sunday 10am to 3pm; and December 23 to January 7 daily 10am to 4pm (closed Christmas and New Year's Day).

Exploring Gouda

Today Gouda (pronounced *Khow*-dah) is famous for its cheese, its summer cheese markets, and its candle festival in mid-December, which sees the Markt and **Stadhuis (Town Hall)** illuminated by flickering candlelight. This handsome town stands on two rivers, which helped it become a wealthy brewing center in the 15th century; the legacy of that is a series of fine public buildings bristling with gables and pinnacles in decorative Gothic style.

Visit on Thursday morning from 10am to 12:30pm between April and August to catch the lively and traditional **Goudse Kaasmarkt (Gouda Cheese Market)** ★. This brings farmers into town driving wagons painted with bright designs and piled high with round cheeses in orange skins; sample them at stalls near the Stadhuis, which is festooned with step gables and red shutters. It is reputed to be Holland's oldest town hall, and parts of its Gothic facade date from 1449.

The foremost reason to visit Gouda is the assembly of outstanding **stained glass windows in Sint-Janskerk** ★★. The church is a step away from Markt and easily identified by its ornate spire peeking above the rooftops. As well as being the longest church in the Netherlands at 23m (76 ft.), this 15th-century Gothic beauty hides some of Europe's loveliest stained-glass windows, considered so beautiful that they were even spared destruction in the Protestant Alteration of 1578. They were donated to the church by a series of rich patrons and number 64 in total, with a total of 2,412 panels depicting biblical scenes and contemporary scenes. To see the contrast between the stained glass of times past and contemporary work, take a peek at the most recent window, no. 28A, commemorating the World War II years in Holland. Sint-Janskerk is located at Achter de Kerk 16 (www.sintjan.com; ℂ **0182/512-684**). Admission is 7.50€ adults, 3.75€ ages 13–17 and 16€ families. It is open March to October Monday to Saturday 9am to 5pm, and November to February Monday to Saturday 10am to 4pm.

Adjacent to Sint-Janskerk, the **Museum Gouda** ★ is housed in the Catharina Gasthuis, a former almshouse built in 1665. It showcases a charming mix of Hague School landscape painting, silver guild relics, altarpieces that survived the Alteration, and original sketches for the stained-glass windows in Sint-Janskerk. You'll find it at Achter de Kerk 14 (www.museumgouda.nl; ℂ **0182/331-000**). Admission is 11€ adults, 4€ ages 5 to 17. The museum is open Tuesday to Sunday 11am to 5pm.

DELFT

55km (34 miles) SW of Amsterdam; 10km (6 miles) SE of The Hague; 14km (9 miles) NW of Rotterdam

Minute Delft is perhaps the prettiest town in all of Holland. The facades of the Renaissance and Gothic houses here reflect age-old beauty, a sense of tranquility pervades the air, and linden trees bend over its gracious canals. Indeed, it's easy to understand why Old Master painter Jan Vermeer chose to spend most of his life surrounded by Delft's gentle charms in the 17th century.

A hefty part of Dutch history is preserved in Delft. William of Orange, who led the Dutch insurrection against Spanish rule, was assassinated in the Prinsenhof and now rests in a magnificent tomb in the Nieuwe Kerk; every member of the Royal House of Oranje-Nassau has since been brought here for burial.

Of course, to many visitors, Delft means only one thing—the prized blue-and-white earthenware still produced by the meticulous methods of yore.

Every piece of genuine Delftware is hand-painted by skilled craftspeople; a trip to Delft really should encompass a visit to a porcelain factory.

Essentials

GETTING THERE There are eight trains an hour to Delft from Amsterdam (all require a transfer in Rotterdam) and up to 10 an hour from Rotterdam. The ride from Amsterdam takes around 1 hour; a round-trip ticket is 27.60€ and there is a supplemental charge of 2.40€ each way on some trains. From Rotterdam, it's 10 minutes and 7€. From The Hague, the train journey is a 15-minute ride that costs 5.20€ round trip. For more details, visit **www.ns.nl**.

By **car,** the town is just off the A13/E19 expressway from The Hague to Rotterdam.

VISITOR INFORMATION Delft's **VVV Delft,** Kerkstraat 3 (www.delft.com; ✆ **015/215-4052**) is located in the center of town near the Nieuwe Kerk. April to September, opening hours are Sunday and Monday 10am to 4pm, Tuesday to Saturday 10am to 5pm; October to March, Sunday and Monday 11am to 3pm, Tuesday to Saturday 10am to 4pm.

Exploring Delft

The best way to absorb Delft's special ambience is by strolling its streets. Around every corner and down every street, you step into scenes that might have been composed for the canvas of a great artist. Supplement your walks with a leisurely tour of the canals via the numerous water taxis that operate during the summer. The town's large main square, the Markt, is a zoo on market day (Thurs), but on quieter days, you get space to see how picturesque it is.

De Koninklijke Porceleyne Fles (Royal Delft) ★★★ WORKSHOP If you love Delftware porcelain, you'll be in heaven at the Royal Delft workshop. A tour of the factory entails a firsthand view of the business of painting porcelain and a visit to the Delft museum, which features antique, multispouted tulip vases. There's also a showroom where factory seconds can be bought at relative bargain prices. And if you thought that Delftware only came in its trademark blue-and-white color scheme, you'll be surprised to see exquisite multicolored patterns. The highlights of any visit are the workshops where you can paint your own porcelain, which is fired, glazed, and ready for pickup (or shipping overseas) in 48 hours. The price quoted for the workshops includes materials but not shipping costs; courses must be reserved at least 24 hours in advance. Your purchases and your creations can both be shipped home directly from the factory.

Rotterdamseweg 196. www.royaldelft.com. ✆ **015/760-0800.** Tour 14€ adults, 8.75€ ages 13–18, free ages 12 and under. Workshops 29–42€ mid-Mar to mid-May daily 9am–6pm; mid-May to Oct daily 9am–5pm; Nov to mid-Mar Mon–Sat 9am–5pm, Sun 12–5pm. Closed Jan 1 and Dec 25–26.

Museum Het Prinsenhof ★★ MUSEUM The Prinsenhof (Prince's Court), on the banks of Delft's oldest canal, Oude Delft, dates from the late

Porcelain from the factories at Delft is beautiful to look at but it doesn't come cheap. It is produced predominantly, but not exclusively, by three Delft-based firms: **De Koninklijke Porceleyne Fles** (see above); **De Delftse Pauw,** Delftweg 133, Rijswijk (www.delftpottery.com; ✆ **015/212-4920**); and **De Candelaer,** Kerkstraat 13 (www.candelaer.nl; ✆ **015/213-1848**). The first two offer tours; those at De Delftse Pauw are free but last just 10 minutes, so for the real deal, head to Royal Delft (see above). At the modest De Candelaer factory, there's a good chance you can catch the artists crafting pieces, though we can't guarantee it.

Genuine Delftware is for sale in specialized stores through the Netherlands (p. 142). Production methods have changed little down the centuries and most of the decorating is still done by hand, which of course accounts for the breathtaking price tags. Some copies of Delftware nearly equal its quality, while most miss the delicacy of the brush strokes, the richness of color, or the sheen of the glazes that make this porcelain so highly prized.

To be sure that you're looking at a *real* Delft item look at the bottom of the piece. De Koninklijke Porceleyne Fles will have a distinctive three-part hallmark: an outline of a small pot, above an initial "J" crossed with a short stroke, above the scripted word DELFT. For De Delftse Pauw, look for three blue stars separated by a drafting compass, above the scripted text D.P. DELFT. And for De Candelaer, there will be the company's candle-and-candlestick symbol, the scripted text D.C. DELFT, and the initials of the artist.

1400s and was originally a convent backed by tranquil gardens that make a pleasant spot to wander. William of Orange, the "Father of the Dutch Nation," maintained his battle HQ here during all the years he fought the Spanish to found the Dutch Republic, and also where an assassin's bullets ended his life in 1584. The musket-ball holes are still visible on the stone stairwell. Three permanent exhibitions look at the life of William of Orange and highlight his influence on modern-day Holland; chart the Dutch entrepreneurial spirit from Golden Age to present day; and examine the creative genius of the nation with impressive tapestries, silverware, pottery, Golden Age glassware, and paintings—including five versions of the "View of Delft" painted by contemporaries of Jan Vermeer.

Sint-Agathaplein 1. www.prinsenhof-delft.nl. ✆ **015/260-2358.** Admission 12.50€ adults, 4€ ages 4–18, free ages 3 and under. March–Aug daily 11am–5pm; Sept–Feb Tues–Sun 11am–5pm. Closed Jan 1, Apr 27, and Dec 25.

Nieuwe Kerk (New Church) ★ CHURCH   The fine spire that graces the Delft skyline belongs to the New Church, which isn't new at all—it was begun in 1383 and completed in 1510. Inside is the magnificent tomb of William of Orange; it was designed by Hendrick de Keyser and is decorated with a sculpture of William in full battle gear as well as figures representing Liberty, Justice, Valor, and Religion. The royal dead of the House of Orange-Nassau lie in a crypt beneath the remains of the founder of their line. The 109m-high (360-ft.) church tower is the second tallest in the country after

Amsterdam's Westerkerk (p. 99); climb it for marvelous views over the town's red rooftops.

Markt 80. www.nieuwekerk-delft.nl. © **015/212-3015.** Church: Mon–Sat 9am–6pm. Tower: Jan Mon–Fri 11am–4pm, Sat 10am–5pm; Feb–Mar Mon–Sat 10am–5pm; Apr–Oct Mon–Sat 9am–6pm; Nov–Dec Mon–Fri 11am–6pm, Sat 10am–5pm. Church admission: 5.50€ adults, 4€ students 12–25, 1.50€ children 6–11, free 5 and under. Tower admission: 4.50€ adults, 3.50€ students 12–25, 2.50€ children 6–11, children 5 and under not allowed.

THE HAGUE

50km (31 miles) SW of Amsterdam; 22km (14 miles) NW of Rotterdam

Stately and dignified, The Hague is an easy day trip from Amsterdam, but some travelers prefer it as a more relaxed sightseeing base. 's-Gravenhage, to give the city its full name, or more commonly Den Haag, is a cosmopolitan town bursting with style and culture, full of parks and elegant homes. Its 18th-century French vibe suits its role as a world-class diplomatic center and the site of the International Court of Justice, housed in the famous Peace Palace.

Essentials

GETTING THERE

BY PLANE Amsterdam's **Schiphol Airport** (p. 152), 40km (25 miles) away, also serves The Hague. Trains run directly from the airport to The Hague, with up to six trains an hour; the ride takes around 35 minutes, and round-trip fare is 17.80€. A taxi from Schiphol to The Hague city center takes 40 minutes in reasonable traffic and costs around 65€.

BY TRAIN The Hague has excellent rail connections from Amsterdam, with fast InterCity trains that take around 50 minutes. The city has two main stations, **Den Haag Centraal Station** and **Den Haag HS;** most city sights are closer to Centraal Station, but some trains stop only at HS. The round-trip fare from Amsterdam is 24.40€. For more details, visit **www.ns.nl**.

BY CAR From Amsterdam and the north, take A4/E19. You'll want to avoid all three *snelwegen* (expressways) during the morning and evening commuter hours, when traffic grinds to a halt. At other times, you should be able to drive to The Hague from Amsterdam in under an hour.

VISITOR INFORMATION

Tourist information is at **The Hague Info Store (THIS),** Spui 68 (https://denhaag.com; © **070/361-8860**), close to the Binnenhof (Parliament). The office is open Monday noon to 8pm, Tuesday to Friday 10am to 8pm, Saturday 10am to 5pm, and Sunday noon to 5pm.

GETTING AROUND

Public transportation in The Hague is operated by **HTM** (www.htm.nl). Centraal Station is the primary interchange point for bus and tram routes, and HS station is the secondary node. The city center is easily walkable but several attractions are best reached by public transport, including the Gemeentemuseum and the

The Hague & Scheveningen

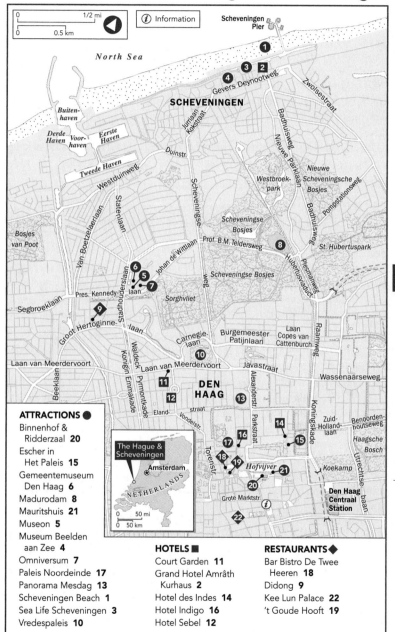

ATTRACTIONS ●

Binnenhof &
  Ridderzaal **20**
Escher in
  Het Paleis **15**
Gemeentemuseum
  Den Haag **6**
Madurodam **8**
Mauritshuis **21**
Museon **5**
Museum Beelden
  aan Zee **4**
Omniversum **7**
Paleis Noordeinde **17**
Panorama Mesdag **13**
Scheveningen Beach **1**
Sea Life Scheveningen **3**
Vredespaleis **10**

HOTELS ■

Court Garden **11**
Grand Hotel Amrâth
  Kurhaus **2**
Hotel des Indes **14**
Hotel Indigo **16**
Hotel Sebel **12**

RESTAURANTS ◆

Bar Bistro De Twee
  Heeren **18**
Didong **9**
Kee Lun Palace **22**
't Goude Hooft **19**

coastal town of Scheveningen. Going by tram is the quickest way to get around town; Tram no. 1 is useful for sightseers as it travels from the North Sea coast at Scheveningen through The Hague and all the way to Delft.

A 2-hour ticket costs 4€; if you will be traveling extensively around the city, a 1-day ticket is 7.10€ and 1.50€ for children ages 4 to 12. As with the public transport in Amsterdam, you need to check in and out when you enter and leave trams and buses. You can purchase tickets at vending machines in the train stations and at the tourist offices or onboard the tram and bus using a credit card or debit card (though keep in mind the machines may not work with non-chip-and-pin cards). You can also buy tickets with cash from the driver.

Regulated **taxis** wait at stands outside both main rail stations and at other strategic points around town; you can also hail them in the streets. Uber is also available.

Exploring The Hague

One of the pleasures of spending a day or more in The Hague is ambling through its genteel streets. Stroll past the mansions that line Lange Voorhout, overlooking a broad avenue of poplar and elm trees, and you'll be struck by how these spacious, restrained mansions differ from Amsterdam's gabled, ornamented canal houses. Take time out in more than 30 sq. km (12 sq. miles) of parks, gardens, and other green spaces within the city limits or head out to The Hague's sophisticated seacoast resort, Scheveningen, on Tram no 1.

Binnenhof & Ridderzaal (Inner Court & Hall of the Knights) ★★
HISTORIC BUILDING   The magnificent Binnenhof, the 13th-century hunting lodge of the counts of Holland, is the center of Holland's political life. It now houses the First and Second Chamber of the Staaten-Generaal (States General), an equivalent to the U.S. House of Representatives and Senate, respectively. At the cobblestoned courtyard's heart is the beautiful, twin-towered Hall of the Knights, the Ridderzaal, which soars 26m (85 ft.) to its oak roof. Since 1904, its immense interior, adorned with provincial flags and leaded-glass windows depicting the coats of arms of Dutch cities, has hosted the queen's annual address to Parliament (third Tues in Sept) and official receptions. Adjacent to the Ridderzaal are the former quarters of the Stadhouder (Head of State).

When Count of Holland Willem II was crowned king of the Romans and emperor-elect of the Holy Roman Empire in 1248, he appointed the Binnenhof, his late father's palace, the official royal residence, thereby providing the city with what is considered its foundation year. Willem's son, Floris V, added the massive Ridderzaal in 1280.

Visit the Parliament exhibit in the reception room of the Hall of Knights, and join a guided tour to visit the hall and, government business permitting, one of the chambers of Parliament. It's worthwhile to visit the courtyard and the Hall of the Knights, which you can do easily in an hour; the tour of Parliament isn't all that exciting, so don't fret if you miss it. Be sure to check out the view from the outside of the Binnenhof, across the rectangular **Hofvijver** (Court Lake) pond, which has a fountain and a tiny island.

Binnenhof 8A. https://prodemos.nl. ℂ **070/757-0200.** Courtyard free admission; 5.50–11€ guided tours (book in advance online). Mon–Sat 10am–4pm. Closed holidays and special events at short notice.

Escher in Het Paleis (Escher at the Palace) ★ MUSEUM   Behind its elegant neoclassical 17th-century facade, the palace was formerly the winter residence of Queen Emma of the Netherlands and later the home of Dutch graphic artist **M.C. Escher.** He lived from 1898 to 1972 and traveled throughout Europe, living in Italy and Switzerland and drawing on influences as disparate as the Alhambra in Granada and the bucolic landscape of Tuscany. Escher became famous for his perspective-skewing lithographs, woodcuts, and engravings as well as drawings and prints. His eccentric works are exhibited throughout his former home.

The museum opened has the world's largest collection of Escher's designs. Highlights include the circular woodcut "Metamorphosis III" as well as the permanent "In the Eye of Escher" exhibition on the second story, where games are played with perspective using mirrors and kaleidoscopes. Permanent displays include his early Italian landscapes, family portraits, and many prints and woodcuts with ingenious optical illusions.

Lange Voorhout 74. www.escherinhetpaleis.nl. ℂ **070/427-7730.** Admission 10€ adults, 6.50€ ages 7–15, free 6 and under, 26.50€ family. Tues–Sun 11am–5pm. Closed Jan 1 and Dec 25.

Gemeentemuseum Den Haag (The Hague Municipal Museum) ★★★ MUSEUM   The outstanding Gemeentemuseum forms part of a museum complex surrounding a small lake along with the science-themed Museon (see below), the Omniversum IMAX movie theater (see below), the Den Haag Museum of Photography, and the Museum of Contemporary Art (the latter two both stage rotating exhibitions). Housed in a honey-hued brick building finished in 1935 by architect H.P. Berlage, and with an interior of harmonious curves and pale yellow and white tiles, this is an outstanding gallery with so much excellence to discover that several hours are required to do the vast displays justice.

Top billing goes to the world's biggest hoard—some 300 works—by De Stijl artist Piet Mondrian, including his last painting, the unfinished "Victory Boogie Woogie" (1944), an abstract representation of New York. Other permanent exhibitions are equally strong, like "Discover the Modern" which covers the very best of 20th-century art from Kandinsky and Schiele to Kirchner, Monet, and Picasso.

Decorative arts are represented with ceramics from Delft, China, and the Middle East; Dutch and Venetian glass; silver; period furniture; and an intricate wooden dollhouse dating from 1743. The music department has antique instruments from around the world and an impressive library of scores, books, and prints, as well as underground galleries hosting temporary fashion exhibits such as dresses by Chanel. Recently updated, the child-friendly interactive

King Willem-Alexander's workplace is the majestic **Paleis Noordeinde** (www. koninklijkhuis.nl), on Noordeinde, just west of Lange Voorhout, which dates from 1553 but was only promoted to a palace in 1609 when it was bequeathed to Louise de Coligny, the fourth wife and widow of William of Orange. Dutch super-architect Jacob van Campen created much of what we see today in the 17th century, including the palace's H-shape form and serene neoclassical facades, but 200 years later, the palace was almost derelict. In 1815 restoration brought it back to a state suitable for a royal residence, and although it isn't open to visitors, you can view it from the street and from the surrounding landscaped gardens; combine a stroll in the Royal Park with a visit to the **Mauritshuis** (see below) and the **Dutch Parliament Buildings** (see above).

exhibition "Wonderkamers" lets kids effectively become part of a space-age computer game as they explore the gallery.

Stadhouderslaan 41. www.gemeentemuseum.nl. ℗ **070/338-1111.** Admission 16€ adults, 12.50€ students, free ages 18 and under. Tues–Sun 11am–5pm. Closed Dec 25.

Mauritshuis ★★★ ART GALLERY   One of the greatest art galleries in the Netherlands the Mauritshuis was once the residence of Count Johan Maurits van Nassau-Siegen, a scion of the ruling House of Orange. This small but delightful neoclassical mansion from 1637 sits astride the Hofvijver lake just outside the Binnenhof complex. In recent years, a modern foyer and underground galleries were added to connect the museum with the newer Art Deco-style Royal Dutch Shell Wing, more than doubling exhibition space.

The Mauritshuis houses a stunning collection of 15th- to 18th-century Low Countries art donated to the nation by King Willem I in 1816. More than 200 works are on display by luminaries including Rembrandt, Frans Hals, Jan Vermeer, Jan Steen, Peter Paul Rubens, and Hans Holbein. The standout pieces from a standout collection are Rembrandt's "The Anatomy Lesson of Dr. Nicolaes Tulp" (1632), Vermeer's meticulous "View of Delft" (ca. 1660), and his iconic "Girl with a Pearl Earring" (ca. 1660). Also among the highlights is "The Goldfinch" by the little-known artist and pupil of Rembrandt Carel Fabritius; the miniscule artwork was the basis for Donna Tartt's 2014 Pulitzer Prize-winning novel of the same name.

The **Galerij Prins Willem V** (Buitenhof 33; ℗ **070/302-3435;** Tues–Sun noon–5pm) is a separate annex to the Mauritshuis. There are few internationally known works, but look out for Jan Steen's shiver-inducing "The Toothpuller" (1651), and give thanks for modern dentistry techniques.

Plein 29. www.mauritshuis.nl. ℗ **070/302-3456.** Admission, including entrance to Galerij Prins Willem V, 15.50€ adults, 12.50€ students, free ages 18 and under. Mon 1–6pm, Tues–Sun 10am–6pm (Thurs till 8pm). Closed Jan 1, Nov 4, and Dec 25.

Panorama Mesdag ★ ART GALLERY   One of the strangest of The Hague's artworks (and the next best thing to visiting seaside Scheveningen) is the Panorama Mesdag, the largest painting in the Netherlands at more than 14m (45 ft.) high and 120m (400 ft.) in length, and the only Dutch "painting in the round" to be in its original location. The extraordinarily precise 360-degree "cyclorama" of the coastal resort of Scheveningen as it was in 1881, painted by Hague School artist Hendrik Willem Mesdag, is a masterly exercise in perspective. The townhouses, churches, lighthouses, coastline, sea, sand dunes, and fishing boats of 19th-century Scheveningen are all represented in minute, accurate detail. The painting is suffused with soft, clear light, and when the painting is viewed from the observation gallery in the center of the exhibition room, artificial dunes separate observers from the painting, creating an illusion that you could simply step right into the landscape.

As well as the Mesdag family collection of 19th-century landscapes and a few examples of Barbazon School works, temporary exhibitions are also held in the gallery—often retrospectives of contemporary Dutch artists.

Zeestraat 65. www.panorama-mesdag.com. ✆ **070/310-6665.** Admission 10.50€ adults, 9€ students, 5.50€ children 4–11. Mon–Sat 10am–5pm, Sun 11am–5pm. Closed Jan 1 and Dec 25–26.

Vredespaleis (Peace Palace) ★ HISTORIC BUILDING American philanthropist Andrew Carnegie donated over a million dollars toward the construction of this immense mock-Gothic palace, home to the International Court of Justice and the Permanent Court of Arbitration. The building was designed by French architect Louis Cordonnier and completed in 1913; today it can be visited only by guided tour with reservations made online ahead of time. Its ornate apartments are filled with grandiose gifts given by each of the participating countries: crystal chandeliers made with real rubies and emeralds and each weighing 1,750kg (3,900 lb.) from Delft; incredible mosaic floors from France; a huge Turkish carpet woven in 1926 in Izmir; and an immense 3,500kg (7,700 lb.) vase from Czar Nicholas of Russia. If the courts are not in session, your guide will take you inside the International Court of Justice, which handles all of the United Nations' judicial cases. The visitor center highlights the history of the Peace Palace with an exhibition and short film.

Carnegieplein 2. www.vredespaleis.nl. ✆ **070/302-4242.** Tour tickets 11€ adults, free for children 7 and under. Visitor Center: Tues–Sun 10am–5pm (mid-Nov to mid-Mar 11am–4pm). Guided tours in English are offered most weekends and must be purchased online. Tours last 45 min.

Especially for Kids

Like Amsterdam, The Hague is a happily child-friendly city, with plenty of rolling parks and the nearby beaches of Scheveningen (p. 151). It's also got several attractions aimed at kids, kicking off with Holland's first **IMAX theater at Omniversum** (President Kennedylaan 5, at Stadhouderslaan; www. omniversum.nl; ✆ **070/354-5454**). A different film is played on a giant dome screen every hour from a roster of six or seven titles covering subjects as diverse as underwater exploration and space travel. The films themselves are in Dutch, but English translations are available via headphones.

Right outside Omniversum is an elongated 10-foot-tall statue of Nelson Mandela, a photo opportunity for parents and kids alike. Almost next door is **Museon** (Stadhouderslaan 37; www.museon.nl; ✆ 070/338-1338), The Hague's hyper-interactive museum of science and nature. Aiming to be both educational and fun, it's a very hands-on affair, with plenty of buttons to press, smells to sniff, and movies. While not enormous, there's enough to distract curious youngsters for a couple of hours. Then for a change of pace, head to the top of **Hague Tower** for afternoon tea in The Penthouse and far-reaching views across the city (next to HS station at Rijkswijkseplein 786; www.the haguetower.com; ✆ 070/305-1000). The Hague's tallest skyscraper reaches an impressive 132m (433 ft.) and is regarded as the city's answer to New York City's Flatiron Building.

But The Hague's biggest attraction for youngsters is a short ride on tram 9 away from the city center towards Scheveningen (p. 151). Here you'll find **Madurodam** ★★ (George Maduroplein 1, at Koninginnegracht; www. madurodam.nl; ✆ 070/416-2400), an enchanting display of a miniature, fictitious city that sprawls over 170 hectares (70 acres) in the Scheveningse Bosjes (Scheveningen Woods). Typical Dutch townscapes and famous landmarks are replicated on a scale of 1:25—you'll feel a bit like Gulliver viewing Lilliput. The wonder of it all is that this is a working miniature world: Trains run, ships move, planes taxi down runways, bells ring, there's a town fair in progress, and 50,000 tiny lamps light up when darkness falls. Children love it, but surprisingly 75 percent of the annual visitors are adults.

Where to Stay & Eat

The oh-so-refined **Hotel Des Indes** ★★ (Lange Voorhout 54–56; www. hoteldesindesthehague.com; ✆ 070/361-2345; doubles 170€–300€) comes highly recommended if you have deep pockets or are traveling on an expense account. The **Grand Hotel Amrâth Kurhaus** (Gevers Deynootplein 30; www.amrathkurhaus.com; ✆ 070/416-2636; doubles 150€–260€) in Scheveningen has wonderful North Sea views and every possible luxury, too. More moderately priced suggestions include the eco-friendly **Court Garden** (Laan van Meerdervort 96; www.hotelcourtgarden.nl; ✆ 070/311-4000; doubles 80€–170€) a stone's throw away from the Peace Palace (see above). Another reasonable choice is the **Hotel Sebel** (Prins Hendrikplein 20; www.hotelsebel. nl; ✆ 070/345-9200; doubles 65€–160€) with simple furnishings and a couple of ground-floor rooms that have access to a leafy garden. The chic, relatively affordable **Hotel Indigo** ★★ (Noordeinde 33; www.ihg.com; ✆ 070/209-9000; doubles 115€–200€) opened in 2018 in the 19th-century former Dutch National Bank and retains many of the building's historic Art Deco details.

Dining and bar options abound around the Grote Markt, with a wide variety of international cuisines. For solid Dutch fare, including a particularly generous breakfast, plus excellent people-watching, head to the terrace of **'t Goude Hooft** (Dagelijkse Groenmarkt 13; www.tgoudehooft.nl; ✆ 070/744-8830; mains 16€–26€). The nearby **Bar Bistro De Twee Heeren** (Oude Molstraat 6; www.barbistrodetweeheeren.nl; ✆ 070/331-1179; mains 18.5-€–20€)

SCHEVENINGEN

A chic beach resort with a tongue-twister name, Scheveningen is 5km (3 miles) northwest of The Hague center and is best reached by Tram no. 9, thanks to interminable traffic jams on weekends, and most every day during the summer. This glossy seaside enclave has a slew of upscale restaurants, accommodations, designer boutiques, and abundant nighttime entertainment. Until early in the 19th century, it was a sleepy fishing village set amid the dunes on the North Sea coast, but as its beaches began to attract vacation crowds, Scheveningen evolved into an internationally known spa with its own distinct identity; as time has gone on it has become a suburb—albeit a charismatic one—of The Hague. The fairytale 19th-century waterfront **Grand Hotel Amrâth Kurhaus** (see above) still draws celebrities from around the globe.

The beach zone is called **Scheveningen Bad**—but it's actually pretty good. A 3km (2-mile) promenade borders the wide, sandy beach. A highlight is the **Scheveningen Pier** (www.pier.nl; ✆ 610/386-859), recently overhauled and now chock-a-block with restaurants and bars. At the end of the pier, the enormous **Skyview Ferris wheel** (www.skyview depier.nl; ✆ 0880/223-333) juts out over the sea, with 36 luxurious enclosed cabins where you can take a 15-minute ride or reserve a full lunch, dinner, or high tea with panoramic views. Skyview is open Monday to Thursday 11am to 8pm, Friday and Saturday until 10pm and Sunday until 9pm. Admission is 9€ for adults and 7€ for children 12 and under.

Attractions start with **Sea Life Scheveningen** ★, Strandweg 13 (www.visit sealife.com; ✆ 070/354-2100) where denizens of the deep, including sharks, swim above visitors' heads in a walk-through underwater tunnel. The aquarium is open Apr–June and Sept and Oct daily 10am to 7pm; July and Aug daily 10am to 8pm; and Nov–Mar 10am to 6pm. Closed Dec 25. When booked in advance online, admission is 15.25€ for adults (17.25€ in person) and 11.25€ for children 3 to 11 (13.25€ in person).

Museum Beelden aan Zee (Sculptures on the Seafront) ★★, Harteveltstraat 1 (www.beeldenaanzee.nl; ✆ 070/358-5857) is an off-beat museum built into the sand dunes steps from Scheveningen's busy boardwalk. Most of the sculptures take the human form and many are portraits, including an installation featuring the Dutch Royal Family. Terraces overlooking the sea are strewn with sculptures, and on the promenade outside the museum you'll find "Fairytale Sculptures by the Sea," a permanent installation that's free of charge, comprised of cartoonlike figures by New Yorker Tom Otterness. The museum is open Tuesday to Sunday 10am to 5pm. Admission is 15€ adults, 7.50€ children 13 to 18. Closed Jan 1, Apr 27, and Dec 25.

A word on the food here: Scheveningen is the most herring-obsessed place in this herring-obsessed land. On the first Saturday in June, in the Dutch equivalent of French restaurants racing to buy the first bottles of Beaujolais Nouveau, fishing boats compete to land the season's first *nieuwe haring* (new herring) during the annual, colorful Vlaggetjesdag (Flag Day) event (p. 40). The fresh-caught fish is considered a delicacy; it's eaten whole (minus the head and the tail) or chopped with minced onion. Year-round the fish are pickled as *maatjes*. Buy herring from sidewalk vendors, beachfront fish stands, and trailers towed onto the beach.

Scheveningen's **tourist information** point is located in the Palace Promenade shopping center at AKO Scheveningen bookshop, Gevers Deynootweg 990-58 (Mon–Fri and Sun 9am–6pm and Sat 9am–8pm).

features a French-inspired menu that changes every month and puts an emphasis on seasonal organic produce. In Chinatown, the **Kee Lun Palace** (Wagenstraat 95; www.kee-lun-palace-den-haag.nl; ✆ **070/384-9988;** mains 16€–32€) rustles up a decent chow mein and top-notch Singapore noodles. Indonesian cuisine is also quite popular in The Hague; one place doing a lighter, more contemporary version is **Didong** (2e Sweelinckstraat 115; www. didong.nl; ✆ **070/364-9887;** mains 7.50€ 15€; rices 17.50€–19€), located just north of the city center in the Duinoord district.

ROTTERDAM ★★

58km (36 miles) SW of Amsterdam; 23km (14 miles) SE of The Hague

A mere hour from Amsterdam by train, Rotterdam is one of Holland's fastest growing cities with a harbor front that's changing by the day. In Rotterdam there are no tangles of old streets, no canals, and no 17th-century town houses; instead, there's an abundance of sleek contemporary architecture, spacious shopping malls, and one of the world's busiest ocean harbors. This bustling metropolis has risen from the ashes of Nazi bombing in 1942, which reduced it to rubble overnight. Any surviving traces of Old Rotterdam are found in Delfshaven (Delft Harbor) and Oude Haven (Old Harbor).

At the war's end, Rotterdammers looked on their misfortune as an opportunity and approached their city as a clean slate. They relished the chance to create an efficient, workable modern city. The results, although not always elegant, have created a city looking forward, full of innovative architecture springing up along the river that brings in so much of its wealth.

Essentials

GETTING THERE Most people fly into Amsterdam's **Schiphol Airport** and take the train to Rotterdam; direct trains take under a half hour (30.80€ round-trip), while those that connect through The Hague take about an hour (26€ round-trip).

From Amsterdam, two to six **trains** depart each hour round the clock. On high-speed Intercity direct trains, the ride takes 40 minutes; on ordinary Inter-City trains, around 70 minutes. The round-trip fare from Amsterdam is 37€ on direct trains, 32€ on regular trains. For more details, visit **www.ns.nl**.

By **car** from Amsterdam, take A4/E19, and then A13/E19; expect delays during commuter times—or to be honest, most of the time.

VISITOR INFORMATION There's a tourist information center at the railway station: **VVV Rotterdam Centraal,** Stationsplein 45 (no phone; www.rotterdam.info), open daily 9am to 6pm. A second tourist office is **ROT-TERDAM.INFO** on Binnenwegplein at Coolsingel 114 (www.rotterdam. info; ✆ **010/790-0185**). The office is open daily 9:30am to 6pm.

GETTING AROUND Rotterdam is far less walkable than Amsterdam, and you will need to use its Metro and tram system to get around (buses will be less useful). The city's public transportation network is **RET** (www.ret.nl). A 2-hour ticket costs 4€; if you will be traveling extensively around the city, a 1-day ticket

Rotterdam

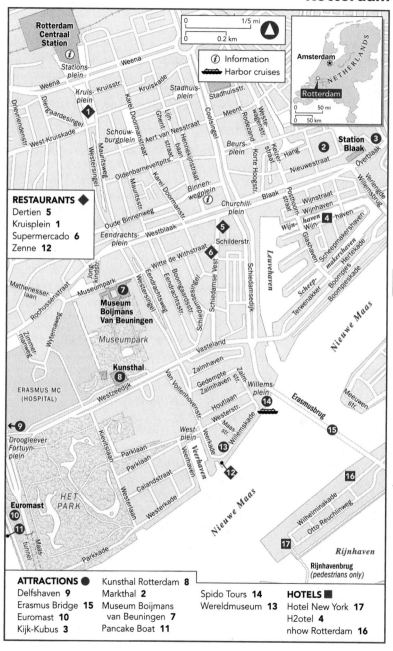

Rotterdam Centraal Station
Stations-plein
(i)

Weena
Weena
Kruis-plein Kruisstr.
Kruiskade
Stadhuis-plein
Stadhuisstr.

Drievriendenstr.
West-Kruiskade
Diergaardesingel
Mauritsweg
Westersingel

Schouw-burgplein
Aert van Nesstraat
Karel Doormanstraat
Lijn-baan
Ghent-straat
Hennekijnstraat
Oldenbarneveltpits.
Karel Doormanstr.
Binnen-wegplein
(i)

Coolsingel
Meent
Weste-wagenstr.
Rodezand
Keizer-straat
Korte Hoogstr.
Beurs-plein

Meent
Nieuwestraat

Station Blaak ❸
Overblaak
Verlengde Willemsbrug

(i) Information
⛴ Harbor cruises

Amsterdam ✪ NETHERLANDS
Rotterdam

RESTAURANTS ◆
Dertien **5**
Kruisplein **1**
Supermercado **6**
Zenne **12**

Oude Binnenweg
Eendrachts-plein
Westblaak

Churchill-plein ❺
Schilderstr.

Blaak
Wijnstraat
Wijnhaven
Wijn-haven ❹ haven
Glashaven

Posthoornstraat
Leuvehaven

Scheepmakershaven
makershaven
Herekade
Boompjes
Boompjeskade
Scheep-
Terwenakker

Nieuwe Maas

Mathenesser-laan
Rochussenstraat
Wytemaweg
Jong-kindstr.
Museumpark
Eendrachtsweg
Eendrachtsstr.
Witte de Withstraat
Boomgaardsstr.
Boomgaardsstr.
Schiedamse Vest
Schiedamsedijk

Museum Boijmans Van Beuningen ❼
Museumpark

Zimmer-manweg
Kunsthal ❽
Westzeedijk

ERASMUS MC (HOSPITAL)

Kievitslaan
Van Vollenhovenstr.
Schiedamsedijk
Vasteland
Zalmhaven
Gedempte Zalmhaven
Zalmhaven str.
Houtlaan
Westerstr.
West-plein
Veerhaven
Maas str.
Willemskade
Willems-plein ⓮

Erasmusbrug
⓯

Meeuwen-str.

←❾
Droogleever Fortuyn-plein

Parklaan
Parklaan
Calandstraat
HET PARK
Westerlaan
Westerkade

Euromast ❿
⓫
Maas-tunnel
Parkkade

West-plein
Veerhaven
⓭ Willemskade
⓬

Nieuwe Maas

⓰

⓱
Wilhelminakade
Otto Reuchlinweg

Rijnhaven
Rijnhavenbrug (pedestrians only)

ATTRACTIONS ●
Delfshaven **9**
Erasmus Bridge **15**
Euromast **10**
Kijk-Kubus **3**

Kunsthal Rotterdam **8**
Markthal **2**
Museum Boijmans van Beuningen **7**
Pancake Boat **11**

Spido Tours **14**
Wereldmuseum **13**

HOTELS ■
Hotel New York **17**
H2otel **4**
nhow Rotterdam **16**

is 8€. As with the public transport in Amsterdam, you need to check in and out when you enter and leave trams, buses, and the Metro. You can purchase tickets at vending machines in the train and Metro stations and at the tourist offices; on the tram and bus, you can buy tickets with cash from the driver.

Explore the Maas waterfront using waterbuses operated by **RET Fast Ferry** (see above) and **Watertaxi Rotterdam** (www.watertaxirotterdam.nl).

Taxi stands are sprinkled throughout the city. You can hail cabs on the street, or by calling **Rotterdamse Taxi Centrale** (✆ **010/462-6333;** www.rtcnv.nl) or **Rotterdam Taxis** (www.rotterdam-taxis.com; ✆ **010/403-0303**).

Exploring Rotterdam

Euromast ★★ HISTORIC BUILDING   This slender, 185m-tall (607-ft.) tower is indisputably the best vantage point for an overall view of Rotterdam and its environs; on clear days, you can see about 30km (20 miles). You can have lunch or dinner halfway up in the tower in the **Euromast Brasserie** while enjoying spectacular views of the port. There are several viewing platforms, including an outdoor platform 112 meters (367ft) up, but the most spectacular views can be had at the very top of the spire, reached by the rotating glass **Euroscoop** elevator. From the Brasserie level, for an additional payment (57.50€), you can abseil or zip line back to the ground—definitely not for the faint of heart.

Parkhaven 20. www.euromast.nl. ✆ **010/436-4811.** Admission to restaurant and viewing platforms: 10.25€ adults, 9.25€ seniors, 6.75€ children 4–11. Apr–Sept daily 9:30am–10pm, Oct–Mar daily 10am–10pm.

Museum Boijmans van Beuningen ★★★ ART GALLERY   *Unfortunately, this important museum is closed for renovations until 2026. But its masterpieces may be viewable elsewhere in the city (see below).* Rotterdam's leading art museum is one of Europe's best and showcases the story of Western art from medieval times to the present. Running from Old Dutch Masters to contemporary glassware, the highlights of this wonderful collection include Pieter Breughel's peerless Old Testament offering "The Tower of Babel" (ca. 1553); scores of delicate drawings by Renaissance artist Fra Bartolommeo; Rembrandt's winsome portrait of his son, entitled "Titus at his Desk"; and a collection of Gerrit Rietveld's distinctive colored wooden furniture. In 2019, the museum began a massive renovation and will be closed for the next 7 years. A public storage facility, called the Depot Boijmans Van Beuningen, will be built next door to the museum and open in 2021; visitors can book a guided tour to see the many of the 151,000 works in the collection. In the meantime, pieces will be shown at institutions around the city, including at the Kunsthal Rotterdam.

Museumpark 18–20. www.boijmans.nl. ✆ **010/441-9400.**

Wereldmuseum ★★★ MUSEUM   Reflecting the rich maritime heritage of the Netherlands, the World Art Museum has cobbled together thousands of historic artifacts from across the world, many picked up by Dutch sailors as they plundered the world during the 17th-century Golden Age. The result is a beautiful, vibrant, and unusual series of displays of tribal artwork not seen anywhere else including Tibetan prayer flags, primitive Australian Aboriginal paintings, beautiful Indonesian hand-printed batiks, African carvings, and a luscious collection of silk textiles embroidered in gold. At press time, the museum was undergoing renovations, so check the website before heading over (it likely will be open, but better safe . . .).

Willemskade 25. www.wereldmuseum.nl. ℗ **010/270-7172.** Admission 15€ adults, 6€ children. Tues–Sun 10am–5pm. Closed Jan 1, Apr 27, and Dec 25.

Contemporary Architecture in Rotterdam

Nicknamed "Manhattan on the Maas," Rotterdam is a shiny, new city rising phoenixlike from the ashes of its destruction in 1 terrible night during World War II. With only wisps of the old gabled townhouses left around Delfshaven and Oude Haven, this is a skyline of innovative buildings, its iconic landmark the elegant lines of the **Erasmusbrug cable bridge,** nicknamed "the Swan" and floodlit at night.

Near Oude Haven is the geometric chaos of cube-shaped, custard-yellow Kubuswoningen (Cube Houses); they were designed by Dutch architect Piet Blom in the early 1970s and are quite a sight. One of these lopsided little abodes, the **Kijk-Kubus (Show-Cube),** Overblaak 70 (www.kubuswoning.nl; ℗ **010/414-2285**), is open for visits daily 11am to 6pm. Admission is 3€ for adults, 2€ for seniors and students, 1.50€ for children 4 to 12.

Skyscrapers glitter in the burgeoning downtown area and around the banks of the River Maas, where abandoned wharves have all but disappeared under a slew of stylish new builds. As the city's heavy industry migrated northwest towards the North Sea, the **old port district** of Wilhelminapier has been revamped with innovative skyscrapers, including the Norman Foster-designed World Port Center, the 44-story Maastoren (currently the Netherlands' tallest office building), the all-white New Orleans apartment tower, and Rem Koolhaas' colossal glassy De Rotterdam complex; all can be seen on a **boat tour of the harbor** (see below).

Koolhaas designed the Museumpark's **Kunsthal Rotterdam** in the 1990s, setting a precedent for stylish public buildings that has been followed by the red-brick New Luxor Theatre, the frothy bubbles of the Drijvend Paviljoen

Rotterdam Harbor

The Port of Rotterdam handles more ships and more cargo every year than any other port in Europe, and it is the world's third-busiest port after Shanghai and Singapore. A dredged channel, the **Nieuwe Waterweg (New Waterway)** connects Rotterdam with the North Sea and forms a 40km-long (25-mile) deep-water harbor known as **Europoort.** The Netherlands owes a fair piece of its prosperity to the port, which employs 180,000 people. The port authority handles around 140,000 ships, 9 million containers, 104 million tons of crude oil, and 469-million metric tons of cargo annually. Container ships, cargo carriers, tankers, and careworn tramp ships are waited on 24 hours a day by a vast retinue of people and automated machines—trucks, trains, and barges all moving hither and thither in a blur of activity. A trip around the harbor may be one of the more unusual experiences to be had in the Netherlands, and the sheer scale of the operation will make your jaw drop.

(Floating Pavilion) in the Rijnhaven, and the dynamic Red Apple apartment block. In 2014 the futuristic, tunnel-shaped indoor food market Markthal (Market Hall) opened, featuring a massive arched ceiling covered with colorful, cartoonish images of produce; the same year, the remodeled Rotterdam Centraal train station unveiled a striking angular metal-clad roof. More innovative architectural projects are slated for the city, including the transformation of the historic former post office—one of the few buildings left standing after the 1940 Rotterdam Blitz.

Delfshaven

But not all of Rotterdam is brand new. Take the Metro to the tiny harbor area known as **Delfshaven (Delft Harbor),** a neighborhood that the German bombers somehow missed when they bombed the city to smithereens in 1940. Historically this is one of the most important places in Europe for U.S. citizens, for it was from here that the Puritan Pilgrim Fathers embarked on the first leg of their trip to found Massachusetts in 1620. Wander into the 15th-century **Pelgrimvaderskerk (Pilgrim Fathers Church),** Aelbrechtskolk 20 (www.oudeofpelgrim vaderskerk.nl), in which the pilgrims prayed before departure, and where they are remembered in special services every Thanksgiving Day. The church is open irregularly, but at least admission is free. Then peek into antiques stores and galleries, and check on the progress of this historic area's housing renovations.

Organized Tours

An essential part of the Rotterdam experience is taking a **Spido Harbor Tour ★★** (www.spido.nl; © **010/275-9988**) of **Europoort** on board a two-tier boat with indoor and outdoor seating and open decks. Mid-March to August, departures from the dock below Erasmus Bridge run daily every 45 minutes

The Windmills of Kinderdijk

Kinderdijk (www.kinderdijk.nl), a tiny community between Rotterdam and Dordrecht, on the south bank of the Lek River, has 19 water-pumping windmills; that means 76 mill sails, each with a 13m (42-ft.) span. It's a spectacular sight, and one important enough for Kinderdijk to have been placed on UNESCO's World Heritage list.

By regulating the level of water, Kinderdijk's windmills guarded the fertile polders (reclaimed land) of the Alblasserwaard. The **Windmill Exposition Center** at Kinderdijk gives a detailed explanation of windmills' technical characteristics and the part they played in the intricate system of water control. It also looks at the people and the culture that developed on the polders.

The mills operate on Saturday afternoons in July and August 2:30 to 5:30pm; the visitors' mill is open March to October daily 9am to 5:30pm and November to February 10am to 4:30pm. The most adrenaline-thumping way to get to Kinderdijk from Rotterdam is by RET high-speed catamaran (www.ret.nl), from the dock adjacent to the Erasmusbrug; this goes to the De Schans dock at Ridderkerk for the local ferry across to Kinderdijk. If you're driving, take N210 east to Krimpen aan de Lek, from where a small car ferry crosses over the Lek River to Kinderdijk.

from 9:30am to 5pm (Sept and Oct from 10:15am); November to mid-March, departures are limited to one to four times a day. The basic harbor tour is a 75-minute sail along the city's waterfront; in July and August, an extended (2½-hr.) trip runs Saturday at 10:30am and 1:30pm. Tours start at 12.75€ for adults, 8.40€ for children 4 to 11.

If you're traveling with kids, head straight for the bright-yellow **Pannen-koekenboot (Pancake Boat)** ★, Parkhaven (www.pannenkoekenboot.nl; ✆ 010/436-7295), moored at the foot of the Euromast to get high on sugary treats. Departures on the family cruise are year-round the first and third Sunday of the month at 1pm and the third Saturday of the month at 8pm. The 2½-hour cruise is 27.50€ for adults, and 22.50€ per child if you book online; onboard tickets are 2€ more.

For sheer novelty value, try cruising down the canals aboard the world's first **HotTug** (www.hottug.nl; ✆ 31/630-39-6822; 2-hour rental 139€), a floating, wood-fired hot tub that keeps you warm and cozy whatever the weather is doing around you. It can seat up to eight people (though you can rent one just for two for a more romantic experience) and it's easy to navigate, but if you want to drink aboard, you'll need to hire a skipper.

Where to Stay & Eat

Some of Rotterdam's best beds can be found at the **Hotel New York** (Koninginnenhoofd 1; www.hotelnewyork.com; ✆ 010/439-0500; doubles 128€–200€), inside the turn-of-the-century former headquarters of the Holland America Line set along the Maas river; if you're a fan of seafood, get a table at their **oyster bar** for a platter of *fines de claires*. A stylish mid-range option is **nhow Rotterdam** (Wilhelminakade 137; www.nhow-rotterdam.com; ✆ 010/206-7600; 110€–185€), set in Rem Koolhaas' glassy De Rotterdam riverfront complex; the skyline rooms offer unbeatable views of the neighboring Erasmusbrug. At the other end of the price (and luxury) spectrum, the floating **H2otel** (Wijnhaven 20A; www.h2otel.nl; ✆ 010/444-5690; 55€–130€) combines budget accommodation with a warm welcome and a brilliant location within walking distance of the shopping center, Spido boat dock (see below), and the oddball Kubuswoningen (see above).

Eating and drinking options include the **cafes** around historic Oude Haven, a sunny spot for eating al fresco, or an array of cutting-edge **restaurants and bars** in and around the trendy thoroughfare **Witte de Withstraat.** Among them are **Supermercado** (Schiedamsevest 91; www.supermercadorotterdam.nl; ✆ 010/404-8070; mains 11€–16€) for surprisingly authentic tacos; **Dertien** (Schiedamse Vest 30; www.dertienrotterdam.nl; ✆ 010/433-3969; 18€–24€) with a hyper-local seasonal menu that excels in vegetarian dishes; and **De Witte Aap** (Witte de Withstraat 78; www.dewitteaap.nl; ✆ 010/414-9565), pouring a nice selection of Dutch and Belgian craft beers. A handy pit stop for lunch after taking a Spido tour, **Zenne** (Willemskade 27; www.zenne.nl; ✆ 010/404-9696; lunch mains 7.25€–9.50€) serves plentiful supplies of simple fare (lamb burgers, kebabs, *bitterballen*) on a terrace overlooking the river and the cute marina at Veerhaven.

6

BRUSSELS

Brussels is all of Europe in one city. Not simply one style or era, but all styles and eras. The medieval and the Renaissance. The Austrian neo-classic and the Spanish flamboyant. The French 19th century and the modern sky-scraper. The accents and tones, in the very sounds that you hear, of both the Latin-influenced languages of Europe (here, the French) and the Germanic strains (here, the Flemish, or Dutch)—a rare, bilingual city.

And not only do you see all of Europe here, and hear much of Europe here, but the very people that you meet—in a metropolis where 30 percent of the population is foreign—are from every cor-ner of Europe, mixing and mingling in a setting that was always a crossroads for both invasions and trade. Brussels is not simply the nominal capital of Europe, it is fast becoming the true capital of Europe, and shows that status in a hundred, intriguing ways.

You may have learned of its richest sights before now. They include the grandest of all the great City Squares. And restaurants so numerous as to make you dizzy. And subways decorated with mod-ern art. And great museums of art. And open-air markets of antiques and foods, of secondhand fashions and leather-bound books . . . and "chocolatiers" . . . and bakers of pastries sublime . . . and beery cafes.

Brussels is all of these . . . but it is more. It is Bruges. And it is Ghent. And it is Antwerp and Liege. And Mons. And Tournai. Because Brussels is also a hub, a base for short day excursions, a metropolis so centrally located that the lures and attractions of a dozen other great cities are also the attractions of remarkable Brussels.

ESSENTIALS

Arriving

BY PLANE **Brussels Airport** (www.brusselsairport.be; ✆ **0900/ 70000;** 0.50€ per minute for general and flight information; ✆ **322/753-7753** from outside Belgium; airport code BRU) is 15km (9 miles) northwest of Brussels city center. This airport handles most of Belgium's international air traffic. There is one terminal that handles all flights, national and international. Moving walk-ways connect passengers with the Arrivals Hall and Passport Con-trol, Baggage Reclaim, and Customs. Conveniences like free luggage carts, currency exchange, ATMs, restaurants, bars, shops, baby rooms, restrooms, and showers are all on tap. The **Sheraton Brussels Airport Hotel** is located directly outside the airport's main entrance.

For tourist information and to make hotel reservations, go to Brussels Airport **Information Desk** in the Arrivals Hall; it is open 6am to 10pm weekdays and weekends until 9pm.

The **Brussels Airport Express train service** to Brussels' three main rail stations (Bruxelles-Nord, Bruxelles-Central, and Bruxelles-Midi) has up to five departures hourly daily between 5:15am and midnight, for a one-way fare of 8.90€. The ride to Bruxelles-Central takes 17 minutes on the direct train and trains leave from the basement level of the airport. Most airport trains have wide corridors and extra space for baggage. Purchase tickets at kiosks in the airport's baggage claim area or in the station.

Every 20 to 30 minutes from the airport's bus platform C outside Arrivals, **Airport Line** no. 12 (Mon–Fri 8am–8pm) and no. 21 (Mon–Fri 8–11pm and Sat–Sun 5am–11pm) depart to the European District in the city. The ride takes a half-hour and the fare is 9€ for a round-trip ticket purchased from a ticket machine before boarding the bus and 12€ for one purchased onboard. For more info: www.stib-mivb.be; ☎ **32/70-232-000.**

Taxis that display an orange sticker depicting a white airplane offer reduced fares (around 45€) from the airport to the center city.

Uber is currently available, however, only for the categories of UberX and UberBLACK, which both employ professional drivers meaning the cost is only slightly less than a taxi. Also, because Uber cars treated as private vehicles, they cannot drop off or pick up passengers at curbside due to security concerns, so you must walk the short distance to one of the car parks.

Brussels-South-Charleroi-Airport (www.charleroi-airport.com; ☎ **0902/02490,** 1€ per minute for general and flight information; ☎ 322/7815-2722 from outside Belgium; airport code CRL) is 55km (35 miles) south of Brussels. It is the domain of European budget flights rather than transatlantic services; there are Brussels City Shuttle (www.brussels-city-shuttle.com) connections every 30 minutes between the airport and Brussels-Midi/Zuid rail station. Round-trip fare is 28.40€.

BY CAR Major expressways to Brussels are E19/A16 from Amsterdam (driving time: 2 hr. 20 min. on a good day) and the E19/E17 from Paris (driving time 3½ hr.). Take the E40/A10 from Bruges and Cologne. If possible, avoid driving on the hell on wheels that has become the R0 Brussels ring road; if you miss your turn off, expect to go all the way around again. Once you're installed in your hotel, leave the car at a parking garage. Brussels is choked with traffic even in the middle of the day, parking is scarce, and one-way systems baffling.

BY TRAIN The Brussels metropolitan area has three main rail stations: **Bruxelles-Central,** Carrefour de l'Europe; **Bruxelles-Midi,** rue de France (the Eurostar, Thalys, TGV, and ICE terminal); and **Bruxelles-Nord,** rue du Progrès. All three are served by Métro, tram, or bus lines, and have taxi stands outside. For train information and reservations, visit www.sncb.be or call ☎ **02/528-2828.**

From London, Brussels is served by **Eurostar** (www.eurostar.com; ℂ **08432/186-186** in Britain; ℂ 44/1233-617-575 from outside the UK); from Paris, Amsterdam, and Cologne by **Thalys** (www.thalys.com; ℂ **320/7066- 7788** 0.30€ per minute); from everywhere in France apart from Paris by **TGV** (www. voyages-sncf.com; ℂ **3635** in France; ℂ 33/892-353-535 from outside France); and from Frankfurt by **ICE** (www.nsinternational.nl; ℂ **31/30-230-0023**).

Warning: Attracted by rich pickings from international travelers, bag snatchers roam the environs of Bruxelles-Midi, and pickpockets work the interior. Although police presence is obvious, keep a close eye on your possessions.

BY BUS   Eurolines (ℂ **08717/818-178** in Britain or 32/02-274-1350; www. eurolines.com) buses from London, Paris, Amsterdam, and other cities arrive at the bus station below Bruxelles-Nord train station.

Visitor Information

The city tourist organization, **Visit Brussels** (www.visitbrussels.be; ℂ **02/513-8940**), has several offices around the city and their website is also excellent for forward planning. The most centrally located office is on the ground floor of the Hôtel de Ville, Grand-Place and is open daily 9am until 6pm. If you're up in place Royale, **Brussels Info Place (BIP)** is open Monday through Friday 9am to 6pm, weekends 10am until 6pm.

There are additional tourist information offices at the Information Desk in the Arrivals hall at Brussels Airport (6am–10pm weekdays and weekends until 9pm) and in the main hall at Gare du Midi rail station (daily 9am–6pm). The office at rue Wiertz 43 is for visitors to the European Parliament and is open daily 10am to 6pm. All offices are closed on January 1 and December 25.

For English-speaking visitors, check out **"The Bulletin"** online (www. thebulletin.be) which contains a weekly guide to events happening around the city under the Culture menu.

City Layout

Brussels is divided into **19 *communes* (districts)**—"Brussels" being both the name of the central commune and of the city as a whole (which comprises Belgium's autonomous Brussels Capital Region). The city center was once ringed by fortified ramparts but is now encircled by the broad boulevards known collectively as the **Petite Ceinture** (Little Belt). Most of the city's premier sightseeing sights are in this zone. Green spaces—parks, woods, and forest—account for just over 11 percent of the zone's total area of 160 sq. km (63 sq. miles).

You'll hear both French and Dutch (well, Flemish) along with a babel of other tongues spoken on the streets of Brussels. The city is bilingual: Bruxelles in French and Brussel in Dutch/Flemish, and confusingly for many a map-reader, street names and places are in both languages. Grand-Place is also Grote Markt; Théâtre Royal de la Monnaie is Koninklijke Munttheater. *Note:* Rather than translate place names into three languages in this chapter, the French place names are utilized.

Brussels is flat in its center and western reaches, where the now-vanished River Senne once flowed. To the east, a range of low hills rises to the upper city, which is crowned by the Royal Palace and has some of the city's most affluent residential and prestigious business and shopping districts. The **Grand-Place** stands at the heart of the city and is both a starting point and reference point for most visitors.

The Neighborhoods in Brief

The Lower Town The **Bas de la Ville,** the core area of the Old Center, has at its heart the **Grand-Place** (p. 178) and its environs. Two of the most traveled lanes nearby are restaurant-lined **rue des Bouchers** and **Petite rue des Bouchers,** part of an area known as the **Îlot Sacré (Sacred Isle).** A block from the Grand-Place is the classical, colonnaded **Bourse (Stock Exchange).** A few blocks north, on **place de la Monnaie,** is the Monnaie opera house and ballet theater (p. 204), named after the coin mint that once stood here. Brussels' busiest shopping street, pedestrianized **rue Neuve,** starts from place de la Monnaie and runs north for several blocks. Just north of the center lies **Gare du Nord** and nearby place Rogier. Central Brussels also includes the **Marché-aux-Poissons (Fish Market)** district.

The Upper Town The **Haut de la Ville** lies east of and uphill from the Grand-Place, along rue Royale and rue de la Régence and abutting the unpretentious, working-class **Marolles** district (p. 202). Lying between the Palais de Justice and Gare du Midi, the Marolles has cozy cafes, drinking-man's bars, and inexpensive restaurants; its denizens even speak their own dialect. The Upper Town is spread along an escarpment east of the center, where you find **place du Grand Sablon** (p. 183) as well as the Royal Museums of Fine Arts (p. 189) and the museums of the place Royal (p. 184). If you head southwest and cross the broad **boulevard de Waterloo,** where you find the most exclusive designer stores, you come to **place Louise.**

Avenue Louise Beyond the city center, things start to get hazier. From place Louise, Brussels' most fashionable thoroughfare, **Avenue Louise,** runs south all the way to a large wooded park called the **Bois de la Cambre.** On either side of Avenue Louise are the classy districts of **Ixelles** and **Uccle;** they're both good areas for casual, inexpensive restaurants, bars, cafes, and shopping, and both border the wide green spaces of the Bois de la Cambre and the Forêt de Soignes.

European District East of the city center lies a part of Brussels whose denizens are regarded by many Bruxellois with the same suspicion they might apply to extraterrestrials. This is, of course, the **European Union district** (p. 185) around place Schuman, where the European Commission, Parliament, and Council of Ministers buildings jostle for space in a warren of offices populated by civil servants, journalists, and lobbyists (the area also is home to a wealth of restaurants and cafes that cater to Euro appetites). A quaint old neighborhood was made to disappear to make way for these noble edifices. North of Ixelles, the modern European Union district surrounds **place Schuman.** The **Cinquantenaire,** a park crisscrossed with tree-lined avenues, extends from just east of the European District to the Porte de Tervuren and is bisected east to west by avenue John F. Kennedy. At the park's eastern end are the museums of the monumental Palais du Cinquantenaire and the Arc du Cinquantenaire.

Bruparck In the north of the city (and something of a leap of the imagination) is the **Bruparck.** Inside this recreation complex, you'll find the Mini-Europe theme park (p. 198); the Kinepolis multiplex movie theater; and the Océade water park. Beside this stands the **Atomium** (p. 197), Brussels Planetarium, Roi Baudoin Soccer Stadium, and the Parc des Expositions congress center.

Getting Around

ON FOOT There's no better way to explore the historical core of Brussels than walking (especially the myriad tiny streets around Grand-Place). It's also a pleasant stroll uptown through the pedestrianized Mont des Arts to place Royale.

For a Stroll: The Parc de Bruxelles

Brussels is a green city with a great expanse of parklands and gardens; it is in fact one of the greenest cities in Europe. One of the loveliest such enclaves is the **Parc de Bruxelles (Brussels Park)** on rue Royale near the Palais Royal (p. 188). Once a hunting preserve of the dukes of Brabant, it was laid out in the 18th century as a landscaped garden. In 1830, Belgian patriots fought Dutch regular troops there during the War of Independence. Later it became a fashionable place to stroll and meet friends. Although not very big, the park manages to contain everything from carefully trimmed borders to rough patches of trees and bushes, and it has fine views along its main paths, which together with the fountain form the outline of Masonic symbols.

Outside these areas, city traffic is both heavy and frantic, but there's excellent public transportation options. For example, it's a cinch to take the Métro out to Merode to explore the museums of Parc du Cinquantenaire (p. 192).

Be careful when crossing roads at black-and-white pedestrian crossings that do not have signals; pedestrians do not have legal priority over cars on these crossings. Likewise watch out for vehicles turning right or left at traffic lights, even when the green flashing lights indicates you are allowed to cross; this is quite legal and catches many a visitor off guard.

BY PUBLIC TRANSPORT Brussels has an excellent, fully integrated transit network—Métro (subway), tram (streetcar), and bus—and the network operates daily 5am to midnight, after which a limited NOCTIS night-bus network takes over until 3am, heading out to the suburbs every 30 minutes. It is run by **STIB** (www.stib-mivb.be).

Maps of the transport system are available free from the city tourist office on Grand-Place (p. 178), and transit maps are posted at all Métro stations as well as bus and tram stops. Timetables are also posted at all tram and bus stops.

The city is relatively compact so unless you plan to use the public transportation frequently, purchase a single ticket each time. Fares for a single-ride ticket on public transport are 2.50€ when purchased onboard (on buses and trams only) and 2.10€ if purchased before boarding from an automated ticket machine. A 24-hour ticket costs 7.50€. Up to 4 children ages 5 and under can ride for free along with a fare-paying adult. The MOBIB chip card system, which is used for purchasing multiple tickets and multi-day cards, can be complex and requires you to buy a 5€ card beforehand.

Validate your ticket by inserting it into the orange electronic machines inside buses and trams and at the access to Métro platforms. If you have a MOBIB card, tap it when entering and exiting the Métro station, bus or tram. Although the single-fare ticket must be revalidated on each leg of your journey, you're allowed multiple transfers within a 1-hour period of the initial validation.

If possible, plan your journey to avoid the crush at morning and evening rush hours. And again, watch out for pickpockets, especially at busy times, and avoid walking alone in deserted access tunnels, particularly after dark—the risk of being mugged is small but not entirely absent.

ART IN THE subways

When Brussels began construction of its subway system in 1969, it set aside 2 percent of the large construction budget for art—especially-commissioned, contemporary art that would adorn and "elevate" the majority of stations in the system. A far-sighted and forceful connoisseur, Emile Langui, then succeeded in persuading the public authorities to permit the art world alone to select the creators of the works that would go into the walls or ceilings of underground stations. An autonomous commission, composed of persons so eminent that they would be free from all outside pressures, was established to make the selections. Artists, it was agreed, would be chosen solely by reputation among their peers, regardless of their politics. And once chosen, they would be given carte blanche. Working from the very outset with the engineers and architects who were planning the form and shape of each station, these top Belgian artists—ranging from the world-famous Paul Delvaux to the newest *enfant terrible*—proceeded to create either murals (often on acrylic-treated metals), sculptures, or bas-reliefs that have given a sense of tingling aliveness to the tasteful and uncluttered subway stations of Brussels.

Stations (and artworks) we think are worth a visit include:

○ **Station Bourse** near the Grand-Place: "Nos Vieux Trams Bruxellois" (Our Old Brussels Trams), in oil, on panels, by the eminent Paul Delvaux which is a night scene of bygone Brussels streetcars, but with atypically-clothed females alongside, and thus lacking the subconscious eroticism and terror of most Delvaux; and "Moving Ceiling," a cascade of stainless steel cylinders (some fixed, some mobile) falling from the roof, by the sarcastic Belgian artist, Pol Bury.

○ **Station Botanique:** "Les Voyageurs" (the travellers) by Pierre Caille some 21 funny, wooden cutouts between panes of glass, of anxious commuters; "Tramification Fluide" (Smooth Tramways) by Emile Souply which shows giant, clustered clothes hangers in brilliant colors against white, a stunning image; and "The Last Migration" by Jean-Pierre Ghysels, a highly abstract flight of birds, in oxidized copper, meant to signify the antithesis of the unnatural, sun-excluding, closed life of the subway.

○ **Station Hankar:** "Notre Temps" by Roger Somville, a 500-square-yard acrylic acrylic painting on concrete requiring 2 years to complete, of the violent movement and march of humanity for social justice, including a caricature of the Chilean dictator Pinochet, all in frenzied streaks and daubs of red and yellow flame-colors that spread across the right angles of the station and visually eliminate those angles.

○ **Station Merode:** "Vive la Sociale" an oil mural by the exciting Roger Raveel of faceless humans in a social setting, next to an Adam and Eve copied from the Van Eycks' "Holy Lamb" in Ghent.

○ **Station Montgomery:** "Thema's" by famous Pol Mara, four pop-art collages devoted to sheer sensuality.

STIB, which runs Brussels' public-transport system, has put together a leaflet on the underground art galleries; download it at www.stib-mivb.be.

—Arthur Frommer

BY TRAM & BUS An extensive network of tram lines provides the ideal way to get around the city. Both trams and urban buses are painted in gray-and-brown colors. Their stops are marked with red-and-white signs and often have a shelter. You stop a tram or bus by extending your arm as it approaches so the driver can see it; if you don't signal, the bus or tram won't stop. Tram lines nos. 92 and 83 pass by key sights along rue Royale and rue de la Régence as far as avenue Louise, and so are especially useful for sightseeing.

BY METRO   The Métro is quick and efficient, and covers many important center-city locations, as well as the suburbs, the Bruparck recreation park (p. 161), and the Heysel congress center. Stations are identified by signs with a white M on a blue background.

BY TAXI   Taxi fares are relatively pricey in Brussels, starting at 2.40€ between 6am and 10pm and at 4.40€ between 10pm and 6am, increasing by 1.80€ per kilometer inside the city (tariff 1) and 2.70€ per kilometer outside Brussels (tariff 2)—so make sure the meter is set to the correct tariff. Tip and taxes are included on the meter price, and you need not add an extra tip unless there has been extra service, such as help with heavy luggage (although drivers won't refuse tips). All taxis are metered. They cannot be hailed on the street, but there are taxi stands on many principal streets, particularly in the center city, and at rail stations. To request a cab by phone, call **Taxis Verts** (www.taxisverts.be; ✆ **02/349-4949**).

BY CAR   Driving in Brussels is nasty and brutish. Normally polite citizens turn into red-eyed demons once they get behind the steering wheel, driving very fast, except at rush hour, and aggressively. At rush hour (which lasts about 2 hr. either side of 9am and 5pm), it is almost impossible to move on main roads inside the city and on the notorious R0 outer ring road (beltway). Sundays and very early mornings are slightly better, and with the exception of Friday night, evenings after about 7pm are not too bad.

This is a long way of saying: don't drive in the city, if you can avoid it. Park your car either at your hotel or in one of the many public parking garages—your hotel can furnish the address of the nearest one—and do not set foot in it again until you're ready to leave Brussels. Parking charges are about 15€ per day; it's worth it. A stout pair of shoes, good public transportation, and an occasional taxi ride will get you anywhere you want inexpensively and hassle-free. If you must drive in Brussels, watch out for the notorious *priorité de droite* (priority from the right) traffic system.

[FastFACTS] BRUSSELS

ATMs   There are ATMs all over Brussels, and most are open 24/7, although you'll want to be a bit cautious about withdrawing cash in quiet areas outside the main tourist areas after dark.

Business Hours   Stores open Monday to Saturday from 9 or 10am to 6pm. On Friday evening, many center-city stores stay open until 8 or 9pm. Most stores close on Sunday, except the tour-ist-orientated ones around the Grand-Place. The major-ity of museums open Tues-day through Sunday from 10am until 5pm, and most close on Monday, which is

the day to head out of town, perhaps to Bruges, Ghent, or Antwerp.

Doctors & Dentists
For doctors, call **Médi Garde** (✆ **02/479-1818**) or **SOS Médecins** (✆ **02/513-0202**) and ask for an Eng-lish-speaking doctor. For

Brussels is generally safe around the tourist attractions, but there is a growing trend of pickpocketing, theft from cars, and muggings in places such as Métro station foot tunnels and streets just out the center of the city. Take sensible precautions with your belongings, particularly in obvious circumstances such as on crowded Métro trains. Be especially vigilant around Bruxelles-Midi and Gare du Nord stations and when withdrawing cash from ATMs at night on quiet streets.

emergency dental care, call 𝄐 **02/426-1026.**

Embassies See p. 275 in chapter 9.

Emergencies Dial 𝄐 **112** for police, ambulance, paramedics, and the fire department. This is a nationwide toll-free call from landline, mobile, or pay phone. For routine police matters, go to **Brussels Central Police Station,** rue du Marché au Charbon 30 (𝄐 **02/279-7979;** Métro: Bourse), just off the Grand-Place. Most officers will speak some English.

Internet Access Most hotels in Brussels offer free Internet access as part of the room price, although perversely some more expensive ones still charge extra. Some areas in central Brussels provide free access to Wi-Fi hotspots; Wifi.Brussels is available in train and Métro stations, major public squares, stores, hotels, bars, and restaurants.

Pharmacies In Belgium, a pharmacy is called either an *apotheek* or a *pharmacie* and sells both prescription and nonprescription medicines. Regular hours are Monday to Saturday from around 9am to 6pm. **Grande Pharmacie De Brouckère,** Passage du Nord 10 (𝄐 **02/218-0575**) is centrally located. Pharmacies post details of nearby **all-night and Sunday pharmacies** on their doors. The website www.pharmacie.be also has that info. Simply type in your area code to find the nearest 24-hour pharmacy; the site is in French and Dutch but it is very easy to navigate. A final method: call 𝄐 **09/039-9000** to find the nearest 24-hour pharmacy.

Post Office The national mail company is known as **bpost** (www.depostlaposte. be; 𝄐 **02/278-5044**); most post offices are open Monday to Friday 9am to 5pm. The office at Bruxelles de Brouckère, boulevard Anspach 1, is open Monday to Friday 8:30am to 6pm and Saturday 10am to 4pm. The office at the Gare du Midi, avenue Fonsny 48a, is open 24 hours a day.

WHERE TO STAY

At every price level, hotels fill up during the week with E.U.-related business travelers and empty out on weekends, as well as during July and August. In these off-peak periods, rates can drop as much as 50 percent, making Brussels the perfect destination for weekend breaks.

The most popular Brussels districts for lodgings are in the extended zone around the **Grand-Place;** in the upper town district around place Stéphanie and boulevard de Waterloo; and along upmarket **avenue Louise.** These areas hold large, glittering three- and four-star establishments, along with many fine medium-priced places. Budget hotels can be found in the streets around the Grand-Place and in the Ixelles district to the south of avenue Louise. The **European District** presents something of a special case: Its hotels are convenient for visiting Eurocrats, politicians, lobbyists, and media people, but tourists may find the businesslike environment, anonymous contemporary architecture, and distance from Grand-Place (about 30 minutes by foot) unappealing. While it's lively during the week, weekends the area empties out and streets are eerily quiet.

Hotels in the upper price range include members of just about every international chain. Most have a wealth of facilities, but the service at them tends to be more impersonal than in similar properties in other European capitals.

Rental Apartments in Brussels

If you would prefer to have a space to call your own in the city, there are plenty of self-catering options in Brussels. **B-aparthotels** (p. 168) has four buildings in the city center; check out www.b-aparthotels.com. Other options include **Rent by Night** (www.rentbynight.com), with three buildings in the historical heart of the city and **Adagio Aparthotel** (www.adagio-city.com), which offers luxurious studios and apartments at two addresses, one near the European Union district (p. 185) and one in the Anspach shopping mall (p. 199). And, of course, **Airbnb** (www.airbnb.com), **FlipKey** (www.flipkey.com) and **VRBO** (www.vrbo.com) have a big footprint in the city, offering apartments of all kinds, from bare bones budget to over-the-top swanky.

Lower Town
EXPENSIVE

Hotel Amigo ★★★   In a prime position just off the Grand-Place, the Amigo is an elegant destination hotel with a surprisingly warm, welcoming ambience. Owned by the Forté family, its chic but understated style shows the sure hand of designer and British TV star Olga Polizzi, who had the good sense to retain the historic flagstone lobby from the building's previous incarnation as a prison. All the public spaces are kitted out with a wealth of antiques, sculptures, and 18th-century Flemish tapestries. Spacious rooms are decorated in tasteful, muted shades with pops of color; each one is adorned with Magritte or Tintin prints. The equally huge bathrooms all have separate showers and baths and the suites get Jacuzzis too. Ask for a room with a view of the Town Hall's fantastic Gothic spire, so close you can almost reach out and touch it. Breakfast is a wonderful experience, with a lavish buffet, as befits the price; by night the breakfast room transforms into the expensive **Bocconi** Italian restaurant. The lobby's **Bar A** brings in well-heeled Brussels couples to enjoy a cocktail or two.

Rue de l'Amigo 1–3. www.roccofortehotels.com. ✆ **02/547-4747.** 173 units. 265€–467€ doubles, 1,272€–4,500€ suites. Suites include buffet breakfast. Valet parking 30€/day. **Amenities:** Restaurant, bar, room service, concierge, fitness center, business center, free Wi-Fi. Métro: Bourse.

Hotel Métropole ★★   Even if you're not staying here, the hotel is worth a visit, as it is the very epitome of Belle Epoque magnificence, just a few blocks from the Grand-Place and still owned by the brewing family who bought it in 1895. An ornate, marble-and-gilt interior complete with soaring ceilings and lavishly ornamented public rooms distinguishes this late-19th-century

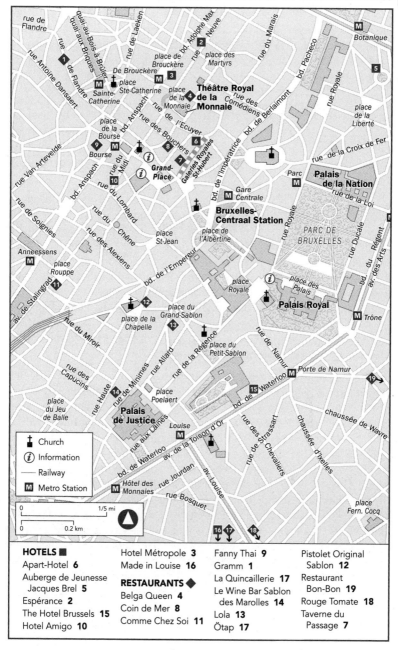

HOTELS ■

Apart-Hotel **6**

Auberge de Jeunesse
  Jacques Brel **5**

Espérance **2**

The Hotel Brussels **15**

Hotel Amigo **10**

Hotel Métropole **3**

Made in Louise **16**

RESTAURANTS ◆

Belga Queen **4**

Coin de Mer **8**

Comme Chez Soi **11**

Fanny Thai **9**

Gramm **1**

La Quincaillerie **17**

Le Wine Bar Sablon
  des Marolles **14**

Lola **13**

Ötap **17**

Pistolet Original
  Sablon **12**

Restaurant
  Bon-Bon **19**

Rouge Tomate **18**

Taverne du
  Passage **7**

glamour puss from the herd of impersonal five-star hotels in Brussels. The sumptuous guest rooms are all individually decorated with classic furnishings and some rather startling color schemes; the suites are positively OTT and many feature Louis XVI-style furniture and antique desks. The hotel is also home to the Art Nouveau brasserie **Cafe Métropole** and the swanky lobby bar **Le 31,** with colorful ceiling frescoes and glittering chandeliers.

Place de Brouckère 31. www.metropolehotel.com. © **02/217-2300.** 251 units. 109€–215€ doubles, 325€–675€ suites. Some room rates include buffet breakfast. Valet parking 27€/day. **Amenities:** Restaurant, bar, business center, concierge, fitness center, free Wi-Fi.

MODERATE

B-aparthotels ★ With 5 buildings scattered through central Brussels, B-aparthotels offer accommodations with all conveniences, from well-equipped kitchens to comfy beds with quality linen bedding, and regular cleaning service (if you stay four or more nights). Just be careful which address you go for; the apartments in rue des Dominicains are set on pretty alleyway just steps away from the Grand-Place and all the restaurants around rue des Bouchers, but the noise level ratchets up to an unbearable level come weekends. And while the rooms here were once decked out with sleek, quality furnishings, time has taken its toll and they are now looking more than a little beaten up. The alternative facilities at boulevard du Regent 58 make better, quieter options and they are just a brief Métro ride away from the action in the Grand-Place.

Rue des Dominicains 25. www.b-aparthotels.com. © **02/743-5111.** 184 units. 114€–179€. Parking 25€/day. **Amenities:** Full kitchens, free Wi-Fi.

Hotel Espérance ★ In a small alleyway off the boulevard Anspach, this former *maison de passé,* where rooms were rented out by the hour to women of the night, is now a small hotel. Its Design Rooms are done up in bold primary colors, while those in the Superior category are more restrained, decorated with muted pastel hues. One guest room preserves the architecture and raffish feeling of the original Art Deco incarnation, and not surprisingly, it's the most expensive. A freestanding bath poses proudly in the middle of that room, with a wooden screen to push into place should you feel modest. The **Taverne bar** downstairs remains a perfect Art Deco specimen with stained-glass windows and aged wooden furniture; it doubles as the breakfast room (included with some rates), as well as a restaurant serving up simple dishes like pasta along with cocktails. The modest hotel is delightful, although the side street can be a little daunting at night. If you are thinking of staying here, bear in mind that there's no elevator and the staircase is steep.

Rue du Finistère 1–3. www.hotel-esperance.be. © **02/219-1028.** 12 units. 95€–160€ doubles. Breakfast included in some room rates. Public parking 16€/day. **Amenities:** Free Wi-Fi. Métro: De Brouckère.

INEXPENSIVE

Auberge de Jeunesse Jacques Brel ★★ This amiable, rather ramshackle hostel is set on a small road leading up to the delightful place des

Barricades and is an easy 15-minute walk to most of the major sites, including Grand-Place and the Royal Fine Arts Museums. Because the hostel has been shoehorned into an old house, rooms are of odd shapes and sizes, so you take potluck. The total bed capacity is 170, spread over 54 rooms, which hold from two to eight beds. Along with dorm rooms are entirely private rooms. The decor is basic; you're here for the value and the company of like-minded youthful travelers. The bar, open from 7pm to 1am, gets packed most evenings. Simple suppers of pasta and pizza are on offer for around 8€, and there's an exceptional, almost purely organic buffet breakfast.

Rue de la Sablonnière 28. www.lesaubergesdejeunesse.be. ℰ **02/219-5676.** 54 units. 22€ shared room–97€ private room. Breakfast included in room rate. No parking. Free Wi-Fi. Métro: Botanique.

Upper Town
EXPENSIVE
The Hotel Brussels ★★★   You can't miss The Hotel. It's the 24-story white building on the boulevard de Waterloo, which is the location of Gucci, Armani, and similar posh boutiques, and the main high-end shopping street of Brussels (p. 199). Its swish rooms are both well designed and practical, with plenty of lighting and mirrors that swivel so you get a back as well as front view. The decor is classy, with lots of blacks, deep browns, white, and beige. Every room has a massive bed, a built-in desk, a large sofa in front of the window with a circular table, and a Nespresso machine. Bathrooms are concealed behind sliding glass panels, so from the washbasin you can brush your teeth and admire the view at the same time. Unless you suffer from vertigo, book one of the rooms on the top floors and go for a corner room with panoramic views on two sides. Those staying in Deluxe rooms and suites have access to the 24th-floor Panorama Lounge with an open bar.

Boulevard de Waterloo 38. www.thehotel-brussels.be. ℰ **02/504-1111.** 420 units. 140€–210€ doubles, 360–1,750€ suites. Breakfast included in some room rates. Parking 35€/day. **Amenities:** Restaurant, bar, spa, fitness room, free Wi-Fi. Métro: Louise/Porte de Namur.

MODERATE
Made in Louise ★★   Located in a residential neighborhood, this former town house is an historic, protected building; its owners have cleverly used what could have been a major restriction to enhance the feel of a private family home. On the ground floor there's a smart black-and-white bar, a generously sized billiards room, and a cafe/breakfast room. The vast central staircase leads to spacious landings filled with artworks and to the elegantly furnished guest rooms, each of which has a unique style. A room with striped wallpaper feels masculine and bold; another, with vivid, blue-flowered wallpaper, is much more feminine; a room with a rough wooden headboard and pale colors has a rustic vibe. All rooms have bathrooms that are of a generous size, with custom-made vanity units designed to look original to the house. The separate cottage, built in 2015, has 9 guest rooms overlooking the internal

169

courtyard; they are similar in style to those in the main building but lack some of its period touches, such as fireplaces.

Rue Veydt 40. www.madeinlouise.com. ℂ **02/537-4033.** 48 units. 90€–325€ doubles. Rates include buffet breakfast. Public parking nearby 10€/day. **Amenities:** Bar, free Wi-Fi. Metro: Louise/Parvis St-Gilles.

WHERE TO EAT

Food is a passion in Brussels, a city that boasts an impressive number of Michelin-star restaurants. People here regard dining as a fine art and their favorite chef as a grand master. It's just about impossible to eat badly, no matter what your price range. The city has more than 3,000 restaurants and even if you're on a tight budget, you should try to set aside the money for at least one big splurge in a fine restaurant—nourishment for both the soul and the stomach.

The Brussels restaurant scene covers the entire city, but there are a couple of culinary pockets you should know about. It has been said that you haven't truly visited this city unless you've dined at least once along **rue des Bouchers** and its offshoot, **Petite rue des Bouchers,** both of which are near the Grand-Place. Both streets are lined with an extraordinary array of ethnic eateries, most with a proudly proclaimed specialty, and all with modest prices. Reservations are not usually necessary in these colorful and crowded restaurants; if you cannot be seated at one, you simply stroll on to the next one. Be prepared for barking waiters eager for business as you wander down the streets, but it's all very good-natured.

There's also the cluster of fine restaurants at the **Marché aux Poissons (Fish Market),** a short walk from the Grand-Place around place Ste-Catherine. This is where fishermen once unloaded their daily catches from a now-covered canal. Seafood, as you'd expect, is the specialty. A well-spent afternoon's occupation is to stroll through the area to examine the bills of fare exhibited in windows and make your reservation for the evening meal. Don't fret if the service is slow: People take their time dining out in Brussels.

Beyond the restaurants described below, we're also big fans of **The Restaurant** (at the Musical Instruments Museum; see p. 191). It keeps the same hours as the museum, so is not open for dinner, unfortunately.

Lower Town
EXPENSIVE

Belga Queen ★★ CONTEMPORARY BELGIAN   This most spectacular of brasseries is blessed with a long dining room swathed in a decorative stained-glass ceiling and marble pillars. It's set in a Belle Epoque building that was formerly a bank and is a beautiful place in which to eat alongside stylish young locals. The food is almost secondary to the decor, but you'll find the dishes, which include buckets full of mussels, towers of seafood, steak tartare, salmon, and duck, are all impeccably prepared. In addition to the restaurant,

quick bites IN BRUSSELS

For a tasty breakfast, lunch, or snack, head for the convivial **Roi des Belges** ★, rue Jules Van Praet 35 (🕿 **02/513-5116**), on the corner of trendy place St-Géry. The soup of the day runs 4€, a generous cheese plate is under 10€, or you can just nurse a coffee while reading the newspaper or chatting with your neighboring diners.

Another seductive invitation is the aroma of **fresh Brussels waffles,** sold from street stands around the city. Generally thicker than American waffles, they cost about 3€ and are smothered in sugar icing. The stands are all equally good and there's not much reason to try one over another. Should you want to sample an impressive range of toppings and accompaniments, head to the specialist **Aux Gaufres de Bruxelles ★★,** rue du Marché aux Herbes 113 (www.belgiumwaffle.com; 🕿 **02/514-0171**).

You could also do a lot worse than try any of the little **Greek, Turkish, Middle**

Eastern, and **Israeli** places around the Grand-Place, where you can fill up on moussaka, kebabs, salad, and falafel for as little as 5€. And if you're after basic fare to fill up on while knocking back the *trippel* beer, **A La Mort Subite** (p. 204) has a menu of very simple cheese and salami-type snacks that don't break the bank.

And don't forget those *frites* (fries). Belgians usually eat their favorite snack with mayonnaise rather than ketchup. Prices run from around 2.50€ to 4€ for a *cornet* (cone); sauces such as pickle, tartare, samurai (hot!), or curry cost extra. Brussels is dotted with dozens of fast-food stands serving *frites* in paper cones. One of the best, **Maison Antoine ★★,** place Jourdan 1 (www.maisonantoine.be; 🕿 **02/230-5456**), in the European District, has been in situ since the 1940s. You'll have to join the line at peak times, but the wait for its fries, made from fresh-peeled potatoes, is worthwhile.

the Belga Queen offers an oyster bar and a beer bar, as well as what must be the last cigar lounge in Belgium, hidden down in the basement. There's an offshoot in Ghent.

Rue du Fossée aux Loups 32. www.belgaqueen.be. 🕿 **02/217-2187.** Reservations recommended on weekends. Lunch main course 18€, lunch prix-fixe 25€–30€, dinner main courses 25€–48€. Mon–Thurs noon–2:30pm and 6:30pm–11pm; Fri noon–2:30pm and 6:30pm–midnight; Sat 6:30pm–midnight. Métro: De Brouckère.

Comme Chez Soi ★★★ FRENCH This fine restaurant has two Michelin stars and offers classic French cuisine at its most refined. Dinner is served in an opulent Art Nouveau dining room resplendent with swirling woodwork and delicate garlands of wrought iron, and under the influence of chef Lionel Rigolet service is attentive but delightfully unstuffy. With menus changing seasonally, most of the ingredients are organic and all are prepared with loving care and attention to the most minute of details; menus might encompass guinea fowl with Wallonian snails or a rack of lamb with honey, sweet onions, and cumin. The wine list is stellar, as you would expect from such an august establishment, which may well be the gastronomic blowout of your trip to Brussels. Book for dinner as far ahead as possible; getting a table at short notice is more likely at lunchtime. You can also choose to eat in the kitchen to watch the chefs at work.

Place Rouppe 23. www.commechezsoi.be. ✆ **02/512-2921.** Reservations required. Lunch 65€, dinner main courses 47€–177€, fixed-price menus 99€–254€. Thurs–Sat noon–1:30pm and Tues–Sat 7–9:30pm.

Gramm ★★ FUSION   Young chef Erwan Kenzo Nakata has a Japanese and Breton background, so it's no surprise that his cooking is an intriguing fusion of Asian and French cultures. Seasonal five- to seven-course tasting menus have featured seared cod in a delicate matcha foam, smoked salmon topped with shavings of spicy black radish, and a ginger-infused cream of beet and carrot accented with a Parmesan crisp. The minimalist dining room— simple folding wood chairs, black tables, plain white walls—isn't much on character, but it keeps the focus on the bold colors and flavors of the dishes.

Rue de Flandre 86. www.grammrestaurant.be. ✆ **0495/101-822.** Fixed-price menus 60€–80€. Tues–Fri noon–2pm and 6:30–10pm, Sat 6:30–10pm.

MODERATE

Fanny Thai ★★ THAI/VIETNAMESE   In spite of the unfortunate name, this is simply the best Thai in Brussels, run by young, enthusiastic wait staff with a vibe so casual it's virtually a cafe. The dining area has one bare brick wall adorned with a giant face of Buddha, who solemnly overlooks proceedings as the waiters scoot daintily around the cramped tables. Go beyond the usual green shrimp curry and try the fish cooked in herbs and wrapped in banana leaves, or chicken stir-fried with basil—all delicious and not too heavy handed with the chili. Fanny Thai gets so busy you might have to wait for a table but there are plenty of drinking dens scattered along the street in this trendy part of town near the Bourse.

Rue Jules Van Praet 36. www.fannythai.com. ✆ **02/502-6422.** Main courses 13€–16€. Mon–Thurs noon–3pm and 6–11pm; Fri noon–3pm and 6–11:30pm; Sat noon– 11:30pm; Sun noon–11pm.

Taverne du Passage ★★ BRASSERIE   Tucked away in the Galeries Royales St-Hubert shopping arcade, this Art Deco gem has been going strong since 1928. While the period setting, replete with checkerboard-tile floors and long leather banquettes, is definitely a draw for tourists, elderly locals and smartly dressed business types also frequent the place, which offers solid

---

Lunchtime Bargains in Brussels

Most restaurants serve lunch between noon and 2pm, and reopen for dinner from 7 to 10pm, with brasseries staying open all day. Almost every eatery in Brussels offers a *menu du jour* at lunchtime, consisting of a fixed menu with a couple of two- or three-course options—often with a glass of table wine thrown in—that are often markedly good values in this expensive city. If you are yearning to try one of the fancier restaurants but can't face the bill, try them out for lunch and save your money for sampling the beer.

French-Belgian brasserie fare at fairly reasonable prices. You can't go wrong with classic *moule-frîtes* or entrecôte but also worth a try is the Flemish specialty *waterzooi,* a hearty, creamy fish-and-vegetable stew. The steak tartare, served with a generous portion of fries and a salad, is practically a meal in itself. Service by white-coated waiters is brisk and efficient, which is especially welcome given the busy lunchtime crowd.

Galerie de la Reine 30. www.taverne-du-passage.be. ℂ **02/512-3731.** Main courses 18€–33€. Tues–Thurs and Sun noon–11pm and Fri–Sat noon–11:30pm.

Upper Town
EXPENSIVE

Lola ★★ BRASSERIE   Genteel elderly couples and smart young things, tourists as well as suits clearly working for the E.U.—all are cheerfully welcomed in this smart contemporary brasserie. The long, narrow canteen-style room is decked in cheery colors and industrial-style piping. The pan-European menu includes Irish steak bathed in Guinness sauce as well as good Belgian shrimp croquettes. For main courses, the duck confit with apple and grape compote and mashed potatoes, and the roasted cod on a bed of fresh peas both hit the spot. The wine list is moderately priced, and the waiters are some of the most professional—and friendliest—in town. Lola deserves her success.

Place du Grand Sablon 33. www.restolola.be. ℂ **02/514-2460.** Mains 18€–32€. Daily noon–2:30pm and 7–11pm. Tram 92, 94 to Petit Sablon.

Rouge Tomate ★★ MODERN FRENCH   Set in a 19th-century mansion on chic, boutique-lined Avenue Louise, this upscale restaurant champions clean eating, with a healthy portion of organic, seasonal produce accompanying nearly every dish. As a result, the menu changes frequently, but expect fine-tuned mains like grilled halibut and soft-shell crab with roasted artichokes, carrots, and potatoes, and spicy duck breast served with smoked carrots and wedges of fried chickpeas. The interior is a sleek, all-white affair with punches of bright red; it's lovely but if the weather is cooperating, the plant-filled back garden can't be beat. One drawback: the service can be downright snooty. For a nightcap, head upstairs to the swanky, 1940s-inspired Alice Cocktail Bar.

Avenue Louise 190. www.rougetomate.be. ℂ **02/647-7044.** Main courses 22€–38€. Fixed-price lunch, one to three courses, 24€–44€; fixed-priced dinner 55€. Mon–Thurs noon–2:30pm and 7–10:30pm, Sat 7–10:30pm.

MODERATE
Le Wine Bar Sablon des Marolles ★★★ TRADITIONAL BELGIAN A glass of wine from the short but good list, and a selection of plates from the menu, is just the thing after a morning spent shopping at the famous *brocante* market in the place du Jeu de Balle or in the antiques shops of the Marolles (p. 202). The surrounding area is scruffy and working class and proud of it, and this wine bar is located in a 17th-century house with wooden floors, chairs, and tables; the simple surroundings are elevated by the vast paintings

and prints on the walls. The short menu is cleverly put together, with starters that are ideal for sharing from 11€ to 20€. Try the chicken liver pâté, sea bream carpaccio, or sardines with olive oil. More substantial dishes could include smoked sausage with Puy lentils or the rack of lamb. There's also a good selection of cheese for dessert as well as a well-priced wine list, which includes champagne by the glass. The weekend lunch, with soup and a main course, is just 15€.

Rue Haute 198. www.winebarsablon.be. ⓒ **02/503-6250.** Main courses 22€–35€. Thurs–Fri 7–11pm, Sat noon–3pm and 7–11pm, Sun noon–4pm and 7–11pm. Metro: Porte de Hal.

INEXPENSIVE

Pistolet Original Sablon ★★★ BELGIAN   A *pistolet* is a filled, crusty bread roll—something that every Belgian child grows up on—so Valérie Lepla struck a rich, nostalgic vein when she named her deli-cafe in the smart Sablon district. It's invariably packed with just about every level of Brussels society, either eating pistolets in the cheerful cafe or lining up at the deli counter to take them home. Pistolet Original makes a perfect spot for lunch after rummaging around the weekend antiques markets. A few of the available fillings: Ardenne ham, shrimp, sharp-tasting pickles with minced pork, chicken curry, roast beef and celery root, blood pudding, white sausage, and butter or chocolate. You could come here on a daily basis and still not go through all the possibilities. Wash things down with beer, wine, coffee, or tea.

> ### Be on Your Guard in the Ilot Sacré
>
> A few restaurants in this colorful restaurant district just off the Grand-Place take advantage of tourists. If you decide to dine at a restaurant not reviewed here and you don't want to get fleeced—be sure to double check the price of everything *before* you order it. Most visitors leave the Ilot Sacré with no more serious complaint than an expanded waistline, but a little caution is in order.

Rue Joseph Steven 24. www.pistolet-original.be. ⓒ **02/880-8098.** Main courses 5€–10€. Mon–Fri 10am–4pm and Sat–Sun 11am–6pm. Metro: Gare Centrale.

Suburbs

Note: The following restaurants are not that far from the city center, but they are technically in areas considered suburbs.

EXPENSIVE

La Quincaillerie ★★★ BELGIAN/FRENCH   Open since 1988, this gorgeous restaurant set the benchmark for the others that followed it into the Châtelain district. Inside a former ironmonger shop built in 1903, La Quincaillerie has a beautiful Art Nouveau exterior and an interior of wrought-iron balconies, polished brass, and a huge clock. It's always buzzing as waiters deliver dishes with style to a chic clientele. The restaurant takes the environmental route with ingredients, using sustainable fish sources; chicken from its own farm in Bresse, France; locally procured vegetables; and organic and biodynamic wines. This is combined with an interesting menu, which may include grilled scallops with marinated pumpkin in a lemony lobster sauce for a starter; and pork knuckle with mashed potatoes and grilled mushrooms as a main. There's also a formidable range of fish and seafood available.

Rue de Page 45. www.quincaillerie.be. ℂ **02/533-9833.** Reservations recommended. Fixed-price two- to three-course menus 20€–48€, dinner main courses 24€–47€. Mon–Fri noon–2:30pm and 7–11pm, Sat 7–11pm, Sun 7–10pm. Tram: 81 to Trinité.

Restaurant Bon-Bon ★★ HAUTE CUISINE   Chef Christophe Hardiquest is one of Belgium's top young chefs, a name to watch as he collects Michelin stars (he's up to two). He opened the first Bon-Bon in Uccle in 2001 before moving in 2011 to an Art Nouveau house in Woluwe-Saint-Pierre, the city's posh diplomatic quarter. The move made the restaurant a hit: You must now book dinner months in advance. Billed as a *salon d'artisan cuisinier* (the salon of an artisan chef), this is a serious monument to dining. Chef believes strongly in the connection between the region and the taste of a product—only ingredients that have the location-specific *appellation d'origine contrôlée* designation are used here. The set menus may include the likes of mille-feuille of avocado and local mushrooms and for dessert, fermented black garlic with balsamic ice cream. The wine list is as serious as the service is impeccable; you can also sit at the bar and watch the chefs toil away in the open kitchen.

Avenue de Tervueren 453. www.bon-bon.be. ℂ **02/346-6615.** Reservations required. Lunch menu 75€, fixed-price dinner menu 185€–245€, dinner main courses 62€–80€. Tues–Fri noon–1:30pm and 7:30–9pm. Closed Sat–Mon. Tram 94 to Trois Couleurs.

MODERATE

Ötap ★★ CONTEMPORARY   Set on a quiet, leafy corner in the Châtelain district, this smart, stylish eatery embraces the trendy shared-plate concept with generally excellent results. The kitchen is headed up by twenty-something chef Paul-Antoine Bertin, whose youthful energy is apparent in the abbreviated, yet highly inventive seasonal menus. Beautifully presented on custom-made ceramic plates, dishes are often Asian-inspired, like the beef tataki with Thai vegetables and nori or the squid tempura. Others are solidly Italian, like the butternut gnocchi tossed with sage and brown butter. Though the menu is divided into appetizers, fish and meat mains, and sides, plates arrive scattershot, which can result in a tangle of flavors that doesn't always jibe. Nevertheless, the service is friendly and the wine card particularly interesting, with several hard-to-find natural labels by the bottle. For two people, expect to order four to five dishes.

Place Albert Leemans 10. www.ötap.com. ℂ **04/7275-4738.** Main courses 12€–15€. Thursday, fixed-price menu 40€. Tues–Sat 6:30–11pm, Sat 11am–2:30pm.

EXPLORING BRUSSELS

Brussels offers so much to the visitor that the city can feel overwhelming; there are more than 80 museums as well as the glorious architecture of King Léopold I's purpose-built city, and one of the best fine-art galleries in the world. Most of the sights are clustered around the Grand-Place in the lower

Arc du Cinquantenaire **5**
Atomium **9**
Autoworld **7**
Bourse **14**
Cathédrale des Sts-Michel-
  et-Gudule **34**
Centre Belge de la
  Bande Dessinée **11**
Eglise Notre-Dame
  du Sablon **22**
Eglise St-Jacques-sur-
  Coudenberg **28**
Eglise St-Nicolas **13**
European District **2**
Fondation Jacques Brel **20**
Grand-Place **16**
Hôtel de Ville
  (Town Hall) **17**
Jardin Botanique **10**
Manneken-Pis **19**
Mini-Europe **9**
Musée Art & Histoire **6**
Musée Bruxellois
  de la Gueuze **8**
Musée David et Alice
  van Buuren **25**
Musée de la Ville
  de Bruxelles **15**
Musée du Costume
  et de la Dentelle **18**
Musée Horta **25**
Musée Magritte **29**
Musée René Magritte **1**
Musée Royal de l'Armée
  et d'Histoire Militaire **4**
Musées Royaux des Beaux-
  Arts de Belgique **26**
Muséum des Sciences
  Naturelles **36**
Musical Instruments
  Museum **30**
Palais de Justice **24**
Palais de la Nation **33**
Palais Royal,
  BELvue Museum
  & Coudenberg **31**
Parc de Bruxelles **32**
Parc du Cinquantenaire **3**
place des Martyrs **12**
place du Grand Sablon **21**
place du Petit Sablon **23**
place Royale **27**
Royal Museum for
  Central Africa **35**

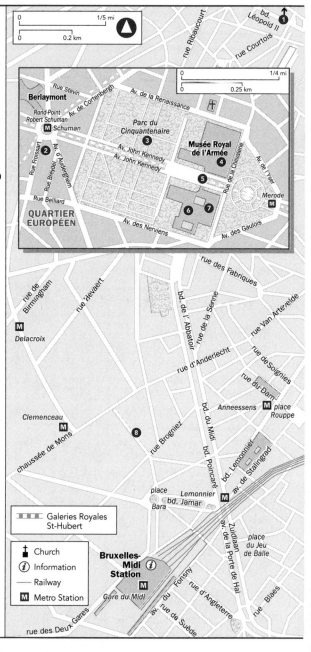

QUARTIER EUROPÉEN

Galeries Royales
St-Hubert

✝ Church
ⓘ Information
— Railway
Ⓜ Metro Station

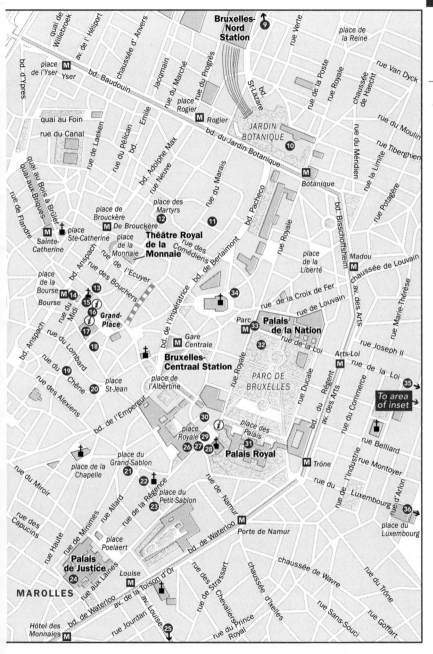

place de Willebroek
quai de Willebroek
av. de l' Héliport
chaussée d'Anvers
Bruxelles-Nord Station 9
rue Verte
place de la Reine
rue Van Dyck
bd. d'Ypres
place de l'Yser M Yser
bd. Baudouin
Jacqmain
Emile
rue du Marché
rue du Progrès
place Rogier M Rogier
bd. St-Lazare
rue de la Poste
rue Royale
chaussée de Haecht
rue du Moulin
rue Tiberghien
quai au Foin
rue du Canal
rue de Laeken
rue du Pélican
bd.
rue Neuve
bd. Adolphe Max
JARDIN BOTANIQUE 10
bd. du Jardin Botanique
bd. Pacheco
rue de la Méridien
rue la Limite
rue du Méridien
rue Potagère
M Botanique
place des Martyrs 12
place de Brouckère M De Brouckère
11
rue du Marais
rue Royale
bd. Bisschoffsheim
place Ste-Catherine
M Sainte-Catherine
place de la Monnaie
Théâtre Royal de la Monnaie
rue des Comédiens
bd. de Berlaimont
place de la Liberté
Madou chaussée de Louvain
quai au Bois à Brûler
quai aux Briques
rue de Flandre
bd. Anspach
rue de l'Ecuyer
rue des Bouchers
av. des Arts
rue Marie-Thérèse
place de la Bourse M 14
13
bd. de l'Impératrice
34
rue de la Croix de Fer
rue de Louvain
rue Joseph II
Bourse
rue du Midi
15 (i)
16 (i)
Grand-Place
Parc M 33
Palais de la Nation
Arts-Loi
rue de la Loi M
rue de la Loi 35
To area of inset
rue de l'Anspach
rue du Lombard
17
18
Gare Centrale M
32
Bruxelles-Centraal Station
PARC DE BRUXELLES
rue Ducale
bd. du Régent
av. des Arts
rue du Commerce
rue du Chêne
19
place St-Jean
place de l'Albertine
rue Royale
place des Palais (i)
rue Belliard
rue des Alexiens
20
30
place Royale 29
26 27 28
31
Palais Royal
M Trône
rue Montoyer
rue de l'Industrie
bd. de l'Empereur
place de la Chapelle
place du Grand-Sablon 21
22
place du Petit-Sablon 23
rue de Namur
rue du Luxembourg
rue d'Arlon
36
place du Luxembourg
rue du Miroir
rue de la Régence
rue Allard
bd. de Waterloo
Porte de Namur M
chaussée de Wavre
rue du Trône
rue des Capucins
rue Haute
rue de Minimes
place Poelaert
Palais de Justice 24
rue aux Laines
Louise M
av. de la Toison d'Or
av. Louise
bd. de Waterloo
rue des Strassart
rue des Chevaliers
chaussée d'Ixelles
rue Sans-Souci
rue Goffart
MAROLLES
Hôtel des Monnaies M
rue Jourdan
rue du Prince Royal
25

Some Brussels museums like the **Musée Art & Histoire** (Art & History Museum, p. 193), **Musée Magritte** (p. 189), the **Museum des Sciences Naturelles** (Museum of Natural Sciences (p. 193) and the **Royal Museums of Fine Art of Belgium** (p. 189), offer free admission the first Wednesday afternoon of every month. Others like the **Musée du Costume et de la Dentelle** (Costume and Lace Museum, p. 187) and the **Musée de la Ville de Bruxelles** (Museum of the City of Brussels, p. 187) have free admission on the first Sunday of the month.

town, and the rue Royale in the upper town; these areas are within easy walking distance of each other, connected by the landscaped Mont des Arts, which leads up to Place Royale from Place de l'Albertine. If you head out into the suburbs, there's a comprehensive public transport system that will get you around easily, but do be aware that this city has its share of social problems and a nighttime walk around areas such as Anderlecht is not a wise idea.

The Grand-Place ★★★ You do not and cannot see the Grand-Place from afar. You must first walk through a narrow, cobblestoned street that gives no hint of what awaits, but suddenly opens onto this great enclosed plaza, flanked on all four sides by the gilded, ornamented, flag-bedecked houses of the ancient Guilds of the Middle Ages, and by the city's fairytale Town Hall. And if you are like most visitors, you instantly stop, as if yanked by a string, mouth agape, silent, and you are consumed by the beauty and age of one of the most extraordinary of all attractions. The market square of Brussels as early as the 12th century, the Grand-Place is today revered as among the greatest summations of medieval architecture and society—though it is not strictly medieval (except for its 15th century Town Hall), but rather medieval with a Renaissance (or Baroque) updating.

We'll start with Town Hall and its Brabantine-Gothic facade, and then proceed counter-clockwise around the square to the many guild houses. What we are viewing, in essence, is the genius of the "Italo-Flamand," or the Baroque, superimposed upon the forms of the Middle Ages. Note that on most of the houses, three stories of pillars decorate each front, and follow on a uniform succession of styles from bottom to top: Doric, Ionian, Corinthian.

The Town Hall—"Tower" of the Grand-Place ★★★ Start with the Town Hall ("Hotel de Ville"). It survived the bombardment of 1695, and is essentially the same, sumptuous, Gothic, medieval structure built in the early 1400s under the Dukes of Burgundy. Have you ever seen a modern structure to compare with it, in beauty of proportion, in lightness, in harmonious detail? Look especially at the tower, surmounted at the very peak of the spire with a 16½-foot-high gilded statue of St. Michael, patron saint of Brussels, sword drawn, atop a vanquished Devil. Square in shape for its first five stories, it then becomes an open construction—a framework of stone ribs—in its next three octagonal stories, before assuming a pyramidal form to culminate at St. Michael. It is as airy as the castle tower of a fairy tale, showing the sky between its stone ribs, and seems to float in the heavens toward which it soars.

When it was then decided, in 1455, to extend the building, only a small space was available for the right-hand wing (as you face it), accounting for the difference in length of the two wings (and the off-center position of the tower). The heavy stone walls of the Belfry Tower also required the placing of an off-center entrance archway underneath the new tower. The assertion that this was an architectural mistake, which caused architect Jan van Ruysbroek to commit suicide when he allegedly discovered the "error," is simply a Brussels joke that has been told for centuries to tourists.

The original entrance to the building was at the staircase flanked by the two lions of Brabant, one holding the escutcheon of St. Michael; young couples walk down those steps on Saturday mornings following their civil weddings inside. On both sides of the lions are scalloped arcades connecting to pillars; but two arcades have no pillars beneath, ending instead in tightly-compressed bas-relief sculptures that simply "hang" in the air—they're called "pendentives." Look closely at them. One tells the story of the righteous Judge Herkenbald who executed his own nephew for the crime of rape. You see the rape, the Judge slitting the nephew's throat, the Judge on his own deathbed receiving Divine approbation for this impartial act of justice. The other tells of Brussels alderman Everard t'Serclaes, who opposed the territorial

THE rebuilding OF A MARKET SQUARE

In 1695, under orders from Louis XIV, the French Marshal de Villeroy directed his gunners to pulverize the central city of Brussels—he told them, in particular, to use the spire of the city's famous Town Hall as their aiming point. Astonishingly, the Town Hall (built in the 1400s) survived the deliberate carnage (though it suffered interior damage), but the guild houses around the square, and the Maison du Roi, were all razed to the ground. It was an act of violence, as Napoleon was to say more than a hundred years later, "aussi barbare qu'inutile" (as barbaric as it was useless).

But it galvanized the magistrates and guilds of Brussels into rebuilding the Grand Place even grander than it was before. In 3-and-a-half years, from 1695 to 1699, they rebuilt the Guild Homes in approximately the same locations, shapes, and sizes as before, but with all-stone facades (they had been partially wood before), of almost uniform height, and with fanciful, decorative touches of the new Baroque designs (the "Italo-Flamand") of the 17th century adorning the top-most gables of the structures. It was as if these proud craftsmen were thumbing their noses at the Great Powers of Europe. In a triangularly-shaped, large, gold inscription under the roof of the "House of the Tailors" (third up from the Maison du Roi, on the left-hand side as you face uphill), these unassuming Belgians who normally sat atop a cloth-strewn table, patiently plying their needles on someone's silk jacket, proudly proclaimed "QUAS FUROR HOSTILIS SUBVERTERATIGNIBUS AEDES, SARTOR RESTAURAT PRAESIDI-BUSQUE DUCAT" (That Which the Enemies' Hostile Fire Destroyed, We the Tailors Have Restored and Offered in Tribute to the City's Magistrate)!

ambitions (threatening to Brussels) of the Lord of Gaasbeek, owner of the famous castle outside Brussels. He was set upon by henchmen of the infamous noble, who cut off his tongue and right foot, and left him to die on a deserted road outside the city. The pendentive depicts the bloody deed, and underneath shows the Devil carrying off the Lord of Gaasbeek's soul to Hell.

The main entrance to the Town Hall today is the large archway under the tower, directly above which are statues of the five major patron saints hereabouts. St. Michael is in the center, his sword above the devil; at his side to the left (looking at the statues), the nearly naked St. Sebastian (patron of the archers), St. Christopher (patron of the arquebusiers), and to his right, St. George (patron of the cross-bowmen, here killing the dragon), and a kneeling St. Gery, the eminent churchman of Brussels. Above these saints, in a semicircle, the seven prophets and a scribe —the latter in a robe of the Capuchin monks, writes on a scroll; sculpted in the 15th century, these are the most remarkable of all the sculptures of the Town Hall, but they are copies of originals displayed in the museum of the Maison du Roi directly across the Grand-Place.

INSIDE THE TOWN HALL: The remaining, front facade of the Town Hall is profusely covered with dozens of sculpted figures of royal personages, like a vast picture gallery. These are all the rulers of Brabant up to nearly the end of the 15th century, in chronological order: the Carolingian emperors starting with Charlemagne come first. Inside the Town Hall you'll find dozens of oil portraits of the same and later rulers, in a succession of richly resplendent halls, chambers and antechambers used by the Burgomaster and Aldermen of the city. Indeed, the chief impression you'll take away from an inside visit is of the rather gentle, warmhearted treatment of Brussels towards the former foreign rulers of Belgium! You'll see giant paintings of various emperors of Germany, the Empress Maria-Theresia of Austria, Charles of Lorraine and several archdukes of Saxony, Napoleon, and others.

Finally, immediately on entering the Town Hall, you will read the two great poster proclamations of resistance (in French and Dutch) by its mayors on the eve of German occupation in both World Wars I and II.

Grand-Place. www.brussels.be. ✆ **02/548-0447.** Admission (guided tours only) 7€ adults; 5€ seniors, students, and children 6–12; free for children 5 and under. Tickets sold at tourist office in Grand-Place (p. 178). Guided tours in English, French, or Dutch Wed 1–3pm, Sun 10am–4pm. Closed Jan 1, May 1, Nov 1, Nov 11, and Dec 25. Metro: Gare Centrale or Bourse.

House of the Star ★★★ Crossing the Rue Charles Buls from the Town Hall, we first encounter the smallest structure on the square, the exquisite "House of the Star" (with a star on top) built, quite incredibly, on stilts. It originally wasn't. Torn down in the mid-1800s by misguided civic officials to widen the street next to the Town Hall (thus gravely harming the architectural unity of the Grand' Place), it was later rebuilt by wiser minds, but on columns to permit carriages and the like to pass underneath. Beneath the arcade created by those columns is the reclining, metal sculpture of the dying Everard t'Serclaes, Brussels' greatest civic hero, whose arm and thigh are rubbed for good luck (and are thus shiny gold) by every well-informed passerby. In the 1300s it was t'Serclaes who led the militia that freed Brussels from occupation by the French-admiring Count of Flanders; t'Serclaes himself tore down the Count's flag from where it flew in front of this very house. Attacked while traveling on a country road, and cruelly multilated by hirelings of the Lord of Gaasbeek, the dying t'Serclaes was carried to this House of the Star, which fittingly commemorates his sacrifice today with the "rubbing statue."

House of the Swan ★★★   Next door (still moving counter-clockwise): the House of the Swan (home of the Butchers' Guild), with a giant swan on front, designed in the classical French style of the man who destroyed the Square, Louis XIV, and not at all Flemish, Italian or Baroque. It is an odd exception (along with the House of the Fox —"Renard") to the generally curvaceous, Baroque designs of the Square. Statues representing Agriculture, the State of Plenty, and the Butchers, stand along the roof.

House of the Brewers ★★★   Next door to the "Swan" is the richly flamboyant "House of the Brewers" ("the Golden Tree"), with unmistakable beer hops climbing up the columns, the helpful inscription "Maison des Brasseurs" (House of the Brewers) along its front, and an equestrian statue of the popular Charles of Lorraine (Austrian governor of the Low Countries) atop its gable.

House of the Dukes of Brabant ★★★   Now turn to the long, continuous building at the top, uphill side of the square: the "House of the Dukes of Brabant," whose busts adorn the 19 pillars at the immediate top of the ground-floor portion. Higher up are colored emblems of the Guilds that occupied these six, connected houses (see the six doors, up the outer staircase) built in the style of one large Italian palace: the Masons, the Cabinet Makers, the Millers, the Tanners, the Wine and Vegetable Merchants, the "Four Crowned Crafts" ("les Quatres Couronnes"; sculptors, stone cutters, roofers, and masons)—you should be able to connect each emblem to the appropriate craft. On the roof of the building: four giant vases emitting flames of burning oil—an allegory of the yearning for peace (for which Brussels continued to yearn in vain since 1695).

House of the Tailors ★★★   Turn now (counter-clockwise) to the side of the Square on which stands the Maison du Roi. On the block above that structure, third from the left (i.e., the middle building) is the "House of the Tailors" we referred to in the box (see above), with its stirring, Latin inscription in the triangular portico under the fanciful, Baroque gable. Atop the gable stands St. Boniface with outstretched arms; in his other arm, he holds a shield adorned with Golden Scissors, symbol of the tailors' guild. Downstairs, over the door that presently leads to the firelight-lit tavern on the ground floor, is a bust of St. Barbara, patron saint of that Guild. The two buildings to the left are classic examples of the hodge-podge of styles—Italian/Brabantine/Baroque, the detailed precision of the Flemish given excitement and movement by fanciful, Italian shapes—that came together so miraculously to create the ravishing beauty of the Grand-Place. On the facades of one are leering theatrical masques inspired by the Commedia dell' Arte of Italy.

Maison du Roi ★★ Next comes the combined Gothic/Renaissance Maison du Roi, originally built by the Emperor Charles V in the 1500s for various communal purposes (tax collection, courts, prison), then rebuilt in the 19th century in neo-Gothic style to approximate the earlier structure. Because Charles was also king of Spain, it was soon called the House of the King, though he never lived there.

Guildhouses on the Downhill End of the Square ★★★ The best for last. On the downhill end of the Square, the lavish frenzy of the Italian/Flemish explodes into a gilded fairyland, strangely beautiful, in which the Guilds used allegorical symbols—an elegant touch—to advertise their own importance. From left to right, looking downhill, you first see the "House of the Haberdashers" on the extreme left, topped by the statue of St. Nicholas, patron saint of merchants, with staff. Underneath, on the top floor, four buxom caryatides (maidens performing as pillars) display the world's wealth: wool, wheat, the vine, flowers. Atop the ground floor are five striking figures: the middle one is Justice, blindfolded, a scale in one hand, a glorious Sun above him. The continents, two by two, stand on each side of him: Africa (ebony and ivory on a turtle shell) and Europe (the horn of plenty) on one side, Asia (an elephant's tusk) and America (gold, the European image of recently discovered America) on the other. Next, the "House of the Boatmen," its facade covered with emblems of sailing, its gable consisting of the richly-decorated stern of a 17th-century ship. At the very top, two lions guard the heraldic shield and image of Charles II of Spain. Lower down: sea horses, fish scales, and a horn, for the alternative name—"Maison du Cornet" (Horn)—of the building.

Next door: the "House of the She-Wolf" ("Maison de la Louve"), serving the Guild of the Archers, who placed a golden Phoenix arising from the Ashes atop the roof, to symbolize the re-birth of the Grand-Place and Brussels. The profession of archery is symbolized in the triangular pediment, in which Apollo shoots the Serpent with his arrows. Statues of Peace, Strife, Falsehood, and Truth adorn the third floor, the bas-relief of a she-wolf suckling Romulus and Remus, founders of Rome, is over the door.

Next door: the incredibly gilded and ornate "House of the Cabinet Makers" ("le Sac"), designed appropriately to resemble an enormous and elaborate wooden chest. A compass stands atop the gable; tools of the Guild decorate the railings over the bottom floors.

Next door: the "House of the Grease (or Tallow) Merchants," with its great variety of columnar styles, some twisted (the only such on the square), others plain and classic. Blue shields over the ground floor contain images of Wheelbarrows ("les brouettes")—the other identifying name for the building in the Middle Ages, when there were no street numbers—and in a niche of the Gable stands St. Gilles, patron saint of these candlestick-makers. Finally, at the extreme right, with a small cupola tower on top, the corporate "House of the Bakers", with a bronze bust of St. Aubert (patron saint of the Bakers' Guild)

ALL ABOUT THE manneken-pis

Near the Grand-Place, on Rue de l'Etuve, look for the corner fountain occupied by the immortal, but tiny, bronze statue of a little boy urinating into the air from a cocky stance atop a ledge of the fountain. Until the early 17th century, a stone statue dating back to the mid-1400s occupied the same niche and performed the same office; it was known then as "little Julian." In 1619, the Brussels sculptor Jerome Duquesnoy created a bronze replacement which all the world now knows as the "Mannekin Pis."

After whom is the little boy modeled? There are at least a dozen competing legends. One is of the little boy-hero of Brussels—Julian—who, using his natural resources, extinguished an incendiary bomb thrown into the street by enemy troops. Another tells of the peasant who came with his little son to a Brussels festival, lost the child in the crowd, found him 5 days later, and expressed his thanks by sculpting a statue of the boy as he looked when rediscovered: the Mannekin Pis. Still another claims he is the son of a nobleman who attempted to seduce the virtuous Ste. Gudule. Heaven's punishment was to condemn his son to remain always a child, and always relieving himself (a poor explanation of the sweet little statue).

Stolen from his niche on numerous occasions, and the subject of other incidents too numerous to describe, Mannekin Pis is today treated as the symbol of Brussels' ironic, impudent outlook, a mirror of the impiety and cynicism of its average resident. Somehow he fits, and it is hard to imagine him standing on the stately squares of those other European cities that have occasionally sought to dominate the world. Instead, in a Brussels that has witnessed every misfortune, suffered every indignity, and lost all illusions, Mannekin Pis is an artistic summation.

in papal hat, above the door, King Charles II of Spain further up, allegorical statues of Wind, Water, Agriculture and Fire along the railing on the roof, and the golden nymph of "Fame" blowing her horn while balanced on one precarious foot, above everything else.

La Grand-Place! What gives it such impact? Perhaps it is the fact that it is totally enclosed. Once inside it, the modem world disappears. And one is immersed in the flow of history, the stages of the world; one senses what people can occasionally accomplish, working together, and impelled by the kind of idealism that resulted in this stupendous achievement.

Other Squares
PLACE DU GRAND SABLON ★★

Although the traffic passing through it diminishes the experience, **place du Grand Sablon** is filled with sidewalk cafes and lined with gabled mansions. The Grand Sablon and its environs are antiques territory; many of its mansions have been turned into antiques stores or art galleries with pricey merchandise on display; others are high-end brands like Christian Louboutin and Pierre Marcolini Chocolate, plus a sprinkling of posh cafes. On Saturday and Sunday mornings an excellent antiques market sets up its stalls in front of **Eglis Notre-Dame du Sablon** (p. 188). This flamboyantly Gothic church has five naves and glorious, slender stained-glass windows; it was built with money donated by the city's wealthy Guild of Crossbowmen in the 15th century.

PLACE DU PETIT SABLON ★

Just across busy rue de la Régence is the Grand Sablon's little sister, a delightful, 19th-century garden honoring the Counts of Egmont and Homes, their arms about each other's shoulders, marching almost jauntily to their deaths at the hands of Philip II (in a well-known, epic statue at the top of the garden). They are flanked by Belgian notables of the 16th century, and the entire little square is surrounded by 48 famous bronze statues of the medieval guilds—it being an outdoor "parlor game" in Brussels to identify each ancient Guild by the clothing and tools of each statuette figure. The six at the very bottom of the Square, along the Rue de la Regence, are, from left to right (facing the square), a gunsmith, a plumber, a stonecutter, a laundryman, a coppersmith, a wheelmaker. Can you identify the others?

PLACE ROYALE ★

Brussels' royal square is at the meeting point of rue de la Régence and rue Royale, the two thoroughfares that hold many of the city's premier sights, including the **Musée Magritte** (p. 189) and **BOZAR** (p. 204). The **Musées Royaux des Beaux-Arts de Belgiques** (see below) are at the west end of place Royale. The classical square overlooking the city is surrounded by stately, white buildings of the city's 18th-century Austrian era, with an **equestrian statue** of crusader Godfrey of Bouillon set incongruously inside, this was the site of the city's former medieval palace of the Coudenberg. On the

A NEW art

A new design style appeared around 1890 and flourished for 2 decades across Europe. In many countries it was called Art Nouveau (in Spain it was called Modernisme). Created in opposition to the industrialization of Europe, it was a style of design that was influenced, primarily, by the forms found in nature, though many note that Japanese woodblock prints, introduced to Europe in the late 19th century, were also a source of inspiration. In Art Nouveau's architectural iteration, its prime materials were glass and iron, which were worked with curved lines and floral and geometric motifs. Belgium produced one of its greatest exponents in **Victor Horta** (1861–1947); his work can be seen all over Brussels and especially at the **Tassel House** (1893; rue Paul Emile Janson 6) and the **Hôtel Solvay** (1895; avenue Louise 224). His own house is open to the public: the **Musée Horta (Horta Museum;** see p. 195) in St-Gilles, a southern suburb of Brussels.

Fans of the city's superb legacy of Art Nouveau architecture should check out the works of **Gustave Strauven** (1878–1919), the Brussels-born student of Horta. Strauven's signature is his use of blue and yellow bricks. He designed around 100 private houses in Brussels, including the slender **Maison Saint-Cyr** (1903) at square Ambiorix 11. This flamboyant, sensuous Gaudí-esque masterpiece of curling wrought-iron, curved windows, and swirling brick was built for the artist Georges Léonard de Saint-Cyr by Strauven when he was a 22-year-old student.

THE european DISTRICT

Home to the European Commission, European Parliament, Council of Ministers, and related institutions, Brussels has no less than 1.2 million sq. m (12.7 million sq. ft.) of office space packed with 25,000-plus Eurocrats to back up its "Capital of Europe" tag. Entire neighborhoods full of character were swept away to make room for them, causing resentment among local residents.

To tour the heartland of European Union governance, take the Métro to Schuman station. If you wish to view that exotic species, the European civil servant, in its native habitat, take the tour Monday to Friday as the district is dead on the weekend.

Your first sight is the X-shaped Palais de Berlaymont, the commission's former headquarters at Rond-Point Schuman. Across rue de la Loi, the Council of Ministers headquarters, the Consilium, is instantly recognizable for its facade's lavish complement of rose-colored granite blocks. On its far side, take a stroll through Parc Léopold, an island of green

tranquility at the heart of the Euro District. This little park is laid out above an ornamental lake and was originally conceived as a zoo and science park. The zoo didn't fly for long, but a cluster of scientific institutes dating from the late 19th and early 20th centuries still occupies part of the terrain. Among these is the **Museum des Sciences Naturelles (Museum of Natural Sciences)**, see p. 193, and the **House of European History** (www.historia-europa.ep.eu), a free museum that provides a brief but interesting overview of how events like the Industrial Revolution, the World Wars, and the Cold War shaped contemporary Europe.

A walk through Parc Léopold brings you to the postmodern European Parliament and its visitors' center, the Parlamentarium; the complex is an architectural odyssey in white marble and tinted glass. Take the passageway through the building's middle to place du Luxembourg, an old square that looks lost and forlorn in comparison to its powerful new neighbors.

north face of the square is the **Eglise St-Jacques-sur-Coudenberg.** Archaeologists have excavated the foundations of the Royal Palace of Emperor Charles V on the square, and the site has been covered over again to form the Coudenberg and BELvue museums (see p. 188).

PLACE DES MARTYRS ★

Some years back, the once-elegant 18th-century **place des Martyrs,** in the Lower Town near the Théâtre Royal de la Monnaie, was in a sorry state and crumbling to the ground. It entombs the "500 Martyrs" of Belgium's 1830 War of Independence. The square has been extensively restored, and although it lost some of its former ragged charm in the process, it is once again an attractive public place.

The Lower Town

Cathédrale des Sts-Michel-et-Gudule ★ CHURCH   Rising above the hectic chaos of the Lower Town on Treurenberg in a no-man's land between the Lower and Upper Towns, this magnificent twin-towered Roman Catholic church is the purest flowering of the Gothic style; its choir is Belgium's earliest Brabantine Gothic work. Begun in 1226, it was only officially consecrated as a cathedral in 1961. The 16th-century Habsburg Emperor Charles V donated the superb stained-glass windows in the Chapelle du St-Sacrément. Apart from these, the spare interior decoration focuses attention on the soaring columns and arches as well as the extravagantly carved wooden pulpit, which depicts Adam and Eve being expelled from Eden, and the statues of the Apostles lined up along the columns supporting the central aisle. It's the official wedding and funeral church of the Belgian Royal Family and contains the glossy black tombs of heroic Brabantine dukes.

In the **crypt** lie the foundations of the earlier Romanesque church dating from the 11th century. The **Trésor (Treasury)** is also worth visiting for its glowing ecclesiastical vessels in gold, silver, and precious stones.

Parvis Ste-Gudule. www.cathedralisbruxellensis.be. © **02/217-8345.** Admission: cathedral free, crypt 3€, archaeological zone 1€, treasury 2€. Cathedral: Mon–Fri 7am–6pm, Sat 8am–3:30pm, Sun 2–6pm.

Centre Belge de la Bande-Dessinée (Belgian Center for Comic-Strip Art) ★★ MUSEUM

In Belgium comics are taken as seriously as any other art form, and they are everywhere: on the walls of buildings, occupying their own special sections in book shops, and in this excellent museum, which is inside an Art Nouveau landmark former department store designed by Victor Horta. Hergé's Tintin and Snowy greet visitors at the top of the elegant staircase—Hergé himself had a hand in the design of the center—and beyond this is a comic-character wonderland, relating the story of cartoons from vague idea to published comic strip (including what is most likely the first comic strip, 1896's "Yellow Kid.") All the big names appear in permanent and special exhibits, including Tintin, Asterix, Lucky Luke, the Smurfs, Charlie Brown, Andy Capp, Superman, and Batman. Of course, the origins of animated storytelling go much further back. Monks may have invented the language of cartoons: They illustrated sacred texts, divided the story into panels, described movement, painted backgrounds, and even wrote dialogues in bubbles. There's an impressively large bookshop, a reading room, and a restaurant on the ground floor. Grown-ups will love this place as much as kids do.

Rue des Sables 20. www.comicscenter.net. © **02/219-1980.** Admission 10€ adults; 8€ seniors; 7€ students and ages 12–25; 3.50€ children 11 and under. Daily 10am–6pm. Closed Jan 1 and Dec 25. Metro: Botanique/Congres/Parc.

Fondation Jacques Brel ★ MUSEUM

Dedicated to Belgium's most famous singer and actor, Jacques Brel, this museum offers an overview of his life and work from his birth in 1929 to his death in 1978. Born into an affluent family, Brel composed songs on the piano as a child and made his first record in 1953; he then hotfooted it to Paris, touring almost incessantly for the next 15 years. Along the way he became one of Europe's foremost singer-songwriters, famously morose and sentimental by turn. In 1966, he held his final concert at the Olympia Theatre in Brussels and moved to America for a spell. He died in Tahiti and is buried close to artist Paul Gauguin. Set up by his daughter, the museum is divided into distinct areas (each priced differently) and includes a smattering of Brel memorabilia, tracks from his albums, snippets from his movies, and an in-depth examination of his life. There's also a cinema with screenings of his concerts. Die-hard fans might also consider the 2-hour, 40-minute Brel-themed walking tour around central Brussels.

Place de Vieille Halle aux Blés 11. www.jacquesbrel.be. ℂ **02/511-1020.** Admission 7€–10€ adults, 5€–8€ seniors and students. Tues–Sun 11am–6:30pm. Closed Jan 1, May 1, Nov 1, Nov 11, and Dec 25.

Musée du Costume et de la Dentelle (Costume and Lace Museum) ★★ MUSEUM

Set up in 1977 to celebrate the long tradition of making textiles and lace in Flanders, this collection is surprisingly engaging. As well as ecclesiastical vestments and fine samples of delicate handmade lace from Bruges and Mechelen, you'll find cabinets full of panama hats (a bit of an obsession in Brussels; scores of stores sell them), Barbie dolls with their many costume changes, and plenty of carefully conserved and elaborately embroidered gowns from the 18th and 19th centuries. Most fun are the cheery displays of 1960s fashion, including tiny miniskirts and bright-red raincoats. But the heart of the collection deals with the 17th century (and earlier) lace-making industry of Brussels which once employed more than 15,000 practitioners of the highly-demanding, incredibly-laborious art. You'll not only see exhibits of the most elaborate and accomplished lace, the kind requiring hundreds of hours of patient hand weaving, but also paintings of various noble figures wearing lace of great intricacy that peeks from underneath collars and cuffs. And suddenly you'll remember all those portraits you've seen of European counts and dukes, duchesses and princes, adorned with yards and yards of lace, all produced painstakingly, over months of time, and for an absurd pittance, by whole armies of exploited female Belgian lacemakers.

Rue de la Violette 12. www.costumeandlacemuseum.be. ℂ **02/213-4450.** Admission 8€ adults, 6€ seniors, 4€ students, free for those under 18; free first Sun each month. Tues–Sun 10am–5pm. Closed Jan 1, May 1, Nov 1 and 11, and Dec 25.

Musée de la Ville de Bruxelles (Museum of the City of Brussels) ★ MUSEUM

Standing on one side of Grand'Place, opposite the equally splendid Town Hall, is the ornate Maison du Roi (King's House, see p. 182). The museum housed inside is a good way to take a gallop through the history of Belgium's capital. A mix of paintings, sculptures, tapestries, earthenware, and silverware are displayed in one area. Another concentrates on the city's development, using large-scale models to help you locate the major historic sites. However, the main attraction here is the folklore section, where some of the clothes of Brussels' most enduring symbol, Mannekin Pis, are on display. The improbable statue of a boy peeing merrily away stands in the small rue l'Etuve, and he's dressed in a different costume just about every day. Here in the museum you can see some of his wardrobe of almost 1,000 outfits, including Santa Claus, mayors of various cities, and a judo fighter.

Grand-Place. www.brusselscitymuseum.brussels. ℂ **02/279-4350.** Admission 8€ adults, 6€ seniors, 4€ students, free for those under 18; free first Sun each month. Tues–Sun 10am–5pm. Closed Jan 1, May 1, Nov 1, Nov 11, and Dec 25. Metro to Bourse/Gare Centrale.

The Upper Town

BELvue Museum & Coudenberg ★ MUSEUM   Two distinct museums—one dedicated to Belgian history, the other an archeological site—are housed in the former Coudenberg Palace. The BELvue occupies the first floor of the neoclassical building, with views out across the Parc de Bruxelles, and relates the story of Belgium through the struggles for independence from the Netherlands and the final breakaway in 1830 to its present (almost) unified political state. Displays include black-and-white film, heaps of old weapons, and some graphic images of Flanders trenches in World War I. The Coudenberg dives down underneath the palace to explore the vast maze of tunnels that were at street level in the 17th century; the tentacles of the museum spread right under the Place Royale, taking in former kitchens, chapels, a few Roman remains, and whole streets that were covered over when King Léopold I started construction of his palatial new city in the 1860s. Don't go down there without a map!

Place des Palais 7. www.belvue.be and www.coudenberg.brussels. ℗ **02/500-4554.** Admission 7€ adults (12€ combo ticket), 6€ seniors (10€), 5€ students 18–25 (8€), free for children 17 and under; BELvue free Wed after 2pm. Tues–Fri 9:30am–5pm, Sat–Sun and July and Aug 10am–6pm. Closed Jan 1 and Dec 25.

eB! ★★ MUSEUM   The acronym stands for "experience Brussels," and this museum provides a lively and informative snapshot of the city   warts and all—touching on everything from Brussels' transportation system to major moments in the city's history to current multicultural tensions. The exhibitions come alive through interactive media, video screens, impressive color photography, and plenty of personal accounts. Best is an enormous interactive 3-D model of the city, which lets you view from above its 19 neighborhoods, network of parks, and most famous buildings.

BIP, place Royale 2–4. http://bip.brussels. ℗ **02/563-6399**. Mon–Fri 9:30am–5:30pm and weekends 10am to 6pm. Free admission. Metro: Porte de Namur/Park, Tram 92, 94 to Royale.

Eglise Notre-Dame du Sablon (Church of Our Lady of the Sablon) ★ CHURCH   In the 1300s, members of Brussels' Cross-Bowmen's Guild used the Place of the Grand Sablon as an archery range, later building a small chapel at the top of the field. According to legend, the Virgin Mary was so touched by this tribute that she directed an Antwerp "beguine" (member of a secular convent), Beatrix Soetkens, to spirit away a small statue of the Madonna from the Antwerp Cathedral and to transport it to the Sablon chapel—a feat soon done. Upon the now-consecrated site, the religious of Brussels built the church of "Notre Dame au Sablon" in the 15th and 16th centuries, adorning its entrance facade with dozens of statuettes of medieval people: knights, court ladies clutching the folds of their long skirts. Gaze upon them, and you may be thrilled to realize that these are contemporaneous portrayals in stone of the society of that time. Though the church isn't of sufficient importance to warrant lengthy inspection, its stained glass and vaulting, its remarkably delicate chapels and statuary, are of considerable beauty, and will assist your introduction to the great cathedrals of other Belgian cities.

Rue Bodenbroek 6. ℭ **02/511-5741**. Free admission. Mon–Fri 9am–6:30pm, Sat–Sun 10am–6:30pm.

Musée Magritte ★★★ MUSEUM   Do not confuse this spectacular collection with the museum in artist René Magritte's Brussels home (p. 195). The Magritte Museum opened in 2009 and is now under the umbrella of the Musées Royaux des Beaux-Arts de Belgique (see below). Located in the Hôtel Altenloh, a neoclassical mansion dating from 1779, the gallery is connected by underground passageway to the main building of the Musées Royaux next door.

The collection holds more than 230 of Magritte's eccentric, surreal works and covers all periods of his oeuvre, exhibiting musical scores and photos of his private life as well as signature works such as his series "The Dominion of Light" and "The Domain of Arnheim." Though you may never have viewed one of his full-scale works, Rene Magritte is already familiar to you, for his powerful images have been shamelessly copied by advertising agencies the world over. His paintings tell of anxiety and isolation in the modern world, of stultifying homogeneity and the inability to communicate, especially in that famous canvas of the group of identical persons staring wordlessly through a window into an open room. Magritte is represented here by his very greatest paintings: "L'Empire des Lumieres" (that night-lit house on a dark canal, under a bright, daytime sky); "Le Mariage de Minuit"; "L'Homme du Large"; "La Saveur des Larmes" (a decaying and corrupted dove); and "La Recherche de la Verite" (a ball, a fish, a scene of infinity).

Place Royale. www.musee-magritte-museum.be. ℭ **02/508-3211**. Admission 10€ adults, 8€ seniors, 3€ students, free for those under 19; combination ticket with all four museums 15€ adults, 10€ seniors, 5€ students; free 1st Wed afternoon each month. Mon–Fri 10am–5pm, Sat–Sun 11am–6pm. Closed Jan 1, May 1, Nov 1, Nov 11, and Dec 25. Metro: Porte de Namur/Park, Tram 92, 94 to Royale.

Musées Royaux des Beaux-Arts de Belgique (Royal Fine Arts Museums of Belgium) ★★★ MUSEUM   This is one of the world's great art museums, and that is not hyperbole. Dedicated to six centuries of art, it comprises six different collections, with four galleries under one roof here in the place Royale. They are: the **Musée d'Art Ancien** (Museum of Old Masters), which covers the 15th to the 17th centuries; the **Musée d'Art Moderne,** with works from the 19th century onward; the **Musée de la Fin de Siècle,** which covers works around the turn of the 20th century; and the **Magritte Museum,** devoted to the Surrealist genius René Magritte.

As you'd expect, this a huge complex, with over 20,000 works. So how to tackle it? I would recommend first visiting the Old Masters Museum, and then coming back another day for the next two. (Since the Magritte Museum is devoted to a single artist, its focus and feel is very different; it's covered under a separate entry above.) The two collections *not* on site here are **Musée Meunier,** celebrating the work of sculptor Constantin Meunier (rue de

6 UNDERSTANDING THE WORKS OF peter bruegel

Peter Bruegel (1525–1567) is today acclaimed as one of the greatest artists of all time, though for centuries he was disparaged and dismissed as a mere "peasant painter." His accomplishments were monumental. Prior to Bruegel, virtually all paintings were of religious scenes or allegories. If they portrayed ordinary life at all, they do so in tiny patches seen through the casement windows of cathedrals or other holy structures. Landscapes in particular were almost totally subordinated to sacred themes (except perhaps in the Van Eycks' "Adoration of the Mystic Lamb").

Bruegel made mankind, and the natural world, the major theme of his paintings. He virtually invented "genre" art—the painting of everyday life. In depicting the activities of ordinary people—their weddings and festivals, their work in the fields—he proclaimed the worth of the common man. He may have gone further. In the troubled time of religious conflict through which he lived—the saddest years in all the history of the Low Lands, witnessing inquisition and executions at the stake, the arrival of occupying foreign armies and repression of free conscience—many of his paintings may be read as cries of protest against the forces of repression. In biblical scenes, portrayed as if they took place in Flemish villages, the armies and authorities he included there can be seen as the Spanish troops of Philip II—although the latter point is hotly disputed by some art experts.

Although his surviving work amounts to only 40 paintings and a hundred or so etchings, they span a remarkable range of artistic themes and styles. What little we know of Bruegel's life is derived from a short essay written by a near contemporary. He was born somewhere in Brabant, received his art training in Antwerp, where he then worked for the foremost etching printer of that city, and later moved to Brussels, possibly to escape involvement in the sharp (and dangerous) religious conflicts of the 1500s, but also to marry the daughter of another prominent artist of that time. He is described as a friend of leading humanists, who frequently accompanied him on excursions into the countryside to witness the weddings and banquets of the village folk. Within 5 years of his death, he became the father of two sons later to become important artists: Pieter Bruegel the Younger (known as "Hell" Bruegel) and Jan Bruegel (known as "Velvet" Bruegel). Following his death, and except as perpetuated by his sons, the realistic artistic traditions he established moved on primarily to Holland and to such painters as Vermeer, while Belgium was captivated by the radically different, florid and curvaceous, Italianate styles of the Baroque, as produced with such drama by the great Peter Paul Rubens. Today Breugel is acknowledged as a Titan of art, the master of Brussels.

–Arthur Frommer

l'Abbaye 59); and the **Musée Wiertz,** displaying the works of Belgium's foremost Romantic artists (rue Vatier 62).

The Museum of Old Masters is a blockbuster, with masterpieces by most of the founders of European art. It's centered around the Southern Netherlands, with many painting from there worth lingering on, including the *Portrait of Anthony of Burgundy* by Rogier van der Weyden. The "Great Bastard of

Burgundy," as its noble subject was known, was one of the illegitimate children of Philip the Good, who ruled over an empire covering most of Belgium in the 15th century. Another standout is Bruegel the Elder's *Census at Bethlehem*, showing Mary riding a donkey through a snowy Brabant village. (Since this is probably the most important collection of Breugel's work anywhere, we have a box on the artist above.) Don't miss the significant collection of works by Peter Paul Rubens, including *The Ascent to Calvary*, plus art by Anthony van Dyck and Jacques Jordaens in the galleries devoted to Flemish art in the 17th and 18th centuries. The rich collection comes courtesy of Napoléon, who in 1801 founded the museum from works seized during the French Revolution. A visit to *Marat Assassiné*, Jacques Louis David's dramatic and iconic portrayal of the French Revolutionary stabbed to death in his bath in 1793, makes a fitting end to a visit.

Next door, in a circular building leading off the main entrance, is the modern art section. It is currently being reorganized, so only a tiny percentage of the collection's treasures are on revolving display: You may see Van Gogh, Delvaux, Matisse, or Dalí. No word on when the complete exhibit will reopen.

In the same complex, but with a different entrance, the **Musée Fin-de-Siècle** displays works between 1868, when the Société libre des Beaux-Arts was founded, and 1914, when World War I began. Brussels was at the heart of the flowering of art nouveau, and this museum's four floors cover all the major artistic disciplines it influenced, including painting, sculpture, photography, film, architecture, furniture, jewelry, and glassware. Some names (van Gogh, Burne-Jones, Bonnard, Sisley) are likely to be familiar, but many others will be happy discoveries, particularly to non-Belgians (Hippolyte Boulenger and Léon Spilliaert are among them). It's a stunning collection showing the exuberance and explosion of arts and crafts during the Belle Epoque.

Place Royale 1–3. www.fine-arts-museum.be. © **02/508-3211.** Admission per museum (excepting Musée Wiertz and Musée Meunier, which are both free) 10€ adults, 8€ seniors, 3€ students, free for those under 19; combination ticket with all four museums 15€ adults, 10€ seniors, 5€ students; free 1st Wed afternoon each month. Tues–Sun 10am–5pm. Closed Jan 1, May 1, Nov 1, Nov 11, and Dec 25. Metro: Porte de Namur/Park, Tram 92, 94 to Royale.

Musical Instruments Museum ★★

The Musical Instruments Museum, or MIM as it's popularly known, is housed a former department store that was designed by the Art Nouveau architect Paul Saintenoy in 1899. With its curving black wrought-ironwork and huge windows, it's an impressive site. Just as impressive are the hundreds of instruments on display here, which are drawn from the museum's vast collection of around 8,000. MIM takes a chronological approach that goes from ancient Egypt to 19th-century experiments with mechanical instruments and on to our modern electric and electronic examples. The instruments make for a fascinating mix: bagpipes from Scotland; instruments made by Tibetan monks from the bones of colleagues; celebrity instruments like Django Reinhardt's guitar and ABBA's synthesizer; and odd

Comic-Strip Brussels

Scores of comic-strip murals have been scattered around Brussels since the city began to celebrate Belgium's passionate love affair with *bande-dessinée* (comic-strip art) in 1993. Among the cartoon characters honored on the sides of houses and stores are **Tintin** (rue de l'Etuve 37), running down a fire escape together with Captain Haddock and Snowy; **Lucky Luke** (rue de la Buanderie 45), as always drawing his Colt faster than his shadow; and just along the street, **Asterix and Obelix** (rue de la Buanderie 33), leading a charge of the gallant Gauls against the rotten Romans.

Unfortunately, many of the other murals off-the-beaten-track districts. Getting there will give you an idea of what Brussels looks like away from its tourist heartlands—not greatly inspiring, it must be said—at the cost of a great deal of Métro-, tram-, and bus-hopping, and considerable shoe leather. The Brussels tourist office has created a 1€ mini-map with a walking itinerary of the city's top murals.

For a general overview of the history of Belgian comic books, the **Centre Belge de la Bande Dessinée** (see p. 186) is a good starting point.

saxophones that the instrument's creator, Adolphe Sax, dreamed up. The instruments are displayed behind glass: put on a headset, approach the cases, and music, often played on the actual instrument you're looking at, fills your ears. There's a good gift shop here and an excellent restaurant (**The Restaurant ★★**) on the top floor with panoramic views over the city from the terrace.

2 rue Montagne de la Cour, www.mim.be. ℰ **02/545-0130.** Admission 10€ adults, 8€ seniors, 4€ students, free for those under 19. Tues–Fri 9:30am–5pm, Sat–Sun 10am–5pm. Closed Jan 1, May 1, Nov 1 and 11, Dec 25.

Parc du Cinquantenaire

Designed to celebrate the half-centenary of Belgium's 1830 independence, the **Cinquantenaire (Golden Jubilee) Park** was a work in progress from the 1870s until well into the 20th century. Extensive gardens surround the triumphal Arc du Cinquantenaire, topped by a bronze chariot representing "Brabant Raising the National Flag" and flanked by colonnaded pavilions housing three fine museums; plan to spend the day here to really do all three justice. Autoworld and the Royal Museum of the Armed Forces and Military History face each other across the gardens; the Art & History Museum is tucked away around the back of Autoworld.

Autoworld ★★ MUSEUM   Even if you're not a "gear head," this display of over 500 historic cars is fascinating. The chronological collection starts with motorized tricycles from 1899 and moves on through the first petrol-engine car designed by Carl Benz in 1886, to bright-yellow racing Bugattis from 1911 and majestic 1922 Bentleys. Performance cars on display from recent years include Ferraris and Fernando Alonso's F1 Renault. The permanent exhibition "Belgium in Autoworld" looks at the relationship of Belgium with the car—who knew that this little country was one of the world's leading car manufacturers in the years leading up to World War I?

Parc du Cinquantenaire 11. www.autoworld.be. ℂ **02/736-4165.** Admission 12€ adults, 10€ seniors, 9€ students, 5€ children 6–12, free for children 5 and under. Apr–Sept daily 10am–6pm; Oct–Mar Tues–Fri 10am–5pm, Sat–Sun 10am–6pm. Closed Jan 1 and Dec 25. Metro: Merode.

Musée Art & Histoire (Art & History Museum) ★★★ MUSEUM

The magnificent collection at this newly rebranded museum (formerly the Musée du Cinquantenaire) journeys through five continents and four main themes: Belgian archaeology, antiquities, European decorative art, and non-European civilizations. The rotation of the huge permanent collection, as well as special exhibits, means that what's on display changes regularly. Founded in 1835, the museum has holdings that were initially drawn from the items owned by the dukes of Brabant and the archdukes of Hapsburg, who ruled Belgium for centuries. Today there are over 650,000 items collected from all over the world.

Start with the national archaeology collection. The Romans, Celts, and Merovingians make an appearance, as does the ancient art of silica mining in Spiennes—now a UNESCO World Heritage Site. *Other highlights*: the fascinating Indonesian collection with its ivory Balinese shadow puppets and wooden models of traditional stilt houses; the Chinese exhibit for hand-carved, wooden, red-and-gold day beds and delicate, hand-painted silk screens; and the Native American displays of feathered headdresses and beaded leather jackets.

Parc du Cinquantenaire 10. www.artandhistory.museum. ℂ **02/741-7331.** Admission 10€ adults, 8€ seniors, 4€ students, free for those 18 and under; free 1st Wed afternoon each month. Tues–Fri 9:30am–5pm, Sat–Sun 10am–5pm. Metro: Merode.

Musée des Sciences Naturelles (Museum of Natural Sciences) ★★

MUSEUM   Just about everyone loves a dinosaur, and the Museum of Natural Sciences has a fabulous collection of them. It has much else besides, but it's Europe's largest dinosaur gallery that pulls in the crowds initially—two highlights are the famous black fossilized skeletons of iguanodons, found in the Belgian commune of Mons in 1870, and a good old T. Rex, which towers above visitors in this industrial space. The museum is invariably full of families, but this is truly an excellent museum for all ages. The Gallery of Evolution takes spans 3.5 billion years of life on earth via six major points of evolution. Hundreds of fossils and animal lead up to the present day, and an imaginative leap jumps ahead to the animals that might be living fifty million years from now. Other don't-miss galleries include a sparkling mineral gallery and "250 Years of Natural Sciences," which tells the story of the museum through 14 major cleverly chosen specimens. A new exhibit, "Living Planet," dedicated to biodiversity in the oceans and on land, is scheduled to open in 2020.

29 rue Vautier. www.naturalsciences.be. ℂ **02/627-4211.** Admission 7€ adults, 6€ seniors, students, 4.50€ children ages 6–17 with adult, free for children 5 and under; free 1st Wed afternoon each month. Temporary exhibitions are extra and admission varies. Tues–Fri 9:30am–5pm, Sat–Sun 10am–6pm. Metro: Merode.

Musée Royal de l'Armée et d'Histoire Militaire (Royal Museum of the Armed Forces and Military History) ★★ MUSEUM   This vast museum is stuffed with a colorful, chaotic hoard of weaponry, uniforms, vehicles, and airplanes spanning a millennia of military history and while it's a joy to explore, it's very confusing to navigate. Attempts have been made to streamline the exhibitions and there are now several themed galleries examining aspects of war from medieval times to World War II (a new wing about the latter, including the occupation of Belgium, was recently added). Still, the most impressive section of the museum is the massive, glass-walled hangar-style atrium containing more than 100 military planes and helicopters from Spitfires, Hurricanes, and Junkers to Soviet MiGs and French Mirages. The European Forum of Contemporary Conflicts takes a salutary look at current wars being fought by European powers across the globe. Expect to spend a minimum of 3 hours here.

Parc du Cinquantenaire 3. www.klm-mra.be. © **02/737-7811.** Admission 10€ adults, 8€ seniors and students, 4€ ages 6–18; free for children 5 and under; free 1st Wed afternoon each month. Tues–Sun 9am–5pm. Closed Jan 1, May 1, Nov 1, and Dec 25. Metro: Merode/Schuman.

Suburbs

Musée Bruxellois de la Gueuze (Museum of Gueuze Brewing) ★★ BREWERY/MUSEUM   The last lambic brewery still operating in Brussels is a family-run affair where organic lambic beers have been produced since 1900. This boutique brewery has built a thriving business in its quaintly old-fashioned premises, running self-guided and guided tours of the traditional cooperage and brewing rooms, offering a bistro menu in the **Carillon restaurant,** and selling T-shirts alongside its 10 brews. Highly prized by beer buffs among these are Rosé de Gambrinus, flavored with raspberries, and the top-quality Grand Cru Bruocsella, which is matured for 3 years in oak casks. While a visit here is informative and entertaining, the location in Anderlecht is not great. Be prepared for some of the rougher elements of Brussels life to be on show.

Brews from Brussels

Brussels is known for its *lambic* beers, which use naturally occurring yeast for fermentation, are often flavored with fruit, and come in bottles with champagne-type corks. They're almost akin to sweet sparkling wine. Try raspberry-flavored *framboise* or cherry-flavored *kriek.* If you prefer something less sweet, order *Gueuze,* a blend of young and aged lambic beers.

Rue Gheude 56, Anderlecht. www.cantillon.be. © **02/520-2891.** Admission 7€ adults, 6€ ages 14–21; free for 13 and under; 9.50€ guided tour. Mon–Tues and Thurs–Sat 10am–5pm. Closed Jan 1, April 22, May 1, May 30, Nov 1, Nov 11, and Dec 25.

Musée Van Buuren ★★ MUSEUM   The collection of the banker David van Buuren and his wife, Alice, is well worth the journey out to the southern suburbs of Brussels. The cultured and wealthy couple designed the house and garden as a harmonious whole, and from 1928 began to fill it with five centuries of art, including rare pieces of furniture, carpets, sculptures, and stained-glass windows. Alice turned it into a museum in 1975. The exterior gives little hint of the beautiful art deco interior, which makes much use of exotic woods and precious materials. Inside are paintings by Peter Brueghel the Elder, the school of Rembrandt, van Gogh, and James Ensor. There's also a collection of 32 paintings by the Belgian artist Gustave van de Woestyne, whose work was a precursor of surrealism. Many people come here just for the extensive gardens, which include a symbolist garden and an art deco rose garden. Three's also a labyrinth whose green rooms were inspired by the Song of Solomon.

Avenue Léo Errera 41, Uccle. www.museumvanbuuren.be. © **02/343-4851.** Admission to garden and museum 10€ adults, 8€ seniors, 5€ students, free for children 11 and under; garden only 5€ adults, 4€ seniors, 2.50€ students, free for children 11 and under. Wed–Mon 2–5:30pm. Closed Jan 1 and Dec 25. Tram 3, 4, 7 to Churchill, Bus 38, 60 to Cavell.

Musée Horta (Horta Museum) ★★ MUSEUM   Visiting the Horta Museum takes you straight back to the golden age of Art Nouveau. Victor Horta (1861–1947), the son of a shoemaker, studied architecture in Paris and then returned to Brussels. From 1892 he was the most important architect of Art Nouveau buildings in the capital. The Horta Museum, which was both his private house and studio, was built between 1898 and 1901 and extended and changed over the following decade. Horta separated the house in 1919 and sold both parts, moving to avenue Louise. From the outside, the rich swirling wrought-iron balconies of the house and the rather more functional-looking facade and huge glass window on the top floor only hint at the purity of the interior, which is a revelation.

The museum has been pretty well left as it was during Horta's day, a small Art Nouveau masterpiece in which, in true Horta fashion, every detail was planned to fit into the overall design. Its magnificent staircase goes up the five floors and ends in a stained-glass skylight, which adds its own warm and rich colors to the interior. There are mosaics, enameled bricks, stained glass, and metal arches throughout, and the original furniture and details are what help make it all fit together in glorious harmony. It gives you a very real feel of the era, something that the Fin-de-Siècle Museum (which you'll still want to visit if you're an Art Nouveau fan) fails to achieve. The recent acquisition of the house next door, designed by Art Nouveau architect Jules Brunfaut, now allows the museum to host temporary exhibitions.

Rue Américaine 25, Saint-Gilles. www.hortamuseum.be. © **02/543-0490.** Admission 10€ adults, 6€ seniors, 5€ students, 3€ children 5–18, free for children 4 and under. Tues–Fri 2–5:30pm. Sat–Sun 11am–5:30pm. Closed Jan 1, Easter Sunday, May 1, Ascension Day, July 21, Aug 15, Nov 1, Nov 11, and Dec 25. Tram 81, 91, 92, 97 to Place Janson, Bus 54 to Place Janson.

Musée René Magritte ★ MUSEUM   The famous Belgian surrealist artist René Magritte lived and worked in a meager town house in suburban Jette in northwest Brussels between 1930 to 1954. Maintained in its original state as a private museum, the house provides a rather slight glimpse at Magritte's career. You have to knock to gain entrance, and of the 19 rooms on view, most are protected with glass screens so you can only peer myopically into the detritus of his life, although you do get to see the dining room-cum-studio where he painted many of his fantastical masterpieces. On the first and second floors are a few original sketches, Magritte's easel and his trademark bowler hat, some letters and photographs. Definitely one only for the ardent lover of Surrealism; everybody else is better off at the Musée Magritte in place Royale (p. 189).

Rue Esseghem 135, Jette. www.magrittemuseum.be. © **02/428-2626.** Admission 8€ adults, 6€ ages 9–22, free for children 8 and under. Wed–Sun 10am–6pm. Closed Jan 1 and Dec 25. Metro: Belgica.

Royal Museum for Central Africa ★★   Set on the grounds of the park of Tervuren, this museum occupies a palatial building designed by King Leopold II (1835-1909) specifically to house the booty and baggage from his imperial conquests in the Congo. It includes African masks, dwellings, canoes, costumes, and maps and mementoes of the Stanley and Livingstone expeditions, the most important ethnographical relics of a then-stone age civilization. The museum was recently renovated to present a more contemporary decolonized vision of Africa, with a new underground gallery that aims to put the collection into context and additional galleries that showcase African artists working today. Among them is Congolese artist Aimé Mpané whose large chiseled-wood sculpture of an African man in profile takes center stage in the building's Great Rotunda.

Leuvensesteenweg 13, Tervuren. www.africamuseum.be. © **02/769-5211.** Admission 12€ adults, 8€ seniors, 4€ ages 18–26, free for children 17 and under. Tues–Fri 11am–5pm, Sat–Sun 10am–6pm. Metro: 1 to Montgomery, Tram 44 to Tervuren.

Organized Tours

BIKE TOURS   Groovy Brussels (www.groovybrussels.com; © **02/484-8989-36**) offers 3½-hour cycling tours leaving from Grand-Place and taking in many of Brussels' major sites. Though you'll only see the attractions from the outside, the guides offer lively, informative commentary and it's a far better way to get an overview of the city than simply sitting on a tour bus. **Bonus:** it includes a halfway stop for *frites* and beer (food and drink cost extra). Tours run April to October daily at 10am, plus 2pm on weekends. 35€. Bookings are required in advance online.

BUS TOURS   Though the city is compact and most of the major sites can be visited on foot, Brussels' steep streets might prove a challenge for some, which is where these bus tours come in handy. Guided bus tours of Brussels last 2½ hours, operate throughout the year, and are available from **Brussels City Tours** (www.brussels-city-tours.com; © **02/513-7744**); they cover most of the city highlights and include farther-flung destinations like the Atomium and the EU district. The tours start at 29€ for adults, 26€ for seniors and students, children 4–12 are half off, and 3 and under are free. Also offered: tours to Bruges, Antwerp, Ghent, and the Flanders battlefields. Reservations can be made through most hotels, and hotel pickup is often available.

CitySightseeing Brussels (www.city-sightseeing.com) offers the now-ubiquitous hop-on, hop-off circular tour of the city; with 2 lines servicing 22 stops at all major attractions, including Cinqantenaire (p. 192), Palais Royal (p. 188), and Atomium (see below). Prices start at 25€; departures vary from every 45 minutes in winter to every 15 minutes in July and August. Again: for most travelers, simply walking from site to site will be more cost- and time-effective, but for those with mobility impairments, this bus can be helpful.

WALKING TOURS **Bravo Discovery** (www.bravodiscovery.com; ✆ **02/ 470-603-505**) operates daily free tours of Brussels that introduce visitors to the history of the city. These are so compelling (and fun), that many travelers go on to book the company's pre-paid themed walking tours, which range in subject matter from beer or chocolate tasting to discovering Jewish Brussels (there are 7 themes in all). Most tours take 2 hours, prices start at 8€.

Sports & Outdoor Activities

BOWLING The top bowling alley (with a laser-games facility, Q-Zar) is **Bowling Crosly,** boulevard de l'Empereur 36 (www.crosly.be; ✆ **02/512-0874**).

HORSEBACK RIDING In the south of Brussels, both the Bois de la Cambre and the Forêt de Soignes are great places for riding. Contact **Centre Equestre de la Cambre,** chaussée de Waterloo 872 (https://manege-la cambre.be; ✆ **02/496-6768-95**); and **Royal Etrier Belge,** champ du Vert Chasseur 19 (www.royaletrierbelge.be; ✆ **02/374-2860**).

ICE-SKATING There's ice-skating from September to late April at **Poseidon,** avenue des Vaillants 4 (www.ijsbaanposeidon.be; ✆ **02/762-1633**).

SOCCER The top local soccer club is **RSC Anderlecht,** avenue Théo Verbeeck 2 (www.rsca.be; ✆ **02/522-1539**). During Continental tournaments, crack European soccer squads can often be seen in action at the stadium in Anderlecht.

Especially for Kids

Brussels is fast-paced, traffic-fumed, and chaotic, and so can be rough on visiting families. However, it is the home of a peeing statue (p. 183) and also to Tintin and his little white dog, Snowy. Kids have great fun spotting the murals of the intrepid pair in the streets (p. 198) and will appreciate the cartoons and comic strips on display in the **Centre Belge de la Bande Dessinée** (p. 186). And let's not forget that Brussels is also a mecca for chocolate; most children will jump at the chance to visit, and see the chocolate-making demonstration, at the **Musée du Cacao et du Chocolat** (Rue de la Tête d'Or 9; www.mucc.be; ✆ **02/514-2048**) as much as they will adore gazing longingly through the windows of the classy confectioners (see below).

But to really give the kids a good time, head out to Bruparck, north of the city center, to visit the **Atomium ★**. There's nothing quite like this cluster of giant silvery orbs representing the atomic structure of an iron crystal enlarged 165 billion times, rising 102m (335 ft.) like a giant plaything of the gods that's fallen to earth. Constructed for the 1958 World's Fair, the Atomium is visible from pretty much all over Brussels and it's a fair bet that when you stand underneath this vast construction, you'll be suitably impressed. There may be something last-century about this paean of praise to the wonders of 1950s science and technology, but the panorama from the Atomium remains spectacular. An elevator shoots up the central column to the five spheres currently open to the public; three provide a permanent record of Expo 58 and the other two host temporary art and science exhibitions. The highest sphere has a glass roof, permitting 360-degree views towards Brussels, and on a clear day Antwerp's cathedral spire can be spotted on the horizon. The Atomium is located at Square de l'Atomium, Bruparck, Heysel (www.atomium.be, ℂ **02/475-4775**). Admission is 15€ adults; 13€ seniors, 8€ students and children over 115cm (4 ft.); free for children under 115cm (4 ft.). Combined tickets with Mini-Europe are available at 25.80€ for adults, 27.60€ seniors, 21.20€ for students and children 13–17, 18.10€for children 12 and under, free for children under 115cm (4 ft.). It's open daily 10am until 6pm.

Conveniently almost next door is **Mini-Europe ★**, which will intrigue kids and adults alike as they stroll around iconic landmarks from member states of the European Union, including Berlin's Brandenburg Gate, the Leaning Tower of Pisa, and Montmartre in Paris. As the E.U. expands, new models appear at Mini-Europe; there is also a new interactive Spirit of Europe exhibition area with virtual games that test your knowledge of the E.U. and the euro. *Son et lumière* (sound and light shows) and firework spectaculars are held on Saturday evenings in July and August. Tickets can be combined with a visit to the Atomium (recommended) and the rather dilapidated, adjacent Océade waterpark (not recommended). Mini-Europe is adjacent to the Atomium (www.minieurope.com, ℂ **02/478-0550**). Admission is 15.80€ adults and seniors, 11.80€ children 11 and under, free for children under 115cm (4 ft.). See above for combined ticket prices with the Atomium. Opening hours are mid-March to June and September daily 9:30am to 6pm, July and August daily 9:30am to

An Adventure with Tintin

Head to Louvain-la-Neuve, 27km (17 miles) southeast of Brussels, to visit the **Musée Hergé ★**, rue du Labrador 26 (www.museeherge.com; ℂ **010/488-421**), which celebrates the work of Tintin creator Georges Remi (1907–83), known to all as Hergé. The building itself is part of the attraction—a minimalist and boxlike gleaming, white affair with a massive image of Tintin emblazoned on one facade. It was designed by the French architect Christian de Portzamparc, and exhibits more than 800 original drawings of Tintin. The museum is open Tuesday to Friday 10:30am to 5:30pm, and weekends 10am to 6pm (closed Jan 1 and Dec 25). Admission is 12€ for adults, 7€ for seniors and students, 5€ for children ages 7 to 14, free for children 6 and under, and free the first Sunday of the month.

8pm, October through mid-January daily 10am until 6pm, with an annual closure between mid-January and mid-March.

SHOPPING

Brussels is not a city where you'll find shopping bargains. It's expensive, certainly as expensive as Paris, and more so than Amsterdam. As a general rule, the upper city around avenue Louise and Porte de Namur is more expensive than the lower city around rue Neuve and the center-city shopping galleries around La Monnaie and place de Brouckère. But that's not hard and fast; the shops on rue Haute in the upper city have some good deals, although as more and more design and antiques stores open, this may cease to be the case. The Galeries Royales St-Hubert, in the lower city, are wildly pricey. Still, there are some unique goods to be found in Brussels (see below).

Shopping Areas

Rue Neuve, which starts at place de la Monnaie and extends north to place Rogier in the lower city, is a busy and popular area that's home to many boutiques and department stores, including the City 2 shopping complex. **Boulevard Anspach,** which runs from the Stock Exchange up to place de Brouckère, offers mid-range fashion boutiques and electronic-appliance stores, plus the **Anspach Center** mall.

Avenue Louise and **boulevard de Waterloo** in the upper city attract those in search of world-renowned, high-quality goods from Cartier, Burberry's, Louis Vuitton, and Valentino. The **place du Grand Sablon** is natural home of chi chi antiques shops and galleries, while trendsters hit edgy **rue Antoine Dansaert** for small, independent boutiques and contemporary designers.

Brussels Specialties

The Bruxellois know a thing or two about **chocolate.** So addictive are their confections that they should be sold with a government health warning. Just ask anyone who has ever bitten into one of those devilish little handmade pralines made by **Wittamer** (see below). You'll find some of the finest confections at **Mary** (see below); **Nihoul,** chaussée de Vleurgat 111 (www.nihoul. be; 𝄞 **02/648-3796); Neuhaus** (see below); **Léonidas,** place du Grand Sablon 41 (www.leonidas.com; 𝄞 **02/513-1466);** and . . . well, it's a long list. Many branches of the city's best chocolatiers are congregated at place du Grand Sablon and the Galeries Royales de St-Hubert.

Lace is another favorite that's widely available in the city, particularly around the Grand-Place. Purchase from **Maison Antoine** (Grand-Place 26; 𝄞 **02/512-4859)** or **Manufacture Belge de Dentelles** (p. 203).

For local beers such as *gueuze, kriek,* and *faro*—among the 450 or so different Belgian beers—head for the **Musée Bruxellois de la Gueuze** (p. 194) or **Beer Mania** (see below). Both can ship beer overseas. Also check out the aisles in local supermarkets, where you'll find a great choice of beers at decent prices, too.

Stores normally open from 9 or 10am to 6pm Monday to Saturday. On Friday evening, many center-city stores stay open until 8 or 9pm. Most stores close on Sunday, except the tourist-orientated ones around the Grand-Place, and out of the center even the supermarkets operate limited Sunday opening hours.

Antiques & Art

Ma Maison de Papier ★★ Owner Marie-Laurence Bernard is an enthusiast of vintage posters and sells only genuine pieces, all coming with a guarantee of authenticity. Her stock ranges from cute 1950s posters of cartoon animals and colorful travel posters used to advertise obscure destinations, to more expensive 19th-century lithographs and even sheet music. Galerie de la Rue de Ruysbroeck 6. www.mamaisondepapier.be. ℂ **02/512-2249.**

Yves Macaux ★★ A specialist in Art Nouveau in the city that spawned the style, Yves Macaux's showrooms offer the finest in *objets d'art* from across Europe. Famed as a discerning dealer, his stock is always changing but the quality remains impeccable, from pairs of hanging lamps by Koloman Moser to silver trays by master craftsman Henry van de Velde. Even if you can't afford to buy here, go visit the gallery for a peerless introduction to the delights of Art Nouveau. Rue des Champs Elysées 19. www.secessions.com. ℂ **02/502-3116.**

Antiques Market

Place du Grand Sablon ★★★ The real deal, with stalls displaying high-end antiques from across northern Europe and an equally smart clientele who come to rifle through the oil paintings, sculptures, silverware, ceramics, and quality jewelry for the find of a lifetime. This is definitely not the place to show off your bargaining skills, as prices are generally deemed to be fair. The market opens Saturday 9am to 5pm, and again Sunday 9am to 3pm. Place du Grand Sablon.

Beer

Beer Mania ★★ With more than 400 beers on sale, from *kriek* to *trippel* brewed in the smallest micro-breweries to the big names like the Trappist beer Chimay, this place is heaven for beef buffs. And what's even better is that you can taste before you buy, so try something new, like Bush Ambrée, made at the Dubuisson Brewery in Hainaut—and at 12 percent, reputedly the strongest beer in Belgium. Chaussée de Wavre 174. www.beermania.be. ℂ **02/512-1788.**

Books & Multimedia

FNAC ★★ This massive and reasonably priced French chain has spread through the main cities of Europe like a rash and carries English-language travel books, novels, DVDs, phone and camera accessories, computer games, and tablets. The branch in the giant **City2** multistory mall on Brussels' main shopping drag is always crammed with ex-pat folks looking for bargains. Concert tickets are also sold here. Rue Neuve 123. www.fnac.com. ℰ **02/275-1111.**

Chocolate

Mary ★★   Established in 1919 by one of the very few female chocolatiers in Belgium, Mary Delluc, this traditional purveyor of pralines started life as a tea room. It has a delightfully old-fashioned air reflected in the sublime taste of its gourmet chocolates and in its pretty packaging, which has remained largely unchanged since the 1920s. From its small beginnings in rue Royal, the Mary empire has now spread as far afield as Kyoto and Chicago. Rue Royal 73. www.marychoc.com. ℰ **02/217-4500.**

Pierre Marcolini ★★★   Extremely youthful by Brussels chocolate-making standards, this chocolatier was only founded in 1995 but has quickly become a legend thanks to its sublime, jewel-like truffles and intensely flavored, handmade chocolates. Marcolini sources premium cocoa beans from small, handpicked producers around the world; other ingredients are also top quality—pink peppercorns from Morocco, Iranian pistachios, and vanilla from Madagascar. Prices are accordingly high, but worth the splurge, especially for the seasonal goodies and limited-edition chocolate boxes designed by the likes of Victoria Beckham and Tom Dixon. There are 11 locations in the city; the flagship is at Place du Grand Sablon. Place du Grand Sablon 39. www.eu.marcolini.com. ℰ **02/513-1783.**

Wittamer ★★★   Wittamer makes some of the best handmade pralines in the world, and even supplies them to the Belgian Royal Family. Its rolls, breads, pastries, and cakes have been winning fans since this store opened in 1910, and its hot pink wrapping paper is as well known in Belgium as the duck-egg-blue of Tiffany. Treats on offer include a huge variety of marzipan flavors in all different shapes, macaroons in rainbow colors, *marron glacés,* and homemade ice cream. Place du Grand Sablon 12. www.wittamer.com. ℰ **02/512-3742.**

Fashion

Delvaux ★★   Founded in 1829, Delvaux is justifiably regarded as one of the finest leather-and-accessory companies in Europe; demand for its high-brand luxury means that the Galeries Royales St-Hubert outpost of this Belgian design company do a roaring trade in some of the priciest handbags in the city. Designs are simple and boxy and will take fashionistas happily from work to weekend. Galerie de la Reine 31. www.delvaux.com. ℰ **02/512-7198.**

Hatshoe ★★   This too-cool-for-school boutique sells luxurious shoes and boots to stylish women, all made by such big-name Flemish designers as Dries van Noten and Ellen Verbeek as well as international names such as Chloé, Jil Sander, and the Spanish great Balenciaga. There's also a small selection of menswear. Rue Antoine Dansaert 89. www.hatshoe.be. ℰ **02/512-4152.**

Natan ★★ One of the only remaining couture houses in Brussels, Natan has an appropriately luxurious setting, inside an elegant mansion on the swanky Avenue Louise. Though it continues to create made-to-measure dresses for European royalty, Natan also offers ready to wear, though be prepared shell out for the designs featuring dreamy silks, exclusive prints, and beautiful tailoring. Avenue Louise 158. www.natan.be. ℭ **02/647-1001.**

Stijl ★★ This legendary boutique has been around since the mid-80s and is still one of the top addresses for high-end cutting-edge fashion. Hanging on metal racks in the industrial-style space are a wealth of Belgian labels including Dries van Noten and Ann Demeulemeester as well as international brands like grungy-chic Rick Owens. There is a second location for menswear in the trendy Sainte-Catherine district, at Place du Nouveau Marché aux Grains 6. Rue Antoine Dansaert 74. www.stijl.be. ℭ **02/512-0313.**

Flea Market

Vieux Marché ★★★ The daily market on a large piazza in once-sleazy Marolles is a joy to rummage around; it has an eccentric bunch of stallholders selling an equally eccentric range of items from vintage clothes to knock-off watches. Those in the know go on Thursday, when there may be a sprinkling of antiques to be unearthed. Bargaining is sometimes acceptable, but play it by ear before diving in with insulting offers. Open daily 6am until 2pm (till 3pm weekends). Place du Jeu de Balle. www.marcheauxpuces.be.

Flowers

Daniël Ost ★ The most exquisite flower shop in Brussels has as its backdrop an equally beautiful Art Nouveau location. Daniël Ost's wildly creative designs are heavily influenced by Japanese flower-arranging principles and are the perfect gift for the hostess if you are invited to supper in Brussels. Rue Royale 13. www.danielost.be. ℭ **02/217-2917.**

Food & Wine

Maison Dandoy ★★ Founded in 1829, Dandoy is still *the* place for sweet-toothed treats after nearly 2 centuries. Sample the traditional Belgian house specialties: spicy cinnamon and brown-sugar *speculoos* cookies, still baked traditionally in wooden molds, or blow off the diet and choose organic ice cream in an array of flavors, crispy waffles coated with jam and cream, or gingerbread made to an ancient recipe with honey. There are 6 locations throughout the city; this is the newest and features a seating area and playful wallpaper of birds eating cookies. Galerie du Roi 2. www.maisondandoy.com. ℭ **02/511-0326.**

La Septième Tasse ★★ Everybody's first port of call for teas in all guises, this cluttered little Bruxellois institution has a lengthy menu to sample. Play safe with Earl Grey or Lapsang Souchong, or have your own brew

One of Europe's oldest shopping malls consists of the three interconnected, glass-roofed arcades of the **Galeries Royales St-Hubert** (www.grsh.be). Constructed in Italian neo-Renaissance style and opened in 1847, architect Pierre Cluysenaer's elegant galleries are light and airy, hosting top-end boutiques Delvaux (see above), Oriande, Manufacture Belge des Dentelles (see below), Long-champ, numerous chocolate shops (Godiva, Neuhaus, Léonidas), sidewalk cafes, and street musicians playing classical music. The Galerie du Roi, Galerie de la Reine, and Galerie des Princes were the forerunners of city malls like Burlington Arcade in London, and lie just north of the Grand-Place, between rue du Marché aux Herbes and rue d'Arenberg.

blended from hundreds of aromatic choices. The shop also has committed, knowledgeable tea masters who are happy to share their knowledge of teas and make recommendations to customers—no mean feat in Brussels stores when service can verge on the brusque. Rue du Bailli 37. www.7etasse.com. ℰ **02/647-1971.**

Gifts

Belge une Fois ★ This concept store on the Rue Haute in the edgy Marolles district features fun graphics and playful phrases in French, Dutch, and English emblazoned on T-shirts, tote bags, mugs, posters, bottle openers, magnets, and more. Our favorite: "Je suis Belge. Don't be jealous." You can also stock up on local beer, condiments, and stationery. Rue Haute 89. www.belgeunefois.com. ℰ **02/503-8541.**

Kids

The Grasshopper ★★ Despite its touristy location steps away from the Grand-Place, this is a lovely warren of a shop behind an elaborate Art Nouveau facade. With several floors, Grasshopper sells toys for kids of all ages, from building bricks for babies to cuddly stuffed animals and traditional wooden train sets to board games. There's a small section upstairs where you'll find English-language books for children, too. Rue Marché aux Herbes 39-43. www.thegrasshoppertoys.be. ℰ **02/511-9622.**

Lace

Manufacture Belge de Dentelles ★ This oh-so-traditional store is based in the Galeries Royal St-Hubert and has been there since it opened in 1847; it is famous for only selling the very finest of handcrafted Belgian lace. Be prepared to dig deep into your pockets for the most delicate of tablecloths, net curtains, handkerchiefs, and intricate women's shirts. One of the sales assistants is usually busily showing off her lace making skills. Galerie de la Reine 6-8. www.mbd.be. ℰ **02/511-4477.**

ENTERTAINMENT & NIGHTLIFE
The Performing Arts

OPERA & BALLET An opera house in flamboyant baroque style, the **Théâtre Royal de la Monnaie ★★★**, place de la Monnaie (www.lamonnaie. be; ℃ 02/229-1211), is home to drama performances and chamber-music concerts as well as the **Opéra Royal de la Monnaie**—regarded as the best in the French-speaking world—and the **Orchestre Symphonique de la Monnaie.** The resident modern dance company, renowned Belgian choreographer Anne Teresa de Keersmaeker's group **Rosas ★★** (www.rosas.be), is noted for its innovative performances. The box office is in the theater's entrance hall on Rue des Princes and is open Tuesday to Friday noon to 6pm, Saturday 11am until 6pm. Ticket prices vary from 20€ to 350€ according to the event.

CLASSICAL MUSIC BOZAR ★★, rue Ravenstein 23 (www.bozar.be; ℃ 02/507-8200), aka the Palais des Beaux-Arts, is a lovely building designed by Victor Horta and now home to a mixed bag of cultural offerings from classical concerts by **Belgium's National Orchestra** to jazz and world music, movies, and a full program of plays. The box office is open Tuesday to Sunday 10am to 7pm, with tickets running from 15€ to 100€, depending on the event.

THEATERS Brussels offers more than 30 theaters presenting performances in French, Dutch, and (occasionally) English. Foremost among these is the **Théâtre Royal du Parc ★★**, rue de la Loi 3 (www.theatreduparc.be; ℃ 02/505-3040), a magnificent edifice occupying a corner of the Parc de Bruxelles, where classic and contemporary drama and comedies are performed. The **Théâtre National de la Communauté Française,** boulevard Emile Jacqmain 111–115 (www.theatrenational.be; ℃ 02/203-5303), offers avant-garde drama; and the **Théâtre Royal des Galeries,** Galerie du Roi 32 (www.trg.be; ℃ 02/512-0407), is known for comedy and musicals. Bringing theater to the city in Flemish is the **Koninklijke Vlaamse Schouwburg,** quai aux Pierres de Taille 9 (www.kvs.be; ℃ 02/210-1112), in a restored neo-Renaissance-style building dating from 1887.

Bars & Pubs

Now you're talking. Bars are where Brussels lives. It's hard to be disappointed, whether you pop into a neighborhood watering hole where a *chope* or *pintje* (a glass of beer) will set you back a mere 3.50€, or fork out several times as much in sleek, designer bars. And many of the bars around Grand-Place are notable for the scenery they overlook, and the grandeur of both their architecture and service. Of the hundreds of bars in Brussels, the following all have their own distinct style and ambience.

A La Mort Subite ★★★ A Brussels institution, this place is always heaving with locals and tourists alike. Its strange name translates as "Sudden Death," which comes from a dice game the regulars used to play in days gone by. The decor is rudimentary, consisting of scruffy old wooden tables and chairs, stained-glass mirrors, and old photos. The real entertainment is watching the wait staff calmly going about their business in the great long drinking hall that's always packed to the rafters. Of the hundreds of bottled and tap beers sold here, the specialties are traditional Brussels brews: *gueuze, lambic, faro,* and *kriek,* and Trappist brews like Chimay. Rue Montagne aux Herbes Potagères 7. www.alamortsubite.com. ℂ **02/513-1318.**

Arthur Orlans ★★   Should you need a break from the typical beer and wine found on most bar menus, this swanky speakeasy set inside a 19th-century tailoring shop shakes up some rather good craft cocktails. The dimly lit bar—outfitted with baroque wallpaper, leather sofas, tartan carpets, and old-timey knick-knacks—has the nostalgic thing down pat (though it opened in 2018). Gin is king here, with Monkey 47 featured prominently on a lengthy cocktail menu that includes the classics (martinis and the like) as well as specialty seasonal drinks. At around 15€ a cocktail, you may want to pace yourself. Rue Antoine Dansaert 67. ℂ **02/499-82-9947.**

Le Cirio ★★★   Just across the road from the Bourse (Stock Exchange), Le Cirio is often full of important-seeming gents who look like they've spent the day making millions. Inside it is a glorious whirl of Art Nouveau mirrors, brass bars, splendid chandeliers, and dark carved wood dating from 1886, where cheery waiters serve a curious concoction of half-wine, half-champagne in the same glass as well as a swathe of well-curated local beers. Rue de la Bourse 18. ℂ **02/512-1395.**

La Chaloupe d'Or ★   The grandest grand cafe in all Brussels occupies the majestic gilded facade of the former tailors' guild on the Grand-Place; don't waste your money eating here (you pay way over the norm for the location) but grab a table on the suntrap terrace in the early evening and watch the

---

Brussels LGBTQ Life

In comparison with the vibe of the Amsterdam gay world, the Brussels LGBT scene is quite subdued, but there are several gay and lesbian bars along **rue des Riches-Claires** and **rue du Marché au Charbon. Macho Sauna,** rue du Marché au Charbon 106 (www.machosauna.be; ℂ **02/513-5667**), houses a gay sauna, pool, steam room, and cafe. It's open Monday to Friday from noon to midnight and around the clock on weekends. The cozy, living-room-like **Station BXL,** rue du Marché au Charbon 27 (ℂ **02/608-3041**) is popular with the older gay crowd.

Brussels Gay Pride takes place in May each year, a vibrant street party

taking over the center of the city. For details of dates and schedules, visit www.pride.be.

For the inside slant on gay life in Brussels, stop by the gay and lesbian community center, **Tels Quels,** rue Haut 46-48 (www.telsquels.be; ℂ **02/512-4587**), open Monday to Friday 8:30am to 12:30pm and 2 to 7pm. There is a gay meeting room, café, and bar at **Rainbow House,** rue du Marché au Charbon 42 (www.rainbowhouse.be; ℂ **02/503-5990**); opening hours vary depending on the space. Both venues are run by volunteers.

world go by. Service is hurried and prices are steeps but the views and the dozens of beer options all contribute to making this bustling bar a uniquely Belgian experience. Grand-Place 24–25. © **02/274-1332.**

La Fleur en Papier Doré ★★   Located in a 16th-century town house and going strong since 1846, this pub always drew in poets, writers, and artists such as Magritte and the CoBrA guys (p. 110) like bees to a honey pot and it continues to do so with occasional poetry readings. This is a wonderfully atmospheric, cluttered old place, where customers gather round the entertaining *patron* for lively conversation and where all comers are welcome as long as they show an interest in the *gueuze* and boutique beers on offer. Rue des Alexiens 55. www.lafleurenpapierdore.be. © **02/511-1659.**

Moeder Lambic ★★   Despite its name, this lively, friendly beer hall serves all kinds of international craft brews, from IPAs and pale ales to stouts and saisons. But it's the long list of Belgian *lambic* and *gueuze* beers, available on tap and in bottles, that's the real draw. Settle in at one of the sleek wood booths and have the knowledgeable staff help you choose among the many lambic varieties, most of which hail from the regional Cantillon brewery and include unusual specimens fermented with rhubarb or flowers. Try a beer flight paired with local cheeses from La Fruitière, a top-notch cheese shop located just around the corner. Place Fontainas 8. www.moederlambic.com. © **02/503-6068.**

BRUGES

A city arrested in time. A Pompeii or a Brigadoon. An urban portrait caught as if by stop-frame photography, of a community that died while it was still young. The most heavily-visited touristic site in all of Belgium, it is the victim of one of the strangest natural events of history—the "silting of the Zwin" (we'll explain below)—which snuffed out its commercial life in the late Middle Ages, caused it to miss the Industrial Revolution, and thus paradoxically saved its unique medieval legacy from the wrecker's ball. If only more ancient cities had suffered such misfortune!

Bruges, in medieval times, was the greatest trading center in northern Europe, a multi-national marketplace for importing and exporting, storing and displaying every variety of goods. Along its canals and in central squares, dozens of wealthy foreign merchants maintained commercial palaces (these, unfortunately, have not survived), virtual embassies of their countries in which they lavishly entertained and dealt with the thousands of traders who flocked to a city renowned for its glitter and importance.

The focus of all this movement, the vital access road, was the "Zwin," an estuary that connected Bruges to the North Sea. In the mid-1300s, at the height of Bruges' renown, and for reasons still not fully understood, the Zwin began to "silt up," to fill with sand denying passage to deep-draft ships. Only slightly dismayed, the city moved its port area to suburban Damme, on a less affected segment of the Zwin 4 miles away, and Damme grew to the size of 60,000 residents. But relief was only temporary. In the 1400s, and while Bruges continued to enjoy unparalleled prosperity (as well as all the attendant artistic activity that comes with such prosperity), the Zwin outside Damme proceeded to silt up, becoming impassable within a few short years.

And Bruges died. Literally died. With the ending of ship traffic, commercial activity virtually ceased, and large portions of the population—some estimate as many as half—left to seek employment in Antwerp and other cities, abandoning their stunning homes, their commercial palaces, their magnificent squares. For most of the remaining residents, poverty set in. While other factors also contributed to the dizzying decline of Bruges—the outmoded and overly-restrictive commercial practices of the long-established merchants and guilds of Bruges, the eventual preference shown by Burgundian dukes for the eastern cities of Brabant, the unsuccessful rebellion of Bruges against the arrival of Maximilian of Austria as the first Hapsburg ruler of Flanders—it was that congealing Zwin that dealt the death blow. Today, at that point on the Zwin where ships once entered the North Sea, you can walk on the Zwin, scattering crumbs to strolling birds on the wet but firm land of a former waterway.

But not everything ended in Bruges, nor was its architectural development frozen in the 1400s. With the onset of religious wars and persecutions in the late 1500s, Catholic nuns and priests, monks and friars, fled to Bruges for safety, building additional churches and accommodations for themselves. Those structures survive to this day. In the 16th century, various wealthy philanthropists dotted the city with almshouses ("godshuizen") built for the poor; they, too, survive. In the 17th century there occurred a weak revival of sorts, and gabled, 17th-century houses and structures, in fair quantity, remain from that era. But Bruges remained a backwater, dozing through the 18th and 19th centuries until a Belgian writer, Georges Rodenbach, inadvertendy broadcast its charms to the world in a novel called "Bruges La Morte" (Dead Bruges) and set off a wave of tourism. Soon thereafter, the city embarked on its second career, this time as a monumental European tourist destination. I have often felt that if the international airport of Belgium were located outside Bruges, rather than Brussels, overseas tourism to Belgium would triple!

Today, it is a city where every walk brings reveries, every stroll results in unexpected discoveries of beauty. You walk behind a gate, and there is a ravishing courtyard, the kind you'd imagine from the last scene of Cyrano de Bergerac. You walk down a lane, and there is a canal and regal swans upon it. You gaze up at buildings, and there are exquisite, carved-stone emblems of the guilds or functions they once served. Everywhere are canals (in this "Venice of the North") and small, arched bridges, cobblestoned streets, ranks of aged medieval structures covered by vines.

And the homes! They all have pointed roofs, and are of brick, but brick used for an aesthetic purpose, set in patterns that draw the eye to a focal point, or create designs of beauty and purpose in even modest dwellings. Just as Italy, in the Middle Ages, excelled in marble, and France in stone, so medieval Bruges was the creator of brickwork never again equaled in its variety and charm.

ESSENTIALS

Arriving
BY PLANE
There are numerous daily flights to **Brussels Airport** (www.brusselsairport. be) from 200 destinations across the world. Bruges is 107km (67 miles) from the airport, easily accessible by train, with one change at Brussels-Midi/Zuid. **Brussels-South-Charleroi Airport** (www.charleroi-airport.com) is the domain of European budget flights; there are regular connections between the airport and Brussels-Midi/Zuid rail station for trains on to Bruges. See p. 158 and 159 for more details.

BY TRAIN

Two trains arrive in Bruges every hour from Brussels, four or five from Ghent, three from Antwerp, and up to three every hour from the ferry ports of Zeebrugge and Ostend (Oostende). The travel time is around 1 hour from Brussels, 25 minutes from Ghent, 1 hour and 20 minutes from Antwerp, and 15 minutes from both Ostend and Zeebrugge. Train information is available from **SNCB** (**Belgian Railways;** www.belgianrail.be; ℗ **02/528-2828**).

From London, passengers can ride the **Eurostar high-speed trains** (www. eurostar.com) through the Eurotunnel and transfer for Bruges either at Lille in northern France or in Brussels. From Paris, **Thalys high-speed trains** (www. thalys.com; ℗ **32/7066-7788**, 0.30€ per minute) go via Brussels to Bruges; on the slower and cheaper international trains, you transfer in Brussels. From Amsterdam, go via Brussels-Midi on the Thalys service.

Although the city is called Bruges in both English and French, look out for its Flemish name, BRUGGE, written on the station name boards. The station is on Stationsplein, 1.5km (1 mile) south of the center of town, a 20-minute walk or a short taxi or bus ride—choose any bus labeled CENTRUM and get out at the Markt to be in the center of the action.

BY BUS

Buses are less useful than trains for getting to Bruges, although there is frequent service from Zeebrugge and Ostend, and other Belgian seacoast resorts. The Bruges bus station adjoins the rail station. Schedule and fare information is available from **De Lijn** (www.delijn.be; ℗ **070/220-200**, 0.30€ per minute).

Flixbus (www.flixbus.com; ℗ **49/30-300-137-300**) operates a cheap daily bus service to Bruges from London, Amsterdam, Paris, or Cologne.

BY CAR

Bruges is 96km (60 miles) northwest of Brussels on the E40/A10; 50km (30 miles) northwest of Ghent on the E40/A10; 107km (66 miles) west of Antwerp on either the E17/A14 and E40/A10, or the E34, which bypasses Ghent; 18km (11 miles) south of the ferry port of Zeebrugge on either the N350 or the N31 and 30km (19 miles) southeast of Ostend on E40/A10. From the Eurotunnel and Calais in France take E40/A16 east to Bruges.

Visitor Information

TOURIST OFFICES   There are three tourist offices in Bruges; the most central is the biggest and it's at the Historium in Markt. Opening hours are daily 10am to 5pm and it's always crowded. A second branch is at the Concertgebouw, 't Zand 34, inside the city's Concert Hall, about midway between the train station and the heart of town; it is open Monday through Saturday 10 to 5pm; Sunday and public holidays 10am to 2pm. The third information center is at the station itself and is open daily 10am to 5pm. Call ℗ **050/444-646** or visit www.brugge.be.

City Layout

Bruges is a circular tangle of medieval streets surrounded by canals and moats; the monumental squares of the Markt and the Burg lie fairly centrally, adjoined by a labyrinth of alleyways and dramatic, imposing buildings. The city's major attractions fan out from there, with many lying to the southwest and another pocket to the northwest.

Outside the canals are the suburban residential neighborhoods—they were formerly separate *gemeenten* (districts) with their own local government and not part of Bruges at all—where most residents have their homes, although of the 120,000 people who live in the city, around 20,000 actually live and work in the ancient center.

Getting Around

The gorgeous center of Bruges is compact and filled with cobbled pedestrians-only streets, which makes walking the best way to get around. Just don't go out for a day's sightseeing wearing kitten heels; those charming cobblestones can be really hard on your feet.

BY BUS

Most city and regional buses are operated by **De Lijn** (www.delijn.be; ✆ **070/220-200**) and depart from the bus station next to the train station on Stationsplein, or from a secondary station at 't Zand near the Concertgebouw (p. 122), and many buses stop at the Markt in the Old Town. You can purchase your single ticket (3€, valid for 1 hour) from the De Lijn sales point in the station, from an automated ticket machine before boarding, or on the bus; the largest bill you can pay with onboard is a 10€ note.

BY BICYCLE

Cycling is a terrific way to get around Bruges, because here cyclists are privileged road users, meaning they can travel in both directions on some—but not

---

events IN BRUGES

One of the most popular and colorful folklore events in Belgium is Bruges' **Heilig-Bloedprocessie (Procession of the Holy Blood)** ★, which dates back to at least 1303 and takes place every year on Ascension Day (fifth Thurs after Easter). During the procession, the bishop of Bruges proceeds through the city streets carrying the golden shrine containing the Relic of the Holy Blood (p. 223). Residents wearing Burgundian-era and biblical costumes follow the relic, acting out biblical and historical scenes along the way. The procession will take place on Thursday, May 21, 2020, and Thursday, May 13, 2021.

The **Praalstoet van de Gouden Boom (Pageant of the Golden Tree)** ★★★ celebrates the 1468 marriage of Charles the Bold, Duke of Burgundy, to Margaret of York with street processions in medieval costume, jousts, and a ceremonial recreation of the entry of Margaret into Bruges. It takes place every 5 years in the second half of August; the next one will be in 2022 (www.brugge.be/gouden-boomstoet-2).

all—of the narrow, one-way streets in the center city. Others are one-way only and you'll be fined if you're caught riding against the traffic flow so keep a close eye on the street signs. Ride with caution, because the streets are filled with throngs of tourists likely to step out in front of you at any minute. But apart from that, the streets are gloriously traffic free and safe for families with older children to navigate by bicycle.

There are 10 bike-rental points in the city, from **Fietspunt Station** on Stationsplein (℡ **050/396-826**) to **B-Bike Concertgebouw** (℡ **050/612-667**) near the tourist office (p. 209) on 't Zand. Prices start at around 4€ per hour, or 12€ for a full day. If you don't fancy pedaling, many of the bike-rental companies, including B-Bike Concertgebouw, rent electric bikes, which start at around 10€ per hour, or 30€ for a full day.

BY CAR

Don't drive. There's no point. Leave your car in your hotel parking garage; one of six **underground parking garages** in the center (expect to pay around 9€ per day); one of four cheap **park-and-ride lots** next to the train station, which charge around 3.50€ per day; or a **free parking zone** outside the city center. It's a short walk into the heart of the Old Town from any of the parking lots. Parking rules are firmly enforced, and unlawfully parked cars will be ticketed, booted, or towed.

BY TAXI

There are taxi stands at the Markt, Vlamingstraat (opposite the City Theater), Kuipersstraat (next to the library), and outside the rail station on Stationsplein. Taxi companies include **ASAP Taxi** (℡ **0494/948-098**) and **Taxi Target** (℡ **0498/443-300**). The meter starts at 2.50€ and charges are 1.25€ or 2.50€ per kilometer for round-trip or one-way trips, respectively. There is an additional nightly rate (between 10pm and 6am) of 2.50€. There were no Uber or Lyft services in Bruges as of press time.

[FastFACTS] BRUGES

ATMs There are ATMs all over Bruges, and since they're on the CIRRUS or PLUS system, your home ATM card should work.

Business Hours Stores usually open from 10am to 6 or 6:30pm Monday through Saturday. Some open Sunday afternoon, and those in the center of the city will open all day on Sunday in summer. Most museums close on Monday, but not the Stadhuis, Belfort, or churches. Everywhere is closed January 1, Ascension Day in the afternoon, and December 25.

Emergencies For any emergency (fire, police, ambulance), the number is ℡ **112** from any land line or cellphone. For urgent but nonemergency medical services during evenings and weekends, call ℡ **1733** and for dental services, call

℡ **0903/39969.** To report a theft, call ℡ **050/448-844.** Residents of E.U. countries must have a European Health Insurance Card (EHIC) to receive full health-care benefits in Belgium.

Internet Access Most hotels in Bruges offer Wi-Fi access for free. There's free, blanket broadband coverage of the city center and most cafes and restaurants also provide Wi-Fi hotspots.

Pharmacies   Pharmacies are called *apotheek* in Flanders. Regular hours are Monday to Saturday 9am to 6pm (some close earlier Sat). Try **Baert S.,** Wollestraat 7

(℃ **050/336-474**), just south of the Markt. All chemists have details of the nearby all-night and Sunday drug-dispensing pharmacies posted on the door.

Post Office   The main post office, BPost, is at Smedenstraat 57-59 (℃ **32/22-01-2345**); it is open Monday to Saturday 9am to 6pm.

WHERE TO STAY

Don't even consider arriving without a room reservation because eight million other visitors have had the same idea as you and they're all heading for Bruges. The city is Belgium's premier tourist destination and even though many visitors are day-trippers from Brussels, it's essential to make your hotel reservations at least 2 weeks in advance, especially at the height of summer. Airbnb, VRBO, Flipkey and other rental companies are also quite active in Bruges, so if you prefer a place with a kitchen (and possibly lower nightly rates, especially for groups), go to one of those websites.

Expensive

Hotel Heritage ★★   One block north of all the action on Market Square, this handsome hotel is tucked on a quiet side street behind the neoclassical façade of a grand 1869 mansion. The beautifully preserved interior oozes plenty of old-world charm, with high ceilings, wood-paneled walls, and antique furnishings throughout; rooms are richly appointed with plush silk headboards, silk draperies, and crystal chandeliers. From the petite rooftop terrace (open seasonally) the Belfort looks close enough to reach out and touch. Down below, vaulted ceilings and stone walls of the 14th-century cellar now house the sauna and fitness area. As you might expect from a Relais & Chateaux property, the restaurant, **Le Mystique,** is top-notch, with a gourmet menu highlighting seasonal French-Belgian cuisine.

Niklaas Desparsstraat 11. www.hotel-heritage.com. ℃ **050/444-444.** 22 units. 210€–350€ double, 320€–500€ suite. Parking 35€. Breakfast not included in room rate (15€ or 29€ buffet). **Amenities:** Bar, restaurant, concierge, sauna, gym, free Wi-Fi.

The Pand Hotel ★★★   On a cobbled side street just off Bruges' handsome central canal and within a stone's throw of the sightseeing action, this privately-run boutique hotel is housed in an elegantly restored 18th-century carriage house. The refined lobby lounge is outfitted with tufted sofas, high-backed armchairs, and an opulent chandelier, while the adjacent wood-paneled library is ideal for cozying up with a book or glass of wine in front of the open fire. There's also an intimate bar and a lovely brick-walled courtyard with a trickling fountain. Each of the 26 rooms and suites are individually decorated in a classic style; some feature toile fabrics and wallpaper while others sport a tartan theme. The plush suites all boast Jacuzzi baths, some also have four-poster beds. Although there is no restaurant, the eateries of Bruges are practically at the doorstep. If you're traveling with youngsters, this is not the hotel for you; no guests under the age of 18 are permitted.

Pandreitje 16. www.pandhotel.com. ℭ **050/340-666.** 26 units. 199€–265€ double, 249€–390€ suite. Parking 24€/day. Breakfast not included in room rate (22€). **Amenities:** Bar, concierge, room service (until 9:30pm), free Wi-Fi.

Moderate

Hotel Jan Brito ★★ A fine example of the type of classy hotel that Bruges does so well, the Jan Brito has elegant period accommodations tucked behind a historic facade; in this case a listed 16th-century town house on a backwater side street. The public rooms are decorated in period style, with vast stone fireplace and burgundy walls; they take on the atmosphere of a private club when full with chattering guests in the evening. Many rooms have vaulted ceilings and all are individually kitted out, perhaps with four-poster beds or gilded walls in heraldic style. While the suites are humongous—even by U.S. standards—this is also a good family-friendly option as several duplex rooms can accommodate up to four. In addition, the Jan Britto has several budget rooms on offer, shoehorned into the old maids' quarters. Secreted away at the back of the hotel is a delightfully ornate Renaissance knot garden; it's just a charming spot to catch your breath after a day attacking the sights of Bruges.

Freren Fonteinstraat 1. www.janbrito.com. ℭ **050/330-601.** 37 units. 99€–220€ double, 199€–380€ suite. Parking 10€/day. Breakfast included in room rate. **Amenities:** Bar, gym, sauna, concierge, free Wi-Fi.

Inexpensive

Martin's Brugge ★ This budget choice doesn't offer much in the way of style or amenities, but the location couldn't be better: it's literally right around the corner from the Markt and the medieval Belfort. Rooms are very clean and comfortably sized and most have been renovated with bright, modern furnishings; the smallest category rooms (Cozy Double) are darker and more dated, though some do feature historical wood beams. There's no restaurant and the nautical-themed bar isn't very appealing but there is a small, pleasant terrace with picnic tables out back.

Oude Burg 5. www.martinshotels.com. ℭ **050/445-111.** 199 units. 90€–140€ double. Parking 30€/day. **Amenities:** Bar, breakfast room, free Wi-Fi.

WHERE TO EAT & DRINK

The foodie choices in Bruges range from Michelin-starred to mobile stands in the Markt selling fries in paper cones, with just about everything between. There's no need to skip the "tourist" restaurants in the central squares; service at them will be quite good, prices can be reasonable (especially if you follow the "menu du jour") and all feature local specialties, which are, after all, what you came to sample. Beyond the restaurants listed below, we're also big fans of the **Le Mystique** (see p. 212), which serves accomplished Belgian cuisine in a lovely setting.

Bruges Hotels & Restaurants

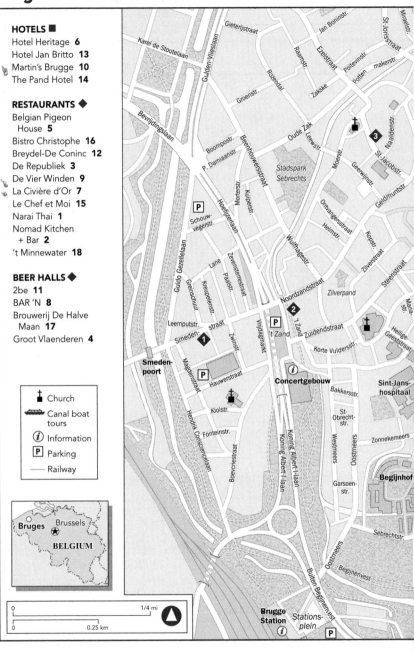

HOTELS ■
Hotel Heritage **6**
Hotel Jan Britto **13**
Martin's Brugge **10**
The Pand Hotel **14**

RESTAURANTS ◆
Belgian Pigeon
  House **5**
Bistro Christophe **16**
Breydel-De Coninc **12**
De Republiek **3**
De Vier Winden **9**
La Civière d'Or **7**
Le Chef et Moi **15**
Narai Thai **1**
Nomad Kitchen
  + Bar **2**
't Minnewater **18**

BEER HALLS ◆
2be **11**
BAR 'N **8**
Brouwerij De Halve
  Maan **17**
Groot Vlaenderen **4**

✝ Church
🚢 Canal boat
    tours
ⓘ Information
P Parking
— Railway

Bruges
BELGIUM
Brussels

0 ————————— 1/4 mi
0 ————————— 0.25 km

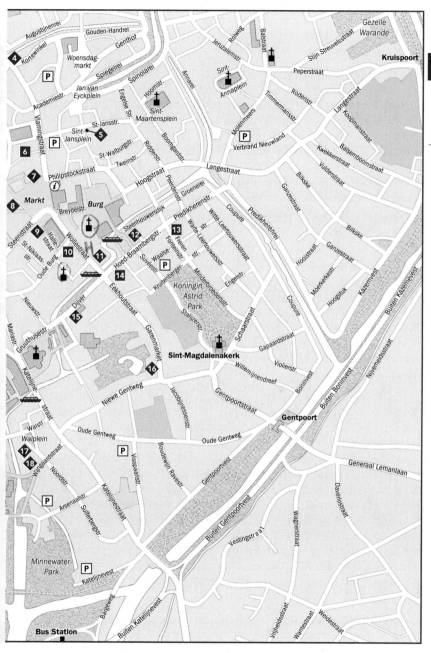

Gezelle
Warande

Kruispoort

Augustijnenrei
Gouden-Handrel
Genthof

4 Kortewinkel
Woensdag-
markt
Spiegelrei

Jan van
Academiestr. Eyckplein
Spinolarei

Vlamingstraat
Hoornstr.
Sint-
Maartensplein

Sint-Jansstr.
5
St-Jansplein
St-Walburgstr.
Tweinstr.
Ridderstr.

6

7 Philipstockstraat
Hoogstraat

8 Markt
Breydelstr. **Burg**
Steenhouwersdijk

Steenstraat
9 Halle-
St-Niklaas- straat
str.
Wollestraat
10 Oude Burg **11**

Nieuwstr.
Dijver
15

Mariastr.
Gruuthusestr.

Katelijne-
straat

Walstr.
Walplein
17
18 Wijngaardstraat
Noordstr.

Arsenaalstr.

Minnewater-
Park

Bus Station

Jeruzalemstr.
Rolweg
Balstraat

Sint-
Annaplein
Timmermanstr.
Rodenstr.
Peperstraat

Annarei
Boomgardstr.
Molenmeers
Verbrand Nieuwland

Langestraat
Langestraat
Koopmanstraat

Stijn Streuvelsstraat
Peperstraat

Kwekkerstraat
Balsemboomstraat

Bilske
Vulderstraat

Ganzestraat

Peerdenstr.
Groenerei
Witte-Leertouwersstraat
Predikherenrei
Coupure
Hooistraat
Ganzestraat
Bilske

Predikherenstr.
Warte-Leertouwersstr.
Freren str.
Fonteinstr.
Moerkerkestr.
Hoogstuk
Kazernvest

12 Hoed-Braambergstr.
Waalse
Suvestr.
Minderbroedersstr.
Engelstr.
Coupure
Buiten Karemevest

13

14 Eekhoutstraat
Knutenberger.
Koningin
Astrid
Park
Stalijestr.
Schaarstraat
Buiten Boninvest

16 Gatenmarkt
Jacobijnessenstr.
Sint-Magdalenakerk
Willemijnendreef
Gapaardstraat
Violierstr.
Boninvest

Niewe Gentweg
Gentpoortstraat
Gentpoort

Oude Gentweg
Oude Gentweg
Gentpoortvest
Buiten Gentpoortvest
Generaal Lemanlaan

Visspaanstr.
Boudewijn Ravestr.
Davenstostraat

Katelijnestraat
Suiterbergstr.

Bargeweg
Vestingstra a t
Wagnerstraat
Vrijheidsstraat
Wantestraat
Weidestraat

Katelijnevest
Buiten Katelijnevest

On the drinks front: Cocktails can be quite pricey in Belgium, so you may want to opt for beer or wine instead. Also, restaurants and bars will not serve tap water, only bottled—this is a rigidly enforced custom, but don't worry, the water is perfectly safe.

Expensive

Belgian Pigeon House ★★ BELGIAN   All manner of carrier pigeon related memorabilia graces this tiny restaurant, which occupies the ground floor and medieval brick-vaulted cellar of an old mansion in the city center. Pigeon statues, pigeon drawings, homing pigeon bands—even the menu and placemats are imprinted with illustrations of the birds. What could be kitschy is actually quite atmospheric, and the concise menu, featuring just a handful of main courses, is remarkably good. There's rabbit stewed in dark beer, North Sea shrimp, and grilled pork, but the star attraction, of course, is the pigeon, slowly cooked in a charcoal oven, which lends a smoky flavor to the tender meat.

Sint-Jansplein 12. www.belgianpigeonhouse.com. ✆ **050/661-690.** Main courses 22€–32€. Thurs–Mon 11am–10pm.

Bistro Christophe ★★ BELGIAN   Two spacious dining rooms with white-washed brick walls dotted with contemporary art, including a cool mural of Picasso, form this stylish bistro on the Garenmarkt. The open kitchen turns out a raft of hearty meat-and-potato dishes—filet mignon, Chateaubriand, lambchops—as well as the occasional seafood plate. The homemade shrimp croquettes make for an excellent starter, as does the house-smoked salmon. While dinner is pricey, the 20€ prix-fixe lunch, which includes an appetizer and a main dish, is quite a bargain.

Garenmarkt 34. www.christophe-brugge.be. ✆ **050/344-892.** Main courses 22€–36€. Thurs–Mon noon–2pm and 6–11pm (Thurs and Mon till 10pm, no lunch Sat).

Breydel-De Coninc ★★★ SEAFOOD   The best seafood restaurant in Bruges, De Coninc is just off the Markt, with a surprisingly pared-down interior, simple wooden tables, and stripped pine floors. A blackboard running round the wall lists specials, but your eye is likely to be held by the large fish tank, where your lunch or dinner may await. You can order steak, but seafood is the raison d'être after all: Sole, scampi, bouillabaisse, fish stew, fried fish, and lobster are all on offer. That said, most people come here either for the eel dishes (try the one with herb sauce for a real Belgian treat) or any of the seven mussel dishes, all served with fries. Starters include excellent fish soup, oysters, and croquettes; finish with desserts that might include fresh seasonal fruit or a typical "white lady," an ice-cream sundae with hot chocolate sauce.

Breidelstraat 24. www.restaurant-breydel.be. ✆ **050/339-746.** Main courses 23€–50€. Daily noon–2:30pm and 6:30–9:30pm (closed Wed).

Le Chef et Moi ★★ BELGIAN   This classic is definitely one for booking ahead of time, both because of the high quality of the cuisine and because it's so tiny. Oil paintings cover the walls, chandeliers drip crystal, and the intimate dining room is lit by candlelight at night. Every sitting runs like clockwork, thanks to the hospitality and skills of owner-chef Stefaan Cardinael and maître d' Caroline Saeys. Menu choice is limited to what is available seasonally and what Cardinael feels like cooking, but the results are always sublime; dishes might include scallops, skate wing, or milk-fed roast lamb. A fine wine list adds to the pleasurable experience.

Dijver 13. www.lechefetmoi.be. ☏ **050/396-011.** Fixed-price lunch 18€–25€, dinner mains 26€–32€, fixed-price market menu 39.50€. Tues–Sat noon–2pm and 6:30–10pm.

Moderate

De Vier Winden ★★ INTERNATIONAL   With a stellar location right at the foot of the Belfort (p. 266), this casual brasserie serves up solid Belgian fare but also offers a nice selection of Italian pastas and pizza. Order a liter of rosé wine, tuck into Flemish stew, mussels, or the meaty lasagna, and finish off your feast with a crème brûlée. Waiters, outfitted in white dress shirts and black vests, have obviously all been doing their job since time began, and manage to mix humor with a firm hand when directing skittish diners around the menu.

Markt 9. www.devierwinden.be. ☏ **050/331-933.** Main courses 18€–26€. Fixed-price menu 22€. Daily 10am–10pm.

La Civière d'Or ★★ BELGIAN   One of four family-owned restaurants set side-by-side and opposite the Belfort (p. 266), La Civière d'Or is the best options in the row of restaurants on the Markt, in terms of price, ambience, and waitstaff charm. Grab a table outside, order a bucket full of mussels, a plate of frites, a Belgian beer, and sit back to watch the action on the dramatic stage that is the Markt. This place has been around since 1947 so it must be doing something right. It's exactly what Bruges is all about.

Markt 33. http://newsites.resto.com/lacivieredor. ☏ **050/343-036.** Main courses 15€–18€, fixed-price menus 18€–29€. Daily 11am–11pm.

Narai Thai ★ THAI   Always busy with diners escaping the ubiquitous mussels and Flemish stew, this Thai is a little way out of the city center, just west of 'Zand and the Concertgebouw (p. 122). Proceedings kick off with a sharp, coriander-and-lemongrass-infused tom yam soup, followed by choices such as piles of beef fried in chili and ginger or traditional Thai green chicken curry, both served with an abundance of noodles or rice. Set menus for sharing are a good value and offer a variety of dishes. For cowardly European palates, levels of spiciness are marked, and even the hottest are well short of volcanic.

Smedenstraat 43. www.naraithai.be. ☏ **050/680-256.** Main courses 14€–23€. Business lunch 25€. Sharing menus 45€–50€ per couple. Daily noon–2:30pm and 6–11pm.

Inexpensive

De Republiek ★★ INTERNATIONAL   If you're wondering where Bruges' hipsters hang out, it's here in this cultural complex, which houses a cinema, artisan workshop, and a bright, airy, industrial-style cafe/bar. The latter buzzes from noon until the wee hours, thanks to its well-priced lunchtime sandwich menu, affordable array of evening tapas, and late-night bar snacks. More substantial dishes include a vegan-friendly stuffed eggplant with quinoa; lamb with sweet potatoes, zucchini, and asparagus; or the catch of the day. The coveted tables on the terrace fill up quickly on sunny days, and on summer nights, it's one of the best spots in the city for an al fresco cocktail.

Sint-Jakobsstraat 36. www.republiekbrugge.be. ℂ **050/734-764.** Sandwiches (lunch only): 9€–10€. Tapas (evening only): 9€–11€. Main courses 17€–23€. Daily noon–midnight (Fri–Sat till 2am; Tues from 3pm).

Nomad Kitchen + Bar ★★ BISTRO   A welcome break from the usual mussels-laden menus, Nomad (which stands for No Ordinary Meals And Drinks) is heavy on fresh, organic produce, with an array of meal-sized salads and vegetarian options, including a terrifically zesty eggplant lasagna. The décor, too, is a departure from Bruges' typical dimly lit, rustic dining rooms; it's light and bright, with white-washed walls and Scandinavian-inspired touches—right down to the cozy furs tossed over the terrace seats. It's a mob scene at breakfast, but far quieter at lunch; unfortunately, Friday is the only time the restaurant is open for dinner. There's also a kids' menu and for adults, a short but well-curated cocktail list.

't Zand 12. www.nomadbrugge.be. ℂ **050/736-488.** Main courses 14€–21€. Sun–Fri 9am–6pm (Fri till 10pm), Sat 8am–6pm.

't Minnewater ★★ BISTRO   The perfect family respite from the surging crowds in Bruges' swarming museum district, this is an easygoing bistro that won't break the bank. Bribe fractious youngsters with a chocolate-smothered crepe or tuck into mussels and pasta arrabiata on the exceptionally reasonable fixed-price lunch menu. In winter there's a welcoming log fire inside, and in summer there are lakeside views from the al fresco terrace out front. It's also a nice pit stop for afternoon tea.

Wijngaardstraat 28. ℂ **050/335-746.** Main courses 13€–23€, fixed-price lunch menu 16€; fixed-price dinner menu 21€–31€. Mon–Tues and Thurs–Sat 11:30am–9:30pm.

Bars & Beer Halls

2be ★★★   With a terrace overlooking the picturesque Rozenhoedkaai canal, this corner pub is crowded all day every day with Belgian beer fans anxious to sample as many brews as possible. There are usually seven draft beers on offer. They change with the seasons, but might include Brugse Zot from the Half Moon Brewery (see below) fruit beers, *trippels,* and white beer. Wait staff are well informed on the pedigree of their beers, but service can be somewhat brusque, mostly owing to the constant crowds. There's little in the way of nourishment to soak up the alcohol so things can get a little boisterous on weekend evenings. The pub also hosts a beer store.

Wollestraat 53. www.2-be.biz. ℂ **050/611-222.** Pub: Daily 11am–7:30pm (Fri–Sat till 8pm, closed Wed).

BAR 'N ★★   Two young sisters preside over this cozy cocktail bar just off the Markt; its edgy decor—wood-lined walls, industrial pendant lights, a giant stuffed cow head—nicely complements the adventurous cocktails. Drinks are crafted using fresh herbs, spices, and fruits, and while you could characterize the beautifully presented concoctions as feminine, they are definitely not sweet. Top marks go to the signature gin and tonic with house-made basil syrup.

Sint-Amandsstraat 2. ✆ **32/472-89-7341.** Mon–Thurs 4pm–1am, Fri–Sat 4pm–2am.

Brouwerij De Halve Maan (Half Moon Brewery) ★★ Many flock here for the brewery tour (p. 230) but the pub at the Half Moon is actually quite good. It holds a swanky modern bistro and covered terrace; pickings from the menu include burgers, salads, and summer BBQs. But the chief reason to come is to savor the beers, including the fruity *Brugse Zot* (Bruges Fools) and fearsomely strong "quadruppel" Straffe Hendrik ales.

Walplein 26. www.halvemaan.be. ✆ **050/444-222.** Pub: Sun–Wed 10am–6pm, Thurs–Sat 10am–11pm.

Groot Vlaenderen ★★★ When it opened in 2012, this was the city's first high-end cocktail lounge and it's still the best, serving sophisticated mixed drinks in an elegant, dimly lit space replete with velvet seating and a towering chandelier. The menu favors classics like the daiquiri and French 75, and the lengthy gin list features around 100 bottles—ideal for crafting a bespoke martini or gin and tonic. Its inventive seasonal cocktails are also a delight.

Vlamingstraat 94. www.grootvlaenderen.be. ✆ **050/684-356.** Tues–Thurs 5pm–1am, Fri–Sat 5pm–2am, Sun 5pm–midnight.

EXPLORING BRUGES

A hot-favorite contender for the title of Europe's most romantic small city, Bruges is a fairy-tale confection of gabled houses, meandering canals, magnificent squares, and narrow cobblestone streets. What is most astonishing is the consistently warm welcome its residents provide to the swarms of visitors who swallow the place up every summer. The basis for this goes beyond mere economics—the good burghers of Bruges have a deep love for their show-stopping city and are only too delighted that others share their enthusiasm.

The Markt

The gigantic open space of Markt is lined with venerable facades swathed in heraldic banners; together with the adjacent Burg (p. 223), these two great squares formed the commercial and administrative heart of Bruges and are today the focal point of its sightseeing adventure. Most of what you'll want to see is less than 10 minutes' walk away from these two squares.

Bruggemuseum-Belfort (Belfry) ★★ HISTORIC BUILDING The Belfort was, and still very much is, the symbol of Bruges' civic pride. What poet Henry Wadsworth Longfellow in 1856 called "the beautiful, wild chimes" of its magnificent 47-bell carillon peal out over the city every quarter-hour, and several times a day in longer concerts during the summer. The ornate tower is the biggest in Belgium and stands 83m (272 ft.) high; its lower

Bruges Attractions

Bruges
Brussels
BELGIUM

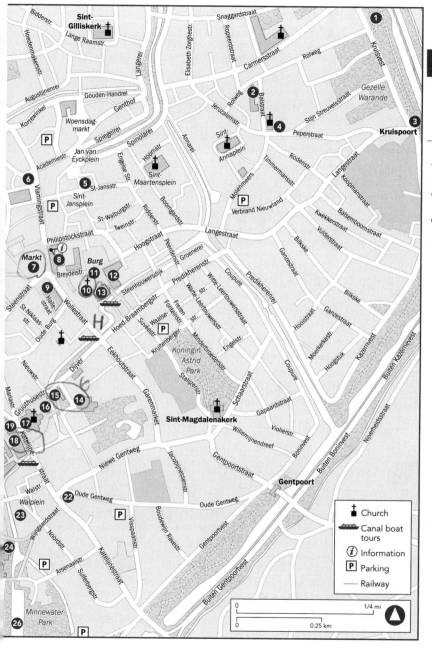

Bidderstr.

Sint-Gilliskerk ✝

Hoedenmakersstr.

Lange Raamstr.

Snaggardstraat

Ropeerdstraat

Carmersstraat

Rolweg

❶

Kruisvest

Elisabeth Zorghestr.

Gezelle Warande

Augustijnenrei

Gouden-Handrel

Genthof

Jeruzalemstr.

Balstraat ❷

Rolweg

Stijn Streuvelsstraat

Kortewinkel

Woensdag-markt

Spiegelrei

Spinolarei

❹

Peperstraat

Stijn Streuvelsstraat

❸

Kruispoort

Ⓟ

Academiestr.

Jan van Eyckplein

Hoornstr.

Sint-Annaplein

Sint-Maartensplein

Rodenstr.

Langestraat

Koopmansstraat

❻

Vlamingstraat

❺ St-Jansstr.

Sint-Jansplein

Annarei

Molenmeers

Timmermansstr.

Balsemboomstraat

Ⓟ

St-Walburgstr.

Tweinstr.

Riddersn.

Boomgaardstr.

Verbrand Nieuwland

Langestraat

Kwekkerstraat

Vulderstraat

Bilkske

Philipstockstraat

ⓘ

Hoogstraat

Peerdenstr.

Groenerei

Ganzenstraat

Bilkske

Markt ❼ ❽

Breydelstr.

Burg ❶❶ ❶❷

❶⓪ ✝ ❶❸

Steenhouwersdijk

Predikherenrei

Predikherenrei

Steenstraat

St-Niklaas str.

Oude Burg

Wollestraat

Hoed-Braambergstr.

Witte-Leertouwersstr.

Wante-Leertouwersstr.

Coupure

Hooistraat

Ganzestraat

Hoogstuk

Moerkerkestr.

Katernvest

Nieuwstr.

❾

Dijver

Eekhoutstraat

Kruitenberger

Suvestr.

Waalse str.

Fonteinstr.

Freren str.

Minderbroedersstr.

Engelstr.

Coupure

Buiten Katernvest

Manastr.

Gruuthusestr.

❶❺ ❶❹

Garenmarkt

Koningin Astrid Park

Stalijzerstr.

Schaartstraat

Gapaardstraat

Nijverheidsstraat

❶❾ ❶❼

❶❻

Sint-Magdalenakerk ✝

Violierstr.

❶❽ Katelijne straat

Niewe Gentweg

Jacobijnessenstr.

Willemijnendreef

Boninvest

Buiten Bonin vest

Walstr.

Walplein

❷❷ Oude Gentweg

Oude Gentweg

Gentpoort

Buiten Gentpoortvest

❷❸

Wijngardstraat

Noordstr.

Ⓟ

Visspaanstr.

Boudewijn Ravestr.

Gentpoortstraat

Gentpoortvest

❷❹

Ⓟ

Arsenaalstr.

Suterbergstr.

Katelijnestraat

Minnewater-Park

❷❻

Ⓟ

✝	Church
🚤	Canal boat tours
ⓘ	Information
Ⓟ	Parking
----	Railway

0 ————————————— 1/4 mi
0 ————————————— 0.25 km

section dates from around 1240, the corner turrets were added in the 14th century, and the upper, octagonal section in the 15th century. Climb an exhausting 366 steep steps to the tower's summit for panoramic views of Bruges and the surrounding countryside all the way to the sea. Pause for breath at the second-floor Treasury, where the town seal and charters were kept behind multiple wrought-iron grilles.

From the 13th to the 16th century, much of the city's commerce was conducted in the Hallen (Market Halls), below the Belfort. Now they are the location of the **Museum-Gallery Xpo-Gallery Dalí,** which allows a fun-filled glimpse into the surreal world of Salvador Dalí, Spain's strangest artist. A vibrant collection of his sculptures, paintings, sketches, and glassware are presented in a suitably bizarre display incorporating mirrors, sparkly blue lighting, and splashes of gold against a backdrop of bright blues and crimsons. Pride of place goes to Dalí's joyfully wacky bronzes, which include his famous spindly elephants. Half the charm of this exhibition is its unexpected contrast to the medieval beauty of the building housing it.

Markt 7. www.visitbruges.be/en/belfort-belfry. ℂ **050/448-743.** Admission 12€ adults, 10€ seniors, children 6–25, free for children 5 and under. Daily 9:30am–6pm. Closed Jan 1, April 24–25.

Historium Brugge ★★ MUSEUM   Housed in an intricate balcony-and-tower–adorned Gothic Revivalist building next to the Provinciaal Hof (Provincial Palace; see p. 222), the Historium is located above the tourist information office (p. 209) and explains all the twists and turns of the city's turbulent history in an approachable and entertaining manner. It's a romp through 15th-century Bruges with a series of interactive experiences using film, music, holograms, sounds, and even smells (multilingual headphones are available). Afterwards catch your breath at the **Duvelorium Grand Beer Café**—which has incomparable views over Markt—in the same building.

Markt 1. www.historium.be. ℂ **050/270-311.** Admission 17.50€ adults, 13.50€ students, 11€ children 6–12, Duvelorium 2€ extra. Daily 10am–6pm. Closed Jan 1 and Dec 25.

Other Sights around the Markt

The **sculpture group** in the center of the Markt depicts a pair of Flemish heroes: butcher Jan Breydel and weaver Pieter de Coninck. The two led an uprising in 1302 against the wealthy merchants and nobles who dominated the guilds, and went on to win an against-the-odds victory over French knights later that same year in the Battle of the Golden Spurs (p. 30). The small, castle-like building called the **Craenenburg** (it's now a restaurant) at the corner of Sint-Amandsstraat was used by a rebel-lious citizenry to imprison the Habsburg Crown Prince and future Emperor Maximilian of Austria in 1488 over increased taxes. In revenge for that humiliation, Maximilian later wounded Bruges' pride by transferring his capital to Ghent and hit the city's pocketbook by transferring its trading rights to Antwerp. The large neo-Gothic Provinciaal Hof (Provincial Palace) dates from the 1800s and houses the government of the province of West Flanders.

The Burg

The Burg is the second of Bruges' vast piazzas, just steps away from the Markt. It parades a similar array of beautiful medieval buildings, which together add up to a time-traveler's trip through the history of European architecture. On this site, Baldwin Iron Arm, Count of Flanders, built a fortified castle (or *burg*) in the late 9th century, around which a village developed into Bruges. The rest, as they say, is history.

Basiliek van het Heilig-Bloed (Basilica of the Holy Blood) ★★★

CHURCH   When knights returned from the Crusades, they often returned with relics—a fragment of the True Cross, a tiny branch from the Crown of Thorns. But when Derek of Alsace, Count of Flanders, returned to Bruges in 1150 from the Second Crusade, he brought back the Relic that staggered all of Europe: a cloth allegedly soaked with the blood of Christ. It was immediately placed in the Chapel of St. Basil, now the "Basilica of the Holy Blood."

The relic is embedded in a rock-crystal vial, which itself is held inside a small glass cylinder adorned at each end with a golden crown. It is kept in a magnificent tabernacle on a side altar in the chapel and is brought out daily (btwn. 11:30am and noon, and 2 and 4pm) so the faithful can pray to it, and even line up to kiss it. Know that if you go up to inspect the vial, you will be expected to donate to the upkeep of the church, a fact that is made all too clear by the attendant clergy.

The Basilica, built in the 1100s, was once a thoroughly Romanesque structure, and its downstairs interior still is—probably the purest example of Romanesque architecture you will see in Belgium, with its distinctive rounded arches and heavy pillars, its squat and horizontal lines, its gloomy, stone interior with poignant statues of the crucified Jesus. Upstairs everything changes! Now the Basilica becomes a green-and-yellow fairyland of emeralds and gilt, of rich paneling, paintings, striped ornaments of every sort, a dazzling display of both Gothic and Renaissance elements that, in later centuries, completely transformed the formerly-Romanesque facade and upper story of the building into a Venetian-like palace-of-a-church. A wide stone staircase worn by the feet of millions of pilgrims leads both to the upper story and adjoining museums housing the ornately-figured reliquaries—golden containers or casques—associated with the Relic.

In the Basilica Museum, the magnificent reliquary created by Bruges goldsmith Jan Crabbe has a gem-encrusted case styled as a medieval castle and topped with a golden statue of the Virgin. This houses the relic on its annual pilgrimage around the streets of Bruges in the colorful **Procession of the Holy Blood** (p. 39) on Ascension Day.

Burg 13. www.holyblood.com. © **050/336-792.** Basilica free admission; museum 2.50€. Daily 9:30am–12:30pm and 2–5:30pm. Mass daily (except Mon) 11am. Museum closed Jan 1, Nov 1, and Dec 25.

Bruggemuseum-Brugse Vrije (Liberty of Bruges) ★ HISTORIC

BUILDING   The center of the city's judiciary until 1984, the Landhuis

Musea Brugge Card

The money-saving **Musea Brugge Card** is available at any one of the 14 participating museums and historical sites, which include the Belfort and Stadhuis (Town Hall) as well as the must-see Groeningemuseum and St. John's Hospital, which houses several masterpieces by the Flemish primitive artist Hans Memling. The card, valid for 3 days, costs 28€ for adults and 22€ for ages 18 to 25. It's worth it if you plan to visit multiple attractions, as individual ticket prices hover around 12€. For more information, go online to the Visit Bruges website **www.visitbruges.be**.

(Palace) of the Liberty of Bruges also served as the administrative HQ of the region of Flanders around Bruges from the Middle Ages onward. Much of it was rebuilt between 1722 and 1727 and the palace now houses the city archives. It's chiefly visited for the exceptional **Renaissancezaal (Renaissance Chamber)** ★★, which has been restored to its original 16th-century condition, and a monumental black marble fireplace decorated with a carved alabaster frieze and topped by an oak chimneypiece carved with statues of Emperor Charles V, who visited Bruges in 1515, and his grandparents: Emperor Maximilian of Austria, Duchess Mary of Burgundy, King Ferdinand II of Aragon, and Queen Isabella I of Castile. That's quite memorable in itself for the size of some of the wooden codpieces. The gloomy oil painting by Gillis van Tilborgh was executed in 1659 and clearly shows the Charles V fireplace on its right-hand side, behind all the aldermen dressed in black robes.

Burg 11a. www.visitbruges.be/nl/brugse-vrije. ℂ **050/448-743.** Courtyard free admission; Renaissance Hall 6€ adults, 5€ seniors and ages 18–25. Daily 9:30am–5pm. Closed Jan 1, Ascension Day afternoon, and Dec 25.

Bruggemuseum-Stadhuis (Town Hall) ★★★ HISTORIC BUILDING Oldest town hall in Belgium (1376), it is certainly one of the most beautiful, a Gothic wedding cake of pointed spires and elaborate statuary adorning the stone facade in uniform rows, the effect marred only by the fact that most of the statues were removed from their niches and destroyed by the soldiers of the French Revolution in 1795—they have not been replaced, though plans are constantly announced to do so. Inside, you wander about through lobby and halls till you see the evocative painting of the Burgomaster receiving Napoleon on his visit to Bruges, then return to the lobby and immediately head up the red-carpeted stone staircase to your left to the immense, scarlet-colored *Gotische Zaal* (Gothic Room), with its stalactite-like ceiling completed in 1402. The immense pride of medieval people in their civic institutions, the majesty and might of medieval cities, literally resounds from the lavish detailing and decor of the walls, ceiling and floor of this richly-ornamented chamber.

A much later addition to the splendor of the Gothic Room are its dozen wall murals completed in 1895; imagine them as bearing consecutive numbers starting near the chimney piece, and you'll enjoy a mini-course in the history of Bruges by perusing: 3 (Derek of Alsace, Count of Flanders, arriving with the Relic of the Holy Blood in 1150); 6 (Philip of Alsace, a later Count of Flanders, granting a charter to Bruges in 1190); 1 (The Triumphant return of the troops of Bruges from the Battle of the Golden Spurs in 1302); 4 (Lodewijk of Male, Count of Flanders, laying the cornerstone of the Town Hall in 1376); 5 (A burgomaster of Bruges visiting the studio of Jan van Eyck in 1433).

Burg 12. www.visitbruges.be/nl/stadhuis. © **050/448-743.** Admission 6€ adults, 5€ seniors and ages 18–25. Daily 9:30am–5pm. Closed Jan 1, Ascension Day afternoon, Dec 25 and 31.

The Dijver—"Museum Street"

The **Groeningemuseum,** the **Arents Museum,** the **Gruuthuse**—you'll pass them in quick order as you walk up the Dijver, along the canal, toward the **Church of Our Lady,** which you will see in the distance. Reaching Mariastraat, you then turn left and find across the street the 12th-century **St. John's Hospital,** with its remarkable collection of works by Hans Memling. If you plan to see several museums, purchase a **Musea Brugge card** (p. 224) at the first one you visit, otherwise you'll pay anywhere from 6€ to 12€ per museum. There is also a combination ticket (14€) for the newly renovated Gruuthuse and Church of Our Lady, which was undergoing restoration at press time and is only partially accessible with a limited number of artworks on view.

The Arents Museum ★ The rather minor Arents Museum ("Arentshuis"), in the rich, patrician home of the Bruges family of that name, displays impressive oil paintings of various historical phases of Bruges, but far less interesting examples of chinaware, silver and pewter, ink sketches and paintings by an English painter of the second rank, Frank Brangwyn—he bequeathed them to Bruges. Although the Arents can be skipped if you're short of time, you will at least want to dart inside the courtyard for a free look at a glassed-in carriage museum of Bruges attached to the main house.

Dijver 16. www.museabrugge.be. © **050/448-743.** Admission 6€ adults, 5€ seniors and ages 18–25, free ages 17 and under; admission included with Groeningemuseum ticket. Tues–Sun 9:30am–5pm. Closed Jan 1, Ascension Day afternoon, and Dec 25.

Gruuthusemuseum ★★ MUSEUM In the brilliant Belgian era of the Dukes of Burgundy (1388 to 1477), then the richest sovereigns of Europe, more wealthy than the kings of France, the most powerful of the Flemish nobles serving those Dukes were the Gruuthuse clan. This is their home, appropriately splendid. And if you'd care to glimpse the gulf that separated such a man as Louis de Gruuthuse from the ordinary citizens of Bruges, head to the Gruuthuse private chapel; its windows cut into the wall of the immense, adjoining Church of Our Lady, so that Louis and the Gruuthuses could witness and attend services from their own home, unsullied by the presence of common folk!

Thousands of household and decorative items of antiquity are displayed in the labyrinth of rooms and winding stone staircases that make up the

Gruuthuse, including paintings by various minor masters of Bruges, illustrated panels of wood and wood sculpture, 15th- to 18th-century furniture, textiles, tapestries, embroidery and lace, weapons, and musical instruments. Though most items postdate the actual time of the Gruuthuses, enough relates to the 15th and 16th centuries to provide you with a sense of the manner in which such over-privileged nobility lived.

Dijver 16. www.visitbruges.be/en/gruuthusemuseum. © **050/448-743.** Admission 12€ adults, 10€ seniors and ages 18–25, free ages 17 and under. Tues–Sun 9:30am–5pm. Closed Jan 1, Ascension Day afternoon, and Dec 25.

Groeningemuseum ★★★ MUSEUM One of the two essential museum experiences of Bruges (the other is St. John's Hospital, which holds numerous works by Hans Memling), this is the home, the shrine, of the so-called Flemish Primitives. Though the "primitives" are displayed in museums and churches all over Belgium, nowhere else are so many major 15th century works (with around 30 of them) clustered as here. Everyone except Dirck Bouts is represented: Van Eyck and Memling, Rogier Van der Weyden, Hugo van der Goes, Petrus Christus, Gerard David, Hieronymous Bosch, and the various anonymous "Masters" of various schools and subjects. Here are the bright and luminous tones resulting from the world's first use of pigments mixed with oil, the photographic realism and exquisite precision, the magnificent grouping of figures, the pure and unquestioning religious belief of "the Age of Faith," the painstaking devotion of long months and indeed years to a single painting, with which the Flemish greats of the 1400s so stunned the artistic world of that time.

The museum itself is a smallish place, like a simple, one-story-high convent in style, its contents compressed into 15 small, whitewashed rooms, bearing consecutive numbers, through which you should walk consecutively—and therefore chronologically. Rooms 1 through 4 house the "primitives," while the higher-numbered rooms then trace the development of Belgian painting (especially from the area of Bruges) into modern times.

Rooms 1 through 4: The supreme work (room 1) is Jan Van Eyck's **Madonna with Canon Joris van der Paele** (1436), commissioned for the now-destroyed St. Donatian Cathedral in Bruges by the eminent, white-chaliced churchman shown kneeling in the painting as he is presented to Mary and the baby Jesus by a hat-tipping St. George, his patron saint. The five figures, and especially the textures of the clothes and chain-mail they wear, are caught as if by a camera, while the expression on Canon van der Paele's face is an unforgettable combination of strain, awe and overwhelming emotion; how else would such a figure react upon being presented to the Divinity he had served all his life? Nearby: the only surviving secular painting by Van Eyck (as best I know)—a brutally honest portrait, blemishes and all, of his wife, Margaret.

Six other works are standouts in the "Hall of the 15th Century Flemish Primitives" (rooms 1 through 4): Rogier van der Weyden's **St. Luke Painting the Virgin** (1435) (since Luke was Patron Saint of the Painter's Guild, the "biographer" of Mary is here portrayed as creating a portrait of her); Gerard David's "diptych" (two paintings) known as **The Judgment of Cambyses** (1498), showing the conviction and punishment of a corrupt Persian judge, condemned to be skinned alive; the painting hung for centuries in the Town Hall of Bruges as an admonition to the politicians of Bruges! Also sublime: David's **Baptism of Christ** (1499?) with its exquisite grouping of little girls, daughters of the donors, shown in the right-hand panel, as you face it; cup your hand about your eye to blot out all but the little girls, and see what an enchanting tableau results; Hugo van der Goes' **Death of the Virgin** (1480) the whole suffused with an unusual and unforgettable bluish-white light—this was van der Goes' last picture, painted shortly before he died of melancholia; Hans Memling's **Moreei Triptych** (1484); and the terrifying, surrealistic **Last Judgment** by Hieronymus Bosch (c. 1482).

As the museum progresses through the Flemish repertoire, more secular themes start to appear, including portraits by Pieter Porbus and Anthony van Dyck, as well as the slightly sinister "Lord Byron on his Deathbed" by Joseph Denis Odevaere (ca. 1826). Later works encompass paintings by James Ensor and the Belgian surrealists René Magritte and Paul Delvaux.

Entrance to the Groeningemuseum also includes access to the adjacent **Arenthuis,** which shows temporary exhibitions and a permanent collection of lithographs and sketches by Anglo-Welsh artist Sir Frank Brangwyn. If time permits be sure at least to see his vibrant "Slave Market," which looks for all the world like a Gustav Klimt painting.

Dijver 12. www.visitbruges.be/en/groeningemuseum-groeninge-museum. ℂ **050/448-743.** Admission (includes Arenthuis) 12€ adults, 10€ seniors and ages 18–25, free ages 17 and under. Tues–Sun 9:30am–5pm. Closed Jan 1, Ascension Day afternoon, and Dec 25.

Sint-Janshospitaal (St. John's Hospital) ★★★ MUSEUM

Built in the 12th century and magnificently preserved, this was a working, charitable hospital of the Middle Ages, one of whose wards is depicted in an ancient painting hung near the main entrance: there you see the very same large room that now stands before you, but lined in those days with compact, wooden, sleeping cubicles in which two and more patients would be crammed for warmth. To the side of the main entrance is the picturesque and fully-furnished Apothecary Room of those ancient days.

But the primary reason you are here is to see the works of **Hans Memling,** the painter who belongs as much to Bruges as Brueughel belongs to Brussels, Van Eyck to Ghent, Rubens to Antwerp. He arrived here in the 1450s to study at the studio of Rogier van der Weyden (by whom he was greatly influenced), stayed on in a city whose cultural life had soared under the Dukes of Burgundy, and soon became the leading painter of Bruges. Housed in the former hospital chapel are just six of his works, but they are enough, in fact they overwhelm the senses.

That's especially true of **The Shrine to St. Ursula,** a small box, less than three feet in length, shaped like a small Gothic cathedral, gilded throughout,

AN INSPIRING saint

No story so captivated the medieval mind as did the tale of St. Ursula and the 11,000 Virgins, a history seemingly corroborated by the discovery in the 12th century of a Cologne ossuary containing hundreds of female bones. Ursula was the ravishingly-beautiful daughter of a king of Brittany in the 4th century, whose hand was desired by the son of a pagan British king. To put him off, the deeply-Christian Ursula agreed to the marriage only if she could first make a 3-year-long pilgrimage to Rome attended by ten maidens, each of whom would be further accompanied by a thousand virgins; and only if her suitor would also go to Rome to be baptized. The small female army traveled there via Cologne and Basle, in the first of which Ursula was advised by an angel of her coming martyrdom. In Rome, the devout group so charmed the Pope that he offered them his protection and impulsively decided to accompany the group on the return trip (perhaps sensing and desiring his own martyrdom).

Arriving in Cologne, they blundered into the armies of Attila the Hun, which proceeded to slaughter all but Ursula. Struck by her beauty, Attila offered to spare her if she would marry him; Ursula, steadfast as ever, refused and was killed. A terrible retribution was instantly visited upon the Huns by the citizens of Cologne.

The story, first transcribed by a monk of the Abbey at St. Omer in 975, swept across Europe, resulting in basilicas, monuments, devotions, paintings to Ursula, her mention in all the martyrologies, the increasing veneration of relics (skulls, ankles, shanks of hair) ascribed to her and her multitude of companions. When Christopher Columbus, sailing the Caribbean in 1493, espied a seeming multitude of small islands, he named them after *las once mil virgines*—the Virgin Islands! It was with this legend that Hans Memling was asked to decorate a small reliquary casque by two sisters, nuns, of the St. John Hospital in 1489. For nearly 350 years thereafter, the casque was stored away in the Hospital and exhibited to the public only on feast days.

–Arthur Frommer

its major illustrations appearing in the arched spaces on both sides and ends. See the box (above) with backstory on the saint. At one end we see St. Ursula, like a giantess, spreading a protecting cloak around her ten main companions, all the while grasping the arrow with which she was killed. At the other end: the oft-repeated theme of the Virgin Mary offering an apple to the Baby Jesus, while at her feet the two nuns who had commissioned the work kneel in prayer. Look closely at panel one, which depicts the arrival at the dock in Cologne—the city's buildings are portrayed exactly as they were.

You may now recall in the Groeningemuseum, earlier visited, a much larger, nine-panel work by an unknown Master of the Ursula legend, also painted in the 1400s, tells the same story, in much greater detail and elaboration, with more numerous instances of genre—little scenes of commercial activity, the comings and goings of people within a cathedral. But in the scant space available to him, Memling has wrought an exquisite miracle. In each of six tiny panels, he has portrayed multiple scenes that unfold in a time sequence within each panel; recreated an entire medieval world of commerce, religion and war; conveyed a message of idealistic commitment; drawn faces, bodies and buildings of haunting loveliness within the space of a few centimeters. In the Hospital of St. John, near the enchanting canals of Bruges: the single greatest masterpiece in a city of artistic wonders.

Mariastraat 38. www.visitbruges.be/en/sint-janshospitaal-saint-johns-hospital. ⓒ **050/ 448-743.** Admission 12€ adults, 10€ seniors and ages 18–25, free ages 17 and under. Tues–Sun 9:30am–5pm. Closed Jan 1, Ascension Day afternoon, and Dec 25.

Onze-Lieve-Vrouwekerk (Church of Our Lady) ★★ CHURCH

Note: At press time, much of the church was closed for renovation, with major works removed for safekeeping. It is unclear when the work will be finished. Emerging from St. John's Hospital, you need only cross the street to visit the soaring, Gothic Church of Our Lady ("Onze-Lieve-Vrouwekerk," "Notre Dame"), built as early as the 12th century, and renowned, among other attributes, for its 360-foot-high, spiked spire, highest in Flanders, and also because it serves as display case for the only statue by Michelangelo **Madonna and Child,** in Carrara white marble—to have permanently departed from Italian soil. Purchased from the Italian genius by a wealthy Flemish merchant, it is perhaps one of his minor works, but a masterpiece nevertheless, which juxtaposes a delightfully human, cherubic and slightly pudgy, 5-year-old Jesus, touchingly clinging to his mother's thumb for security, with a more abstract and other-worldly Mary, obviously troubled by the eventual fate of her son; the statue is found in the right-hand apse of the church, behind a protective shield of glass. Halfway down the nave, a particularly glorious **oak pulpit and canopy** (designed by the Jan Garemijn) seems to be supported, improbably, on the right toes of the two angels flanking the pulpit. The massive, several-ton work is in fact suspended from the metallic sunburst above the canopy, a detail among hundreds that one might note in a church that surely must be ranked among the most impressive in Belgium.

Its most chilling possessions are in **the choir;** lying side by side, the two massive mausoleum tombs, topped by reclining bronze effigies, of Mary of Burgundy and her father, Charles the Bold, Duke of Burgundy, beneath which a portion of the church floor has been cut away, replaced by a thick pane of glass, and spotlighted, to reveal the actual simple coffin which recent studies have apparently shown to contain the actual remains of Mary of Burgundy (and a container with the heart of her son). Overlooking all: the second story balcony of the Gruuthuse home, built into the wall of the church ambulatory (to the left as you face the mausoleums), from which Louis de Gruuthuse and family participated in the Masses observed downstairs.

Onze-Lieve-Vrouwekerkhof Zuid. www.visitbruges.be/en/onze-lieve-vrouwekerk-church-of-our-lady. ⓒ **050/448-743.** Admission 4€ adults, 3€ seniors and ages 18–25 during restoration, then 6€ and 5€, respectively. Mon–Sat 9:30am–5pm, Sun 1:30–5pm. Closed Jan 1, Ascension Day, and Dec 25.

St. Saviour's Cathedral ★★★ From the Church of Our Lady, the 13th-century Cathedral of St. Saviour ("Sint Salvator", "Saint Saveur") is a 2-minute walk up the Mariastraat into the Heilige Geeststraat. Already, you've undoubtedly glimpsed this great Gothic headquarters of the Bishop of Bruges;

its extraordinary tower is topped by a strange, later, neo-Romanesque construction of several turrets, spires, multiple, columned buildings standing in the sky—the effect that of a little celestial city, yet utterly appropriate to its setting, and an example of how the mixture of architectural styles can nevertheless create impact and beauty. Inside, we are back to the Gothic, with numerous decorations from a later age, and with a particularly beautiful choir area of 48 stalls overhung with magnificent tapestries and surmounted with the coats of arms of members of the Order of the Golden Fleece, who met here in 1478. The highlight is a seven-room **treasury** immediately to the right of the nave as you enter, where numerous reliquaries, displays of vestments, and paintings, include two important triptychs: Dirck Bouts' graphic **Martyrdom of St. Hippolytus** (1470) and Peter Pourbus' **Last Supper** (1599). The work by Bouts is a particular masterpiece from the age of the Flemish primitives, its central panel depicting the saint as he is about to be rent asunder by horses tied to each of his arms and legs, while the left-hand panel is of the donors of the painting, the right-hand one of a pagan emperor vainly attempting to persuade Hippolytus to renounce his faith.

Sint-Salvatorskerkhof (off of Steenstraat); www.sintsalvator.be. ☏ **050/336-188.** Admission free. Cathedral hours: Mon–Fri 10am–1pm and 2–5:30pm, Sat 10am–1pm and 2–3:30pm, Sun 11:30am–noon and 2–5pm; closed to casual visitors during services. Treasury: Sun–Fri 2–5pm.

Other Sights in Bruges

Most visitors to Bruges don't have enough time to see all of its splendid sights. So don't waste your time at the **Diamantmuseum Brugge** (Bruges Diamond Museum), which is simply a tourist trap, and not worth the cost of admission.

Brouwerij De Halve Maan (Half Moon Brewery) ★★ BREWERY
The Half Moon is one of Bruges' last family-owned working breweries and has operated on its present site near the Begijnhof since 1856. Today, it produces the famous *Brugse Zot* (Bruges Fools) and *Straffe Hendrik,* which averages around 14 percent alcohol; all can be sampled in the brewery's own brasserie. If you're an enthusiastic beer buff, the brewery tour is worth it for the detailed information about historical and modern brewing techniques; a bonus is you get to climb to the rooftop, which yields great city views. Otherwise, just get down to sampling some of the potent brews in the smart brasserie or on the pretty courtyard terrace.

Walplein 26. www.halvemaan.be. ☏ **050/444-222.** Tours 12€ adults, 6€ children 6–12. Guided tours last 45 minutes on the hour daily 11am–4pm and Sat 11am–5pm. Closed Jan 1 and Dec 25.

Bruggemuseum-Volkskunde (Folklore Museum) ★★ MUSEUM
Housed in a row of 8 whitewashed houses formerly belonging to the Shoemakers Guild, in a peaceful residential area within the city walls, the Folklore Museum recreates a slice of Bruges from the turn of the 20th century. Displays include a school classroom, a milliner's workshop, a pharmacy, and a

The Old Walls of Bruges

Medieval Bruges was heavily fortified, totally encircled by its circular walls and further protected by a moat and defense towers. The walls were largely knocked down in the 19th century and today only the moat and four of the nine 14th-century, powerfully fortified gates have survived. Of these, the **Kruispoort** is the most monumental, looking like a mini-castle complete with drawbridge and defending the city's eastern approach routes. The others are (clockwise from the railway station in the southwest) the imposing **Smeden-poort; Ezelpoort,** which is known for the many swans that grace the moat beside it; **Kruispoort;** and **Gentpoort.**

candy store, where sweets are made on the first and third Thursday afternoon of the month. There's a collection of clay pipes, puppet shows, and a pretty selection of handmade lace as well as the chance to sample a traditional Flemish beer in the **De Zwarte Kat** (The Black Cat) inn.

Balstraat 43. www.visitbruges.be/en/volkskundemuseum-folklore-museum. ℂ **050/ 448-743.** Admission 6€ adults, 5€ seniors and ages 18–25, free 17 and under. Tues–Sun 9:30am–5pm. Closed Jan 1, Ascension Day afternoon, and Dec 25.

Choco-Story: The Chocolate Museum ★★ MUSEUM This privately owned museum takes advantage of Bruges' reputation as a center of chocolaty excellence and strolls through the cocoa bean's backstory from its origins among the Aztecs to the chocolate drink taking Europe's royal courts by storm in the 1500s. There are a few Aztec artifacts, display of delicate Limoges china, and a couple of interesting facts along the way. For example, did you know that saucers were developed to stop fine Parisian ladies from dripping hot chocolate down their *embonpoint?* It's fun for kids and there's a chocolate-making demonstration at the end, where you get to taste the products. Courses in the delicate art of chocolate making can be booked ahead of time online.

Wijnzakstraat 2. www.choco-story.be. ℂ **050/612-237.** Admission 9.50€ adults, 7.50€ seniors and students, 5.50€ children 6–11, free for children 5 and under. Daily 10am–5pm. July–Aug 10am–6pm. Closed Jan 1, the 3rd week of Jan, and Dec 25.

Expo Picasso ★★ ART GALLERY More former wards of the Sint-Janshospitaal (p. 227) have been requisitioned for this unsung modern-art museum situated around a tranquil central garden. On view are more than 300 works by Picasso created between 1930 and 1970; his line drawing "Colombe Bleue" from 1961 charms in its simplicity, while the subject matter of his emotive and dynamic bullfighting prints, executed for Federico García Lorca, may not appeal, there is no denying their beauty and elegance. Many rooms are given over to temporary exhibitions, which have included everything from Egyptian mummies to Andy Warhol's colorful Pop Art creations.

Mariastraat 38. www.expo-brugge.be. ℂ **050/476-100.** Admission 10€ adults, 8€ seniors and children 6–18, free 5 and under; temporary exhibits vary in price. Daily 10am–5pm; July–Aug daily 10am–6pm. Closed Jan 1 and Dec 25.

Friet Museum (Fries Museum) ★★ MUSEUM   Owned by the same crew as Choco-Story, the fries museum showcases facts and figures about the rise of the humble potato to its current position as one of Belgium's best-loved dishes. Highlights include a dissertation on the Irish potato famine and an entertaining film about the progress of the spud from ground to frozen fry. Two stars are accorded for this being the only fries museum in the world and for its beautiful setting inside a 14th-century building.

Vlamingstraat 33. www.frietmuseum.be. ⓒ **050/340-150.** Admission 7€ adults, 6€ seniors and students, 5€ children 6–11, free for children 5 and under. Daily 10am–5pm. Closed Jan 1, 2nd week of Jan, and Dec 25.

Kantcentrum (Lace Center) ★ MUSEUM/SHOP   At one time there were more than 2,000 lace makers in Bruges, and today this combination of workshop, museum, and shameless retail opportunity is where the ancient art of lace creation is passed on to the next generation. There are lace-making demonstrations each afternoon between 2 and 5pm and the store also sells everything you need to make lace, from bobbins to thread. Courses are available if booked online in advance.

Balstraat 16. www.kantcentrum.eu. ⓒ **050/330-072.** Admission 6€ adults; 5€ seniors, students, and children 12–25; free for children 11 and under. Mon–Sat 9:30am–5pm. Closed Jan 1 and 2, April 22, May 1, June 10, July 21, Aug 15, Nov 1 and 11, and Dec 25–26 and 31.

Especially for Kids

Bruges is absolute heaven for kids. They can explore the city by **canal boat** or **pony-and-trap** (see below), and also navigate the pedestrianized streets safely by **bike** (see p. 210). In fact, the city itself is the attraction for some

A Quiet Corner of Bruges

Since it was founded in 1245 by the Countess Margaret of Constantinople, the **Prinselijk Begijnhof ten Wijngaarde (Princely Beguinage of the Vineyard)** ★★, Wijngaardstraat (www.monasteria.org; ⓒ **050/330-011**), at the Minnewater (Lake of Love), has been one of the most tranquil spots in Bruges, and so it remains today. *Begijns* were religious women, similar to nuns, who accepted vows of chastity and obedience but drew the line at poverty, preferring to earn a living by looking after the sick and making lace.

The *begijns* may be no more but the Begijnhof has been occupied by Benedictine nuns since 1928, and they strive to keep the old traditions alive. This beautiful little cluster of 17th-century whitewashed houses surrounds a lawn shaded by poplar trees and makes a marvelous escape from the din of the outside world. One of the houses, the **Begijnhuisje (Beguine's House),** is now a museum. The Begijnhof courtyard is always open and admission is free. The Beguine's House is open daily 10am to 5pm. Admission is 2€ for adults, 1.50€ for seniors, 1€ for students and children 8 to 11.

BRUGES' windmills

Where once 25 windmills graced the outskirts of Bruges, now only four survive. They are found in the park that abuts the old city walls on their eastern flank between Kruispoort and Dampoort; of these, two are open to the public in summer and both are grain mills coming under the banner of Musea Brugge, which also runs the city's main museums. The **Koeleweimolen** was built in 1765 and was moved to its present spot from the Dampoort in 1996, while the **Sint-Janshuismolen** has been in situ since 1770. Both windmills are found along Kruisvest and share the same opening times and admission April to September Tuesday through Sunday 9:30am to 12:30pm and 1:30 to 5pm; admission 4€ adults, 3€ seniors and ages 18 to 25, free for children 17 and under.

children, who love the notion that around every corner there's a 1,000-year-old building or some hidden courtyard.

And nowhere else will you find museums with such child-appeal factor as the **Fries Museum** (p. 232), which tells the story of the humble potato, or **Choco-Story** (p. 231) where they can learn about the process of making the world's favorite sweet treat and take a master class in the art. The **Historium** (p. 222) offers the city's most child-appropriate introduction to Bruges, with a dynamic and entertaining walk-through exhibition encompassing film, multimedia, and interactive exhibits. The **Archeologiemuseum (Archaeological Museum)** at Mariastraat 36a (www.visitbruges.be/en/archeologiemuseum-archeological-museum; ✆ **050/448-743**) is also designed with kids in mind, with interactive displays, the occasional skeleton, and medieval costumes to dress up in.

The cuisine of Belgium, with its waffles, fries, omelets, and toasted sandwiches, lends itself to junior appetites—try the *frietkoten* (**fries stands**) in the Markt—as do the numerous yummy **chocolate stores** (see "Shopping," below). And winter visits to Bruges turn up Christmas fairs and an ice rink in the Markt plus wacky installations on Stationesplein during the **Snow & Ice Sculpture Festival**, which lasts from mid-November to early January (p. 42).

Organized Tours & Excursions

It's practically law that every visitor to Bruges should take a **boat cruise ★★** around the city canals. There are five landing stages, the most convenient for tourists being the two along Dijver, but all are marked with an anchor icon on maps available at the tourist office (p. 209). These open-top canal boats can be scorching in hot weather and bracing in cold, but they only last 30 minutes, the commentary is multi-lingual, *and* they reveal a uniquely satisfying view of the city. They operate March to mid-November daily 10am to 6pm, with weather-dependent departures between December and February. A half-hour cruise is 10€ for adults, and 6€ for children 4 to 11 when accompanied by an adult.

Wherever you are in Bruges, you'll hear the clip-clop of horses' hooves, so if you fancy a tour of the city by **horse-drawn carriage** (*caleche* in Flemish), the year-round departure point is on the Markt (in the Burg on Wed mornings) between 9am and 6pm (and sometimes later in summer). The 35-minute ride is 50€ per carriage for up to five people; there's a jumping off point for you and a resting point for the horses at the Beguinage (see above); see if you can spot the fountain nearby that's adorned with two horses' heads.

If you'd appreciate a little help uncovering the secrets of Bruges, hire a **local guide.** Guides can be found on such marketplace sites as **ToursBy Locals.com, Airbnb.com/Experiences** and **Viator.com.** The tourist office (p. 209) runs informative walking tours from April through September costing 12.50€ (free for kids 11 and under) for a 2-hour stroll through the pretty streets to all the main sights plus a trip up to the Concertgebouw rooftop for panoramic city views. Tours depart at 2:30pm daily from the Concertgebouw (see below), with Sunday kick off at 10:30pm in July and August. During October the tours only run on the weekend, leaving at 2:30pm.

Guided day tours of Bruges from Brussels are offered by **Sandemans New Europe** (www.neweuropetours.eu; ℰ **49/305-105-0030**), leaving daily during the high season and every day except Tuesday and Thursday in the winter season; the trip (40€) includes round-trip transportation by train and a guided tour of the city but not food or drinks. Also departing from Brussels, **Bravo Discovery** (www.bravodiscovery.com; ℰ **32/470-60-3505**) offers guided day trips (30€) on Friday and Saturday (and Wednesday and Thursday in July and August); it includes round-trip train tickets and a guided tour of the city but not food or drinks. Bravo Discovery also offers a combination Bruges/Ghent day tour (45€) from Brussels on Sunday.

SHOPPING

Bruges is too tiny to keep pace with Brussels or Antwerp when it comes to shopping, but it certainly has its moments. This little city is a monument to the skills of lace-makers, chocolatiers, and brewers. You'll find souvenir shops selling machine-made lace concentrated around Mark and Burg, but the best, and way more expensive, handmade types of lace are bobbin, ribbon, princess, or needlepoint. If you're after a handcrafted chemise or tablecloth, check out **Rococo** at Wollestraat 9 (www.rococobrugge.be).

Souvenirs of a more perishable nature include Oud-Brugge cheese from **Diksmuids Boterhuis** at Geldmuntstraat 23 (www.diksmuidsboterhuis.be), and marzipan from **Brown Sugar** at Mariastraat 21 (www.marzipan-nougat shop.be), but best of all chocolate, which Bruges is simply mad for. Pick up delicious arrays of calorie-laden confectionary from **Mary** at Katelijnestraat 21 (www.mary.be), or the four branches of **ChocOHolic** (www.choco-holic. be) on Katelijnestraat, Wollestraat, and Stoofstraat.

Local **beers** such as *Straffe Hendrik, Brugs Tarwebier,* and *Brugge Tripel* can be tracked down at **2be** on Wollestraat 53 (p. 218), or **Bacchus Cornelius**

A day IN DAMME ★

Photogenic Damme is just a 7km (4½ miles) hop from Bruges and was once the city's outer harbor where trading ships plied their cargoes, but the inlet of the River Zwin silted up in 1520 and the city lost much of its strategic importance. The marriage of Charles the Bold, Duke of Burgundy, to Margaret of York took place here celebrated with great pomp and ceremony.

Today, it's a place to spend a happy day pottering around, enjoying the red-brick Gothic architecture and the landscape cut through with canals. Start off in the **Markt** by admiring the Gothic (Stadhuis) Town Hall and the statues of Charles and Margaret on the facade. In the middle of the market square stands a statue of 13th-century Flemish poet Jacob van Maerlant (1230–96) and opposite the Stadhuis, at Jacob van Maerlantstraat 13, is the 15th-century **Saint-Jean d'Angély Huis ★**, where Charles and Margaret made their dynastic marriage in 1468.

Damme's **Visitor Centre** (Jacob van Maerlantstraat 3; www.visitdamme.be; ℰ **050/288-610**) is found in the stately 15th-century Huyse de Groote Sterre, which also shares space with the strange **Uilenspiegelmuseum (Tijl Uilenspiegel Museum).** Uilenspiegel was a 14th-century Flemish troubadour who was adopted as a lucky mascot by the village of Damme; his eponymous museum relates his story and there are several statues dedicated to him around the village. Admission is 2.50€ for adults, 5€ for a family. Opening hours for both tourist office and museum are April to September daily 9:30am to 12:30pm and 1 to 5pm; October to March Monday through Friday 9:30am to 12:30pm and 1 to 5pm, Saturday and Sunday 1 to 5pm.

You can easily get to Damme by road from Bruges (drive, cycle, or catch the De Lijn [p. 209] **bus no. 43** that departs seven times daily from Bruges train station and the Markt) but the most memorable way to arrive is by boat; the small sternwheeler **Lamme Goedzaak ★★** departs from Noorweegse Kaai 31 in the north of Bruges, Tuesday to Saturday five times daily from April to October. The half-hour cruise along the poplar-lined canal passes through a landscape straight out of an old Flemish painting. Tickets are 10.50€ for adults (14.50 round-trip), 10€ (12.50€) for seniors, 9€ (11.50€) for children 3 to 11, and free for younger children. Schedules and other details are available from **Rederij Doornzele** (www.bootdamme-brugge.be; ℰ **05/288-610**)

at Academiestraat 17 (www.bacchuscornelius.com), where you'll also find a selection of stone-bottled, ginlike liqueur *jenever* (p. 28).

If you're looking for unusual gifts for back home, try the slice of Christmas that is **De Witter Pelikaan** at Vlamingstraat 23 (www.dewittepelikaan.be) for festive baubles and handmade wooden toys.

Most stores are open Monday to Saturday 9am to 6pm, with hours extended to 9pm on Friday. Many open on Sunday as well, especially in summer.

If you're after a piece of silverware or pre-loved diamond rings, the weekend **Antiques and Flea Market** on Dijver puts on a fine show alongside the canal from mid-March to mid-November, Saturday and Sunday from 10am to 6pm and also every Friday from June to September.

BRUGES AFTER DARK

The Performing Arts

The ultramodern **Concertgebouw** ★★ ('t Zand 34; www.concertgebouw.be; *©* **070/221-212**) the home base of the **Symfonieorkest van Vlaanderen (Flanders Symphony Orchestra;** www.symfonieorkest.be; *©* **050/840-587**), is the city's main venue for opera, classical music, theater, and dance. This has left the former principal venue for these events in Bruges, the circa-1869 **Stadsschouwburg (City Theater;** Vlamingstraat 29; www.ccbrugge.be; *©* **050/443-060**), to back up the mother ship by mounting smaller-scale performances. Theater at both venues is likely to be in Dutch or French, and rarely, if ever, in English.

Contemporary dance, drama by rising artists, rock and pop concerts, festivals, and lots of children's activities are held in the futuristic **Magdalena Concert Hall (MaZ** for short; Magdalenastraat 27; www.ccbrugge.be; *©* **050/443-060**).

For **jazz fans:** The cozy club **27Bflat** (Sint-Jakobsstraat 15; www. 27bflat. be; *©* **32/479-29-7429**) hosts live weekly jazz and blues shows in the heart of the city. **Kunstencentrum (Arts Center) De Werf** (Werfstraat 108; www. kaap.be; *©* **050/330-529**) has around 40 jazz concerts annually, mostly from Belgian talents; also on the agenda here are productions for children, contemporary drama, and dance.

Those traveling with children might enjoy the fire-eating, falconry, juggling, and feasting at a **mock medieval banquet** to "celebrate the wedding of Charles the Bold, Duke of Burgundy, to Margaret of York" in the hallowed setting of the neo-Gothic former **Heilig-Hartkerk (Sacred Heart Church).** Shows take place year-round on Saturday and also on Friday from April and October. Tickets for this historical extravaganza range from 59€ to 74€ (half price for children 11–14; children 6–10 12.50€; free for children under 5) from Celebrations Entertainment (Vlamingstraat 86; www.celebrations-entertainment.be; *©* **050/347-572**). Shows start at 7pm.

SIDE TRIPS FROM BRUSSELS & BRUGES

B russels and Bruges may be Belgium's Big Two visitor destinations, but to ignore the delights of other cities would be doing both yourself and this cultured country a huge disservice. Although not many places can match Bruges for sheer medieval good looks, **Ghent** and **Antwerp** make a very good attempt, and many Belgians consider them the true heartland of Flemish culture; certainly when it comes to contemporary dynamism, they are hands-down winners.

And there's more. Historic **Mons** is the capital of French-speaking Hainaut, the green and pleasant, lake-speckled land that stretches along most of Belgium's border with France. It had a sprucing up in 2015, when it was named a European City of Culture, and its array of UNESCO sites ranges from a towering baroque belfry to a grand Neoclassical colliery complex. **Mechelen** in Flanders is an underrated gem, boasting a magnificent cathedral, a lovely main square, and numerous canals—along with a fraction of the crowds of nearby Bruges. And history buffs will want to attend the emotional daily Last Post service in **Ypres** to commemorate those who died in the trenches of Flanders Fields during World War I.

All the side trips suggested in this chapter are achievable as day trips from Brussels or Bruges, but the gritty resurgence of Ghent and the sleek sophistication of Antwerp really merit an overnight visit, so a couple of dining and sleeping suggestions are included for both cities. And while it's perfectly possible to visit the battlefields of Flanders in a (long) day from Brussels, the journey west from Bruges to Ypres and Passendale is considerably shorter, a distinct plus point, especially if you're traveling with kids.

ANTWERP ★★

48km (30 miles) N of Brussels

Until a few years ago, Antwerp was one of western Europe's secret places, known only to a lucky few, but now it's been discovered big time. Owing its historical wealth to its location on the Schelde (Scheldt) River, the city's reputation as a thriving port and diamond-trade center is well deserved, but that's far from all there is to say about this booming, high-brow, and—in some small parts—seedy city. The capital town of the province of Antwerpen boasts monuments from its wealthy medieval, Renaissance, and baroque periods; a remarkable cathedral; a maze of medieval streets; thriving nightlife; cutting-edge architecture; and cool cultural and fashion scenes. Given all this, it's no surprise that international visitors to Belgium have been remedying their former neglect of the city. Yep, Antwerp is on the rise.

Essentials

GETTING THERE

BY PLANE   **Brussels Airport** is the main international airport for Antwerp (p. 158). A few budget flights (including Flybe from London Southend) arrive at **Antwerp Airport** (www.antwerp-airport.be; ✆ **03/285-6500;** airport code ANR) in Deurne 7km (4½ miles) east of the city. De Lijn buses no. 51, 52, and 53 take 15 minutes between the airport and Rooseveltplein, close to Antwerp Centraal Station. The taxi fare to downtown is around 22€.

BY TRAIN   **SNCB trains** run in approximately 50 minutes between Brussels-Midi and Antwerp Centraal Station, which is 1.5km (1 mile) east of the Grote Markt. Trains leave every 15 minutes and fares are 15€ round-trip. For more details, go to www.belgianrail.be.

BY CAR   Two main arteries connect Antwerp and Brussels: the A1/E19 via Mechelen (p. 268) and the A12. Journey time is about 1 hour.

VISITOR INFORMATION

Antwerp Tourism & Convention is at Grote Markt 13 (www.visitantwerpen. be; ✆ **03/232-0103**) and is open daily from 10am to 5pm. The **Information Desk** at Centraal Station is open daily from 9am to 5pm. (Both are closed Jan 1 and Dec 25.)

GETTING AROUND

The integrated public-transportation system of **bus, tram,** and **Premetro (partially underground) trams** in Antwerp is run by **De Lijn** (www.delijn. be; ✆ **070/22-0200**). Other than pounding the pavement of this pocket-size metropolis, trams are the best way to get around. The most useful services for tourists are lines 3, 5, 9, and 15, which run between Centraal Station and Groenplaats near the cathedral; and lines 11 and 24, which run near the Grote Markt. Purchase your ticket (3€ for 1 hour) from the De Lijn sales point in the station or from an automated ticket machine before boarding the tram or bus; the largest bill you can pay with onboard is a 10€ note.

Regulated **taxis** wait outside Centraal Station and in Groenplaats; otherwise call **Antwerp Tax** (www.antwerp-tax.be; ✆ **03/238-3838**). After 10pm, an extra 2.50€ is added to the fare.

ANTWERP'S PORT

When you come down to it, if there were no River Schelde, there would be no Antwerp. The city's location close to the point where the river meets the tidal

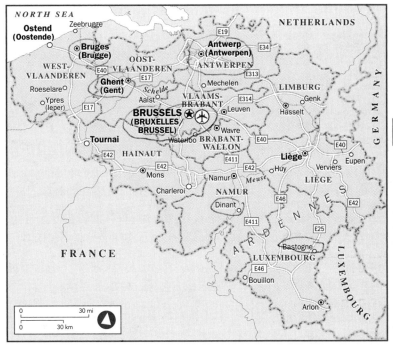

Westerchelde estuary made it a strategic port as far back as the 2nd century B.C. Antwerp was a trading station within the powerful medieval Hanseatic League but, unlike Bruges, did not have the status of a full-fledged *Kontor,* with its own separate district and mercantile installations. In the early days, ships moored along the city's wharves, where Het Steen (see below) now stands; nowadays the port has moved 13km (8 miles) downstream to docks that jam up against the Dutch border. After Rotterdam, Antwerp is Europe's second biggest port for goods handled, and the third biggest (after Rotterdam and Hamburg) for containers.

Given the port's size and importance, it was determined that new offices were needed to consolidate administrative and technical staff of the port authority. The **Port House,** Zaha Hadidplein 1 (www.portofantwerp.com/en/port-house), designed by the late Zaha Hadid and unveiled in 2016, has since become the city's most iconic new architectural landmark. Set deep in the city's harbor, the wedge-shaped faceted-glass structure resembles both a sparkling diamond and the prow of a ship—two things most closely associated with Antwerp's identity. Guided tours of the interior (in English) must be booked at least a month in advance (reserve by calling Visit Antwerp at ✆ 03/232-0103 or emailing info@visitantwerpen.be), but the most intriguing aspect is its glittering exterior, best viewed from the rooftops of the MAS and Red Star Line (see below).

Antwerp

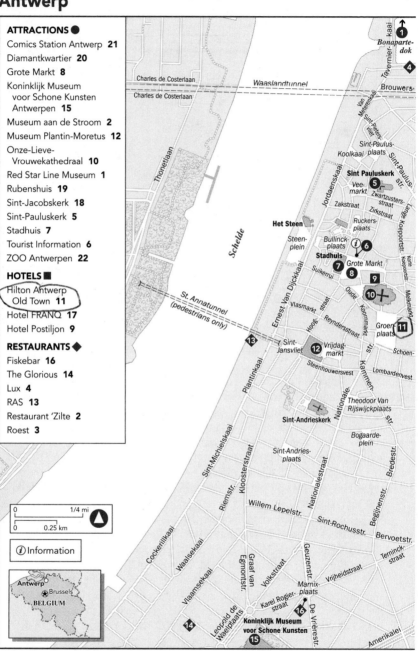

ATTRACTIONS ●

Comics Station Antwerp **21**

Diamantkwartier **20**

Grote Markt **8**

Koninklijk Museum
  voor Schone Kunsten
  Antwerpen **15**

Museum aan de Stroom **2**

Museum Plantin-Moretus **12**

Onze-Lieve-
  Vrouwekathedraal **10**

Red Star Line Museum **1**

Rubenshuis **19**

Sint-Jacobskerk **18**

Sint-Pauluskerk **5**

Stadhuis **7**

Tourist Information **6**

ZOO Antwerpen **22**

HOTELS ■

Hilton Antwerp
Old Town **11**

Hotel FRANQ **17**

Hotel Postiljon **9**

RESTAURANTS ◆

Fiskebar **16**

The Glorious **14**

Lux **4**

RAS **13**

Restaurant 'Zilte **2**

Roest **3**

0 ____ 1/4 mi

0 ____ 0.25 km

ⓘ Information

Antwerp
Brussels
BELGIUM

Bonaparte-dok

Charles de Costerlaan

Waaslandtunnel

Brouwers-

Charles de Costerlaan

Sint-Paulus-
Koolkaai plaats

Sint Pauluskerk ❺

Vee-
markt   Zwartzusters-
Zakstraat   straat
    Zirkstraat

Het Steen   Ruckers-
    plaats

Steen-   Bullinck-   ⓘ❻
plein   plaats
Stadhuis
❼ Grote Markt
❽   ❾

Schelde

St. Annatunnel
(pedestrians only)   Vlasmarkt

❿ ✝

Groen- ⓫
plaats
Schoen-

Sint-   ⓭
Jansvliet   Vrijdag-   ⓬   markt
    Steenhouwersvest   Lombardenvest

Theodoor Van
Rijswijckplaats

Sint-Andrieskerk ✝

Bogaarde-
plein

Sint-Andries-
plaats

Willem Lepelstr.   Sint-Rochusstr.   Bervoetstr.

Terninck-
straat

Vrijheidstraat

Marnix-
plaats

Karel Rogier- ⓰
straat

⓮   **Koninklijk Museum**
voor Schone Kunsten
⓯

Amerikalei

240

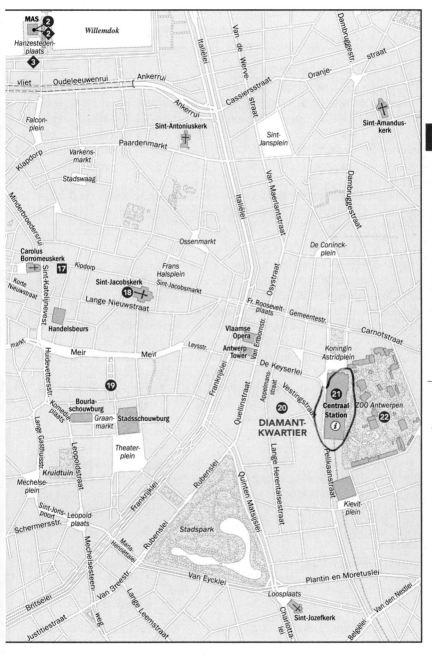

On the waterfront in the center of town, Antwerp's oldest building, **Het Steen (The Castle),** Steenplein 1, a 13th-century stone fortress on the banks of the river that once overlooked Antwerp's port. It is currently closed and entirely under scaffolding as it undergoes renovations and remodeling, with plans to reopen in late 2020 as a both a tourist center and a cruise ship terminal.

Exploring Antwerp

Most visitors to Antwerp head straight for the warren of winding streets in the medieval Old Town, which fan out from the Grote Markt. South of there, the old shipping warehouses along Vlaamsekaai and Waalsekaai have burst back into life as edgy bars, restaurants, and art galleries. The area around Centraal Station, east of De Keyserlei and Koningin Astridplein, is more than a little seedy and has problems with drug dealing and prostitution; best leave that area well alone at night.

An important note: We do *not* recommend the Antwerp City Card. Most travelers will not be able to see enough attractions in the time allotted to make back the cost of the pass.

Grote Markt ★★★ HISTORIC SQUARE   A lovely 16th-century square lined with buzzing sidewalk cafes and restaurants filled with Antwerp's sleek residents, the Grote Markt is the city's social and cultural epicenter. Dominated by the neoclassical Brabo Fountain, it is surrounded by majestic buildings like the many-gabled **Huis den Spieghel** at Grote Markt 9. This was a meeting place for great Renaissance thinkers such as Erasmus and Sir Thomas More, who was in Antwerp when he began to write "Utopia" in 1515.

The Renaissance **Stadhius (City Hall)** takes up the entire west side of the Grote Markt and was designed by Cornelius Floris de Vriendt; it is an outstanding example of the Flemish mannerism that replaced Antwerp's early Gothic architectural style in the 16th century; it has a splendid central tower and a pleasing, symmetrical frontage. The hall was burned during the city's sack by invading troops in the "Spanish Fury" of 1576 and rebuilt in 1579. If you are lucky enough to get inside, look out for the frescoes by Hendrik Leys, a 19th-century Antwerp painter; otherwise content yourself with admiring the building's orderly proportions and gilded coats of arms as well as counting the flags of the ever-growing European Union that flutter constantly from the

---

Antwerp Touristram

Save your feet on all those cobbled streets and take a **circular tour** of Antwerp's attractions in a **mini electric tram;** you'll start off in the Groenplaats, trundle around the cobbled lanes of the Old Town, pass the Gothic facades in Grote Markt, venture through the main shopping thoroughfares, and potter along the Schelde riverfront to MAS (see below). There are seven departures a day during summer, on the hour from 11am until 5pm; tickets cost 8€ for adults, 6€ for children ages 4 to 12, and is free for those 3 and under. See **www.touristram.be** for details.

facade. The building is currently under renovation and is closed to the public until late 2020.

Grote Markt. ✆ **03/221-1333.**

Koninklijk Museum voor Schone Kunsten Antwerpen (Antwerp Royal Museum of Fine Arts) ★★★ MUSEUM   *Note: The museum is closed until 2021 for renovations.* Hidden behind this massive neoclassical edifice is the world's biggest and best collection of paintings and frescoes by Peter Paul Rubens. Other artists displayed here include the Flemish Primitives Jan van Eyck, Rogier van der Weyden, Hans Memling, and Pieter Brueghel, as well as more recent Belgian favorites James Ensor and Paul Delvaux. Alas this glorious gallery, normally stuffed with the loot of 500 years of great painting, is closed for restoration until 2021 so if peerless Flemish art is your addiction, you'll have to get your fix at the Groeningemuseum in Bruges (p. 226), although a few works from KMSKA are on display in the **Golden Cabinet at Museum Rockoxhuis** (Keizerstraat 10-12; www.rockoxhuis.be; ✆ **03/201-9250**).

Leopold de Waelplaats 2. www.kmska.be. ✆ **03/224-9550.**

Museum aan de Stroom (MAS) ★★★ MUSEUM   In its architectural brashness, the Museum aan de Stroom has become an icon of contemporary Antwerp. Designed by Dutch architects Neutelings and Riedijk, it looks like a pile of untidy red Lego bricks clamped loosely together with teeth of glass. What's inside is as invigorating: MAS is a multi-floored homage to Antwerp, its people, and its culture today. Over five floors of interactive and entertaining artworks, photos, newspaper cuttings, video, newsreel, and nearly half a million other artifacts, MAS offers an insightful explanation of how much the city owes to its position on the River Schelde, to its immigrants, and to its diamond industry (p. 245). Temporary exhibitions are found in the small galleries on the walkway outside the main building. On the ninth floor are scintillating views over the city and the sprawling harbor (the museum is right in the heart of the once abandoned, and now vibrant, Willemdok harbor area, sitting on a dock commissioned by Napoleon). If you're hungry: stay put! Onsite is **Restaurant 'Zilte** ★★★, one of the finest places in the city for a meal. Altogether this is a carefully conceived museum showcasing a thoroughly modern city and its multiracial occupants.

Hanzestedenplaats 1. www.mas.be. ✆ **03/338-4400**. Admission 5€ adults, 3€ seniors and ages 12–25, free for children 11 and under; temporary exhibition prices vary. Free the last Wed of the month. Apr–Oct Tues–Fri 10am–5pm, Sat–Sun 10am–6pm. Nov–Mar Tues–Sun 10am–5pm. Closed Jan 1, May 1, Assumption Day, Nov 1, and Dec 25.

Museum Plantin-Moretus ★★ MUSEUM   In 1555, Christoffle Plantin established an influential printing workshop in this stately patrician mansion in the city center. Its output included an astonishing multilanguage (Hebrew, Greek, Syriac, Latin, and Aramaic) edition of the Bible and translations of other great works of literature. Plantin's name survives in today's publishing world as a widely used typeface. His grandson, Balthasar Moretus, was a contemporary and close friend of Rubens, who illustrated many of the books published by the Plantin-Moretus workshop and who painted the family portraits you see displayed here, along with panel paintings that include The Dying Seneca (1616). The museum's exhibits include original printing presses dating as far back as the 16th century and a Gutenberg Bible dating from 1455. The building was inscribed a UNESCO World Heritage Site for its historic importance.

Vrijdagmarkt 22–23. www.museumplantinmoretus.be. ☏ **03/221-1450.** Admission 8€ adults, 6€ seniors and ages 12–25, free for children 11 and under. Tues–Sun 10am–5pm. Closed Jan 1, May 1, Ascension Day, Nov 1, and Dec 25.

Onze-Lieve-Vrouwekathedraal (Cathedral of Our Lady) ★★

CHURCH   Antwerp's iconic landmark is a masterpiece of Brabantine Gothic architecture—and in fact the largest Gothic structure in Belgium. And the cathedral breaks more records too—it also boasts the tallest church spire in the country, an ornate affair looming 123m (404 ft.) over the city's ancient heart. Looking from the main entrance to the cathedral, you'll see that a second tower, intended to be of similar size, was never completed, giving the facade an oddly lopsided aspect. Begun in 1352 to a design by Jean Appelmans, whose statue stands outside, the cathedral was finally completed in 1521; its backstory includes a destructive fire in 1533, devastation by Protestant rebels during the religious wars of the 16th century, de-consecration by anticlerical French revolutionaries in 1794, and a slow rebirth after Napoleon's final defeat in 1815.

Its interior is a gleaming, white affair with seven aisles supported by 125 pillars, its embellishment a heady mix of baroque and neoclassical stained-glass windows, carved wood pulpits and lecterns, and tombs of the Bourbon royal family, but pole position goes to the four exquisite Rubens altarpieces: The two standout pieces are his "The Raising of the Cross" (1610) and "The Descent from the Cross" (1614).

Groenplaats 21. www.dekathedraal.be. ☏ **03/213-9951.** Admission 6€. Children under 12 are free. Mon–Fri 10am–5pm, Sat 10am–3pm, Sun 1–5pm. Closed to tourist visits during services.

Red Star Line Museum ★★★ MUSEUM

From 1873 to 1934, some 2 million passengers sailed from Antwerp to the U.S. and Canada aboard the Red Star Line. Many were Russian and Eastern European Jews escaping the rise of Nazism in Europe. Housed in a stunningly renovated building that was once the defunct shipping company's headquarters, a 10-minute walk from MAS, the museum traces the stories of these intrepid souls through photographs, letters, journals, and personal possessions—all enlivened via audiovisual displays. Two of the Red Star Line's most famous emigres were photographer Edward Steichen and Irving Berlin, née Israel Isidore Baline, whose family donated one of his pianos to the museum. Don't miss a trip up to the sail-like observation tower, which offers panoramic views of the surrounding port and in the distance, the city's newest architectural icon, Zaha Hadid's glittering Port House (see p. 239).

Montevideostraat 3. www.redstarline.be. ☏ **03/298-2770.** Admission 8€ adults, 6€ seniors and students ages 19–26, 1€ free for children 18 and under. Tues–Sun 10am–5pm. From Apr–Nov, weekends until 6pm. Closed Jan 1, May 1, Ascension Day, Nov 1, and Dec 25.

Rubenshuis (Rubens House) ★★★ HISTORIC SITE Touch Antwerp's cultural heart at the house where the city's most illustrious son lived and worked. Far from being the stereotypical starving artist in a garret, the artist Peter Paul Rubens (1577–1640) amassed a tidy fortune from his light-kissed paintings, which allowed him to build an impressive mansion in 1610 when he was just 33. Today you have to beat off the tourist hordes to file through one gloriously OTT period apartment after another, all richly decorated with fine furniture, marble Roman sculptures, and examples of Rubens's exquisite portraiture, including one of Anthony van Dyck, who was his pupil. Go when it first opens, if you can, to avoid the crowds. If you can't do that, know that you'll be able to take a breather in the Renaissance courtyard garden, whose pavilion was recently restored, and reflect on the sumptuous lifestyle of patrician Flemish gentlemen in the 17th century.

Wapper 9–11. www.rubenshuis.be. ✆ **03/201-1555.** Admission 10€ adults, 8€ seniors and students ages 12–25, free for children 11 and under. Free the last Wed of the month. Tues–Sun 10am–5pm. Closed Jan 1, May 1, Ascension Day, Nov 1, and Dec 25.

Sint-Jacobskerk (St. James's Church) ★★ CHURCH This flamboyant Gothic church with a baroque interior is best known as the final resting place of Peter Paul Rubens, whose white marble tomb is embellished with the artist's own painting "Our Lady Surrounded by Saints." It occupies one of seven chapels bordering the opulent semicircular ambulatory behind the high altar. Several more of Rubens's works are here, as well as pieces by Van Dyck and other prominent artists. *Note:* The church is currently undergoing major restoration work and portions of the interior will be closed until 2027.

Lange Nieuwstraat 73. www.sintjacobantwerpen.be. ✆ **03/232-1032.** Admission 3€ adults, 2€ students. Daily 2–5pm. Mass Mon–Sat 11am, Sun 9am and 10am.

diamonds ARE ANTWERP'S BEST FRIENDS

Antwerp remains the world's leading market for cut diamonds and second only to London as an outlet for raw and industrial diamonds, despite intense competition from India, Dubai, and Israel. The raw facts are sparkling enough: 84 percent of all the world's diamonds pass through Antwerp at some point on their journey from rough stone to polished, set gem. There are four diamond-trading houses in Antwerp and together they comprise an industry that turns over 147 million euros for the city each year. The trade, with its diamond cutters and polishers, workshops, brokers, and merchants, is centered on the few heavily guarded streets that form the city's **Diamantkwartier**

(Diamond Quarter), located steps away from Centraal Station. It is regulated by the Antwerp World Diamond Center (www.awdc.be) and mostly run by members of the city's Hasidic Jewish community, who found a niche market when they arrived in Antwerp in the 15th century.

To buy diamonds or watch them being cut, visit the constellation of jewelry stores in the Diamond Quarter. **Diamondland,** Appelmansstraat 33a (www.diamondland.be; ✆ **03/369-0780**) is the city's biggest diamond salesroom and offers free guided tours of its workshops as well as trustworthy, personalized, and knowledgeable service for serious buyers (all tax-free for non-E.U. visitors).

Sint-Pauluskerk (St. Paul's Church) ★★ CHURCH   Although there was a monastery on this site as early as 1256, the present St. Paul's Church dates from the late 17th century and exhibits a cheerful clash of spindly Gothic exterior and a calm, white interior with hints of gilded baroque flourish. It is chiefly notable for the unsung collection of paintings by Rubens and his pupil Anthony van Dyck that line the outer aisles. The works of Rubens are "The Flagellation" (painting number 7 of the "Stations of the Cross" sequence in the left-hand aisle) and "The Adoration of the Shepherds" just in front of the choir on the same side. Van Dyck's contribution was "The Bearing of the Cross" (number 9 in the "Stations of the Cross"). If you get lucky, the choir may perform a 13th-century plainsong during Mass on Sunday morning.

Sint-Paulusstraat 22. www.sint-paulusparochie.be. ✆ **03/221-3321.** Free admission. Apr–Oct daily 2–5pm. Nov–Mar Sat–Sun 2–5pm. Mass Sun 10:30am.

Especially for Kids

Antwerp may not be the most exciting destination for kids, but it offers enough to keep them happy for a couple of days. Try **harbor cruise** with **Rederij Flandria** (www.flandria.nu; ✆ **03/472-21-4056**) and a ride on the **electric tram** (p. 242). Older kids will enjoy visiting the **Rubenshuis** and the **MAS** (see above for both), for little tots hightail it to **ZOO Antwerpen** ★★ (Koningin Astridplein 20–26; www.zooantwerpen.be; ✆ **03/224-8910**), a 10-hectare (25-acre) zoological garden that is one of Europe's oldest, dating back to 1843, with many beautiful Art Nouveau buildings which have been granted monument status. The 950 species include red pandas, Arabian oryx, gorillas, panthers, and cuddly koalas, along with a reptile house and a petting zoo for toddlers. Many updates were made in 2017, including a newly designed aviary, an expanded outdoor area for great apes, a buffalo savannah, and a new conservatory for endangered okapi. Admission is 26.50€ adults, 25.50€ seniors and students, and 20€ children 3 to 11 (under 3 are free). It's open daily 10am to 6pm.

For indoor fun, head to **Comics Station Antwerp** ★★ (Antwerp Centraal Station, Kievitplein; www.comicsstation.be; ✆ **03/232-3308**), a theme park set inside the main railway station and featuring a number of popular Belgian cartoon characters such as The Smurfs and Lucky Luke. It's huge—spread out across four floors and six different zones—and geared toward younger kids (ages 3–12), with interactive games, comic-themed rides, 4-D movies, and perhaps most exciting, what's said to be the world's biggest indoor slide at 22.5m (73 ft) high and 51m (167 ft) long. Open daily from 10am to 5pm; admission for those over age 3 is 21.50€.

> ### Room for Misunderstanding
>
> A word of warning to budget travelers: The phrase "tourist room," which in other cities means an accommodations bargain in a private home, means something rather different in Antwerp—it's a discreet way of advertising very personal services that have nothing to do with sleeping and everything to do with a room for an hour.

Where to Stay & Eat

Antwerp has carved a niche for itself in the sleek, contemporary hotels market; it abounds with boutique stays that reflect its status as a world capital of cool. One such example is **Hotel FRANQ** ★★ (Kipdorp 10–12; www.hotel franq.com; ✆ **03/555-3180;** doubles 175€–245€), a neoclassical former bank building transformed into a chic design hotel. While the public areas are quite grand—a soaring atrium and marble pillars—its 39 rooms are more restrained, with clean lines and low-key modern furnishings. As befits its Relais & Châteaux status, the property touts a gourmet French/Belgian restaurant, but if you're looking for more affordable eats, it's just a 5-minute walk to the dining and bar hub of Grote Markt.

A more classic choice is the **Hilton Antwerp Old Town** ★★ (Groenplaats 32; www.hilton.com; ✆ **03/204-1212;** doubles 140€–230€), occupying an ornate19th-century building right on Groenplaats square. Behind the historic façade is a contemporary interior, with wonderfully roomy accommodations and stately marble bathrooms; suites and executive rooms allow access to the executive lounge, which has a sunny roof terrace open seasonally.

A good budget option in the city center, **Hotel Postiljon** ★ (Blauwmoezelstraat 6; www.hotelpostiljon.be; ✆ **03/231-7575;** doubles 75€–123€) offers small, simply furnished rooms (and only some with private bathrooms), but its prime location right next to the Cathedral of Our Lady can't be beat.

On the food front: In Grote Markt, there's no shortage of traditional Belgian spots serving staples like mussels and *stoofvlees* (Flemish beef and beer stew), but the more dynamic dining scenes are found beyond the medieval center. To the north, the formerly seedy port area of Eilandje—now home to the MAS and Red Star Line Museum (see p. 244)—has seen trendy cafes, restaurants, and bars popping up in formerly derelict harbor-front buildings. On the gourmet end there's **Lux** ★★ (Adriaan Brouwerstraat 13; www.luxantwerp.com; ✆ **03/233-3030;** mains 43€–49€, fixed-price menus 60€–80€), set inside the marble-clad 17th-century offices of a shipping company; the four- to six-course tasting menus champion local seafood and produce like Zeeland oysters with Mechelen asparagus. Nearby, a renovated warehouse is now home to the rustic, plant-filled **Roest** (Sint-Aldegondiskaai 64; www.roest.be; ✆ **03/298-7359;** mains 15€–23€), whose simple menu of sandwiches, salads, and soups is elevated by top-notch organic ingredients.

A 20-minute walk south of Grote Markt, the Zuid district, known for its plethora of art and antiques galleries, is blossoming as a hip dining destination. See what came off the boat that day at **Fiskebar** ★★ (Marnixplaats 11; www.fiskebar.be; ✆ **03/257-1357;** mains 17€–28€), which specializes in heaping plates of fresh shellfish, including North Sea crab, langoustine, and shrimp. **The Glorious** ★★ (De Burburestraat 4A; www.theglorius.be; ✆ **03/237-0613;** mains 36€–48€), serves classic French-Belgian cuisine in a swanky, lounge-like setting; there's a terrific dry-aged steak and a wine list offering some 30 wines by the glass.

A bit off-the-beaten-path on the riverfront promenade, **RAS ★★★** (Ernest Van Dijckkaai 37; www.ras.today; ℂ **03/234-1275;** mains 24€–32€) presents beautifully composed seafood and vegetable dishes in a modern glass dining room overlooking the River Schelde; request a seat on the tranquil waterfront terrace for spectacular sunset views. And if you're at the MAS museum, you can't do better than **Restaurant 'Zilte ★★★** (p. 243), which serves creative, delicious food in a view-rich setting.

Shopping

Antwerp now has a worldwide reputation for design savvy. It rivals Brussels as a shopping destination, largely thanks to world-renowned graduates of the city's Royal Academy of Fine Arts. Known as the Antwerp Six, the group of avant-garde designers includes **Ann Demeulemeester** (Leopold de Waelplaats 1; www.anndemeulemeester.com; ℂ **03/216-0133**), famed for her edgy, Japanese-inspired fashions, and **Dries van Noten** (Nationalestraat 16; www.dries vannoten.be; ℂ **03/470-2510**), whose quirky prints have become legendary.

The long shopping street of **Meir** has mid-range international chains and department stores, while the upmarket stores and boutiques have colonized the area **south of the Grote Markt between Steenhouwersvest and Komedieplaats;** here you'll find Diane von Furstenberg, Gucci, Ralph Lauren, Filippa K, and many others. For lace, scour the streets surrounding the cathedral and for diamonds, head for **Appelmansstraat** and nearby streets around Centraal Station.

Antwerp After Dark

Antwerp is as dynamic after dark as it is busy during the day. The main entertainment zones for visitors are Grote Markt and Groenplaats, which are both packed with **bars, cafes, and theaters;** the former port area of Eilandje, where trendy **cafes, pubs, and nightclubs** have taken over old warehouses; Het Zuid, home to stylish, upscale **cocktail lounges;** and the Centraal Station area for **discos, nightclubs, and gay bars.** The red-light district, set in **Schipperskwartier,** is concentrated in just three streets; it's much seedier than the one in Amsterdam and is definitely *not* a tourist attraction.

THE PERFORMING ARTS

Antwerp takes pride in being a citadel of Flemish culture. Two of the region's stellar performance companies are based here: the **Vlaamse Opera (Flanders Opera;** www.operaballet.be; ℂ **070/22-0202**), run in conjunction with the opera house in Ghent (p. 259), and the **Koninklijk Ballet Vlaanderen (Royal Ballet Flanders;** www.operaballet.be; ℂ **070/22-0202**); both perform at the historic **Vlaamse Opera** (Frankrijklei 1) with additional ballet performances at the modern **Theater 't Eilandje** (Kattendijkdok-Westkaai 16).

Contemporary music, hard-hitting drama, and dance is the province of performances at the multi-staged **deSingel,** Desguinlei 25 (www.desingel.be; ℂ **03/248-2828**), and big-name concerts (Elton John, The Eagles, and Julio

Iglesias played here in 2019) are held at the **Sportpaleis Antwerp** (Schijnpoortweg 119; www.sportpaleis.be; ℒ **03/400-4040**).

GHENT ★★

48km (30 miles) NW of Brussels

Life moves fast in the capital town of Oost-Vlaanderen (East Flanders) province; it's got a pretty face, yes, but currently it's a bit careworn, not all powdered and puffed like Bruges. Tourists are welcomed here with open arms but they don't make the city tick as they do in Bruges, as Ghent is also an important university city, an inland port, and an industrial center. Largely thanks to its 44,000-strong student population, Ghent compensates for its less precious appearance with a vigorous, somewhat gritty social and cultural scene, with bars, restaurants, and clubbing options aplenty.

Essentials

GETTING THERE

BY PLANE **Brussels Airport** is the main international airport in Belgium (p. 158) but a coach service runs 9 times a day between **Brussels-South-Charleroi Airport** (p. 159) and Bruges via Ghent, making this small airport easier to access. Ticket prices vary; booking in advance online at www.flibco.com usually means a cheaper fare. A one-way fare ticket purchased at the airport is 19€.

BY TRAIN Ghent is a 30-minute train ride from Brussels, and depending on the time of day, there are anywhere from three to seven direct trains every hour between the two, with a round-trip fare of 22€. The main station of **Gent-Sint-Pieters** is on Koningin Maria-Hendrikaplein, 2km (1½ miles) south of the center city. Tram No. 1 runs into the Korenmarkt.

BY CAR Take A10/E40 from Brussels; the journey takes 45 minutes when the traffic is clear.

VISITOR INFORMATION

The **Visit Ghent tourist office** is a fabulously modern affair with a James Bond–esque computer table offering multilingual information. It's in the former Fishmarket (Sint-Veerleplein 5; www.visitgent.be; ℒ **09/266-5660**) and is open daily 10am to 6pm.

GETTING AROUND

Once you get to the historical center of Ghent, most of the major sites are within walking distance, but both the city's main train station, **Gent-Sint-Pieters,** and the **Museum voor Schone Kunsten Gent** are quite far from the center—at least a half-hour by foot. Ghent has an integrated **tram and bus network** and the single **electric trolley-bus** line, all operated by **De Lijn** (www.delijn.be; ℒ **070/220-200**). The four tramlines (1, 4, 21, and 22) stop at **Gent-Sint-Pieters station** and at multiple points throughout the city center. Purchase your ticket (3€ for 1 hour) from the De Lijn sales point in the station

Party Time in Ghent

If you hit town in July, you've crashed in on party heaven in Ghent. For 10 days around July 21, Belgium's greatest extended street party, the **Gentse Feesten** (**Ghent Festivities;** www.gentsefeesten.be; ℂ **09/210-1010**) swirl through the city with concerts, from classical to indie and dance, street theater, performance art, puppet shows, a street fair, special museum exhibits, and riotous fun and games.

or from an automated ticket machine before boarding the tram or bus; the largest bill you can pay with onboard is a 10€ note.

There are plenty of regulated **taxis** with ranks in the streets; you'll find them outside **Gent-Sint-Pieters** and **Ghent Dampoort stations** as well as on Korenmarkt. Otherwise call **Vtax** (www.v-tax.be; ℂ **09/222-2222**).

Exploring Ghent

This is a city best seen by walking its streets, gazing at its gabled guild houses and private mansions, and stopping on its bridges to take in the waterside views. Ghent's historical monuments have not all been prettified; some of them look downright gray and forbidding, which, oddly enough, gives them a more authentic feel. The city's heart surrounds the funnel-shaped piazza of **Korenmarkt,** and this is where local big wigs had their residences in times past. Most of the city's major sights—including the **Stadhuis** (p. 255), **St. Bavo's Cathedral** (p. 254), and the **Belfort** (p. 250)—are close by. To the north lies the foreboding **Gravensteen Castle,** and beyond that is the revamped medieval enclave of **Patershol,** today something of a hot drinking and dining spot. The River Leie winds through the city center on its way to join the River Schelde and a network of canals leading to the port. Citadel-park, location of the **Museum voor Schone Kunsten Gent** (p. 253) is in the south of the city near Gent-Sint-Pieters station, and is one to avoid at night thanks to drug dealers and muggers.

Note: As in other cities, the official pass (**Citycard Gent**) doesn't pay off for more sightseers. Unless you plan to take in an exhausting number of attractions in a day, you'll lose money by buying the card.

Belfort en Lakenhalle (Belfry and Cloth Hall) ★★ HISTORIC SITE   Just across the square from the cathedral, in the heart of Ghent, the richly ornate Gothic Cloth Hall and Belfry tower above it together form a glorious medieval ensemble. The 14th-century **Belfry** holds the great bells that have rung out Ghent's civic pride down the centuries; the most beloved was a giant bell known as Roland (1315), which was used as the city's alarm bell. It was destroyed by Emperor Charles V in 1540 as punishment for Ghent's insubordination against the Spanish. No fewer than 28 of the 54 bells that now make up the tower's huge carillon were cast from Roland's broken pieces. The massive Triomfanten bell, cast in 1660 to replace the Roland, now rests in a small park at the foot of the Belfry, still bearing the crack it sustained when it broke in 1914. Take the elevator to the Belfry's upper gallery, 66m (217 ft.) to

Ghent

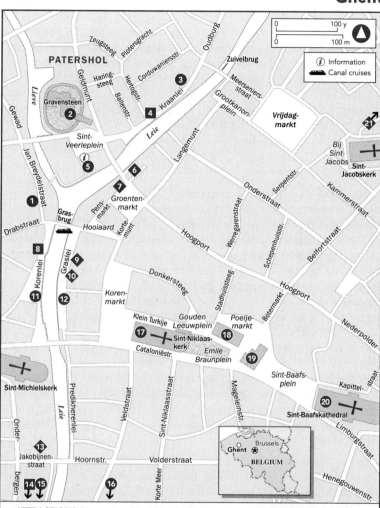

ATTRACTIONS ●

Belfort en Lakenhalle **19**
Design Museum Gent **1**
Graslei **12**
Gravensteen **2**
Het Huis van Alijn **3**
Korenlei **11**
Museum voor Schone
  Kunsten Gent **16**
Sint-Baafskathedraal **20**

Sint-Niklaaskerk **17**
Stadhuis **18**
Stadsmuseum van Gent **15**
Stedelijk Museum voor
  Actuele Kunst Gent **16**
Tourist Information **5**

HOTELS ■

Ghent Marriott Hotel **8**
Hotel Harmony **4**
Hotel NH Gent Sint-Pieters **14**

RESTAURANTS & BARS ◆

Balls & Glory **13**
Café 't Galgenhuisje **7**
De Graslei **9**
Holy Food Market **21**
't Dreupelkot **6**
Tolhuisje Gent **10**

see the bells and take in fantastic **panoramic views of the city;** it's a great way to get your bearings. A great iron chest was kept in the Belfry's *Secreet* (strongroom) to hold the all-important charters that spelled out privileges the guilds and the burghers of medieval Ghent wrested from the counts of Flanders.

The **Cloth Hall** at the foot of the Belfry dates from 1425, is where cloth was stored and traded, and was the gathering place of wool and cloth merchants. A baroque extension from 1741 on Goudenleeuwplein was used until 1902 as a prison, dubbed *De Mammelokker* (the Suckler). The name comes from a relief above the doorway that depicts the Roman legend of Cimon, starving to death in prison, being suckled by his daughter Pero. Appropriately, this newer section is now the office for the city's *ombudsvrouw* (ombudswoman).

Sint-Baafsplein. www.belfortgent.be. ℂ **09/233-3954.** Admission 8€ adults, 6€ seniors, 2.70€ ages 19–26, free for ages 18 and under. Daily 10am–6pm. Closed Dec 25 and Jan 1.

Gravensteen (Castle of the Counts) ★★ HISTORIC SITE

"Menacing" is the word that springs to mind for this circular, gray fortress crouching like a great stone lion over the split in the River Leie. Gravensteen was clearly designed by the ruling counts of Flanders to keep the populace in line by sending out a harsh message to a rebellion-inclined citizenry. Although a wooden castle had existed for several centuries in this location, the turreted fortress we see today was built in 1180 by Philip of Alsace, the Count of Flanders. He had just returned from the Crusades and clearly intended to recreate the stern, foreboding crusader castles that are strewn on rocky crags across the eastern Mediterranean. If its 2m/6-foot–thick walls, battlements, and turrets failed to intimidate attackers, a well-equipped torture chamber awaited inside. Relics of the chamber—a guillotine, spiked iron collars, branding irons, thumb screws—are displayed in a small museum. Climb up to the battlements for great views of Ghent's rooftops and canals.

Sint-Veerleplein 11. www.gravensteengent.be. ℂ **09/225-9306.** Admission 10€ adults, 7.50€ seniors, 6€ ages 19–25, free for children 18 and under. Daily 10am–6pm. Closed Dec 24–25 and Dec 31–Jan 1.

Design Museum Gent ★★ MUSEUM

Located in the Hotel de Coninck (ca. 1755), a baroque mansion with a lovely courtyard garden dominated by a huge ceramic urn and a modern extension grafted on to the rear, this decorative arts museum showcases the very best in world design. In the old wing, the exhibits range through period salons decked out with swagged curtains, frescoed ceilings, elaborate chandeliers, fine French furniture, and Chinese porcelain in typically aristocratic 18th- and 19th-century Flemish style. Oddly out of context here is a "book table" by contemporary Dutch designer Richard Hutten, entirely comprised of hardcover books and lacquered to give it a shiny, hard finish. In marked contrast to all that heavy, ornate, period luxury, the bright, light-filled new wing sings to a contemporary tune and features sublime examples of Art Nouveau furniture by Henry van de Velde and Paul Hankar, and even the Belgian master of the genre, Victor Horta. Seminal work from the 20th and early 21st centuries feature Alessi silverware, stools in

SIDE TRIPS FROM BRUSSELS & BRUGES

Ghent's main square is **Vrijdagmarkt**—huge, tree shaded, ever bustling, and surrounded by old guild houses hosting stores selling Ghent noses (a syrupy confection like an overgrown jelly baby in fruity flavors) and restaurants that sprout across sidewalks when the sun shines. There are markets here most weekends but historically this square has been the scene of much turbulence, a fact marked by the central bronze statue of 14th-century rebel leader Jacob van Artevelde, who fought the English ban on Flemish wool exports in the 14th century. The statue was erected in 1863 to commemorate Van Artevelde's assassination in 1345.

The beguiling **Patershol** neighborhood along the west bank of the Leie River and north of the Lieve Canal provides a charming taste of Old Ghent. The nest of narrow, pedestrianized streets and tightly packed brick cottages were built in the 17th century for the city's weavers, craftsmen, and tradesmen; about 100 of these buildings are protected monuments and have been delightfully revamped. Restaurants and bars have now flooded in to the area, making it a popular late-night drinking and clubbing spot.

recycled plastic by Bar und Knell Design, and chairs by Richard Gehry. Temporary exhibitions take on controversial subjects such as the use of plastic and pollution.

Jan Breydelstraat 5. www.design.museum.gent.be. © **09/267-9999**. Admission 8€ adults, 6€ seniors, 2€ ages 19–26, free for children 18 and under. Mon–Tues and Thurs–Fri 9:30am–5:30pm; weekends 10am–6pm. Closed Dec 25 and Jan 1.

Het Huis van Alijn (House of Alijn) ★★ MUSEUM

Though Ghent's intriguing folklore museum takes its visitors on a journey through 20th-century life it's actually located in the only medieval *godshuis* (almshouse) still standing in the city. The House of Alijn dates back to the 12th century, stands around a neat courtyard garden, and over its long lifetime has functioned as a children's home and a hospital. Inside the clutch of whitewashed, gabled, and restored cottages are replicas of Ghent weaving and metalwork workshops as well as shop interiors of a sweet shops and a bakery, but the most fascinating rooms are those dating from the 1950s and 1980s—and oh, how dated the '80s decor looks. One long corridor features flickering home movies, mundane in subject but rich in vicarious detail from this story of every-day Belgian folk going about their lives. You might want to end your day's sightseeing here over a beer in the traditional tavern, **'t Cafeetse,** beside the River Leie.

Kraanlei 65. www.huisvanalijn.be. © **09/235-3800**. Admission 6€ adults, 4.50€ seniors, 2€ ages 19–26, free for children 18 and under. Mon–Tues and Thurs–Fri 9am–5pm; weekends 10am–6pm. The tavern opens at 10:30am and closes with the museum. Closed Dec 24–25 and Dec 31–Jan 1.

Museum voor Schone Kunsten Gent (Ghent Fine Arts Museum) ★★ MUSEUM

Tucked behind a pillared, neoclassical facade on the edge of Citadelpark, the fine arts museum traces the story of Belgian art from the glowing, almost Byzantine religious art of the Middle Ages to modern day. Although it has its fair share of work by the Flemish Primitives, including

The Naked Truth

Prudish 18th-century Austrian Emperor Joseph II ordered the naked figures of Adam and Eve in **"The Adoration of the Mystic Lamb"** to be replaced by others with fig leafs covering their genitals. Today, the original Adam and Eve are back in their birthday-suit glory, and you can view the faintly ridiculous replacement panels attached to columns near the cathedral's entrance.

the recently restored Bosch painting "Saint Jerome" (ca. 1485), plus Rubens and Van Dyck—where this museum really excels is in its later offerings. The late 19th century was a period of great artistic flowering in Ghent, and this is reflected in the works by *fin de siècle* artists such as James Ensor and Theo van Rysselberghe, whose work bears an uncanny resemblance to the paintings of his American contemporary John Singer Sargent. All artwork hangs evocatively highlighted against dark walls embellished with bright-white neoclassical friezes. If contemporary artwork is your thing, there's an offshoot of MSK close by in Citadelpark at **SMAK** (see below). Fernand Scribedreef 1, Citadelpark. www.mskgent.be. ✆ **09/240-0700.** Admission 8€ adults, 6€ seniors, 2€ ages 19–26, free for children 18 and under. Tues–Fri 9:30am–5:30pm and Sat–Sun 10am–6pm. Closed Dec 25–26 and Jan 1–2.

Sint-Baafskathedraal (St. Bavo's Cathedral) ★★★ CHURCH   Even if you see nothing else in Ghent, you shouldn't miss this massive cathedral. Don't be put off by its rather unimpressive exterior, an uncertain mixture of Romanesque, Gothic, and baroque architecture, which lacks a certain fluidity of form. The interior is filled with priceless paintings, sculptures, screens, memorials, and carved tombs. About midway along the vaulted nave is a remarkable pulpit (1741) in white marble entwined with oak, reminiscent of Bernini. The baroque organ from 1653 is the biggest in the Low Countries, and it sure sounds like the loudest when it's in full voice.

St. Bavo's showpiece is the 24-panel altarpiece **The Adoration of the Mystic Lamb,** completed by Jan van Eyck in 1432. Van Eyck's luminous use of oils and naturalistic portrayal of nature and people represented a giant step away from the rigid style of Gothic religious art. For an example of what we mean, take a look at the flowers painted on the central panel. Horticulturists who have examined the tiny plants with magnifying glasses have found each of them scientifically exact, have even affirmed that the flowers found growing in shadows are only those species that could in fact blossom without light. But besides its importance in the history of art, the Mystic Lamb is spellbinding in its own right. The work was commissioned for this very chapel by a wealthy alderman in 1420. The original artist was Jan's brother Hubert van Eyck, but the piece was completed by Jan after Hubert's death in 1426.

Other art treasures include Rubens's **The Conversion of St. Bavo** (1623), in the Rubens Chapel on the semicircular ambulatory behind the high altar. The Romanesque crypt holds a wealth of religious antiquities, vestments, sculptures, and paintings. Look for faint frescoes still on some of the arches (some frescos were cleaned away entirely during previous restorations).

Though the church was constructed in the 14th and 15th centuries, the crypt contains traces of the earlier 12th-century Church of St. John.

A new visitor's center for the cathedral, which will include simulations of the building throughout the ages as well as its artwork, is due to open in 2020.

Sint-Baafsplein. www.sintbaafskathedraal.be. ℗ **09/269-2045.** Admission: cathedral free; "Mystic Lamb" chapel 4€ adults (includes audio guide in English), 1.50€ school children. Cathedral: Apr–Oct Mon–Sat 8:30am–6pm, Sun 10am–6pm; Nov–Mar Mon–Sat 8:30am–5pm, Sun 1–5pm; "Mystic Lamb" chapel: Apr–Oct daily 9:30am–5pm, Sun 1–5pm; Nov–Mar Mon–Sat 10:30am–4pm, Sun 1–4pm.

Sint-Niklaaskerk (St. Nicholas's Church) ★★ CHURCH   The first to be constructed of the triumvirate of church spires that dominate central Ghent, St. Nicholas displays a mixture of Romanesque elements and the Flemish Schelde Gothic architectural style. An impressive 13th- to 15th-century church, it is a veritable mountain of Tournai bluestone and was paid for by Ghent's wealthy medieval merchants as an ostentatious signal of their wealth to other Flemish cities. A baroque high altar and other rich decorations embellish the interior; these date from after the Protestant *Beeldenstorm* (Iconoclastic Fury) of 1566, during which Catholic churches across the Low Countries were ransacked. One of the best ways to appreciate the Gothic detailing of St. Nicholas's flying buttresses and slender stained-glass windows is from the viewing platform of the Belfort (see p. 250).

Korenmarkt. ℗ **09/234-2869.** Free admission. Tues–Sun 10–5pm, Mon 2–5pm.

Stadsmuseum van Gent (Ghent City Museum) ★★★ MUSEUM   STAM offers the perfect introduction to Ghent, as it details the development of the city from its medieval beginnings to the cultured city we meet today. It's housed in an eccentric space that flows from the 14th-century Bijloke Abbey through its neat knot of gardens and into a contemporary block of airy exhibition space with exterior walls made of glass, mirroring the historical progress of the city as it moves from medieval to modern. A chronological

---

The Two-Faced Town Hall

Ghent's large *Stadhuis* (Town Hall), turns a rather plain Renaissance profile to Botermarkt, and an almost garishly ornamented Gothic face to Hoogpoort. Its schizophrenic appearance probably came about because its construction, started in 1518 under the direction of Mechelen architect Rombout Kelder-mans, was interrupted by Emperor Charles V in 1539, began again at the end of that century, was halted once more in the early 1600s, and wasn't completed until the 18th century. The changing public tastes and available monies of those years are reflected in the building's styles. In its *Pacificatiezaal* (Pacification Room), the Pacification of Ghent was signed in 1567. This document declared to the world the repudiation by the Low Countries provinces of Spanish Habsburg rule and their intention to permit freedom of religion within their boundaries. The Town Hall can only be visited with a guided tour. Contact Ghent Guides at www.gentsegidsen.be or 09/233-0772.

trail meanders through multimedia exhibits, images, archeological finds, artwork, and "listening benches" to bring Ghent's rich history to life in a museum that's stylishly curated and educational, yet also succeeds in being entertaining.

Godshuizenlaan 2. www.stamgent.be. ℂ **09/267-1400.** Admission 8€ adults, 6€ seniors, 2€ ages 19–26, free for ages 18 and under. Mon–Tues and Thurs–Fri 9am–5pm, Sat–Sun 10am–6pm. Closed Dec 24–25 and Dec 31–Jan 1.

Stedelijk Museum voor Actuele Kunst Gent (Museum of Contemporary Art) ★★ MUSEUM Better known by yet another acronym, SMAK is Ghent's primary attraction for contemporary art fans, located in a 1930s building in Citadelpark near the Fine Arts Museum (see above). The permanent collection contains intriguing works by Karel Appel of CoBrA fame and big international names like Andy Warhol and Christo, but they're not always on show. You're more likely to find wacky, weird, and sometimes wonderful temporary exhibitions that showcase the work of leading international contemporary artists (recently that included Gerhard Richter and Michael E. SmithStandards can be hit or miss so check what's on before a visit.

Citadelpark, Jan Hoetplein 1. www.smak.be. ℂ **09/240-7601.** Admission 15€ adults, 13€ seniors, 2€ ages 19–26, free for children 18 and under. Tues–Fri 9:30am–5:30pm, Sat–Sun 10am–6pm. Closed Dec 25–26 and Dec 31–Jan 1.

The Medieval Harbor ★★★

Undoubtedly the most beautiful parts of Ghent are the medieval quays of **Graslei** and **Korenlei** just west of Korenmarkt. Facing each other across the Leie waterway, they were the site of Tusschen Brugghen, the city's medieval harbor. Both embankments are lined with rows of intricately gabled former guild houses, warehouses, and elegant town houses built in a variety of architectural styles between the 1200s and 1600s. It is fair to say that if all Ghent was as lovely as these two streets, it would give Bruges a run for its money. Although a considerable amount of restorative nip and tuck has been performed over the centuries, none of these majestic buildings have lost their medieval allure. To see them all lit up at night under the **Ghent Light Plan** (see below) is a genuinely breathtaking experience. By day, both quays are lined with tour-boat docks (see box below).

GRASLEI

Graslei today is one of the city's most picturesque meeting points, awash with **bars and restaurants** and surrounded by graceful gabled gild houses. At no. 8, the Brabantine Gothic **Gildehuis van de Metselaars (Stonemasons' Guild House)** has graceful pinnacles and is decorated with a medallion of an angel and reliefs of the "Quatuor Coronati," four Roman martyrs who were the guild's patrons. It dates from 1527 but what you see is actually a 1912 reconstruction of a 16th-century guild house originally located on Cataloniëstraat.

No. 9, dating from 1435, was the first **Korenmetershuis (House of the Grain Measurers),** where officials weighed imported grain before it was transported to the Korenmarkt. Next door, at no. 10, is the solidly constructed **Het Spijker (Stockpile House),** dating from around 1200, where corn was stored. The front of its forward-leaning Romanesque facade reaches up to the world's oldest step gable.

The tiny building squashed in at no. 11 is the **Tolhuisje (Little Customs House),** which was constructed in 1682 in the Flemish Renaissance style as the office of the city's corn revenue agent. It now houses a great little cafe, **Het Tolhuisje** (see below). Next door, nos. 12–13 were an annex to the **Korenmetershuis (House of the Grain Measurers)** and date from 1540; the patterned red-and-white brickwork was added in 1698.

No. 14, with a facade dating from 1531 covering the 14th-century building underneath, was the ornate Brabantine Gothic **Gildehuis van de Vrije Schippers (Guild House of the Free Boatmen)** ★. This is one of the finest sights on Graslei, decorated with symbols of sailing ships and sailors on its sandstone facade.

KORENLEI

Across the water from Graslei by the Sint-Michielsbrug (St. Michael's Bridge), Korenlei is a fine vantage point from which to appreciate the architectural wonders on the opposite bank. However, this street has many treasures of its own, most built later than the historic facades along Graslei.

The step-gabled 16th-century house constructed of red brick at no. 23 on the corner by the bridge was the **Brewers' Guild House.** The ultramodern **Ghent Marriott Hotel** (see below) has installed itself in a bunch of restored guild houses, with the main entrance at Korenlei no. 10. Next door, the redbrick, step-gabled building called **De Swaene (the Swans),** at no. 9, dates from 1609; it has a pair of gilded swan medallions on the facade, and in its time has been a brewery and a bordello.

At no. 7 is the pink-and-white-shaded **Gildehuis van de Onvrije Schippers (Guild House of the Tied Boatmen)** ★. Dating from 1739 and dubbed Den Ancker (the Anchor), it is a masterpiece of Flemish baroque architecture, with a graceful bell gable and carved dolphins and lions on the facade; that's all topped with a gilded weathervane of a sailing ship at full mast on the roof.

Cruising Ghent

A 50-minute **cruise** ★ on the canals with either **Rederij De Gentenaer** (www.rederijdegentenaer.be; © **09/269-0869**) or **Gent Watertoerist** (www.

Ghent Light Plan

In 1998, Ghent city fathers hatched a plan to light the city after dark. This had dual purposes: to increase safety at night and to show off the city's phenomenal architecture to its best advantage. Now you can follow the route through the streets on a 2-hour circular walk from Kouter in the south to Vrijdagmarkt in the north, but by far the most spectacular sights are the medieval guild houses in Korenlei and Graslei. But don't get too sidetracked in Ghent's enticing bars as the illuminations, like Cinderella, disappear at midnight. You can download the walk for free from https://visit.gent.be/en/see-do/magical-ghent-evening.

gent-watertoerist.be; ℘ **09/269-0869**) is well worth it to see the historic buildings lining the medieval waterways. Tour boats sail from Graslei and Korenlei, and opening hours and costs are the same for both cruise companies: April to mid-October daily 10am to 6:30pm, mid-October through March daily 11am to 4pm. Cruises cost 7€ for adults, 4€ for children 3 to 11.

Especially for Kids

As well as **canal tours** to explore the medieval canals (see above) and views from the top of the **Belfort** (p. 250), several of Ghent's major museums, including the **House of Alijn** (p. 253), **Design Museum Ghent** (p. 252), and **Ghent City Museum** (p. 255), have tours specially designed to appeal to kids. The torture chamber at **Gravensteen Castle** (p. 252) is guaranteed to enthrall gloomy, emo-inclined teenagers. As much of the city center is pedestrianized, it's safe to explore by bike; rent from De **Fietsambassade Gent** (www. fietsambassade.gent.be), prices start at 7€ per half day. If all else fails, bribe the kids with must-have treats including fruity, pyramid-shaped *neuzekes* (Ghent noses) from the shops around the Vrijdagmarkt or Temmerman (Kraanlei 79).

Where to Stay, Eat & Drink

Many of Ghent's hotels are sandwiched into ancient buildings but hide interiors that are the very latest in contemporary design and comfort. Travelers with cash to spare need look no further than the immaculate temple to modern design and comfort that is the **Ghent Marriott Hotel** (www.marriottghent.be; ℘ **09/233-9393;** doubles 150€–235€), located in medieval mansions at Korenlei 10. The **Hotel Harmony** (Kraanlei 37; www.hotel-harmony.be; ℘ **09/324-2680;** doubles 175€–250€) is another such gem, overlooking the Leie on the fringes of Patershol. The stylish rooms of this family-run establishment are so vast you can lose whole families in them and there's a tiny plunge pool squeezed in the garden at the back. The **Hotel NH Gent Sint Pieters** (Koning Albertlaan 121; www.nh-hotels.com; ℘ **09/222-6065;** 86€–120€) is a short walk to the main train station but it's less convenient to the historic center—at least 25 minutes on foot (or an 18-minute tram ride). But this chain hotel is clean and comfortable, with nice touches including hardwood floors in every room, and it offers some real bargain rates (plus a 3pm checkout on Sundays).

A night out in Ghent is always a pleasure, thanks to a proliferation of dining and drinking options from traditional grand cafes to gin-tasting houses. For lovely nighttime views over gracious guild houses, choose **De Graslei** (Graslei 7; www.restaurantdegraslei.be; **09/225-5147;** mains 16€–32€); the place buzzes in many languages and offers a typically Flemish menu of teeming seafood platters or *waterzooi* served with piles of fries. After an afternoon of shopping in the Veldstraat, fuel up nearby at Belgium's famous meatball joint **Balls & Glory** (Jakobijnenstraat 6; www.ballsnglory.be; ℘ **32/486-67-8776;** mains 14.50€–19.50€), which serves up hearty handmade "Glory Balls" stuffed with classic pork, chicken, or veggies. Order one with a side of stoemp (a mash of potatoes, carrots, and seasonal greens) and join the crowd of young locals at the lively communal table. From lunch until late into the evening, hipsters flock to the **Holy Food Market** (Beverhoutplein 15; www.holyfood market.be; ☏ **32/494-28-2562**), an indoor food hall set in a converted 17th-century chapel replete with stained-glass windows; its 17 stalls hawk everything from Portuguese tapas to sushi to classic moules-frites and the center bar is a popular gathering spot.

Ghent After Dark

Although Ghent is up for a good night out on the town any time of year, its cultural calendar really hits the heights from October to mid-June, when international opera is performed in the 19th-century **De Vlaamse Opera,** Schouwburgstraat 9 (www.operaballet.be; ☏ **09/268-1011**), run in conjunction with the opera house in Antwerp (p. 248). This is regarded as one of the most spectacular concert halls in Europe, built in the 1840s and with an auditorium encrusted with gilding, red velvet, and frescoed ceilings.

Ghent's favorite after-dark entertainment is found among hundreds of atmospheric bars and taverns. Groentenmarkt, Korelei, and Graslei make the best trawling ground for a pub crawl in an easily navigable (and safe) area. The oldest drinking haunt in the city is **Café 't Galgenhuisje** (Groentenmarkt 5; ☏ **32/474-93-0034**), normally crammed with students spilling out onto the square. A vast choice of Belgian beers is on offer at the miniscule tavern **Tolhuisje Gent** (Graslei 11; ☏ **32/488-59-9330**), which is cleverly inserted into the smallest building on floodlit Graslei. But if there is one place that encapsulates the party vibe of Ghent, it's **'t Dreupelkot** (Groentenmarkt 12; www. dreupelkot.be; ☏ **09/224-2120**), where you can spend an addictive hour or two sampling some 100 or so varieties of the ginlike liqueur *jenever* (p. 28); horrifically, it's even available flavored with chocolate.

MONS ★

51km (32 miles) SW of Brussels

Hainaut's provincial capital—and the *cultural* capital of French-speaking Wallonia—sits in the southwest of Belgium abutting the French border. Mons started life as a fortified camp constructed by Julius Caesar's Roman legions high in a landscape of rolling hills, and today, it's home to SHAPE (Supreme Headquarters Allied Powers Europe). Between those two military bookends, it has enjoyed a rich and eventful history. The Roman encampment morphed into a town when St. Waltrude, the daughter of a local nobleman, founded a convent here in the 600s.

Occupied repeatedly by opposing French and Austrian forces down the centuries, Mons eventually found its forte and grew wealthy through industrialization. The mining that brought in the money to help Mons expand has long since dried up and this pretty little place is often wrongly overlooked on the tourist trail. However, there's plenty to please here, as Mons is blessed with one of the most handsome townscapes in Belgium. Start your exploration in the harmonious central Grand-Place, which is a masterpiece of civic and religious buildings dating from the 11th century onward. By the way, if you want to travel to Mons from a Flemish-speaking destination, it's called Bergen.

Essentials

GETTING THERE Mons is an easy day trip from Brussels, with trains departing between the two twice hourly; the ride takes about 50 minutes and the round-trip fare is 19€. The station is on place Léopold, a short walk west from the center of town. For more details, go to **www.belgiantrain.be**. To get to Mons by **car** from Brussels, take E19; the journey takes around an hour.

VISITOR INFORMATION The **Maison du Tourisme du Pays du Mons** is at Grand-Place 22 (www.visitmons.be; ℂ **065/335-580**). The office is open Monday to Saturday 9:30am to 5:30pm and Sunday 9:30am to 4:30pm.

GETTING AROUND Walking is the best way to get around in the Old Town, but free **Mons Intra Muros** mini-buses run on four routes between the station and the Grand-Place every 6 minutes Monday through Saturday 7am to 9pm.

Exploring Mons

BAM ★ MUSEUM The Beaux-Arts Mons (Museum of Fine Arts) occupies a purpose-built gallery on a side street off Mons' fine Grand-Place. As well as hosting concerts, the museum has a permanent collection of 19th- and 20th-century paintings and sculpture drawn from around Hainaut. Much more interesting to most visitors are the temporary exhibitions, which have focused on big names like Warhol and van Gogh.

Rue Neuve 8. www.bam.mons.be. ℂ **065/405-330.** Admission: permanent exhibitions 4€ adults, 2€ ages 6–17, free children 5 and under. temporary exhibitions 9€ adults, 6€ ages 6–17, free children 5 and under. Free first Sun each month. Tues–Sun 10am–6pm.

Beffroi ★★ HISTORIC SITE The first thing anyone notices about Mons is the baroque Beffroi (Belfry), a landmark UNESCO World Heritage Site that stands 87m (270 ft.) above the highest point of town on the square du Château. Don't worry if you feel an urge to giggle at your first sight of this tower; it does look a bit comical, and as Victor Hugo remarked, somewhat like "an enormous coffee pot, flanked below belly-level by four medium-size teapots." With typical Gallic bureaucracy it's only open by writing in advance to the tourist office (see above). Opposite the Belfry is the Chapelle St-Calixte, the oldest structure in town, dating from 1051. The chapel has a very meager **Musée du Château Comtal (Museum of the Castle of the Counts)** containing a few ancient bits of crumbling statuary.

Square du Château. ℂ **065/335-580.** Admission 2.50€ adults, 1.25€ seniors and students 12 to 18, free for children 11 and under. Free first Sun each month. Tues–Sun noon–6pm.

Collégiale Ste-Waudru (Collegiate Church of St. Waltrude) ★★

CHURCH Dating from 1450, this remarkably lovely church in Brabantine Gothic style stands just below the Belfry. Inside its vast vaulted space is crammed with 16th-century sculptures and wooden wall carvings by Mons artist Jacques Du Brœucq (1505–84), while around the choir 16th-century stained-glass windows depict biblical scenes and banners hang in the slender Gothic window recesses. The church's treasury contains richly ornamented religious objects in gold—chalices, monstrances, and reliquaries—many of them dedicated in honor of St. Waltrude, along with sculptures, paintings, and vestments. At the entrance to the church, the ceremonial **Car d'Or (Golden Coach)** anticipates its annual spring outing, when it is paraded around town in a religious festival called **Ducasse de Mons** on Trinity Sunday.

Place du Chapitre. www.waudru.be. ✆ **065/335-580.** Free admission. Church: Mon–Sat 9am–6pm, Sun 9:30am–6pm; treasury: Tues–Sun noon–6pm.

Grand-Place ★★ HISTORIC SITE   Almost everything you'll want to see in Mons is on or around the fountain-filled Grand-Place, a lovely spot to take half an hour out over coffee or a beer in the terrace cafes. The piazza is lined by a noble mix of splendid town houses and surrounded by steep, cobbled streets, and its centerpiece is the 15th-century Gothic **Hôtel de Ville (Town Hall),** topped with an unusual bronze bell tower. Inside the Town Hall are antique tapestries and paintings; access to the stately apartments is by free, guided tour arranged through the Visit Ghent tourist office (p. 249). At the rear of the Hôtel de Ville you'll find the tranquil **Jardin du Mayeur (Mayor's Garden),** filled with calming shrubs, flowers, and fountains. As you go through the arched doorway toward the gardens, it's customary to stop and rub the head of the monkey of the "Grand-Garde," an iron statue that's been granting good luck since the 15th century. Needless to say, he has a very shiny pate.

Town Hall: Grand-Place 22. Guided tours July–Aug Tues–Sat 2:30pm.

Musée des Arts Décoratifs (Museum of Decorative Arts) François Duesberg ★★ MUSEUM   Arguably the most pleasing museum in Mons, this privately owned decorative-arts collection is housed in a former bank opposite the Collegiate Church of St. Waltrude and has squirreled together a fine collection of neoclassical French and Belgian *objets d'art.* Standout pieces include fine sets of Meissen porcelain, silverware from rich guilds, and hundreds of gilt-embellished 18th-century timepieces—they are all beautifully displayed in glass cabinets reminiscent of the "curiosity cabinets" so popular with 18th- and 19th-century collectors.

Sq. Franklin Roosevelt 12. www.duesberg.mons.be. ✆ **065/363-164.** Admission 5€ adults, free for children 12 and under. Tues, Thurs, Sat–Sun 2–7pm.

Around Mons

Château de Beloeil (Beloeil Castle) ★★★ CASTLE   The "Versailles of Belgium" is the magnificent ancestral home of the aristocratic de Ligne family, a great moated palace sitting amid formal baroque-style gardens overlooking an ornamental lake. The Princes of de Ligne have called this magnificent castle their home since the 14th century but there was a fortified residence for at least 300 years before that. In summer the family open their sumptuous home to the public to show off the considerable style in which they live; each vast apartment is furnished in glamorous 18th-century French style, swathed with elaborately frescoed and gilded ornamentation and filled with priceless antiques, fine-spun carpets and tapestries, Old Master paintings, a lock of hapless Queen Marie Antoinette's hair, and more than 20,000 books.

Rue du Château 11, Beloeil (22km/14 miles northwest of Mons). www.chateaudebeloeil.com. © **069/689-426.** Admission: château and park 10€ adults, 9€ seniors and ages 12–18, 5€ children 6–11, free children 5 and under; park only 4€ adults, 3€ seniors and ages 12–18, 2€ children 6–11, free children 5 and under. Apr–June and Sept Sat–Sun 1–6pm. July–Aug daily 1–6pm.

Grand-Hornu ★★ HISTORIC SITE   As the Industrial Revolution hit the area around Mons, many families grew rich on the backs of their workers. One entrepreneur with a social conscience was mine-owner Henri de Gorge (1774–1832), who constructed Grand-Hornu between 1810 and 1830 in neo-classical style and attached to it 450 houses for his workers. Following the collapse of industry in the region, Gorge's utopian dream fell into dereliction before being restored in the 1970s. It's a fascinating, unlikely mixture of anti-quarian sensibility and gritty industrial reality that showcases the Victorian entrepreneurial tradition at its best. A part of the site has been given over to the **Musée des Arts Contemporains** of Belgium's Francophone community and its exhibits of contemporary art.

Rue Ste-Louise 82, Hornu (13km/8 miles southwest of Mons). www.grand-hornu.be. © **065/652-121.** Admission 10€ adults, 6€ seniors, 2€ children 6–18, free for children 5 and under. Tues–Sun 10am–6pm. Closed Jan 1 and Dec 25.

Maison Van Gogh (Van Gogh House) ★ MUSEUM   During his days as a none-too-successful church missionary (ca. 1879–80), the tortured Dutch artist Vincent van Gogh lived in a bleak miner's cottage called the Maison du Marais (the "March House") in the Borinage coal-mining district. From this squat, brick-built house he preached the gospel to poverty-stricken mining families while honing his talent painting and drawing in the bleak, boggy countryside. His house has been restored as a monument to his skills, with an audiovisual presentation but sadly only one original Van Gogh sketch, "The Diggers" (1880). Unless you're a fervent devotee of Van Gogh, this place is not worth the detour.

Rue du Pavillon 3, Cuesmes (3km/2 miles south of Mons). http://en.maisonvangogh.mons.be. © **065/355-611.** Admission 4€ adults, 3€ children 12–17, free for children 11 and under. Tues–Sun 10am–4pm. Closed Jan 1 and Dec 25.

NAMUR ★★

56km (35 miles) SE of Brussels

The handsome old riverside town of Namur is the administrative capital of French-speaking Wallonia in southern Belgium. Sitting at the confluence of the Meuse and Sambre rivers, the town makes the perfect jumping off point for exploring the rolling hills and gastronomic delights of the Ardennes as well as the lavish chateaux of the Meuse Valley. But before you rush on, stop awhile in Namur, presided over by its massive citadel with all its family-friendly attractions, and offering some fine attractions of its own—museums and churches, and an abundance of cafes and restaurants in the narrow, atmospheric alleyways of Le Corbeil, the attractive old quarter of 17th-century brick houses strewn along the Sambre waterfront. If you visit when the weather is fine, take a *namourette* boat ride across the rivers; there are docks along the waterside.

Essentials

GETTING THERE   There are two **trains** every hour from Brussels to the Gare de Namur, an easy walk from the center of town; the journey takes 60 minutes and round-trip fares are 18€. For more details, go to **www.belgiant rain.be**. The **bus station** is out front (www.infotec.be). By **car** from Brussels, take the A4/E411 southeast; you'll be there in under an hour.

VISITOR INFORMATION   The **Maison du Tourisme du Pays de Namur** is at Place de la Station (www.namurtourisme.be; ✆ **081/246-449**), close to the rail station. The office is open Monday to Saturday 9:30am to 6pm and Sundays 11am to 3pm.

GETTING AROUND   Namur is easily accessible on foot.

What to See & Do

Cathédrale St-Aubain (St. Aubain's Cathédral) ★ CHURCH   The domed cathedral was designed by Italian architect Pisoni between 1751 and 1767 in a light, ethereal, late baroque style with an ebullience of columns, pilasters, cornices, and balustrades. It was constructed on the site of an earlier Romanesque church and its ancient belfry is incorporated into the present structure. The **Musée Diocésain et Trésor (Diocesan Museum and Treasury),** place du Chapitre 1 (www.musee-diocesain.be; ✆ **04/987-10-316**), just outside the cathedral, holds a small but impressive collection of ecclesiastical relics, gold plates, and jewel-encrusted diadems. As many of the items and the space itself are gradually being refurbished, the museum is only open part of the year (see below) and only on Thursdays.

Place St-Aubain. www.cana.be. ✆ **081/220-320.** Admission: church free; Diocesan Museum 2€ adults, under 18 free. Church: Tues–Sat 8:30am–5pm, Sun 8:30am–6:30pm. Museum: Apr–Oct Thurs 2–5pm.

Citadelle (Citadel) ★★ HISTORIC SITE   A fortification has stood atop Namur's bluff crag since pre-Roman times, and the Citadel in various guises has seen much military action down the years. Today, however, its function is purely peaceful: the fortified castle has become a rural entertainments complex with plenty of amusements to offer families. Kick off a visit by taking the **cable car** that runs up to the Citadel ramparts and jump on the **electric train** that chugs around the castle. A high-tech visitor center set in the former barracks offers an overview of European military history alongside the history of Namur and the Citadel. Themed **walking tours** detail the history of the citadel and there are two medieval-styled scented **gardens** to explore as well as **underground passages** where Napoleon's troops once hid. A traditional **perfumery** and a small

amusement park for young children are also found within the fortified walls. Although the Citadel is open to roam all year around, as is the visitor center, its attractions only open with the tourist season from April until October.

Rte. Merveilleuse. https://citadelle.namur.be. © 081/247-370. Admission: Citadel free; museums, guided visits, and excursion train 13€ adults; 11€ seniors, students, and children 6–17; free for children 5 and under. Citadel daily 8am–6pm; park Apr–Oct daily 10am–5pm; visitor center Apr–Nov daily 10am–6pm, Nov–Mar Tues–Sun 10am–5pm. Closed Dec 24–Jan 1.

Musée Félicien Rops (Félicien Rops Museum) ★ MUSEUM
Namur's best-known son was a 19th-century painter and engraver of the bizarre and the erotic. Félicien Rops led a dissolute life, mostly among the fleshpots of Paris and Brussels but despite his flirtation with drugs and absinthe he was extraordinarily skillful and prolific, a fact attested to by the 3,000-odd drawings, aquatints, lithographs, and prints exhibited in his museum, which is safely tucked away from sensitive eyes on a narrow side street near his birthplace in the old quarter of town. Rops was indisputably one of the most outstanding engravers of the late 19th century and also a vastly underrated painter; the

THE grand châteaux OF THE MEUSE VALLEY

The banks of the River Meuse are liberally sprinkled with grand historic châteaux, often with moats and towers. Among the finest that you can visit are:

o **Château d'Annevoie** ★★★, rue des Jardins 37, Annevoie (www.annevoie.be; © 082/679-797), is east of the Meuse on the N92 in between Namur and Dinant and offers charming formal water gardens in Italian, French, and English styles.

o **Château de Freÿr** ★, Freÿr 12, Hastière (www.freyr.be; © 082/222-200), on the left bank of the Meuse, along N96 between Hastière-Lavaux and Dinant. The 17th-century summer retreat of the dukes of Beaufort-Spontin has a scenic riverside location and magnificent ornamental gardens.

o **Château de Jehay** ★★, rue du Parc 1, Amay (www.chateaujehay.be; © 085/824-400), 18km (11 miles) southwest of Liège, off N614. Its lawns and gardens are beautified with sculptures and fountains.

Inside, rooms are filled with paintings, tapestries, lace, silver and gold pieces, jewels, porcelain and glass, antique furniture, and family heirlooms. The interior is being restored at press time and is currently not open to the public.

o **Château de Modave** ★★, rue du Parc 4, Modave (www.modave-castle.be; © 085/411-369), 12km (7½ miles) south of Huy, off N641. Once the property of Liègeois prince-bishops and then cardinals of the Catholic church, this fine example of the Louis XIVth French style has a delightfully flamboyant interior and neatly planted terraced gardens.

o **Château de Vêves,** rue du Furfooz 2, Celles-Houyet (www.chateau-de-veves.be; © 082/666-395), 8km (5 miles) east of the Meuse, off N94. An 18th-century folly styled as a medieval castle, Vêves looks almost more romantic than the real thing and offers plenty of medieval-themed entertainment that will enthrall kids.

works hung in the museum include some of his pornographic images as well as his delicate, almost wistful, landscapes. Temporary exhibitions often compare his works with other greats of his time, such as Auguste Rodin.

Rue Fumal 12. www.museerops.be. ℂ **081/776-755.** Admission 3€ adults (5€ for temporary exhibitions); 1.50€ seniors, students, and children 12–18 (2.50€ for temporary exhibitions); free for children 11 and under. July–Aug daily 10am–6pm, Sept–June Tues–Sun 10am–6pm. Closed Dec 24–25 and Dec 31–Jan 1.

YPRES ★★

110km (68 miles) W of Brussels; 45km (28 miles) SW of Bruges

Set among the low, gentle slopes of the West Flanders Heuvelland (Hill Country), Flemish-speaking Ypres (Ieper in Dutch, and often pronounced "Wipers" in English) owed its early prosperity to the Flemish textile industry that peaked in the 13th century. Over the centuries, the handsome town was wholeheartedly trashed in one war after another, but by far the most devastating was World War I (1914–18); hardly a brick was left standing after 4 years of violent bombardment as Ypres became one of the slaughterhouses of the Western Front. In the few square miles of the Ypres Salient (see below), 250,000 soldiers from the British Empire, France, and Belgium were killed, along with an equal number of Germans. The tally of wounded on all sides reached 1.2 million.

Most visitors come to Ypres—today perfectly restored brick by brick to its former considerable grandeur—to remember those who fell on the surrounding battlefields and who rest eternally on the green breast of the Heuvelland. In the rolling countryside around the town, there are no fewer than 185 serene World War I military cemeteries, the last resting place of soldiers from across the globe. Pay homage to the brave of this most horrendous of wars in the deeply emotional, daily "Last Post" ceremony, which takes place at 8pm, come rain, shine, plague, or pestilence, under the hallowed arches of the town's neoclassical Menin Gate (see below).

Essentials

GETTING THERE Many visitors combine a visit to Ypres with a stay in Bruges although it is perfectly possible to get there and back from Brussels in a (long) day for a round-trip train fare of 18€. **Trains** depart hourly from Bruges for the hour's trip to Ypres and round-trip fares are 24€; some services require a change at Kortrijk. Visit **www.belgiantrain.be** for full details of schedules. From Brussels, take the A17/E40 to Ghent, then the A14 and the A19 west; the drive takes around 90 minutes. For the 50-minute **drive** from Bruges, take A17/E403 south to the Kortrijk interchange, and then A19 west; from the coast at De Panne, take N8 south.

VISITOR INFORMATION **Toerisme Ieper** is in the Lakenhalle, Grote Markt 34 (www.toerismeieper.be; ℂ **057/239-220**), in the center of town. The office is open April to mid-November Monday to Friday 9am to 6pm, and weekends 10am to 6pm; mid-November through March, hours are Monday to Friday 9am to 5pm and weekends 10am to 5pm.

GETTING AROUND Sights in town are easily reached on foot, though if you're arriving by train, you'll save time by taking almost any **De Lijn** bus (www.delijn.be; ℂ **070/220-200**) from the bus station next to the train station for the 5-minute ride to the Grote Markt. Regulated taxis are available outside the train station.

SPECIAL EVENTS Every 3 years on the second Sunday in May, Ypres celebrates a colorful pageant, the **Kattenstoet (Festival of the Cats;** see p. 39), during which the town jester throws cats from the Belfry to the people below. The custom originated centuries ago when cats were considered a "familiar" of witches, and evolved into the tradition of today's lively carnival, procession, and street partying. Thankfully these days the flying felines are fluffy toys. The next Kattenstoet is on May 9, 2021.

Exploring Ypres

Most of the gabled guild houses and mansions around the gorgeous Grote Markt are occupied now by restaurants, cafes, and hotels. At the western end of this central square, Ypres's medieval wealth is reflected in its extravagant Gothic **Lakenhalle (Cloth Hall)** ★★. The original was constructed between 1250 and 1304 along the Ieperlee River (long since banished underground) but was blown to pieces between 1914 and 1918 and reconstructed with painstaking care, although the work wasn't finished until 1967. Gilded statues once more adorn the roof, and a statue of Our Lady of Thuyne, the patron of Ypres, stands over the main entrance. Inside, you'll find the tourist office, and the upper floor houses the **In Flanders Fields Museum,** which is one of the most thought-provoking and visually stunning war museums in Flanders (see below).

The Cloth Hall's central **Belfort (Belfry)** is the oldest part of the building, dating from 1201, and has four corner turrets and a spire that rears up to 70m (230 ft.). You get fine views over the town from here, provided you're willing and able to climb the 264 steps to the upper gallery. Concerts chime out across the square from Belfort's 49-bell carillon between June and September on Saturday from 11am and Sunday from 3:30pm.

The arcaded Nieuwerck is an extension of the Cloth Hall dating from 1619 and houses Ypres's **Stadhuis (Town Hall).** You can visit the council chamber and view its fine stained-glass window for free Monday to Friday whenever the town hall is open.

The spire of the 13th-century Gothic **Sint-Martenskathedraal (St. Martin's Cathedral)** ★★, on Sint-Maartensplein, is another town landmark. Inside is the tomb of Cornelius Jansen (1585–1638), a bishop of Ypres who was condemned for heresy in 1642, as well as a much-revered statue of Our Lady of Thuyne. Britain's armed forces donated the stained-glass rose window in honor of Belgium's World War I soldier king, Albert I. The cathedral is open to visitors daily 8am to noon, and 2 until 8pm except during services. Admission is free.

Behind the cathedral, the **Munster Memorial** is in the shape of the Celtic Cross and honors Irish soldiers killed in World War I. Across the way, British and Commonwealth veterans made the **St. George's Memorial Church** (1929) in Elverdingsestraat a shrine to their fallen comrades. Wall-mounted banners and pew kneelers decorated with colorful corps and regimental badges add an almost festive air to what might otherwise be a somber scene. The church is open daily from 10am to 6pm, and admission is free.

The town's great offering to the war dead is the **Meensepoort (Menin Gate)** ★★★, the immense marble memorial arch at the east entrance to the Grote Markt. Inscribed on its walls are the names of the 54,896 British troops killed around Ypres between 1914 and 1917 that have no known grave. Every evening at 8pm, traffic through the gate is stopped while war veterans in dress uniform sound the plaintive notes of "The Last Post" on silver bugles, in a brief but moving ceremony that dates from 1928. Every evening this service attracts hundreds of spectators, who come to pay their respects to the fallen. Adjacent to the Menin Gate is the **Australian Memorial** in honor of more than 43,000 Aussies who lost their lives in the Ypres Salient (see below).

The impressive 17th-century **city ramparts** were designed by the French military engineer Vauban and are fronted by a moat that once surrounded the town; these are among the few structures not demolished during World War I. You reach them via stairs at the Menin Gate and walk around the battlements to the **Rijselsepoort (Lille Gate).**

into THE SALIENT

In addition to companies based in Ypres, many Brussels and Bruges tour operators (p. 196 and 223) run day trips to Flanders Fields. **Flanders Battlefield Tours** (www.ypres-fbt.be) and **Salient Tours** (www.salienttours.be) both run bus tours of the battlefields and memorials around Ypres, ranging from 2 hours to a full day. Prices begin at 30€ for a 2-hour tour. The Ypres tourist office (see above) offers details for the **In Flanders Fields Route,** a self-guided tour of 80km (50 miles) on signposted roads that cover all the main sights.

For a less ambitious, 1- to 2-hour self-guided tour by car, head out of town through the Menin Gate and take the N8 and turn off to Canadalaan, close to **Bellewaerde Park** (see below). Near the end of the lane, near **Sanctuary Wood Cemetery,** is a preserved stretch of trenches peppered with shell holes and shattered trees. Amazingly, almost no other sign remains of the vast network of muddy, waterlogged trenches—nature has reclaimed the once-tortured landscape. Nearby stands the **Canadian Monument** on Hill 62.

Return to the N8 and turn right. Take the N303 through Zonnebeke in the direction of Passendale (Passchendaele in French), and stop off at the **Tyne Cot Commonwealth Military Cemetery,** with its 12,000 graves surmounted by a Cross of Remembrance in white Portland stone. In 1917, Passendale was dubbed "Passiondale" by British and Commonwealth troops, who took the village at a cost of 140,000 lives. Head northwest from Zonnebeke towards Langemark, and on the crossroads with the N313, you'll find the Canadian St. Julien Memorial. On the north side of Langemark is the site of 44,000 graves at the **Deutscher Soldatenfriedhof (German Military Cemetery).** Return to the N313 and turn right to head back to Ypres.

In Flanders Fields Museum ★★★ MUSEUM "War is hell" is the clear message of this superb interactive museum. It presents a heart-rending take on World War I brought alive by the judicious use of film, personal accounts, images of decimated and desolate Flanders battlefields, and sickening facts and figures that lay heavy on the heart. Most moving is the account of the Christmas Truce, in which Allied and German troops laid down their weapons and played soccer in No-Man's Land. Along with the tragic tales of bloodshed, the museum offers the hope of reconciliation and world peace.

Cloth Hall, Grote Markt 34. www.inflandersfields.be. ℘ **057/239-220.** Admission 10€ adults, 6€ ages 19–25, 5€ children 7–18, free for children 6 and under. Apr to mid-Nov daily 10am–6pm, mid-Nov to Mar Tues–Sun 10am–5pm. Closed first 3 weeks of Jan and Dec 25.

ESPECIALLY FOR KIDS

Bellewaerde Park, Meenseweg 497 (www.bellewaerde.be; ℘ **057/468-686**), offers kids the chance to have a blowout after the solemnity of the war museums and cemeteries. This theme park combines white-knuckle rides with a wildlife reserve occupying various recreated natural environments, and plenty of gentle rides for the tiniest tots, plus audiovisual specials like the 4-D film "Turtle Vision." Bellewaerde is set in what was once the wasteland of the World War I front lines. The park is open April to June daily 10am to 5pm (6pm weekends), July daily 10am to 6pm (7pm weekends), August daily 10am to 7pm (10pm Sat), and September to November weekends 10am to 6pm. Admission is 32€ adults, 27€ seniors, 28€ for children 100cm (3ft) to 140cm (4.5ft), free for children under 100cm (3ft).

MECHELEN ★

34km (20 miles) E of Brussels

This unsung mini-city in Flanders is a stone's throw away from Brussels but light years away in attitude and ambience; once the capital of the Low Countries, its wealth came from the cloth trade in the 13th and 14th centuries, which were Mechelen's glory days. When the political capital of Belgium headed to Brussels, Mechelen slowly slipped back into charming obscurity.

Thanks to its illustrious history, Mechelen has a gaggle of remarkable Gothic and baroque buildings at its heart, with its most important landmarks being the architecturally schizophrenic **Stadhuis (Town Hall)** and **St. Rumbold's Cathedral** on the gargantuan **Grote Markt.** Today much of the local action is centered around the **Vismarkt,** a cobbled square that lies along the River Dijle and is bordered with canopied restaurants and bars; it connects to Grote Markt along the buzzy, busy parallel shopping streets of Begijnenstraat and IJzerenleen.

Essentials

GETTING THERE Mechelen is a short hop from Brussels, with **trains** departing five to eight times hourly; the journey takes under half an hour and the round-trip fare is 9.20€. Check **www.belgiantrain.be** for schedules. You can get to Mechelen from Brussels by **car** in under half an hour if the traffic is not choked; jump on the A1/E19.

VISITOR INFORMATION   **Tourism Mechelen** is at Vleeshouwersstraat 6 (https://visit.mechelen.be; ☏ **32/152-976-54**), just off the Grote Markt. The office is open April through October Monday to Saturday 10am–5pm, Sunday 12:30–4pm; November to March Monday to Saturday 10am–4pm, Sunday 12:30–4pm.

GETTING AROUND   Walking is the easiest and most pleasant way to get around in Mechelen.

Exploring Mechelen

Standing out among the cluster of gabled and gaily painted town houses around Grote Markt, the spire of Mechelen's UNESCO-listed **Sint-Rombout-skathedraal (St. Rumbold's Cathedral)** is the town's much-loved icon. From Sunday to Friday between 1 and 6pm and Saturday between 10am and 6pm, it's possible to clamber up all 514 steps to the panoramic Skywalk for views over the surrounding, pancake-flat countryside. Admission is 8€ adults, 3€ ages 4 to 27, 20 percent discount for families. Dating from 1452, the cathedral also has a famous 98-bell carillon that rings out every 15 minutes.

Opposite St. Rumbold's stands the UNESCO-listed 14th-century **Belfort (Belfry)** of the Stadhuis (Town Hall), which stood roofless for almost 200 years after the cloth trade in Mechelen died out. A provisional roof was added some 200 years later but only finally completed in 1911, based on original 16th-century plans. To its left is the pinnacled, lacy facade of the Palace of the Great Council. A regular 1-hour **guided walk** of Mechelen (6.50€ for adults, 2.50€ for ages 12–26) is offered on weekends at 2pm from March to November (also Wednesday at 2pm during Easter, public holidays, and in July and August) from the tourist office (see above).

Of the town's 18 museums and art galleries, the two worth hitting on a day trip are the **Kazerne Dossin Holocaust Centre ★★★** at Goswin de Stassartstraat 153 (www.kazernedossin.eu; ☏ **015/290-660**) and the **Toy Museum ★★**. The Kazerne Dossin is housed in a squat, white purpose-built museum on the site of the former Dossin barracks, where Mechelen's Jews and gypsies were held before deportation to the concentration camps of Poland during World War II. It presents a hard-hitting, often hard-to-take story using interactive exhibits, gruesome images, and deeply moving personal accounts of the Nazi atrocities. The museum is open Thursday through Tuesday, 10am to 5pm (closed Jan 1, Dec 25, and Jewish holidays). Entrance costs 10€ for adults, 4€ for ages 10 to 21, and free for ages 9 and under (we think the museum is too disturbing for young children). Kazerne Dossin won European Museum of the Year in 2014 for its heart-rending ruminations on war.

Altogether more upbeat in its subject matter, the **Speelgoedmuseum Mechelen ★★** (**Toy Museum Mechelen;** Nekkerspoelstraat 21; www.speelgoed museum.be; ☏ **015/557-075**) is a charming place that will appeal to all ages. It boasts Europe's biggest collection of toys, ranging from model Napoleonic soldiers to Victoriana dolls and on through Matchbox cars to plastic Barbies and Kens; it will provide a warm blast of nostalgia for anyone over 40. Open Tuesday through Sunday 10am to 5pm, admission 9.80€ for adults, 8.80€ seniors and students, 7.30€ for children between 3 and 12.

PLANNING YOUR TRIP

Amsterdam, Brussels, and Bruges are not hard cities to come to grips with; they are human-sized, have excellent public transportation systems, and most people speak English. Nevertheless, all trips benefit from some advance planning. This chapter is designed to help you on your way with some of the nitty-gritty details that can make or break a vacation (or a vacation budget).

9

The information in this chapter is intended to cover trips to all three cities so it's valuable reading whether you are visiting one, two, or all of them. For additional planning info, such as when to go, what the weather's like—and for more specific on-the-ground resources in Amsterdam, Brussels, and Bruges—see the "Essentials" and "Fast Facts" sections in chapters 4, 6, and 7.

GETTING THERE & AROUND

BY PLANE With few exceptions, round-trip air from most gateways in the United States will be slightly cheaper (about $50) into Brussels than it will be into Amsterdam. That doesn't hold if you're flying out of the New York City area, however: thanks to a competitive array of non-stop flights to Amsterdam, flights to Holland can be up to $100 cheaper than flights into Belgium. From other U.S. gateways, accepting a flight with a stopover in, say London (on British Airways), Reykjavik (on Icelandair), or Stockholm (on SAS), will result in the cheapest airfares. So if you're considering combining the two in one itinerary, it may be a better idea to choose the Belgian gateway. And while it is a time-saver to fly into one gateway and out of the other (say, into Brussels and out of Amsterdam), that will usually add on to the overall costs by $50 to $100 from the United States depending on the gateway. We say "usually" because in rare instances choosing this type of so-called "open jaw" ticket costs roughly the same as a regular round-trip. The key to saving, therefore, will lie in pricing several different routes; being flexible on arrival and departure dates can also be a money saver.

For Amsterdam most visitors will fly into **Amsterdam Airport Schiphol;** see p. 55 for airport info and info on getting from the

FINDING A GOOD airfare

Book at the right time. It sounds odd, but you can often save a good amount by booking airfare about 6 weeks in advance of departure. That figure comes from a study of 35 million airfare transactions that an industry group called the Airlines Reporting Corporation undertook in 2019. Book earlier than that, and you won't have access to the lowest-priced seats, as the airlines only release them when they have an idea of how the plane is selling. Book too close to departure, and the airline knows they've "got you" and will charge more.

Fly when others don't and take an itinerary the business travelers don't want. Those who fly Sunday, Tuesday, or Wednesday, and who stay over a Saturday night, generally pay less than those who fly at more popular times.

Do a smart Web search. In a recent Frommers.com study of hundreds of airfares, we found that Momondo.com and Skyscanner.net beat the competition when it came to finding affordable prices. Both search all of the discount sites as well as the airline sites directly, so that you get a broader and more impartial search.

Be anonymous in your search. Clear your cookies, or better yet, use a different browser or computer than you usually do when searching for airfares. The airlines and airfare booking sites do track users (though they deny it), and are getting increasing expert in serving up the fares tailored to customers' past buying history. To see the actual lowest rates you may need to cloak your identity.

airport into town. For visits to Brussels, Bruges, and anywhere else in Belgium, transatlantic travelers fly into **Brussels Airport** (see p. 158). **Brussels-South-Charleroi-Airport** (see full info on p. 159) receives European budget flights, not transatlantic ones.

BY CAR For info on driving to Amsterdam, see p. 58; for Brussels see p. 159; and for Bruges see p. 209. In general, we don't recommend driving in *any* of these cities. The historic centers of all three cities are easily—and most enjoyably—explored on foot; if you get tired, public transport is readily available in the form of trams, buses, and in Amsterdam and Brussels, the Metro. Only rent a car if you're keen on visiting battlefields, or rural sights that aren't easily reached by rail.

All the international car rental firms, including **Avis** (www.avis.com), **Budget** (www.budget.com), **Europcar** (www.europcar.com), and **Hertz** (www.hertz.com) have offices in the airports, in the city centers, and in the Channel ports. But we find that the website **AutoSlash** (www.autoslash.com) tends to better the rates that you'll find going directly to a rental car agency. That's because AutoSlash applies every coupon on the market to the original booking. Then, they monitor the booking. If the rental rate falls, they automatically rebook their customers at the lower rate.

To rent a car in Belgium and the Netherlands, you need a credit or debit card (for the deposit), a passport, and a driver's license. The car registration papers must be kept in the vehicle. The minimum age for drivers is 18, and on expressways, speed limits are 70kmph (43 mph) minimum, 130kmph (81 mph) maximum; in all cities and urban areas, the maximum speed limit is 50kmph (31 mph). Lower limits might be posted. Seat belts must be worn in both the front seats and in the back. In the car, you need to have a fire extinguisher, a basic medical kit, a red reflective warning triangle, and a reflective jacket; the rental car companies will supply this compulsory equipment but check to make sure it's there before driving off.

BY TRAIN Rail services to Amsterdam, Brussels and Bruges are frequent and fast. In fact, we think traveling by train is the preferred method of getting around this corner of Europe. You'll find complete information on rail travel into and out of Amsterdam on p. 59. For Brussels, consult p. 159. Information on rail into Bruges is on p. 209. Remember that **Eurostar high-speed trains** are an excellent way to travel between London and the cities in this guide.

BY BUS International and domestic coaches serve all the cities in this guide, and while affordable, traveling by train is faster. That being said, most regional bus companies have express lines between major destinations such as Rotterdam and Amsterdam. Regional and intercity bus services in the

responsible TOURISM

The Dutch live in a tiny country that's so heavily populated they need to recover land from the sea, and they take protection of their environment very seriously. More than 60 percent of household waste is sorted, collected, and recycled. As a visitor, you are expected to play your part in this process and not toss stuff without checking if it's recyclable or reusable.

Cities in Belgium and the Netherlands all have excellent integrated public transportation systems; using them helps reduce greenhouse-gas emissions. Even if you rent a car for getting around, most main car-rental firms (see above) now offer green options, from renting a low-emissions car to making a payment to a CO_2-offset program.

All those bicycles you see in Amsterdam take cars off the street. Anyone who's not riding a bike is likely to be walking or getting around by tram, and visitors are encouraged to do likewise. There are many places where you can

rent bikes (p. 112), and public transportation is easy to use and efficient (p. 61).

Belgium's Dutch-speaking Flanders region, including Bruges, comes close to sharing the Dutch commitment to getting around by bike, but in hilly, traffic-choked Brussels, the bike is a less-enticing mode of transportation. There's no need to drive, though, as the tram and Métro systems work well.

Many Dutch and Belgian hotels have signed up for becoming more energy efficient in all areas of operation, conserving water, decreasing the amount of unsorted waste, and more. Visit eco-friendly champions **Green Key (www. green-key.org)** to see what you can do to help, and check hotel reviews throughout this book for details on specific sustainable properties, in particular the Conscious Hotel Vondelpark and Court Garden Den Haag (p. 73 and 150), who both are ahead of the pack in leading the way into the future of green tourism.

Public Holidays

New Year's Day	January 1
March/April/May	Easter Sunday and Monday
April 27	King's Day (Holland Only)
May 1	Labor Day (Belgium Only)
May 4	National Remembrance Day (Holland)
May 5	Liberation Day (every 5 years in Holland, celebrated in 2020)
May/June	Ascension Day and Pentecost
July 11	Flemish-speaking community holiday (Belgium)
July 21	Independence Day (Belgium)
September 27	French community holiday (Belgium)
November 11	Armistice Day (Belgium)
November 15	German-speaking community holiday Belgium)
December 25	Christmas Day
December 26	Boxing Day (Holland)

Netherlands are operated by **Connexxion** (www.connexxion.nl), **Arriva** (www.arriva.nl), and **Qbuzz** (www.qbuzz.nl). In Belgium bus travel between cities is headache inducing thanks to complicated timetables and insufficient routes. To get to many places in Belgian by bus often involves too many intermediate stops. Fares and schedules are available from **STIB** (www.stib.be) for Brussels, and **De Lijn** (www.delijn.be) for Bruges and Flanders.

ENTRY REQUIREMENTS

Visas

Citizens of the United States, Canada, the United Kingdom, Ireland, Australia, and New Zealand do not need a Visa for a visit to either Belgium or the Netherlands of less than 3 months. If you're a citizen of another country, check **www.diplomatie.be** for Belgium or **www.government.nl** for the Netherlands.

Passports

Citizens of the United States, Canada, the United Kingdom, Ireland, Australia, and New Zealand need a valid passport to visit Belgium and the Netherlands.

It is advisable to have one or two consecutive blank pages in your passport to allow space for entrance and exit visas and stamps. You must have at least 3 months left on your passport *after* your trip has ended for customs in Belgium or the Netherlands to allow you in to the E.U.

Medical Requirements

No health and vaccination certificates are required for entry in to Belgium or the Netherlands, nor do you need any vaccinations before your trip.

| Best Strategies for Booking Hotels Online |

While our hotel recommendations have been personally vetted, and cover a wide breadth of styles and prices, you'll still need to go on the trusty World Wide Web to book. So, for just a moment, put down this guide (long live print!) and make use of our pro tips for booking accommodations. A 2019 study by Frommers.com found that **Booking.com** offered the best rates for Europe, by far. Other good options include **Hotels.com** and **Agoda.com**. On the former, you'll earn 1 free night for every 10 nights booked on their free rewards program. And, finally: **Ask for a discount!** While it's not a particularly helpful strategy at big chains, don't hesitate to politely request a small discount in person, especially for last-minute deals or during off-peak tourism times. Be sure you're asking the right person though: Usually you'll need to speak with a manager or owner to get the money off.

TIPS ON PLACES TO STAY

Across Belgium and the Netherlands, but particularly in Amsterdam and Brussels, **Airbnb** (www.airbnb.com) and in Brussels, **Wimdu.com**, are blooming in popularity. If you're a budget traveler or are traveling with a group, these options can offer outstanding value, especially if you're willing to stay in a home where the host is still in residence. For strictly unhosted apartments **VBRO** (www.vbro.com), **FlipKey** (www.flipkey.com), or **HomeAway** (www.homeaway.com) can also be useful.

[FastFACTS] AMSTERDAM, BRUSSELS & BRUGES

Area Codes It's **20** for Amsterdam, **2** for Brussels, and **50** for Bruges.

ATMs As in most of the rest of the world, the easiest way to get cash is from an ATM. Be sure you know daily withdrawal limit before departure. Look for ATMs with the Cirrus (www.mastercard.com) or PLUS (www.visa.com) network symbols, as these accept foreign-issued cards.

Disabled Travelers Some hotels and restaurants in Holland and Belgium provide access for people with disabilities, but the old town house hotels in the cities are often short on facilities for people with mobility issues. Both Brussels Airport and Amsterdam's Schiphol Airport have services to help travelers with disabilities through the airport. There's also comprehensive assistance for travelers with disabilities throughout the railway systems surrounding all three cities.

Most, but not all, trams in Brussels, Antwerp, Amsterdam, The Hague, and Rotterdam are accessible for travelers in wheelchairs; all new trams being introduced into service have low central doors that are fully accessible. The Metro systems in Brussels, Amsterdam, and Rotterdam, and the Premetro in Antwerp, are fully accessible. Bruges is so easily explored on foot that you'll have no need for public transport.

There's assistance for travelers in Belgium on **SNCB** (www.b-rail.be; ✆ **02/528-2828**) trains and in stations, and in the Netherlands with **NS** (www.ns.nl; ✆ **030/235-7822**).

Drinking Laws The minimum drinking age in the E.U. is 18; proof of age is often requested at bars, nightclubs, and restaurants, so it's a good idea to bring passport or driver's license when you go out.

Electricity Holland and Belgium both run on 230 volts and 50 Hz. Most mobile phones, cameras, MP3 players, and laptops will need adaptors for the two- or three-pin plugs.

Embassies **Dutch embassies** are all in The Hague, the administrative capital of the Netherlands: **Australia,** Carnegielaan 4 (www.netherlands.embassy.gov.au; (✆ 070/310-8200); **Canada,** Sophialaan 7 (www.netherlands.gc.ca; ✆ 070/311-1600); **Ireland,** Scheveningseweg 112 (www.irishembassy.nl; ✆ 070/363-0993); **New Zealand,** Eisenhowerlaan 77N (www.nzembassy.com/netherlands; ✆ 070/346-9324); **United Kingdom,** Lange Voorhout 10 (www.gov.uk/world/organisations/british-embassy-the-hague; ✆ 070/427-0427); **United States,** John Adams Park 1 (http://nl.usembassy.gov; ✆ 070/310-2209).

Belgian embassies are all located in the capital, Brussels: **Australia:** Level 7, av. des Arts 56 (https://belgium.embassy.gov.au/bsls/home.html; ✆ 02/286-0500); **Canada:** av. des Arts 58 (www.canadainternational.gc.ca; ✆ 02/741-0611); **Ireland:** rue Froissart 50 (www.dfa.ie/irish-embassy/belgium; ✆ 02/282-3400); **New**

Zealand: Level 7, av. des Nerviens 9–31 (www.mfat.govt.nz; ✆ 02/512-1040); **United Kingdom:** av. d'Auderghem 10 (www.gov.uk/government/world/belgium; ✆ 02/287-6211); **United States:** bd. du Régent 27 (https://be.us embassy.gov; ✆ 02/811-4000).

Emergencies In the Netherlands and Belgium, dial ✆ 112 for police, ambulance, paramedics, and the fire department. This is a nationwide toll-free call from landline, mobile, or pay phone.

Insurance All travelers should invest in travel insurance when visiting Europe. A typical policy provides cover for the loss of baggage, tickets, and—up to a certain limit—cash, as well as cancellation or delay of your journey. Sickness and accident benefits are often extra. Note that some all-risk home-insurance policies may cover your possessions when overseas, and many private medical plans include coverage when abroad. To find a good policy, look at such marketplace websites as **SquareMouth.com** or **InsureMyTrip.com**.

Internet Access Most hotels in Holland and Belgium offer Wi-Fi access for free, although some of the more expensive ones charge a daily fee. KPN hotspots are scattered throughout Amsterdam; cost starts at 5€ for 1 hour (p. 64). Some areas in central Brussels permit free access to Wi-Fi hotspots (p. 165); the same

holds true in Bruges' city center (p. 211).

Legal Aid If you get into trouble with the law, your first point of contact is likely to be the police. Many Dutch and Belgian (but by no means all in Brussels) police officers are disposed to go easy with foreigners on minor matters, and many of them speak English. If the problem is serious and you are arrested, you have rights similar to those in any Western democracy. You are not required to say anything self-incriminatory, and you will be given access to a court-appointed lawyer or permitted to contact your embassy or consulate (p. 64).

LGBT Travelers There is little-to-no discrimination towards LGBT travelers in Belgium or the Netherlands. You shouldn't have trouble finding information about the gay scene as it's well publicized in Amsterdam. "Gay News" (www.gay-news.com), a monthly magazine in both Dutch and English, is available free in gay establishments around the city. Amsterdam hosts one of the world's most flamboyant Gay Pride events (p. 41) in August. For further information in Amsterdam, try COC Amsterdam, Stadhouderskade 89 (www.cocamsterdam.nl; ✆ 020/626-3087). The Gay and Lesbian Switchboard (www.switchboard.nl; ✆ 020/623-6565) can also provide advice. Both websites are in Dutch only although English speakers staff the offices and answer the phones.

In Brussels, contact the gay and lesbian community centers **Tels Quels,** rue Haute 46-48 (www.telsquels. be; ✆ **02/512-4587**); and **Rainbow House**, rue du Marché-au-Charbon 42 (www.rainbowhouse.be, ✆ **02/503-5990**). For the scene in Bruges, contact **Lumi** (www.lumi.be). Belgium's main Gay Pride event takes place in Brussels in May.

Mobile Phones Tri-band devices and iPhones work across Europe. Call charges are often high when making international calls and roaming charges, especially for data download, can be extortionate; even checking voicemail can result in an expensive phone bill. If you have a GSM phone and use it a lot, buy a European SIM card to use during your stay. And check with your phone company about charges. Generally T-Mobile has the best rates for European calls.

U.K. mobiles work in Belgium and Holland; a 2017 EU regulation abolished roaming charges but voice calls and text messages will be charged.

To rent a GSM mobile phone in Belgium, go to **Rent2Connect** (www.rent2 connect.com; ✆ **02/652-1414**), in the Arrivals hall at Brussels Airport.

If you have web access, use **Skype (www.skype. com)** or download the apps **WhatsApp** or **Facebook Messenger** to make free international calls from your laptop or mobile device to those on your contact list.

Money & Credit Cards

Debit cards are the most widely used form of payment in the Netherlands and Belgium. Major attractions and stores and restaurants that cater to tourists will take credit cards but local stores and small businesses, especially in the Netherlands, may well only accept cash or PIN-only debit cards supported by Maestro, so be aware that your American debit card will likely not work. The most common are Visa and MasterCard, although American Express and Diners Club are also accepted.

It's highly recommended that you travel with at least one major credit card. You must have one to rent a car, and hotels and airlines usually require a credit card imprint as a deposit against expenses.

The value of the euro varies against other currencies. For current exchange rates, check **www.xe.com**.

Safety In Amsterdam, Rotterdam, and even The Hague, be wary of pickpockets on trams, buses, at the main railway stations (especially Centraal Station in Amsterdam, which is a hotbed of nefarious activity); on busy shopping streets and in busy stores.

Outside the capital, Belgium is generally safe; even the big cities are low-crime areas. However, in the metro and train stations in Brussels, primarily Bruxelles-Midi, pickpocketing and petty crime take place with some regularity (even with a police

presence and video surveillance). So be aware of your surroundings and keep a close eye on your bags.

Both Brussels (Gard du Nord, Boulevard Adolphe Max, and Avenue Louise) and Antwerp (Schippersstraat, Vingerlingstraat, and Verversrui) have red-light zones, in which caution is in order. Don't confuse these places with the Red Light District in Amsterdam, which is a tourist attraction in its own right and usually safe for casual visitors. Brussels' red-light zone around Gard du Nord in particular is a lowlife place, and although Antwerp's is not quite so bad, it's not the place for sightseers after dark.

Senior Travel Belgium and Holland both offer discounts for seniors on public transportation—by far the easiest way to get around the cities covered in this book. For train travel, these discounts begin at age 65 in Belgium, and at 60 in the Netherlands. Bus companies have different starting ages for discounted tickets and passes. Many sightseeing attractions and tour companies offer senior discounts, but these might apply only to local residents when they produce ID. Be sure to ask when you buy your ticket.

Smoking There's a blanket ban on smoking in public places across Europe, although not in the streets. It's fine to smoke a joint in the coffee shops of Amsterdam, but not a cigarette (p. 123).

Student Travel   Most attractions in Amsterdam, Brussels, and Bruges offer student discounts on admission; these are noted throughout the destination chapters. Check out the **International Student Travel Confederation (ISTC;** www.aboutistc.org) for travel information and the **International Student Identity Card (ISIC;** www.isic.org), for a card that permits savings on rail passes, plane tickets, and entrance fees. It also provides basic health and life insurance. The card is valid for a maximum of 12 months. Apply for the card online. If you're no longer a student but under 31, you can get an **International Youth Travel Card** from **STA Travel** (www.statravel.com), which entitles you to some discounts.

Taxes   A value-added tax (BTW in Holland, TVA in Brussels) runs at 21 percent on most good bought in stores. Visitors residing outside the European Union can recover this upon departure. Stores that offer tax-free shopping advertise with a **Global Blue (www.global blue.com)** tax-free shopping sign in the window and will furnish shoppers with the correct forms and information to recoup their refund. Refunds are available only when you spend more than 50€ in a participating store.

Tipping   Tipping is not a big deal in Europe, as in many instances a 15 percent service charge is already added to a bill. Round up bills in cabs, small bars, and cafes to the nearest Euro, and leave between 10 and 15 percent in restaurants only if service has been exemplary. In French-speaking Wallonia and Brussels, tipping is more common than in Flanders, where it is not expected.

Time   Amsterdam, Brussels, and Belgium operate on Greenwich Mean Time (GMT) + one: 1 hour ahead of the U.K., 6 hours ahead of Eastern Daylight Time, and 8 and 12 hours behind Australian Eastern Standard Time.

Toilets   Public lavatories are few and far between in Belgium and Holland, and when you do find them, you'll often have to pay 0.50€ for the privilege of using them. In Amsterdam, there are free public urinals scattered throughout the city, but obviously, those are reserved for men. If you want to use the toilet at a cafe, restaurant, or bar, you'll need to be a paying customer.

Water   The water in your hotel and at public drinking fountains is safe to drink.

Index

Map List

Photo Credits

Published by
FROMMER MEDIA LLC

Frommer's EasyGuide to Amsterdam, Brussels and Bruges, 2nd Edition
ISBN 978-1-62887-454-9 (paper), 978-1-62887-455-6 (e-book)

Editorial Director: Pauline Frommer
Editor: Pauline Frommer
Production Editor: Lindsay Conner
Photo Editor: Meghan Lamb
Assistant Photo Editor: Phil Vinke
Cartographer: Elizabeth Puhl
Cover Design: Howard Grossman

Front cover photo © Olena Z / Shutterstock.com

For information on our other products or services, see www.frommers.com.

FrommerMedia LLC also publishes its books in a variety of electronic formats. Some content that appears
in print may not be available in electronic formats.

Manufactured in the United States of America

5   4   3   2   1

ABOUT THE AUTHOR

Jennifer Ceaser is a freelance writer and editor who has specialized in travel journalism for two decades. A former New Yorker and staff editor at the *New York Post*, Jennifer now splits her time between Berlin and Barcelona. She contributes to a variety of publications including *Conde Nast Traveler, AFAR, New York Magazine, BBC, Time Out, Coastal Living, and Wine Enthusiast.*

ABOUT THE FROMMER TRAVEL GUIDES

For most of the past 50 years, Frommer's has been the leading series of travel guides in North America, accounting for as many as 24% of all guidebooks sold. I think I know why.

Though we hope our books are entertaining, we nevertheless deal with travel in a serious fashion. Our guidebooks have never looked on such journeys as a mere recreation, but as a far more important human function, a time of learning and introspection, an essential part of a civilized life. We stress the culture, lifestyle, history, and beliefs of the destinations we cover, and urge our readers to seek out people and new ideas as the chief rewards of travel.

We have never shied from controversy. We have, from the beginning, encouraged our authors to be intensely judgmental, critical—both pro and con—in their comments, and wholly independent. Our only clients are our readers, and we have triggered the ire of countless prominent sorts, from a tourist newspaper we called "practically worthless" (it unsuccessfully sued us) to the many rip-offs we've condemned.

And because we believe that travel should be available to everyone regardless of their incomes, we have always been cost-conscious at every level of expenditure. Though we have broadened our recommendations beyond the budget category, we insist that every lodging we include be sensibly priced. We use every form of media to assist our readers, and are particularly proud of our feisty daily website, the award-winning Frommers.com.

I have high hopes for the future of Frommer's. May these guidebooks, in all the years ahead, continue to reflect the joy of travel and the freedom that travel represents. May they always pursue a cost-conscious path, so that people of all incomes can enjoy the rewards of travel. And may they create, for both the traveler and the persons among whom we travel, a community of friends, where all human beings live in harmony and peace.

Arthur Frommer